*f*P

ALSO BY C. A. TRIPP

The Homosexual Matrix

The Intimate World of

Abraham
LINCOLN

C. A. TRIPP

EDITED BY LEWIS GANNETT

FREE PRESS
NEW YORK LONDON TORONTO SYDNEY

FREE PRESS

A Division of Simon & Schuster, Inc.

1230 Avenue of the Americas

New York, NY 10020

FREE PRESS and colophon are
trademarks of Simon & Schuster, Inc.

For information about special discounts for bulk purchases,
please contact Simon & Schuster Special Sales:
1-800-456-6798 or business@simonandschuster.com

Designed by Joseph Rutt
Insert designed by K. J. Cho

Manufactured in the United States of America

1   3   5   7   9   10   8   6   4   2

Library of Congress Cataloging-in-Publication Data

Tripp, C. A.
The intimate world of Abraham Lincoln / C. A. Tripp; edited by Lewis Gannett.
p. cm.
Includes bibliographical references and index.
1. Lincoln, Abraham, 1809–1865—Psychology. 2. Lincoln, Abraham, 1809–1865—
Friends and associates. 3. Lincoln, Abraham, 1809–1865—Relations with women.
4. Presidents—United States—Biography. 5. Intimacy (Psychology)—Case studies.
6. Character—Case studies.   I. Gannett, Lewis. II. Title.

E457.2 .T75 2005
973.7'092—dc22   2004057605

ISBN 0-7432-6639-0

To Future Lincoln Scholars
With hopes that Planck was incorrect:

A New Scientific truth does not triumph
By convincing its opponents,
But rather because its opponents die,
And a new generation grows up that is familiar with it.

— MAX PLANCK

Contents

Introduction

By Jean Baker, Goucher College

The debate over Abraham Lincoln's sexuality has become an insistent inquiry. During the 1990s the issue has been considered on call-in shows, in magazines, on websites, and in the private conversations among scholars who have devoted their lives and reputations to understanding the sixteenth president. Whisper campaigns have even included talk of a newly discovered diary written by Lincoln's lover, which turned out to be fictitious. Clearly the matter has seized the public's attention, and it needs to be addressed. But no one has seriously researched the question until C. A. Tripp's *The Intimate World of Abraham Lincoln*. Fortunately Tripp's book is much more than an effort to answer the limited question, by applying today's categories to past sexual behavior, of whether Lincoln was a homosexual. What follows is neither polemic nor exposé, but a full-fledged character study that places Lincoln's sexuality into a larger, more significant framework of trying to understand this elusive man.

Of course Lincoln, labeled by his law partner William Herndon "the most shut-mouthed man I knew," has offered little assistance in answering questions about his love life. In fact the president left few clues about any aspect of his personal affairs, much less his sexual preferences. Such reticence extends into his relationships with his parents (scholars still argue about his feelings toward his father); his marriage (about which there seems to be unending debate); and even his paternal views of his four sons (although he did once describe his eldest son Robert as a "rare ripe sort . . . smarter at about five than ever after"). In the autobiography encouraged by his Republican supporters in the fall of 1859 when he was emerging as a candidate for that party's nomination, Lincoln, already among the best-known men of his generation, produced a spare, less than six-hundred-word description of his first fifty years. His autobiography was short, he averred, because "there is not much of me."

Historians have taken Lincoln's comment as an example of his humility. Yet such brevity and evasiveness also demonstrate his lifelong public silence about personal matters, a conventional response among men during the nineteenth century, though less so, then as now, among aspiring politicians. In any case discussions about sex, even between long-married heterosexual couples, were rare in the nineteenth century. Physical intimacy remained a private matter about which nineteenth-century Americans, little given to the confessional outpourings of their twenty-first-century descendants, left few hints. We would not expect Abraham Lincoln to tell us that he favored sex with men, although he may have left some clues. And because scholars have only recently begun investigating sex as a time- and place-bound experience, we have little context for assessing sexual practices in Lincoln's time.

Today's focus on sex—some call it an American obsession—is radically different. Retrospective considerations of the sexuality of nineteenth-century historical figures—including Lincoln's presidential predecessor James Buchanan, whom some proclaim our first gay president—abound. Gay activism has helped stir historians to investigate what had been an invisible, unfathomable subject, unimaginable to some, improper and meaningless for others.

Homosexuals—male and female—now seek civil rights, and grudgingly some courts and legislatures have moved to protect these rights. A similar, but much slower transformation in private attitudes supporting homosexuality, has accompanied such changes, but heterosexual acceptance of "the other" is still limited and tenuous. As late as the mid-1980s over 60 percent of all Americans found homosexuality an unacceptable lifestyle. Evidence "outing" the iconic Lincoln, among many historians and much of the general public, will come as bad news dishonoring a revered figure. Some will protest that the case C. A. Tripp makes in *The Intimate World of Abraham Lincoln* has not been proven and is largely circumstantial; others will turn away in disgust, for homosexuality is a subject that stirs deep emotions. But many will applaud efforts to answer questions that threaten to obscure all others, on the eve of the bicentennial celebration in 2009 of Lincoln's birth. In the end Lincoln is too important a figure in our national past to censor, especially since in the argument presented here, Lincoln's sexuality is integral to understanding his presidential leadership. Whatever the response, Tripp's *The Intimate World of Abraham Lincoln* deserves a fair reading.

No one asks if Andrew Jackson, Franklin Pierce, Ulysses S. Grant, or Andrew Johnson were homosexuals. They seemed "too robustly sexual," meaning, of course, that they responded to women. On the other hand, even if Lincoln himself has left few obvious indications of his possible homosexuality, there were always hints observed and commented upon by historians. Some, like Ida Tarbell writing her two-volume *The Life of Abraham Lincoln* in 1900 and Margaret Leech in her 1941 *Reveille in Washington 1860–1865*, discovered evidence of Lincoln in bed with another man in 1862, but for reasons of prudery, implausibility or ignorance about homosexuality, they declined to develop this material into any argument about Lincoln's homosexuality. (In terms of Lincoln scholarship it is not surprising that two women, among the disproportionate host of male historians, found these clues.)

In 1924, Carl Sandburg, in the first volume of *The Prairie Years*, poetically described Lincoln's "streak of lavender and spots soft as May violets," but Sandburg pursued the issue no farther. There is also fragmentary evidence about Lincoln's homosexuality in the comments of Lincoln's contemporaries made to that oral historian par excellence, William Herndon, when the latter was gathering material about the president after his assassination. To some, Lincoln was not a garden-variety heterosexual.

What others have avoided, ignored, denied, dismissed, and overlooked C. A. Tripp confronts openly in *The Intimate World of Abraham Lincoln*. While Tripp is not the first recent observer to do so, he is the most systematic and simultaneously the most speculative. Earlier Charley Shively considered the issue of Lincoln's sexual preferences in his 1989 study of the poet Walt Whitman. Published by the Gay Sunshine Press, Shively's conclusions in *Drum Beats* were little noted, save by gays who discovered in Lincoln's possible preferences an affiliation with an illustrious and greatly admired American president.

Not by chance did a group of Republican gay advocates in 1996 choose a name that associated them with Lincoln, proclaiming themselves "Log-Cabin Republicans." In 2001 Jonathan Ned Katz featured Lincoln's relationship with Joshua Speed, his first friend in Springfield in 1837 and his four-year bedmate, as a love story—or as Katz puts it, an example of "sex between men before the invention of homosexuality."

In *The Intimate World of Abraham Lincoln* C. A. Tripp goes farther than any earlier studies to present the greatest amount of evidence and the strongest argument currently available that Lincoln's primary erotic response was that of a homosexual. As he says in his preface, Lincoln's personal history reflects "a plentiful homosexual response and action. . . ." It is safe to say that short of the dubious proposition of finding new Lincoln letters or a previously undiscovered nineteenth-century diary written by one of the president's lovers, or discovering a somehow previously overlooked observation from a contemporary of the president's, Tripp's *The Intimate World* will define the issue for years to come.

Born in Texas in 1919, trained as a photographer at the Rochester Institute of Technology, C. A. Tripp became part of Alfred Kinsey's staff after World War II. After reading Kinsey's *Sexual Behavior in The Human Male* in 1948, in a style maintained throughout his life, he audaciously phoned the famous sex researcher, and at Kinsey's invitation immediately visited the Institute for Sex Research in Bloomington, Indiana. Tripp was promptly hired, and became part of a team engaged in pivotal work on human sexuality. With his impressive empirical studies based on surveying the sexual practices of 3,500 men and his groundbreaking approach to the hidden topic of sex, Kinsey indelibly influenced Tripp. The older man (Kinsey died in 1956) pushed Tripp to see sexology as a scientific field, and sexual behavior as a discernable part of human experience that should be studied.

Tripp became convinced that Kinsey's data would promote greater understanding among Americans who had little knowledge and much misinformation about sex. Moreover Kinsey's figures on the pervasiveness of the homosexual experiences of men dazzled the ever-inquisitive Tripp. (More than one-third of Kinsey's sample had engaged in a homosexual act during their lifetime and while a slim 4 to 6 percent identified themselves as exclusively homosexual, only about a half of the entire sample were exclusively heterosexual.) The idea of the universality and ubiquity of men loving men confirmed Tripp's intuitive judgments, and ratified his own homosexual experience. So too did the associated findings that as a matter of science, sexual behavior could not be classified as normal and abnormal, that Freud's deductive categories of human behavior such as the Oedipus complex rested on hopelessly weak evidential reeds, and that the sex drive of all humans was an intermixing of biological, psychological, and sociological factors, with biological ones mostly holding the trumps. Yet the vagaries of experience—in some cases a satisfying early adventure—encouraged some men to engage in homosexual acts more readily than others.

Kinsey eventually persuaded Tripp that he should go back to school, and in 1951, age thirty-four, Tripp returned to college, majoring in sociology and psychology at the New School for Social Research in New York, an institution he later proclaimed the best he ever attended. Two years later C. A. Tripp (who was universally known as "Tripp" among his friends) entered New York University's doctoral program, emerging in 1957 with a doctorate in clinical psychology. Several internships followed, and by 1960 he had developed a successful practice as a psychotherapist amid the competitive overabundance of listening rooms in New York City. As was often the case at a time when homosexuality was seen as a condition to be corrected therapeutically, many of his patients were homosexuals.

These patients provided the evidence and understandings for Tripp's first book, *The Homosexual Matrix*. So too did his ten-year study of the literature of homosexuality. Published in 1975, reviewed unfavorably by the *New York Times* but an overnight bestseller, *The Homosexual Matrix* provided an informed, opinionated, yet commonsense look at every aspect of homosexuality from the similarity of sexual developmental processes among heterosexuals and homosexuals, to the meanings of sexual techniques, especially inversions, to the downgrading of parental pathology as the cause of homosexuality. No longer were overbearing mothers and timid fathers the cause of homosexuality in males, as Freudian psychiatrists had long argued.

Tripp's book became a manual of what every American wanted to ask (and was afraid to) about gays and lesbians, with the added benefit of Tripp's insights into the origins of heterosexuality. "Perhaps the most troubling assumption," wrote Tripp, "has been that every mature person would be heterosexual were it not for various fears and neuroses developed from parental and social misfortunes." Homosexuals were not impaired heterosexuals waiting to be released from their abnormal orientation. Conservatives and religious fundamentalists disliked *The Homosexual Matrix* because it humanized homosexuality as a pervasive natural practice of physical loving, while monogamous heterosexuals disputed Tripp's dismissal of their sexual relationships as ultimately unsatisfying, lacking the tension and resistance of successful sex. Suspicious feminists found demeaning and incorrect Tripp's insistence that too much independence on the part of women "blotted out the image of ultimate submission that sexual allure [to men] requires." But the public bought the book, and *The Homosexual Matrix*, after four printings, sold 500,000 copies.

Sometime during the 1990s the ever-inquisitive Tripp began to study Abraham Lincoln, who, as has been the case for so many Americans, fascinated him. Tripp did so from the perspective of a meticulous sex researcher well-versed in the conceptual apparatus of Kinsey's work. Like all Americans, Tripp intended "to get right with Lincoln" (in David Donald's phrase), which, for him, meant reclaiming the president's intimate life for a new generation. The fact that Lincoln was a homosexual was not, for Tripp, the dispositive matter in understanding this inscrutable president. Sexual preference and activity never defined anyone, he believed, although in the case of homosexuals— male and female—society often made it so. Instead Lincoln's homosexuality was part of a cluster of attributes that explain his leadership during the Civil War.

Tripp's evaluation of evidence long familiar to Lincoln scholars, such as the Ann Rutledge story and the meaning of the Speed-Lincoln friendship, clearly diverged from that of mainstream scholars. Given his background, Tripp saw things obscured to those untrained in sexuality. On the other hand, his notion of factual verification defied the canons of the discipline of history, and because of the nature of the subject, there is considerable circumstantial evidence in *The Intimate World*. Tripp paid little attention to what David Hackett Fischer once called fallacies of substantive distraction, that is shifting the argument to sometimes irrelevant issues. (This is especially true in the digressions in the last chapter.) Yet the final result is an intriguing public and private Lincoln. No previous writer on Lincoln's homosexuality had molded this sexual orientation into a complete biographical understanding.

No doubt reviewers will point to Tripp's deficiencies, but it is worth remembering that with regard to his central finding, Tripp came to the evidence believing that homosexuality is, and must be considered as, an entirely normal condition. Lincoln may have functioned as a heterosexual, but his marriage did not preclude an intense homosexual drive. Using the same speculative framework as heterosexual historians, save for the birth of the Lincoln children, one could, in Tripp's view, challenge the assumed heterosexuality of Lincoln. For the evidence of what went on in Mary and Abraham's marriage bed is as evidentially obscure as that of Lincoln's affairs with men.

What others saw as innocent, perhaps homoerotic bed-sharing in an era when there were few mattresses emerged in Tripp's analysis as evidence of an autonomous, autodidactic lover of men. Only the blinkered eyes of historians had prevented them from seeing what seemed so obvious to a sex researcher. Tripp expected as much. For years he had been sensitive to the ways in which the public's comfort level led to censorship of homosexual content, a process of bowdlerization readily apparent even in Jowett's famous translation of Plato. Now he came to believe that historians had similarly diminished and misinterpreted the evidence of Lincoln's homosexuality.

Only after ten years was Tripp ready to publish *The Intimate World*. During this time Tripp had proceeded slowly and meticulously, reading the extensive and ever-growing literature on the sixteenth president, and even calling some scholars on the phone to invite their comments (which were mostly negative) on his early chapters. Never interested in turning Lincoln into a representative of gay pride (Tripp refused to use the word), instead Tripp intended to encase Lincoln's sexuality within a larger portrait. Readers of *The Intimate World* will find that this is not a work of sexual or biological reductionism, but rather a significant effort to understand a complicated man.

During the 1990s, applying scientific methods to the vast amount of writing on Lincoln, Tripp began constructing a database of Lincolnalia, which is currently available at the Lincoln Library in Springfield. Through an index, librarians there can access material by topic and subject. Certainly this database helped Tripp's research, but it also serves as testimony to his seriousness of purpose. Now including a great many books that have been scanned, this powerful research tool will remain one of Tripp's legacies to the future study of Lincoln. Indeed *The Intimate World* is dedicated to future Lincoln scholars, with the wry accompanying Max Planck epigram to the effect that it takes two generations for new ideas to take hold—because the first generation of opponents must die.

On the basis of inductive reasoning familiar to him as a Kinsey researcher and in the spirit of social science, Tripp intrepidly measures Lincoln's homosexuality and presents his findings in the first chapter. To do so he employs Kinsey's famous classification system that ranks an individual's homosexuality on a seven-point continuum, where 0 = exclusively heterosexual and 6 = exclusively homosexual.[1] Lincoln, according to Tripp, ranks as a 5, i.e. "predominantly homosexual, but incidentally heterosexual." While this scale has recently been criticized as offering few advantages over the three common terms heterosexual, bisexual, and homosexual, its application to Lincoln is a clear indication of Tripp's position. There is no hedging in this book.

Tripp died in May 2003, after he finished *The Intimate World*, but before he had time to edit and revise. Had he lived he might have changed the eclectic organization of chapters that follow no clear linear or substantive progression. He might have edited a last chapter that takes readers, as if on a magic carpet, to twentieth-century intelligence gathering, Roosevelt, Churchill, and the little-known Alan Turing. Tripp probably would have added additional data; he might even have presented his material as a series of essays. But there can be no doubt that he would have enjoyed responding to the criticisms of this book.

The Intimate World begins with a chapter on Lincoln's seduction of a forty-four-year-old captain of the Pennsylvania Bucktails in the fall of 1862. Captain David Derickson, detailed to guard the president at his summer retreat at the Old Soldier's Home in northeast Washington, is found sleeping in the president's bed during one of Mary Lincoln's absences. The captain is observed wearing the president's nightshirt, and this sharing of the bed is not a one-time incident. To Tripp it goes without saying that the two men had sex together and that this relationship is one of at least five verifiable cases of Lincoln's sexual activity with other males. If Lincoln had been found in bed with a woman, few would doubt that sex was involved and that the president was cheating on his wife. But for complex reasons involving homophobia, many historians consider this bedsharing an innocent incident of "spooning," or else Lincoln's desire for non-tactile companionship, or perhaps even the president's need for warmth during Washington's chilly fall nights. Undoubtedly the determination of homosexual practice is held to a higher evidentiary standard among historians than is heterosexuality. In any case the president was not embarrassed and told another officer that "the Captain and I are getting quite thick."[2]

We will never know if Lincoln's male relationships were genitally chaste. There were, of course, innocent spiritual same-sex affiliations among young men and women of the nineteenth century, just as there were sexual relations. The fact that no one paid much attention at the time to Lincoln's presidential bed-sharing or any other of Lincoln's possibly homosexual encounters tells us nothing. The fact is nineteenth-century Americans simply did not give as much attention to sex as we do today. Sex did not define an existence, as it does today particularly in the case of male and female homosexuals. The essential historical chasm between the nineteenth and the twenty-first centuries is that during Lincoln's lifetime, homosexuality, as an identity or the naming of a sexual category, did not exist. Lincoln was dead when in 1868 the word homosexuality was first coined in Austria and later popularized by German sexologists to describe the erotic practices of men with other men. It was not until the end of the nineteenth century that Americans "discovered" homosexuality, became cognizant of what was dubbed "perversion," and tried to stamp it out.

In Lincoln's time if he was participating in anal intercourse, he was technically committing, in the nineteenth-century's euphemism, "a crime against nature" or "the sin that cannot be named." On the other hand, oral-genital sex was not prohibited in state laws until much later in the century. Legally, if he had anal sex, he was engaging in sodomy—even if the acts were consensual. Along with bestiality and buggery—sex with animals by men and women—sodomy had been a capital crime during the colonial period of American history, and the penalty was inflicted in at least ten instances, mainly in the seventeenth century. After the American Revolution, Thomas Jefferson urged castration for the guilty rather than hanging, and Virginia and most other states revised their sodomy statutes, providing lesser penalties. By the 1840s in Midwestern states, penalties ranged from ten years to life in prison. There was only one approved behavior in Lincoln's sexual times: marital coition for procreation, but not even too much of that. Sex was never approved for recreation. Yet as Graham Robb has pointed out about both Europe and the United States in his recent book *Strangers: Homosexual Love in the Nineteenth Century,* "Nineteenth century homosexuals lived under a cloud, but it seldom rained." Only in cities where men visited male brothels was there any conspicuous display of homosexuality at a time when most Americans were neither cognizant nor suspicious of it. In terms of prosecutions bestiality was as much an issue as sex between men. Of course in religious terms Lincoln was a sinner, the label sodomite coming from the name of the sinful city of Sodom in the Old Testament Book of Genesis. But as Tripp argues, Lincoln's sexual orientation encouraged him early in his life to challenge the biblical strictures against homosexuality and eventually organized religion.

Americans of Lincoln's time were much more concerned with masturbation. Lincoln lived in a period when "self-pollution" or the "solitary vice" was the sexual taboo on everyone's mind. In nineteenth-century prescriptive manuals, doctors and public opinion held it to be the cause of insanity and associated physical diseases. As a sexual practice, and usually a solitary one at that, masturbation challenged parental controls; certainly it threatened the prevailing notions of a given amount of semen to be usefully expended only in the creation of children. In such a society homosexuality might be hidden in plain sight. It was rarely discussed. It was rarely suspected.

In subsequent chapters Tripp turns to Lincoln's youth, introducing a critical concept borrowed from Kinsey. Lincoln, if we can believe a neighbor who testified to Lincoln's sudden growth spurt, underwent puberty at an early age—possibly at nine. This is four years before the average of other males, although the transporting of such actuarial data to the early nineteenth century may be problematic. In Kinsey's survey data early-puberty males had higher sex rates over time (referring to the number of their orgasms) than late bloomers. They were also more likely to engage in homosexual behavior. Too young to be inoculated against sex by anxious parents and too unsophisticated to turn to girls, masturbation and contact with other males (and in the nineteenth century with a surprising number and variety of animals) provided their sexual outlets. In Tripp's taxonomy of sexuality, a pleasurable homosexual experience early in life could forever eroticize maleness over femaleness.

Lincoln's sexual precociousness and hypersexuality help to explain his notable smuttiness. Throughout his life he told dirty jokes; often they had anal punch lines. Donn Piatt, an Ohio journalist and politician, once said that Lincoln told the dirtiest stories that ever fell from human lips. Asked to publish them, Lincoln himself pronounced them too dirty; they would stink as an outhouse, he said. But his friend Leonard Swett always insisted it was the wit, not the vulgarity of the story, which Lincoln appreciated.

Certainly, as Tripp argues in subsequent chapters in *The Intimate World*, twenty-year old Abraham Lincoln knew about homosexuality. In his obscene and sometimes bowdlerized poem "First Chronicles of Reuben," Lincoln referred to a man marrying another man ("But Billy has married a boy"). Subsequently the two produce a "jelly baby," that is, in the vernacular, a pregnancy imagined from homosexual intercourse. Arrived in New Salem in 1831, Lincoln soon shared a bed (and learned grammar) with Billy Greene who earlier had admired his thighs, part of a sexual practice among men called "femoral intercourse." In *The Intimate World* Tripp provides examples of less well-developed homosexual contacts with A. Y. Ellis and later Henry Whitney who once said that Lincoln seemed always to be courting him. According to Whitney, Lincoln also said that sexual contact was "a harp of a thousand strings."

Most surprising and innovative in Tripp's catalogue of Lincoln's male interests are the president's strongly erotic feelings for the handsome, heterosexual, twenty-four year old Colonel Elmer

Ellsworth. Unsuccessfully Lincoln had encouraged Ellsworth to join his law office in Springfield. Later when the war began, the president insisted that Secretary of War Cameron appoint Ellsworth the inspector general of the United States Militia. Posted to Washington because of Lincoln's intervention, and an admirer of Lincoln, Ellsworth vowed to remove the insulting Confederate flag waving over a hotel in Alexandria that was visible from the White House.

The young colonel was killed in this operation, devastating the president. Lincoln's emotional reaction suggests to Tripp a profound romantic affection. To his contemporaries Lincoln described his association with Ellsworth as intimate, a common enough nineteenth-century term for nonphysical attachments. But while others have seen the Lincoln-Ellsworth affiliation as one of a father to a surrogate son, Tripp presents the relationship as yet another example of Lincoln's sexual response to males. Unlike his other affairs, the Lincoln-Ellsworth affair remained unconsummated, a desired physical romance with a spiritual component that explained the president's excessive grief.

The most important friendship in Lincoln's life was his relationship with Joshua Speed, with whom he slept for four years from 1837 to 1841. "No two men were ever so intimate," acknowledged Speed about what is characterized by most historians as a classic example of the close spiritual bonding significant for young men of the nineteenth century on the eve of their marriages. The term used is homosocial—or, raised another notch, homoerotic—suggesting a chaste romance like that of Daniel Webster and James Bingham or Ralph Waldo Emerson and his handsome fellow student Martin Gay, a condition similar to the well-known crushes or smashes of young women. In the Aristotelean typology recently used by David Herbert Donald in *"We Are Lincoln Men": Abraham Lincoln and His Friends*, these are complete friendships in which the secrets of the heart are exchanged.

Tripp saw this relationship differently. Far less squeamish about matters of sex than the fraternity of scholars studying Lincoln, he found the difference between homosexuality and homoeroticism to be little more than an orgasm—the spilling of seed. In the bed that Lincoln shared with Speed for so long, the small space made sex as inevitable as the skin-to-skin contact necessary to fit on the mattress. After a close evaluation of the famous and variously interpreted letters from Lincoln to Speed, Tripp argues that rather than melancholy over the status of his romance with Mary Todd, Lincoln suffered one of his depressions (Lincoln called them "hypochondriaisms") when his principal love object, Speed, was returning to Kentucky. Tripp confuses Speed's possible infertility with his impotence. Nonetheless, the author of *The Intimate World* expands our understanding of what Speed meant to Lincoln, and why.

Of course the case for Lincoln's homosexuality rests on his corollary lack of attention to women, and it is one of the striking features of Lincoln's boyhood that his contemporaries invariably commented on this disinterest. "He was not very fond of girls," remembered his stepmother. But there were, of course, three women in Lincoln's life, and in separate chapters Tripp removes their importance as Lincoln love objects. The chapter on Ann Rutledge, for example, suggests other reasons than her death for Lincoln's depression. The chapter on Mary Owens reveals how ambivalent Lincoln was about marrying her.

But Lincoln did marry Mary Todd. In an overly long, brutally harsh chapter, Tripp removes the final woman from Lincoln's affections. Using the familiar rants of previous historians, Tripp employs selective evidence to eviscerate Mary Lincoln as someone who literally can do no right. She is "an outlaw type" whom Tripp compares to psychopaths like Hitler. This is unfair, and the chapter is surely not worthy of the careful, balanced interpretations of which Tripp is capable. Indeed there is more than a whiff of Tripp's misogyny in this depiction, although Lincoln's supposedly miserable marriage does serve the author's purpose of explaining why the strongly homosexual Lincoln married at all and how he stood such a shrew. The president could put up with his wife because he did not care. His love interests rested with men.

In his final chapters Tripp considers Lincoln's religion and the distinction he drew between morality and ethics. Tripp's observation that Lincoln's failure to use any prayerful consolation in his agonized grieving for his dead son Willie suggests a profound alienation from conventional religion, traceable through the president's homosexuality to a young man's "freedom from constraint and a degree of wildness that lives at the edge of social conformity."

Throughout *The Intimate World* Tripp depends on Kinsey's dated findings to frame his position. Certainly the argument about Lincoln's early puberty and its determinative effect on the future president rests on slender evidentiary grounds. Moreover having promised that sexuality does not define anyone, Tripp contradicts himself by using homosexuality deterministically. He is as deductive in his hypothesis-testing and conclusion-finding as Freud ever was, and despite his scrupulous research, he is selective in how he approaches the evidence, sometimes resembling the man who looks for his lost keys only under the nearby street lamp.

Yet while Tripp may be wrong in his interpretation of some particulars, he may still be right on the larger question. For myself, I believe that Lincoln was bisexual. The evidence from the Joshua Speed and David Derickson incidents, one occurring when Lincoln was in his late twenties and the other when he was fifty-three, suggests that he engaged in both heterosexual and homosexual practices and that his attraction to men did not end with his marriage. I also believe that he loved his wife, Mary, and I know that he had sexual intercourse with her. Readers will have to decide for themselves how conclusive Tripp's evidence is, as indeed they always do. But even amid the disagreements this book will generate, Tripp deserves credit for a thought-provoking, richly researched, and intelligently argued book that will frame future discussions of our sixteenth president.

In the end Tripp's Lincoln, who succeeded so majestically as a leader, is in some ways not so different from other historians' Lincoln. It is simply that the author's explanations emerge from a different cluster of attributes. Lincoln's early puberty, his homosexuality and his ability to educate himself placed him on a path toward independence and self-reliance. Ultimately, in his essential role as a guardian of the nation during the Civil War, Lincoln provided bold leadership for a nation in crisis. He proved he could step back from conventionality and hold countervailing views simultaneously. He could walk, as Tripp puts it, both sides of the street. Tripp's Lincoln operates with an independent moral and ethical system that emerges from his sexual otherness. He was not bound by the proscriptions hampering others. The words of the homosexual poet Walt Whitman say it well: "Apart from the pulling and hauling stands what I am / stands amused complacent compassionate, idle, unitary."

Editor's Note

───────────────────────────

C. A. Tripp died in May 2003. He worked on the manuscript for this book until shortly before his death and likely would have continued working on it if he had lived longer. The manuscript was edited posthumously.

Preface

For more than a quarter century, especially in the late 1990s, print media have carried numerous reports that Abraham Lincoln may have been homosexual, or even "gay." Lincoln was certainly not the latter. For while his personal history does, indeed, reflect a plentiful homosexual response and action, as will be shown, exactly none of it had the lightness and frivolity, let alone the note of social protest, implied in "gay." The first mention of Lincoln's homosexuality was apparently in an article written and privately printed in 1971 by an energetic collector of sexual facts, one of the first and most effective "gay liberation" activists, James Kepner.[1] During the next quarter century, and especially in the 1990s, numerous knockoff articles followed; these seldom mentioned Kepner by name, but several carried his imprint by accident. His original article contained a small error (a slightly incorrect reference to Carl Sandburg) that, when repeated in subsequent reports, flagged the source.[2]

Kepner's article on the Lincoln and Joshua Speed relationship was not his first effort of this kind. Previously he had "outed" Eleanor Roosevelt in sufficient detail about her relationship with Lorena Hickok to put him in serious trouble with the Roosevelt family (legal action was threatened). These difficulties came to a sudden halt with the publication in 1980 of Doris Faber's *The Life of Lorena Hickok: E.R.'s Friend,* which more than confirmed Kepner's comments with excerpts from a trove of no less than 3,360 letters, 2,336 of them from Eleanor Roosevelt herself.[3]

Still, anyone wanting to entertain doubts and disbelief about Lincoln's special friendship with Speed, as mentioned by Kepner and by now a host of others, might still find easy pickings. Beyond the fact that Kepner and his followers had their eyes squarely on possible gains for the gay liberation movement—itself hardly noted for impartiality—there have always been flaws and holes in the story (such as unmentioned details that can sharply reduce its impact). Yet when carefully examined, the Lincoln and Speed relationship turns out to be a rich source of exactly the kinds of sexual evidence those early writers would have prized. So why did they keep using the same few examples while ignoring far stronger ones close at hand? Simplistic as it sounds, the reason seems to lie mostly with the ease of copy-catting, as opposed to a more laborious sifting of a copious Lincoln literature. Meanwhile, historical research at every level has improved over the years.

In 1989 Professor Charles Shively of the University of Massachusetts wrote *Drum Beats*, a book more about Walt Whitman than Lincoln, but it did contain a large, important section—Chapter 7—in which many facts of Lincoln's sex life were cited and analyzed. Although Shively's work had its shortcomings, it nevertheless broke new ground and examined a number of matters never previously explored. What may have helped short-circuit formal acknowledgment of Shively (which might otherwise have helped win him support and recognition) was his use of very impolite language in spots, coupled with a stamp of gay liberation advocacy.[4] Perhaps equally harmful was his choice of a not exactly neutral-sounding publisher—the *Gay Sunshine Press* in San Francisco—along with the additional fact that Shively was "out" himself, which might mean that the whole effort was part of a gay agenda.

Together, these negatives were perhaps enough to blight any research effort. But would it have succeeded in turning around scholarly opinion if it had had none of these drawbacks, no exaggerations at all, and had been published in, say, a top-level journal? Nobody knows, but in view of the temper of the times and the amount of opposition arrayed against its conclusions, probably not. Yet pressures were building for what was about to happen.

The 1990s were marked by an ever increasing tolerance for, if not homosexuality itself, at least discussing and writing about it at upper media levels. On October 1, 1995, the *New York Times* ran a half-page spread under the title IN SEARCH OF HISTORY, with large pictures of Eleanor Roosevelt, Abraham Lincoln, and his friend Joshua Speed. The article began, as many others have, with Lincoln moving to Springfield in 1837, meeting the store clerk Speed who, when Lincoln proved unable to afford the price of a new bed, invited his customer to share his own, which Lincoln did for the next four years. (Bed-sharing was common enough in those days, though to stay on for years was not.) As the *Times* put it:

> A century and a half later, that seemingly ambiguous relationship has been invoked to suggest that the Republican Party, which is often uncomfortable with accepting homosexuality, is failing to acknowledge its own past. Although the party is dominated by social conservatives who reject the notion that homosexuals should be sheltered by special civil rights laws, it is also home to people who are just as fiscally conservative but happen to be gay, many openly so.
>
> Intimations about Lincoln's sexuality were raised anew last month after Senator Bob Dole's Presidential campaign rejected a contribution from the Log Cabin Republicans, a gay group whose name was inspired by the humble beginnings (but not the youthful sleeping habits) of the party's first President. Scott Thompson, a prominent member of the Log Cabin Republicans, a Reagan appointee to the United States Institute of Peace, and a professor at Tufts University's Fletcher School of Law and Diplomacy, retorted that homosexuals ought to feel welcome in the party, "given that the founder was gay."

George Chauncey, associate professor of history at the University of Chicago, responded: "Almost every stigmatized group has sought to elevate its reputation by pointing to illustrious members." The Lincoln scholar Michael Burlingame added, "I don't see how the whole question of Lincoln's gayness would explain anything other than making gay people feel better . . . [a]nd I don't think the function of history is to make people feel good. Celebratory history is propaganda."

Other half-page articles trumpeted similar themes along with the usual counterarguments. A later account in the *Los Angeles Times,* dramatizing another headline, this time from Springfield, Illinois, Lincoln's hometown, blared: LINCOLN COUNTRY AGHAST AS LOCAL PAPER PRINTS GAY ALLEGATION. Then, just as a surprising shift was apparently ready to occur nationally, a prominent gay activist, Larry Kramer, managed to arouse both public and scholarly attention by loudly proclaiming not only that Lincoln was gay (pointing to that same Lincoln and Speed story), but this time with the added fillip that he, Kramer, had uncovered a never before heard of diary of Joshua Speed, complete with a few lurid lines of love quoted with no diary in hand. (Seeing is believing, should that diary ever show up; the passages claimed for it have not the slightest Lincolnian ring.) Yet for reasons not instantly clear, Kramer's voice carried far and wide, with numerous Lincoln scholars castigating both his method and his message.

By an irony of chance, less than a week after the *Los Angeles Times* article appeared, the whole issue was repeated on national television under remarkable circumstances. On June 28, 1999, as Brian Lamb, host of C-SPAN's *American Presidents* Lincoln celebration, was broadcasting from Springfield, a caller asked if there was any truth to reports of Lincoln's homosexuality. When one of the scholars stumbled in responding, Brian Lamb quickly stepped in and summarized the whole matter with full and direct quotes from Kramer's specific charges. (Driving the effect further, C-SPAN rebroadcast the entire program month after month—seven times between June and the end of December.) In part because of this high media attention, the issues discussed received what Shively's work had not: very respectable publicity, plus opportune timing. It was as if a few refined verbal exchanges struck some pendulum of public opinion at a moment when it was primed to swing toward the idea, if not toward the fact, of an entirely changed view of Lincoln's sexual side.

Castles built of papier-mâché, perhaps, and yet the results appear to overcome the clout of ordinary persuasions. Thus, when C-SPAN's Brian Lamb received that caller's inquiry, and restated it as a straightforward question to the two Lincoln scholars present (David Long and Cullom Davis), he elicited from them a maturity of view that might otherwise have taken years to reach. Facing the homosexual question, now stripped of hype, Professor Long merely shrugged and asked, "So what? Would that make the Emancipation Proclamation any less eloquent?" The reaction of Cullom Davis was even more to the point: "What difference does it make?" (This was not the first time the question and those answers had come up; they had been asked before, and answered by the top Lincoln scholar Thomas Schwartz, but only as a news bite, not in a setting of such quality as Brian Lamb offered.) If this realistic position were to continue to hold at upper levels, as now seems probable, it might neatly separate the facts of Lincoln's private life from much moralistic wrenching.

At the moment, however, the question "So what?" is passed along to the present inquiry, with an added observation: In looking through all that is known of Lincoln it is hard to find any case in which his sexual orientation impinged in any way on his political judgment, pro or con. Even slavery leaves us in the lurch, since it cannot be shown that a single slave was freed sooner—or kept in chains longer—as a result of any specific aspect of Lincoln's private life. True, his special empathy and sympathy may have helped, may well have fed his moral enthusiasm and sped him toward what many see as his finest hour. But such secondary gains are hardly traceable to his sex life—and even if they were, who is to say they were not balanced out by unknown drawbacks elsewhere?

In short, if the "contributions" of Lincoln's sex life are as yet not specifiable, with many factions expressing profound discomfort at such revelations, and insisting they would rather not hear any such evidence—plus the further risk of damaging a pristine icon— why, indeed, not back away from this disagreeable search? One quick answer is that nowhere in science or psychology has it ever proved useful either to hide truth or to follow a false flag. Indeed, the benefits of uncovering facts in the case of Lincoln are especially great, owing in no small measure to his own supersecrecy, and the rest to an overlay of romantic fictions. Lincoln is much too important to deserve that, too central a figure in history to keep obscuring basic facts of his life.

In any case, present readers have a choice. If they are mainly interested in a single aspect of Lincoln's sex life—the nature and extent of his homosexual side—then they may find all they care to know here in Chapters 1, 2, and 3. Later chapters are for those who share, or who may come to share, our fascination with countless surprises in Lincoln's often astonishing mind and personality.

LOOKING BACK, AND FORWARD

By common logic one might have expected various restraints on Lincoln's personal history to have been tightest upon the older, less up-to-date scholars. But the marvel is that in a bygone era of staggering sexual ignorance, there were at least a handful of early Lincolnists—in particular, Ida Tarbell, Carl Sandburg, Robert Kincaid, and Margaret Leech—each of whom showed enough curiosity and perception first to detect and then to note at least a few homosexual elements in Lincoln's life. Did any of them come right out and label Lincoln homosexual? Absolutely not, nor can it be proved that any, even when face-to-face with the clearest evidence, ever held the thought in just that form. But this makes all the more interesting how they dealt with certain edgy facts.

It has sometimes been charged that scholars, heeding propriety, have held back for reasons of cover-up or censorship. But of course if these had been the motives in Lincoln's case, then nothing would have been easier, or safer, than to opt for the classical stance held by virtually every Lincoln scholar alive today: simply to stay silent on the whole question.

Our own interpretation of the "policy" decisions made by the early scholars who chose not to remain silent is that for reasons of personal integrity they felt duty-bound to record, and often to reveal, a part of what they discovered in Lincoln's life, rather than hold it back. Was what they withheld purely the result of prudery? Some observers think so; I do not. (Prudery seldom bargains by halves; it seeks to kill at the root, and wilt every leaf on any unwanted tree.) No, as will become apparent, the stakes are much higher than what Alfred Kinsey used to call "defending the mores"—a fierce guarding of tradition and of questionable moral positions.

It is notable that various scholars and historians, while seeing different images of the same thing, did not agree with each other on what the rules of revelation should be. Far from it. Margaret Leech, as will be seen, was quick and startlingly frank to put Lincoln squarely in bed with the captain of his guard inside the White House, but then pulled back on small details, as if these, rather than the action itself, held the key. Ida Tarbell, on the other hand, stayed entirely away from allusions to Lincoln's bedroom, but was quick to identify the captain by name: David V. Derickson. Her collected notes suggest that she may have achieved a remarkably detailed image of Lincoln's private life during his final years. True, most of this failed to find its way into Tarbell's Lincoln biography—or left much of its intimacy bypassed where it did survive. Whether this was mainly for safety or brevity is arguable. But one must not be too critical here; where silence is sacred—as it is in a wide swath of Lincoln land—credit still goes to those who speak softly, as opposed to many others who to this day have said nothing.

Carl Sandburg said not a word of anything mentioned by either Margaret Leech or Ida Tarbell. He saw Derickson as hardly more than a footnote, and added nothing to that record. But he spoke knowingly of Lincoln having "invisible companionships" (more on those in a moment) and the kinds of compatibilities that drive them. Kincaid did the same, but much more specifically, and from an entirely different angle (as Shively in our day was first to note). What these very different scholars had in common—besides dealing with at least a little of Lincoln's homosexual side—was a certain hit-and-run quality. In each case a few sharp details are followed by quick exits from dangerous territory. Were these hasty retreats designed to pander to prudery? That may be part of it, but many scholars are entirely innocent of that charge. The problem lies elsewhere.

From the moment anything comes along with the possible power to destabilize large areas of Lincoln scholarship, it can be viewed as a major threat by historians who have invested much of their lives sifting and sorting conventional interpretations. Not that anything sexual is by itself that important, particularly not in the case of a larger-than-life figure like Lincoln, whose essential qualities are undimmable. But scholarship itself is damnably dimmable. Over the years in various shifts back and forth, Lincoln has become implicated in one romantic fiction after the other, often based on little or no significant evidence. Such reporting has led to an ever more improbable picture of Lincoln—one which, in the face of contradictory information, now creates a double embarrassment. To fit the reality, his heterosexual side needs a careful, much more conservative recasting—one that honors facts such as his lifelong discomfort in intimate contacts with eligible women.[5] At the same time, allowance must now be made for new, previously unrecognized homosexual components in his life.

It is apparently this prospect—the double jeopardy of a major recasting of the Lincoln literature, along with accepting the unacceptable—that seems to have caused nearly all Lincoln scholars to bolt and run at the first whiff of homosexual evidence. Conversely, it would seem unfair to fault the handful of scholars who *have* collected or mentioned small bits of such evidence, even though they, too, have often exited the kitchen with the cake half cooked.

Particularly interesting—and revealing—is the example of Carl Sandburg, who created a masterpiece of sorts in his six-volume biography of Lincoln. At a very prominent place—the final sentence of the preface to his 1926 edition—in words he kept there for twenty-eight years through many editions, until finally cut in a major abridgment, he wrote:

> Month by month in stacks and bundles of fact and legend, I found invisible companionships that surprised me. Perhaps a few of these presences lurk and murmur in this book.[6]

No chance at all that these "invisible companionships" were heterosexual, for in that case they would have been paraded out with trumpets blaring. Nor could they have been liaisons between casual or political friends; those would neither qualify as "companionships" nor have to be hidden by being mentioned obliquely. But homosexual relationships fit the facts exactly. Poet that he was, Carl Sandburg no doubt held his words in sharp focus and meant precisely what he said when he spoke of "invisible companionships" that "surprised" him—some of them clandestine enough to qualify as presences that "lurk" and "murmur."

This interpretation is no stretch. When describing the most intimate relationship Lincoln ever had—the one with Joshua Fry Speed—Sandburg unmistakably labels it homosexual by making the commonplace assumption that by this very fact, the relationship must mean that a "streak" of effeminacy ran through the partners. Thus he concluded:

> Joshua Speed was a deep-chested man of large sockets, with broad measurement between the ears. A streak of lavender ran through him; he had spots soft as May violets. And he and

Abraham Lincoln told each other their secrets about women. Lincoln too had tough physical shanks and large sockets, also a streak of lavender, and spots soft as May violets.

"I do not feel my own sorrows more keenly than I do yours," Lincoln wrote Speed in one letter. And again: "You know my desire to befriend you is everlasting."[7]

Then a few pages later:

Their births, the loins and tissues of their fathers and mothers, accident, fate, providence, had given these two men streaks of lavender, spots soft as May violets.[8]

Remarkably, Sandburg had the "sockets" part exactly right. The whole business of complementation—each partner "importing" admired traits from the other to fill or repair a felt lack—is entirely correct. Indeed, the well-matched fit of compatible partners is quite like a ball-and-socket. The same idea was spelled out by the Lincoln scholar Robert Kincaid more than fifty years ago:

Speed saw in Lincoln the rough-hewn product of the frontier . . . [and] in Joshua Fry Speed, Abraham Lincoln saw a youth who was truly a "gentleman to the manor born" . . . their kindred hopes and ambitions fused into a unity and understanding which was never broken. . . . They went to parties together; they attended debating clubs and political forums; they occasionally took rides into the country.[9]

Unfortunately, Sandburg's "streaks of lavender, spots soft as May violets" invite serious misunderstanding. For while Lincoln clearly had his soft spots—the wellsprings of his lifelong kindness and generosity—there was certainly nothing "lavender" (effeminate) about these. In fact, a measure of just this kind of softness is apparent or inherent in the toughest of men; it relieves what might otherwise be a brittle, more easily snapped maleness. Moreover, the very notion of a bony, gnarly, rough-hewed Lincoln having the lightness to glide around with the animations and quick changeableness of effeminacy is plainly untrue, and too ludicrous to contemplate.

But just as Sandburg fell into the conventional stereotype of equating male homosexuality with effeminacy, the same assumption may well have suggested itself to other scholars, adding to their hesitations to acknowledge even the clearest homosexual indications in Lincoln.

On the other hand, it would be incorrect to suppose that all problems of dealing with Lincoln's sexuality are necessarily part of the past, or are primitive enough to match the conventions of fifty or a hundred years ago. On the contrary, some of the most pressing questions are as alive, as undiminished, and as fully in force today as they ever were. For instance, there is still nothing intuitively clear in the proposition that a married man with four children could possibly be primarily homosexual. While such a prospect is well within the purview of trained observers, if they wish to be both clear and convincing, they have their work cut out for them. Just such evidence is on the way.

The Intimate World of

Abraham

LINCOLN

CHAPTER ONE

"What Stuff!"*

Virginia Woodbury Fox, the wife of Assistant Secretary of the Navy Gustavus V. Fox, traveled in high sociopolitical circles and kept a detailed diary noted for its specificity and impartiality from 1856 to 1876. She was a close Lincoln confidant, and her diary has become a much quoted source found throughout Lincoln literature. The Library of Congress files contain literally hundreds of her comments and references to them. Yet one of her notes has been overlooked, until very recently. It is an entry dated November 16, 1862: "Tish says, 'there is a Bucktail soldier here devoted to the President, drives with him, and when Mrs. L. is not home, sleeps with him.' What stuff!"

"Tish" was Letitia McKean, a player in Washington's fashionable society and the daughter of an admiral. It is unknown how she came by her information, but hearsay is likely. Should it be dismissed as such?

The Bucktail soldier was David V. Derickson. He was five-feet-nine-inches tall, with intense eyes, a strong nose, and thick black hair, and was from a socially prominent family in Meadville, Pennsylvania. He was a captain in the army. He was born on April 9, 1818. (He was nine years younger than Lincoln.) The military was well-known to the Derickson clan. The captain's father was himself an officer, Capt. Samuel Derickson of the 137th Regiment Pennsylvania Militia (1787–1827). His middle brother, George, was killed in 1854 in the Mexican War. The youngest, Richard, held an array of state military posts, rising to become brigadier general of the state volunteers in 1849, and eventually signing up with Pennsylvania's Erie Regiment as a private in the Civil War.

A scattered record offers some clues to the nature of the Lincoln-Derickson relationship, and attests that McKean's rumor was more than mere hearsay. Margaret Leech's 1941 Pulitzer Prize–winning *Reveille in Washington, 1860–1865*, includes one mention of Derickson on page 303[1]:

> [Lincoln] grew to like the Bucktails, especially Company K, with whose captain he became so friendly that he invited him to share his bed on autumn nights when Mrs. Lincoln was away from home. When the question arose about a guard at the White House on the family's return to town, the President especially requested that Company K continue on duty. The congenial captain was presently transferred to another command, but the soldiers remained with the President throughout the war.

Ms. Leech never identified this "congenial captain," and she cryptically left the fellow almost as soon as she introduced him; all in a mere three sentences. Perhaps it was the off-handed manner in which it was presented or because she never named the captain that the incident comes across as unremarkable. Or maybe it was the suggestion that because the captain was transferred, he was no longer in the picture.

Leech's bibliography references a rare and scholarly book that discusses Derickson in far more detail: *History of the One Hundred and Fiftieth Regiment, Pennsylvania Volunteers, Second Regiment, Bucktail Brigade*. Published in 1895, it was written by Lt. Col. Thomas Chamberlin, immediate commanding officer to Capt. Derickson in Washington.

Every detail about Chamberlin points to his legitimacy as a historian. As he wrote in the preface to his book:

> Nothing has been set down here without careful authentication and, where the memory of witnesses has clashed in respect to any important incident, everything possible has been done to reconcile disagreements and reach an actual fact. . . . And if [my] book, which is truly a *labor of love*, have [sic] no other merit, it is at least, or aims to be, *a faithful presentation of the truth*. (italics in the original)[2]

Chamberlin had graduated with high honors from Lewisburg College, his hometown school, in 1858 and had then gone on to graduate studies in both law and philosophy in Germany. When war came, he elected to serve as company captain in the Pennsylvania Reserves. He was wounded twice in combat, including at Gettysburg on July 1, 1863, which turned out to be the finish of his military career. It also left him partially disabled for the duration of his life, until 1917.

A sizable contingent of the Bucktail Survivors read Chamberlin's history of the regiment. They congratulated him and even gave him an award for the quality and accuracy of his reporting.

Chapter 4 of his book discusses Lincoln and Derickson:

To him [Chamberlin] was immediately entrusted the care of companies at the Soldier's Home, and up to the 22nd of October he visited them each day, inspecting the camp and guards and exercising the men in all the more important company and battalion movements. Here he several times witnessed the arrival of the President, who, after the onerous duties of the day at the White House, was driven to his summer retreat in an open carriage, accompanied by an insignificant detail of cavalry from "Scotts' Nine Hundred." Here, too, he frequently met little Thomas Lincoln, vulgarly known as "Tad," who spent much of his time in the camp, in which he seemed to have a weighty sense of proprietorship.

The President was also not an infrequent visitor in the late afternoon hours, and endeared himself to his guards by his genial, kind ways. He was not long in placing the officers in his two companies at their ease in his presence, and Captains Derickson and Crozier were shortly on a footing of such marked friendship with him that they were often summoned to dinner or breakfast at the presidential board. Captain Derickson, in particular, advanced so far in the President's confidence and esteem that in Mrs. Lincoln's absence he frequently spent the night at his cottage, sleeping in the same bed with him, and—it is said—making use of his Excellency's night-shirt! Thus began an intimacy which continued unbroken until the following spring, when

Captain Derickson was appointed provost marshall of the Nineteenth Pennsylvania District, with head-quarters in Meadville.[3]

With two independent mentions of Mrs. Lincoln's absences, and Derickson's bed-sharing, the matter clearly deserves scrutiny. The implications of Mary Lincoln's absence, for starters, are perhaps different from what one might suppose. The Lincolns presumably had little if any sex for ten years, due to severe physical damage (probably vaginal tearing) that Mary had sustained while giving birth to Tad, with his especially large head, damage that made later sexual intercourse painful. As she herself confided to a friend, "My disease is of a womanly nature."[4] Nor had the Lincolns shared the same bedroom for years; his many nighttime visits from friends and colleagues to discuss politics far into the night had long since caused Mary to want her own bedroom. Thus the importance of her absence during Derickson's nighttime visits rested squarely on not wanting her to be present as a witness.

According to *Lincoln Day By Day: A Chronology 1809–1865*, Mrs. Lincoln left for New York and Boston on October 25, 1862, returning on November 27. Virginia Fox's diary entry falls within this window. Before and after these dates, it is difficult to be certain of Mrs. Lincoln's sleeping arrangements. And yet—as is no surprise—the nature of sexual attraction is such that its appetite is inclined to be whetted rather than blocked by impossible time slots and other barriers that would challenge or stand in its way.

The Lincoln-Derickson relationship had been discussed separately in 1895 in Ida M. Tarbell's popular and widely read *The Life of Abraham Lincoln*, originally a series of pieces written for *McClure's* magazine. Tarbell had discovered a four-thousand word memoir by Captain D. V. Derickson, published in the May 12, 1888, edition of the Meadville (Pennsylvania) *Tribune-Republican*, titled ABRAHAM LINCOLN'S BODYGUARD. The article left the distinct impression that Lincoln's attraction to him began practically at first sight. Their first encounter at the Soldier's Home on September 8, 1862, is described in several paragraphs by Tarbell, quoting Derickson at length, but cutting certain of his passages (restored here, in bold):

"The next morning after our arrival," says Mr. Derickson, "the President sent a messenger with a note to my quarters, stating that he would like to see the Captain of the Guard at his residence. I immediately reported. After an informal introduction and handshaking, he asked me if I would have any objection to riding with him to the city. I replied that it would give me much pleasure to do so, when he invited me to take a seat into his carriage. On our way to the city, he made numerous inquiries, as to my name, where I came from, what regiment I belonged to, etc. **I told him my name and place of residence. He replied, 'Oh, I already know about you. We appointed you one of the internal revenue assessors a few days ago.' He inquired how I got into military service, and I explained my situation to him. He told me how it came that my appointment as assessor was so long delayed.**

"When we entered the city, Mr. Lincoln said he would call at General Halleck's headquarters and get what news he had received from the Army during the night. I informed him that General Cullum, chief aide to General Halleck, was raised in Meadville and that I knew him when I was a boy. He replied, 'Then we must see both gentlemen.' When the carriage stopped, he requested me to remain seated, and said he would bring the gentlemen down to see me, the office being on the second floor. In a short time the President came down, followed by the other gentlemen. When he introduced them to me, General Cullum recognized and seemed pleased to see me. In General Halleck I thought I discovered a kind of quizzical look, as much as to say, 'Isn't this rather a big joke to ask the Commander-in-Chief of the Army [sic] down to the street to be introduced to a country captain?'

"On arriving at the White House the President invited me into the executive chamber, where I spent a half-hour very pleasantly. During that time he explained to me all the situation of both armies, and read the official telegrams that have been received during the night

from the different headquarters of the Army. I was much pleased with my interview with the President. I returned in the carriage to my camp quarters.

"Supposing that the invitation to ride to the city with the President was as much to give him the opportunity to look over and interview the new captain as for any other purpose, I did not report [to regular duty] the next morning. During the day I was informed that it was the desire of the President that I should breakfast with him and accompany him to the White House every morning, and return with him in the evening. This duty I entered upon with much pleasure, and was on hand in good time next morning; and I continued to perform this duty until we moved to the White House in November. It was Mr. Lincoln's custom, on account of the pressure of business, to breakfast before the other members of the family were up; and I usually entered his room at half-past six or seven o'clock in the morning, where I often found him reading the Bible or some work on the art of war. On my entering, he would read aloud and offer comments of his own as he read.

"I usually went down to the city at 4 o'clock and returned with the President at 5. He often carried a small portfolio containing papers relating to the business of the day, and spent many hours on them in the evening. **Frequently on our way home, he discussed points that seemed to trouble him.**

"I found Mr. Lincoln to be one of the most kind-hearted, pleasant gentlemen that I had ever met. He never spoke unkindly of any one and always spoke of the rebels 'as those southern gentlemen.' "

Derickson's full account is a fascinating document. It goes on to discuss the events of November 1, 1862, when the Lincoln family was due to leave the Soldier's Home and return to the White House. Company K was slated to be removed as the President's Guard and be assigned elsewhere, and other companies were vying to succeed it. However, the president intervened:

During the fall of '62 several efforts were made to supersede our company, by parties wanting the position, which became so annoying to the President that he issued the following order, which placed the matter at rest:

EXECUTIVE MANSION,

Washington, Nov. 1, 1862

Whom it may concern.
Captain Derrickson [sic], with his company, has been for some time keeping guard at my residence, now at the Soldier's Retreat. He and his company are very agreeable to me, and while it is deemed proper for any guard to remain, none would be more satisfactory to me than Capt. D. and his company.

A. LINCOLN

This was apparently an urgent reason for Lincoln wanting to retain the Bucktails and their captain, though to common soldiers who knew nothing of the emotions involved, it may have seemed as if he only wanted to grant a favor to his young son, Tad, amid a sea of military politics. In any case, near the turn of the century, as Tarbell continued gathering leftover memories, she heard from one Milo M. Millen who, on July 13, 1897, wrote that he had recently heard from his uncle, one of the original Bucktails, former sergeant Billy F. Ellis:

I have just interviewed my uncle. . . . It seems that several times during the stay of Company K at the Soldiers' House [sic] orders were issued by the War Department to have the company join the regiment in the field, as there was need of all the men that could be spared. About the last day of October 1862, another order came and was read to the company. The boys at once began to make preparations for leaving, as this time "marching orders" were imperative. Shortly after the hustle of making ready began in the camp on the morning of the first of November, "Little Tad," who was a great favorite with the "guard" came down with tears in his eyes and asked what was up. The men replied "We are going to leave you, Tad, we've got marching orders." "No," replied Tad, "you mustn't go." "Yes, we must," replied the soldier boys, "we have received orders from the War Department to report at the head quarters of our regiment and we can't disobey." Little Tad thought for a moment and said that he would see that they did not go and ran as fast as his little limbs would carry him towards the house. He related the news to his father who at once penned [his order, dated November 1, 1862]. Lincoln sent "Little Tad" with this to the War Department and presently returned very proudly being [bringing?] a message from the Secretary [of War], countermanding the order to march.[5]

Chamberlin, unlike Tarbell, distinguished between occasion and intent. The decision to retain the Bucktails, he confirmed, was a matter strictly of the heart: "Captain Derickson's excellent standing with the President sufficiently explains this written expression of the latter's feeling."

For whatever reason, Tarbell did not explore the Derickson-Lincoln relationship in detail. Her only mention of it was to spread the wealth. She described it as nothing more than another example of the president's well-known warmth and generosity toward the whole of Company K: "This kindly relation, begun with the captain, the President extended to every man in the company."[6] She elaborated:

The welfare of the men, their troubles, escapades, amusements, were treated by the President as a kind of family matter. He never forgot to ask after the sick, often secured a pass or a furlough for someone, and took genuine delight in the camp fun. . . . No doubt much of the President's interest in Company K was due to his son Tad. The boy was a great favorite with the men, and probably carried to his father many a tale of the camp. He considered himself, in fact, no unimportant part of the organization, for he wore a uniform, carried a lieutenant's commission, often drilled with the men or rode on his pony at their head in reviews.[7]

Yet Derickson's account of his relationship is suggestive of something different. Derickson received the president's request to meet him, and went right over to do so; after a handshake Lincoln asked if he "would have any objection to riding with him to the city." It's clear that almost as soon as he entered Lincoln's carriage for their first ride to the city, their connection was immediate. There was a charged atmosphere of mutual esteem, one well-primed for moving toward some kind of culmination. As Derickson described it, their conversation proceeded through many small but rapid steps, with Lincoln's questions about his background. These are precisely the kinds of redundant questions in pursuit of small increments of intimacy that quickly become tiresome in ordinary conversation—but not here, perhaps because the interest was not on facts but rather on the chance they offered the partners to increase the quality and extent of their closeness within an almost classical seduction scene. Derickson felt very complimented, and it didn't take long for both to realize there was mutual interest.

Some observers might be inclined to deny that all this was any kind of seduction—or at least to put off that possibility, perhaps awaiting more tangible evidence further along in the relationship. In keeping with such doubts it is indeed remarkable that Lincoln chose to move quite as rapidly and as assertively as he did toward Derickson on their very first day. Not that the action was entirely one-sided on Lincoln's part. Once initiated, the escalation of events in such a situation as this was bound to have been boosted from both sides, since even a momentary blip in the continuity of backing and filling tends to markedly de-escalate it. But hardly here; Lincoln was soon wound up if not revved up, ready to exploit any next opportunity. He did not have to wait long.

When Lincoln stated his intention to call at General Halleck's headquarters to get the latest news, Derickson accidentally supplied just such an opportunity with his casual mention of having known General Cullum back home when he was a boy. Without this remark it is doubtful whether Derickson would have been introduced to either of the high brass—and certainly doubtful that the generals would have been invited down to the street to meet him. But Lincoln, seeing a golden opportunity to impress his new captain, instantly revised his previous plan, placing a new one at the service of his quickly developing relationship with Derickson. Only a moment before, the plan had been simply to call on General Halleck for the latest news; but now, under a banner of old home week, it suddenly became possible to both thrill Derickson and advance their closeness by turning the whole occasion into an unforgettable event.

When they returned to the White House, Lincoln found countless opportunities to forge their closeness by confiding in Derickson, sharing official telegrams newly received from the field, even laying out the military positions of opposing armies. Little wonder Derickson was "much pleased" and tremendously impressed. From that first handshake in the morning to finally being driven back to his camp in the presidential carriage it had been quite a day. Beyond being packed with events, it overflowed with precisely the kinds of gentle and concentrated high-focus attention from Lincoln that Henry C. Whitney, from having himself once been on the receiving end, well described: "[It was] as if he wooed me to close intimacy and familiarity," a kind of courtship, as indeed it was. [8]

In the ensuing days and weeks Derickson continued to loom ever larger in Lincoln's life. Besides their closeness in bed, they shared a wide variety of confidences and daily social interactions. Derickson recalled them in separate scenes, scenes that are clearer if viewed together:

- "He [Lincoln] was not a member of any church, but usually attended Dr. Paxton's (Presbyterian) church, where I frequently accompanied him." With strong religious doubts, Lincoln was ordinarily much disinclined to attend such services; but with his wife out of town, he was "frequently" inclined to attend with Derickson.
- "The President frequently requested me to remain in the executive chamber on the morning of [a] cabinet meeting, to be introduced to members of his cabinet, as they usually dropped in one by one half an hour or so before the hour of meeting."
- "A short time after the battle of Antietam, the President visited the battle fields of Harper's Ferry, Antietam and South Mountain, and invited me to accompany him, which I was pleased to do."

- "There was no fear or timidity in Mr. Lincoln's make up. In fact I thought him rather careless or thoughtless as to his personal safety. He frequently walked to the theater with no escort but myself and his little son."

- "Mr. Lincoln made no effort to conceal his humble origin, but rather delighted to dwell upon the incidents and trials of his early life. He often interested me by rehearsing many of the stories and incidents of his youth, most of which have been published. . . . But I will give one as he related it to me, that I have never seen in print." Here Derickson described a Black Hawk War experience.

- "Although she had two brothers in the Confederate Army, Mrs. Lincoln was a hearty loyal woman, and one of the best rebel-haters that I met during my stay in Washington. She approached to me, on more than one occasion, to urge the President to arrest and confine a certain official connected to a government institution in Washington whom she believed to be a rebel sympathizer. I spoke to Mr. Lincoln about it one day, when he replied that Mrs. Lincoln had mentioned the matter to him several times, but if he were to arrest and imprison all within our lines known to be in sympathy with the rebel cause, to say nothing about those who were suspected, it would keep the quartermaster's department employed most of the time in building new prisons."

The ready access of Derickson to Lincoln was beyond easy. His instant avenue to the president made for a relationship remarkable for its confident low-intensity informality. Derickson knew how to maintain smooth relations with everybody, including Mrs. Lincoln (no small feat in itself), delivering messages with efficiency, meeting countless demands from little Tad, and all the while enjoying the run of the place. Remarkable, too, was how entirely free Derickson felt not only to pop in and out of the White House, but into Lincoln's office as well. He could stop and chat easily, then without hesitation rush right in to tell Lincoln of yet another good deed awaiting his help. Sometimes the message was as lighthearted as a joke: "There's a man outside who has thirty-six feet of sons [six six-footers] in the army." Lincoln's instant reply: "Invite him up, Captain; I want to see him just as much as he wants to see me."

Quite beyond all this, the usually supersecret Lincoln shared with Derickson small and larger details about himself that he seldom if ever revealed to anyone else. Yet Derickson sometimes went out of his way to insist with more than a modicum of modesty that some of what he heard Lincoln relate about his humble origins and the trials of his early life were only "stories and incidents of his youth, most of which have been published time and again, so I will not repeat them."

With these careful words, Derickson leaned so far backward from claiming privileged information as to suggest he may well be a rich repository of it. Nevertheless, some of the revelations he heard from Lincoln are astonishing, especially when not discussed elsewhere, and carry a certain cadence of confidentiality, if not of pillow talk:

> I said to him one day, "Mr. Lincoln, when you were a candidate for President in 1860, your friends made much of the fact that you were a rail-splitter. How many rails did you ever split in a day?" His reply was that when he was a lad about twelve years old, his stepfather [sic] moved the family from Kentucky to the state of Indiana, where he bought a farm of fifty acres. On it there was a field of five acres cleared and partly fenced, and enough rail timber cut to enclose the lot. He said that he and his [father] had split rails enough to complete the fence, and that this was all the rail-splitting he had ever done.

Beyond those with whom he shared his private life, Lincoln seemed seldom if ever to have mentioned the fiction of his fame as a railsplitter. In the *Collected Works*, for instance, only once, and then only to his special confidant Noah Brooks, does he mention a word of it.[9] Perhaps its rural ring appealed to him enough to keep him from protesting its inaccuracy; or possibly it may have felt embarrassing, or even rude, to pull back from an image that early on had seemed a perfect fit to so large a public. These and other possibilities might have been part of it—we shall never know—but to just leave the label in place as virtually the logo of his life, with scarcely a fragment of fact in it, still seems remarkable. Everywhere his image as very much the railsplitter stared back at him in the form of election placards, newspaper cartoons, historical societies, little books, and bulletins by the name of Railsplitter; indeed, as his bodyguard and longtime friend and colleague Ward Hill Lamon recalled, it was a logo "heard everywhere and rails were to be seen on nearly everything, even on stationery."[10] How like Lincoln to share the plain truth only with intimates, yet with all others to simply stand by as both supporters and opponents used the emblem to laud or to skewer him; the whole of it as much in line with his code of supersilence in public and his utter frankness in private, along with a boyish glee he sometimes took in watching people guess wrong.

In 1996, the prominent Lincoln scholars Don and Virginia Fehrenbacher published their important *Recollected Words of Abraham Lincoln*, in which they rated the authenticity of various statements and stories attributed to him. Nowhere do they mention David Derickson (as few Lincolnists ever do), but they did raise and rank a question once asked about railsplitting by Noah Brooks. Lincoln had answered:

> Now let me tell you about that. I am not a bit anxious about my reputation in that line of business; but if there is any thing in this world that I am a judge of, it is a good felling of timber, but I don't remember having worked by myself at splitting rails for one whole day in my life. . . . I recollect that sometime during the canvass for the office I now hold, there was a great mass meeting where I was present, and with a great flourish several rails were brought into the meeting, and being informed where they came from, I was asked to identify them, which I did, with some qualms of conscience, having helped my father split rails, as at other jobs. I said if there were any rails which I had split, I shouldn't wonder if those were the rails.[11]

Strange to say, the Fehrenbachers rated this highly specific and decidedly Lincolnesque statement as a "D"—one "about whose authenticity there is more than average doubt." Remarkable! If rated here, it would rank at a high level of certainty. For not only is it in striking accord with Lincoln's account to Derickson, it is unmistakably Lincoln-like even in the twists and turns he takes to avoid speaking an untruth, as is almost painfully apparent in his final sentence above.

Lincoln and Derickson's daily contact lasted nearly eight months, and the circumstances of its ending deserve attention. Derickson wanted a transfer and promotion, as well as an army posting back home in Meadville. As he described it, Lincoln was instrumental:

> In the spring of 1863, Congress passed what was known as the Enrollment Act, establishing the Provost Marshall's Bureau. Finding my duties very light, I told the President that I thought my lieutenants could take care of him and the company and suggested that he appoint me provost. His reply was that if he had the appointment he would give it to me at once; "but," said he, "the members of congress think these appointments all belong to them." He asked me if I knew our member of congress and whether he was my friend. I replied that I knew him very well, but that he was not a citizen of our county, and I had not spoken to him on the subject. He said, "Well, you had better write him, anyway. "I did do, and in a short time received a reply, stating that before receiving my letter, he had received fifteen other applications; and among so many good men, it was hard for him to make the choice. I handed this reply to the president, who after reading it said, "Very well, if he cannot make the choice, we will have to make one for him."[12]

It is apparent that Lincoln did not resent the captain's request to leave, or at least not enough to let it interfere with his promise to him. Lincoln kept his word, and on April 17, 1863, after a formal inspection of Company K, together with Secretary of State William H. Seward, gave the captain what was surely welcome news:

> At the hour appointed, Mr. Lincoln's son Tad, then about 12 years old, came to where I had the company in charge and

informed me that the president and the governor were waiting at the lawn on the south side of the White House. I immediately marched up and saluted the inspecting officers,
and after maneuvering the company for a short time, I put it
in charge of Lieutenant Getchell, who marched the company
to their quarters. After a handshaking and a few words com-
plimentary to the company, Mr. Lincoln said to me quietly,
"Captain, I was over to the war department, yesterday, and
that little matter of ours is all right." I thanked him for his
kindness, when we separated. The next day, I received my
appointment, and made my arrangements to leave for home.
I bid a final farewell to the president and his family, feeling
conscious and proud of the fact that I had friend and acquaintance one of the kindest and greatest men this country
has ever produced.[13]

After the war, now *Major* Derickson retired and took full advantage
of his many excellent connections. He decided on a career in politics
and public service. With a nod from President Grant, he was appointed the postmastership in Meadville in 1869, following that with
a term spent as a state legislator, from 1881 to 1882. He also served
as a member of the board of directors for the Pennsylvania & Ohio
Railroad, simultaneously giving his time to the Meadville City Hospital, doing charity work to help the poor.

Understandably, Derickson was exceedingly judicious about what
he included, and omitted, in his hometown paper, never mentioning
the nights he'd shared a bed with Lincoln or even the day-to-day social
interactions. The marvel is not in what he left out, but how much he
managed to convey and the accuracy of it. His four-thousand-word article of 1888 was much in line with a brief account of Company K included in Samuel P. Bates's multivolume *History of Pennsylvania
Volunteers*, 1861–65, published in 1870. (Not that this was surprising;
Bates was from Meadville and Derickson had probably spoken about
his friendship with Lincoln.)

A curious characteristic of this entire case is that when carefully examined, one surprise after another keeps tumbling out of it. Derickson was married (as were nearly all men in those days), yet his

personal history still startles and stands apart. After his first wife died he married again. By the time he began his relationship with Lincoln, he had nine children. After Lincoln died, he had still another child. For reasons soon to be examined, his heterosexual and homosexual sides were neither as unusual nor as contradictory as they may at first seem, yet other parts of the picture invite questions. For instance, at the very time Derickson was in the Bucktail Brigade and closely involved with Lincoln, he had a grown son, Charles Milton Derickson, who actually marched with his father as part of Company K, after enlisting at age eighteen. The son served the president right up until Lincoln was assassinated. But neither father nor son seemed customary in their responses to one another. What possible explanation could there be for a father who so rarely mentions or acknowledges a son who is also a comrade and soldier? And why would the son act similarly about his father, in fact, acknowledging his father even less? In a ten-page, handwritten letter written to Tarbell (dated December 15, 1897, six years after the death of his father), Charles refers to "Captain Derickson" three times, with no hint of him being any relation, in fact, without the merest trace of ill-will *or* kind feelings between them. Surely this was more than just good breeding and the formal writing practices of the day.

Interestingly, Charles Milton Derickson, the son, also wrote about visiting Lincoln in his private quarters, in one innocuous instance:

> The President evidently paid very little attention to his own personal welfare as the front hall door of his residence at the Soldiers' House [sic] was scarcely ever locked. I remember one night about twelve or one o'clock a cavalry man rode up to the front door and said he had a message to deliver in person to the President. As I was Sergeant of the Guard, I asked him to give it to me; he at first refused but finally complied (having been previously instructed in similar cases). I opened the front door, went upstairs, knocked at the President's bedroom door, which was unlocked, walked in, turned up the gas, handed him his spectacles, and the message, which he read and receipted for, without leaving his bed. I turned

down the gas, closed the door and thought how little he thought of his own safety.

Evidently, both Lincoln and his son Tad felt some affection for the teenage sergeant and felt at ease with him:

Little Tad sent for me to come to the White House to see him, his father and he both being somewhat indisposed, it was the time the President was reported to have small pox. [Actually, varioloid, a less deadly but still dangerous form of smallpox he first felt November 19, 1863, while giving his Gettysburg Address.] I spent two or three hours with them that afternoon, very pleasantly, in referring to the [recent runaway horse] accident and congratulating the President on his escape. He said that he had been in several runaways and was never frightened by horses, but about the worse scared he ever was, was when he was a young man, he had been hauling wood with a yoke of steers and going through the woods with an empty wagon, sitting on the hounds with his legs hanging down on either side; something frightened the steers, they started to run and every time the wheels would strike the root of a tree he would bound up in the air; he held on the best he could; they finally got out into an open field where he got them stopped. He also told me about Colonel Ellsworth and how he tried to have him not go into the service at that time but could not prevail on him to wait a while. He said Ellsworth read law in his office and was the first officer killed in Virginia, he got a field glass and pointed out to the house in Alexandria in which he was killed. He also related several other stories which I cannot now recall.[14]

Scattered among the vast Lincoln literature are many bits and pieces, some of them as mildly interesting as those above, that mention separate small facts concerning members of the extended Derickson family, but none of these brings us any closer to solving the mutual coolness of this father and son. Could Charles have had a prudish response to reports of his father repeatedly being in bed with Lincoln?

We don't know, although Charles never showed any coolness toward Lincoln to jibe with any embarrassment. Faced with this dead-end, it seems better to leave the topic unanalyzed and leave it be, rather than fill in the blanks with mere conjecture.

The gossip factor, as they say, is a horse of different color—although it, too, rides off in a cloud of dust that shrouds many a mystery. Unlike the case with Chamberlin, where it remains unclear why he told as much as he did in the first place, or how members of the Survivors Association managed to swig it all down without a cough, other dangers appear to have been eradicated up front by a swift and timely move. Company K had seen Lincoln lavish attention on their captain, including meals, social events, bedroom sharing, and even trips. What were they to make of it?

Lincoln's note requesting that "Capt. D and his company" be left in place proved a masterstroke of public relations. It was sent to military headquarters—with the news soon relayed back to the company, but more than the mere news found its way back. Apparently, in no time Lincoln's order had circulated among the troops. Supplied by whom? Unknown. On whose orders? Also unknown for sure, but quite possibly supplied by Lincoln himself. (He had a track record of supplying copies of his statements—even excerpts in his own hand from his speeches—and sending them off to people he thought might especially appreciate them.) Right on cue, as if by yet another stroke of magic, the entire company appears to have read and reread his note as roses for themselves, and pridefully began to memorize it word for word—so much so, in fact, that thirty-eight years later when Tarbell published *The Life of Abraham Lincoln*, she noted, "Every member of the guard now living can quote verbatim the note which the President wrote settling the matter [of keeping Company K]."[15]

Could this sequence of events so favorable to Lincoln's luck have occurred by some extraordinary coincidence? The situation suggests, admittedly without tangible proof (such as physical copies of the note the soldiers read), that very quickly, probably on the very day Lincoln wrote the order acknowledging his high favor for Company K, he also scribbled out at least a few copies for the soldiers themselves. Taken alone, it's an innocent and polite gesture. But Lincoln also had an extraordinary quality, sometimes much apparent: the ability to detect complications at a great distance, and to guard his flanks far sooner than others saw any danger. In this he often followed a fundamental principle well in advance of Anatole France's later formulation: "In facing life's dangers, the secret is to listen for the guns, and walk toward them."

However, neither this style of handling danger, by engaging it head-on, nor Lincoln's many uses of supersecrecy in his personal life, is the most remarkable. No, ironically, the outstanding characteristic of his relationship with Derickson is something close to exactly the opposite of rigorous secrecy and control. After taking a few commonsense precautions (such as inviting Derickson to spend the night only when they could be alone) he then proceeds to move rapidly and straight away toward what he wants, seemingly oblivious to criticism—or to any and all worries of other kinds.

It is unlikely that Lincoln wasn't aware of the potential for dangerous talk; gossip that could start at every turn. He and Derickson were constantly seen together. Should we just assume he wasn't worried? He never appeared to pull away from peril, or to cover his tracks. His display of affection toward Derickson could be considered brazen, even by the most liberal observers. As was true in other of Lincoln's less lengthy homosexual attachments, he seems never to have felt at all guilty about sex (clear as well in his wit). Almost the opposite, actually. It is possible he may simply have been unaware of how obvious his actions had become? In any case, could Lincoln's unguardedness and his seeming self-acceptance have emboldened members of Company K to think and speak more openly than they might have otherwise? This may be why years later Chamberlin wrote the story as frankly as he told his military history.

Ultimately, what can be said of the sexual status of Lincoln and Derickson? Both could be seen as within some huge, undifferentiated "bisexual" category—all the more so when it is remembered that nearly all men in that era were married and had children—meaning that virtually every homosexual act or impulse might easily fall into a single, enormous bisexual category. And yet to force people of widely different motives and behaviors into such an immense, indiscriminate pigeonhole is to obfuscate more than to clarify their differences.

A half century ago the sex researcher Alfred Kinsey confronted the problem of classifying mixed sex patterns by devising his 0-to-6 scale, which allows the ranking of any homosexual component in a person's life from none to entirely homosexual. By this measure Lincoln qualifies as a classical 5: predominantly homosexual, but incidentally heterosexual.[16]

Derickson, with his much more enthusiastic heterosexual side in the form of multiple wives and children, would no doubt rank considerably lower. True, there is no way of knowing exactly what went on in their bedroom (nor would any particular acts have affected their ratings anyway). But for Derickson to have attained sufficient affectional and physical arousal for it to have been mutually and repeatedly satisfying would imply, indeed demonstrate, a marked homosexual response—the essence of his bisexuality—amounting to a Kinsey rating of at least a 2: predominantly heterosexual, but more than incidentally homosexual.[17] Both of these ratings are conservative in the sense that each might well be a notch higher—at least during the period of their affair.

The mutual affection between Lincoln and Derickson almost certainly continued after they were officially separated in April 1863. Whether the two ever saw each other again is not known. However, a letter of June 3, 1864, from Provost Marshall Derickson to his commander-in-chief, preserved in the Library of Congress, expressed Derickson's abiding warmth:

> I have the honor to inform you that I have been appointed Delegate from this District to the Baltimore [Republican] convention.
>
> It would give me much pleasure to be present and vote for your renomination, but owing to the condition of the Draft in my District, it is not proper for me to be absent at this time. I have therefore appointed J. H. Lenhart, Esq of this place as my Substitute, who will vote on all occasions as your friends may desire.
>
> I enclose the proceedings of the conference from which you will see that I received a unanimous vote, for which compliment I am indebted [more] to the fact that I was known to be your warm friend than to my own personal popularity. I mention this

fact mearly [sic] to show you that our whole District are in favour of your re[e]lection. [18]

On April 28, 1865, Derickson bade his final farwell when Lincoln's funeral train made its stop in Cleveland. Carl Sandburg noted the occasion: "From Meadville, Pennsylvania, had come two hundred [men] marshalled by Captain Derickson and some of his boys who had served with Lincoln's White House bodyguard."[19]

TWO

Beginnings

Early Puberty, Reuben Chronicles

On the very day Lincoln was born, February 12, 1809, his nine-year-old cousin Dennis Hanks came to see and hold the new baby. Lincoln's mother cautioned, "Be keerful, Dennis, fur you air the fust boy he's ever seen." Right off, Dennis noticed a near lifetime trait, that little Abe was "solemn as a papoose"—adding that "he looked like any other baby, at fust—like red cherry pulp squeezed dry. An' he didn't improve none as he growed older." Indeed, Lincoln was not much for looks then or for the rest of his life, and was many times somber and quiet, even depressed. Still, as Dennis reported, "He was mighty good comp'ny . . . interested in everything. An' he always did have fits of cuttin' up. I've seen him when he was a little feller, settin' on a stool, starin' at a visitor. All of a sudden he'd bu'st out laughin' fit to kill. If he told us what he was laughin' at, half the time we couldn't see no joke."[1]

In December 1816, when Abe was seven, the Lincolns left Kentucky and set out for Indiana (where land titles were more secure). At a spot now in Spencer County Thomas Lincoln unaccountably chose a harsh homesite, almost a mile from any water. With winter bearing down he quickly made a three-sided "half-faced camp," a cabin of sorts, with its fourth side entirely open, protected night and day only by a constantly raging fire. Later he built a regular eighteen-foot-square log cabin, through the leaky logs of which Abe soon shot at a flock of turkeys, and killed one. This was a shock that left its mark on the tender-minded boy, for as Lincoln later said in a short autobiography, he "has never since pulled a trigger on any larger game."[2]

Nothing in young Lincoln's personality ever proved stronger than his tendency to see the world through the eyes of another, be it animal or human, and thus vicariously to suffer its pain. This empathy—the stuff of sympathy—lay behind Lincoln's often unbounded lenience and compassion.

Another side of his gentle nature was a marked disinterest in any display of machismo. Friendly competition, as in wrestling and tests of strength, could be fun, but not the sharp edge of team sports. (Curiously, he never paid a price for standing apart in this way, perhaps because he was amusing, and too tall to tease.) He never went in for any form of heroics, or for attempting to win over an adversary who might be roundly beaten. In fact, he never seemed to do anything for ego or for glory. Yet when fired with moral indignation at some injustice—as he often later was in legal cases—he could be fierce. As his friend Judge Davis noticed, when seeking justice Lincoln was ready to be resoundingly "hurtful in denunciation and merciless in castigation." In one lawsuit he destroyed a crooked lawyer for stealing from a helpless widow. He not only won the case and had the stolen money returned, he also put up surety for her court costs, charged her no fee, paid her Springfield hotel bill, and then bought her ticket home.[3]

But all this came later. Lincoln's early life was hard, filled with drudgery and tragedy. As he himself once said, most of it could be condensed into a single phrase: "the short and simple annals of the poor." Only a few scenes stuck in his memory. One was of working all day with his father planting seed, only to have a cloudburst during the night wash everything away. And he remembered something of a terrible plague—the so-called "milk sick" (probably brucellosis)—caused by bad milk from cows that had eaten poisonous snakeroot; it was usually fatal within days. When he was but nine years old his mother, Nancy Lincoln, came down with the milk sick. As she lay dying she placed her hand on little Abe's head and told him to be kind to his father and sister. To all three she said, "be good to one another," and died.[4] The day was October 5, 1818.

Once again hard times were upon the Lincolns. Twelve-year-old Sarah cooked, swept, mended, and did her best, while Thomas, Abe, and Dennis Hanks, who moved in with the Lincolns when his parents died, hewed away at the forest and tended meager crops. Still, their fortunes ebbed. Deprived of much that Nancy Lincoln had once supplied, the household sank into squalor. Even Thomas became alarmed. So in the winter of 1819 he left the children to their own devices and returned to Kentucky, where he found Sarah Bush Johnston, a tall, attractive widow with three children who, years before, had turned down his marriage proposal. But now she too was a struggling single parent. This time she accepted his proposal, and on December 2, 1819, they married. She had accumulated considerable household goods over the years, a modest enough dowry but far better than anything the Lincolns had ever known. Thomas Lincoln loaded his new wife, her three children, and her various stores into a borrowed wagon with a four-horse team, and set out once more for Indiana. There would now be eight persons to share the rough-hewn, one-room, dirt-floored Lincoln cabin.[5] Nobody yet knew it, but Sarah Bush Lincoln possessed surprising qualities that were to bloom like exotic flowers in the common dirt of Indiana.

There is no record of what the new Mrs. Lincoln thought of the doorless, floorless, windowless shack; she voiced no complaints or even surprise. As William Herndon, Lincoln's law partner and premier biographer, put it:

> With true womanly courage and zeal she set resolutely to work to make right that which seemed wrong. . . . The work of renovation in and around the cabin continued until even Thomas Lincoln himself, under the general stimulus of the new wife's presence, caught the inspiration, and developed signs of intense activity. The advent of Sarah Bush was certainly a red-letter day for the Lincolns. She was not only industrious and thrifty, but gentle and affectionate; and her newly adopted children for the first time, perhaps, realized the benign influence of a mother's love. Of young Abe she was especially fond, and we have her testimony that her kindness and care for him were warmly and bountifully returned.[6]

The tasks she took on soon resulted in a quantum leap forward. Her husband Thomas was put to laying a wood floor in the cabin, as well as to filling the open doorway with a slab of planks hung by leather straps as hinges. The open gap of a window was covered with oiled paper to stop the wind, and to let in a little light. The cracks between the logs were plastered shut with mud—"daubed" as the locals called it—and there were pleasant improvements in daily life. "[T]he mat of corn husks and leaves on which the children had slept in the corner gave way to the comfortable luxuriance of a feather bed. She washed the two orphans, and fitted them out in clothes taken from the stores of her own."[7] Little wonder that for the rest of his life Abraham Lincoln greatly cared for her, visited her when he could, and felt for her as deeply as he once had for the "Angel Mother" he lost at age nine.

As rich as Sarah Lincoln's contribution was, it is still understated. Besides her unbounded energy and overflowing kindness, she was extraordinarily perceptive. In 1865, when Lincoln's biographer William Herndon started searching out every possible Lincoln fact, he was delighted to learn that the adored stepmother was still alive and not very far away—some eight miles south of Charleston, Illinois. He reached her on September 6, but soon began to lose hope:

> She seemed so old and feeble; she asked me my name two or three times and where I lived as often, and would say: "Where Mr. Lincoln lived once, his friend too." She breathed badly at first, but seemed to be struggling at last to arouse herself, or to fix her mind on the subject. Gradually by introducing simple questions to her, about her age, marriage, Kentucky, Thomas Lincoln, her former husband Johnston, her children and grand children, she awoke, as it were, a New Being. Her eyes were clear and calm, her flesh white and pure. . . . She even stood tall [again].[8]

A New Being, indeed! Out of this newly revived Sarah Bush Lincoln there poured forth a treasure trove of detail—perhaps the single most important compendium ever—of facts and tableaus of Lincoln's boyhood, including how early some of his sovereign traits showed up. And there were hidden surprises as well. She began simply enough:

Thomas Lincoln and myself, were married in 1819—left Kentucky. When we landed in Indiana Mr. Lincoln had erected a good log cabin, tolerably comfortable. Abe was then young, so was his sister. I dressed Abe and his sister up—looked more human. Abe slept upstairs—went up on pins stuck in the logs, like a ladder.

Abe was about nine . . . when I landed in Indiana. The country was wild and desolate. Abe was a good boy—didn't like physical labor—was diligent for knowledge—wished to know, and if pains and labor would get it he was sure to get it. He read all the books he could lay his hands on—read the Bible some, though not as much as [is] said, sought more congenial books suitable for his age. I think news papers were had in Indiana as early as 1824 & up to 1830 when we moved to Illinois—Abe was a constant reader of them—I am sure of this for the years of 1827-28-29-30. Abe read histories, papers—and other books—can't name any one, have forgotten. Abe had no particular religion—didn't think of that question at that time, if he ever did. He never talked about it. He read diligently, studied in the day time—didn't after night much—went to bed Early—got up Early and then read. Abe read all the books he could lay his hands on—and when he came across a passage that struck him he would write it down on boards if he had no paper and keep it there till he did get paper, then he would re-write it, look at it, repeat it. He had a copy book, a kind of scrap book in which he would put down all things and this preserved them. He ciphered on boards when he had no paper, and when the board would get too black he would shave it off with a drawing knife and go on again.

Abe, when old folks were about was a silent and attentive observer—never speaking or asking questions till they were gone and then he must understand Every thing—even to the smallest thing—Minutely & Exactly; he would then repeat it over to himself again & again—sometimes in one form and then in another and when it was fixed in his mind to suit him, he became Easy and never lost that fact or his understanding of it. Sometimes he seemed perturbed to give Expression to his ideas and got mad almost at one who couldn't Explain plainly what he wanted to convey. He would hear sermons preached—come home—take the children out—get on a stump or log and almost repeat it word for word. He made other Speeches—Such as interested him and the children. I can say what scarcely one woman in a thousand can: Abe never gave me a cross word or look and never refused in fact, or Even in appearance, to do any thing I requested of him. He was kind to Every body and to every thing—accompanied others if he could, would do so willingly. His mind and mine, what little I had, seemed to run together—more in the same channel. Abe could Easily learn and long remember, and when he did learn anything he learned it well and stored away in his memory, which was Extremely good. . .

Abe was a moderate eater; he sat down and ate what was set before him, making no complaint; he seemed Careless about this . . . always had good health—never was sick—was very careful of his person, was tolerably neat and clean only—Cared nothing for clothes [only] that they were clean and neat—fashion cut no figure with him—nor color—nor material—was Careless about these things . . . I saw him every year or two after he was Elected President. (Here the old lady stopped, turned around and cried, wiped her eyes, and proceeded.)

Abe was always fond of fun—sport—wit and jokes—He was sometimes very witty indeed. He never drank whiskey or other strong drink—was temperate in all things—too much so I thought sometimes. He never told me a lie in his life—never Evaded—never Equivocated never dodged—nor turned a Corner to avoid any chastisement or other responsibility. He never swore or used profane language in my presence nor in others' that I now remember of—He duly reverenced old age—loved those best about his own age—played with those under his age—he listened to the aged—argued with his Equals—but played with the children. He loved animals generally and treated them kindly; he loved children well, very well. There seemed to be nothing unusual in his love for animals or his own kind—though he treated Every body and Every thing Kindly—humanely.

Abe didn't care much for crowds of people; he chose his own Company which was always good. He was not very fond of girls as he seemed to me. He sometimes attended Church—would repeat the sermon over again to the children. The sight of such a thing amused all and did Especially tickle the Children. He was dutiful to me—loved me truly, I think. I had a son John who was raised with Abe. Both were good boys, but I must say—Both now being dead, that Abe was the best boy I Ever Saw or Ever Expect to see. I wish I had died when my husband died. I did not want Abe to run for President—did not want him elected—was afraid Somehow or other—felt it in my heart that Something would happen to him and when he came down to see me after he was Elected President I still felt that Something told me that Something would befall Abe and that I should see him no more. Abe and his father are in Heaven I have no doubt, and I want to go there—go where they are—God bless Abraham.[9]

At first glance it might seem these many images flickering at us through the eyes of Sarah Bush Lincoln hardly more than reiterate what is already known of him from other sources. Not quite so. Nearly every one of her observations carries an added fillip, usually revealing some half-hidden corner of his mind. Among countless comments from others during Lincoln's life was the claim that he read far into the night or even by the glow of embers in a fireplace— quite a different picture from his old mother saying he liked no such thing, went to bed early, and got up early to continue. Or take the matter of young Lincoln coming home from church and repeating the sermon in a way which "amused all, and did especially tickle the children." The mimicry itself suggests that he put little stock in religion and even less in the preacher, yet with nary a harsh word against either (else his performance would not have "amused all"). That his takeoff would "especially tickle the children" suggests that he all too accurately pantomimed the gestures of ranting preachers. Such examples add substance to the continuing argument concerning Lincoln's religion, or lack thereof.

Or take Sarah Lincoln's observation, "He was not very fond of girls as he seemed to me," which throws light on both the fact itself, and on something of her own motivation in noticing it in the first place. That last little turn—"as he seemed to me"—signals that she looked, and looked again without finding (or having to worry about) his response to girls.

Like other frontier mothers with a houseful of male and female children, Sarah Lincoln no doubt tried to maintain morals by staying on guard against sex and sin. In rural settings especially, it was nothing short of a calamity for a young girl to be "fast," and worse still to get pregnant, and boys were watched over too. To keep the sexes properly apart was a main concern, and not easy in crowded one-room cabins surrounded by woods. That Abe was impassive toward girls no doubt comforted Sarah; it meant not having to worry about him on that front.

No worry about homosexuality either. To think of it as an actuality or active possibility in those days was simply out of the question. The word itself was not to exist for another half century, nor was there any clear concept of it, so little, in fact, that men of all ages and stations, even strangers, regularly shared the same bed without raising eyebrows. And anyway, the prevailing assumption was that sooner or later nature would step in and take its course, automatically causing males and females to be attracted to each other.

Yet in seeming contradiction to at least part of this, certain nameless, unspoken same-sex practices existed with some frequency on the American frontier, and have continued right into modern times. Here is a sample of what the sex researcher Alfred Kinsey found as typical in some of these environments:

> [T]he highest frequencies of the homosexual which we have ever secured anywhere have been in particular rural communities in some of the more remote sections of the country. The boy on the isolated farm has few companions except his brothers, the boys on an adjacent farm or two, visiting male cousins, and the somewhat older farm hand. His mother may see to it that he does not spend much time with his sisters,

and the moral codes of the rural community may impose considerable limitations upon the association of boys and girls under other circumstances. Moreover, farm activities call for masculine capacities, and associations with girls are rated sissy by most of the boys in such a community. All of these things are conducive to a considerable amount of homosexuality among the teen-age males in the most isolated of the rural areas. There is much less of it in the smaller farm country of the Eastern United States.[10]

Thus, with or without a label, and with or without any social mention of it, a considerable amount of homosexual activity, then as now, occurs among young males. In fact, when the Kinsey group began to take histories of ever younger boys in order to balance their sample, the homosexual rate quickly rose from about half (48 percent) who had early homosexual experience on up to 60 percent and even 70 percent and beyond, not because of any true increase, but because these younger males were questioned nearer the time of such events and did not have to "remember back" as far.[11]

Where does Lincoln fit in here? Although there is no record of his earliest sexual actions and/or desires, this does not leave us as empty handed as one might suppose. Surprising as it may seem, the very *timing* of puberty (the age at which a boy is first able to ejaculate, soon followed by his growth spurt) was found by Kinsey to be an extremely sensitive barometer of far-reaching sexual and, indeed, psychological consequences. Thanks to an accident of history, Lincoln's age at puberty happens to be precisely known.

In March 1819 the Turnham family, longtime friends of the Lincolns back in Kentucky, moved "next door" to them in Indiana, less than a mile away. David Turnham was sixteen years old at the time; Abe had turned ten just the previous month. David later remembered Abe as "a long, tall, dangling, awkward, droll-looking boy," marking Abe's growth spurt as obvious enough by then to have been well under way for several months, with his first ejaculatory capacity predating even that; thus, Lincoln may have arrived at puberty before David Turnham first met him in March.[12] In short, Lincoln hit puberty at age nine.

Here Lincoln was highly unusual. Most males reach puberty

within a narrow two-year-span, from a year sooner to a year later than the average age of 13.7 years. Thus, Lincoln was far ahead of the curve, reaching puberty several months *before* he was ten years old—fully four years before average!

This is a significant. Sex research has established that the forces that drive a boy's sexual machinery toward puberty, especially early puberty—his hormones, neurology, heredity, the lot—largely set the level of his sexual response, both at the time and for the rest of his life. As Kinsey put the latter, such factors continue to operate for "at least 35 or 40 [subsequent] years."[13] Plainly put, the earlier a boy arrives at puberty, the more "sexual" he tends to be, not only in the ease and speed of his arousal, but in his actual frequency of orgasm—his sex rate. These variations have been measured in great detail. For instance, a difference of as little as five months in arriving at puberty can result in a significant lifelong difference in sexual response. When one considers that Lincoln arrived at puberty *four years* earlier than average (approximately ten times greater than five months), it becomes clear why he was as sex-minded as he was; more on that later.

It is true, as some critics have complained, that the Kinsey researchers based their main calculations only on white Americans. However, they also collected data on a "small" number of several hundred other subjects showing that matters of maturity—including the age at puberty—are not significantly affected by racial or national differences. (The timing of puberty leaves no apparent trace in female sexual histories, only males.) On the other hand, what can, indeed, markedly delay puberty is any protracted nutritional deficiency while growing up. Thus, an important Kinsey finding was that "lower-level" males (those with an eighth-grade education or less), many of whom were maturing during the Great Depression of the 1930s, arrived at puberty fully seven months later than did the well-fed college-educated males. Although education has no direct link to biology, its economic implications easily carry over to diet and to a delay in puberty that Kinsey detected as "the outcome of nutritional inequalities."[14]

Much remains to be said regarding Lincoln's boyhood transition into adolescence. But as a familiar "rite of passage" it stirred particular comments from both Herndon and Carl Sandburg. More than a century ago, borrowing from his own notes on David Turnham, Herndon gave this account of Abe's coming of age:

> In his eleventh year [age ten] he began that marvelous and rapid growth in stature for which he was so widely noted in the Pigeon Creek settlement. "As he shot up," says Turnham, "he seemed to change in appearance and action. Although quick-witted and ready with an answer, he began to exhibit deep thoughtfulness, and was so often lost in studied reflection we could not help noticing the strange sensitiveness, especially in the presence of men and women, and although cheerful enough in the presence of the boys, he did not appear to seek our company as earnestly as before." It was only the development we find in the history of every boy. Nature was a little abrupt in the case of Abraham Lincoln; she tossed him from the nimbleness of boyhood to the gravity of manhood in a single night.[15]

In 1926 Sandburg added to the picture using some of Herndon's details and a slightly overstated age: "When he was eleven years old, Abe Lincoln's young body began to change. The juices and glands began to make a long, tall boy out of him. As the months and years went by, he noticed his lean wrists getting longer, his legs too . . . he was now looking over the heads of other boys. Men said, 'Land o'Goshen, that boy air a-growin'!' "[16]

These mentions of Lincoln having "shot up" from juices and glands that made "a long, tall boy" of him do indeed attest to his adolescent growth spurt. But Herndon went farther. With his mention of a "rare timidity and sensitiveness" and even a touch of social hesitance coming along with "the gravity of manhood," Herndon's description was at the very edge of what is often seen as one of the transformations of puberty. Kinsey was to say much the same from his own study: "[T]he newly adolescent boy's capacity to ejaculate [and] his newly acquired physical characters of other sorts, do something to him which brings child play to an end and leaves him awkward about making further sociosexual contacts.[17] This sudden "awkwardness" at the start of adolescence reflects both the new intensity of sex (as opposed to casual sex play), and yet certain hesitations in approaching others—ordinarily girls—with this pressing new interest.

But these facts fail to fit the fortunes of early-puberty males who are, of course, too young to indulge in conventional pursuits such as dating. Nor do such young boys encounter the same guardedness or resistance from adults that ordinary adolescents feel, since overt sexual interests are not expected from the very young. Nevertheless, there *are* sharp differences between boys who reach puberty as early as eleven (or even sooner, as did Lincoln) and those who reach their maturity by age fifteen or later. The early bloomers tend to be precocious in matters far beyond their increased sex rate.[18] They show a notably erotic mental set—a quick and easy self-starting sexual arousal, with a sex-mindedness widely evident in both their speech and fantasy. A quick wit is often evident, along with various tangible actions that set them apart. For instance, early maturers not only begin masturbating as soon as they can make it work, but typically begin it a full year or more *ahead* of being able to ejaculate.[19] Conversely, late maturers not only fail to jump the gun in this way, but when they finally do discover masturbation they often pronounce it pleasurable, and yet turn out to be in no rush to repeat it—or do so with much moderation.

In theory, these differences in attitude and practice apply to all boys, regardless of whether they do have, or will have, or will never have any homosexual experience; certainly early puberty has its impact irrespective of a person's present or eventual orientation. And yet in reality no such evenhandedness prevails; the playing field is decidedly "unleveled" by the obvious fact that young boys have more access to other boys than to girls, a situation that favors same-sex tryouts (some of which become pattern setting). Thus, as Kinsey shows in the graph on p. 35, there is fully twice as much homosexual experience among early-maturing as among late-maturing males—with those who mature at in-between ages showing a homosexual incidence remarkably proportional to the earliness of their puberty.

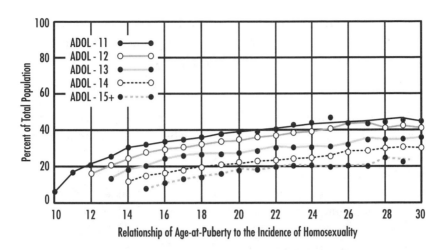

Relationship of Age-at-Puberty to the Incidence of Homosexuality

Source: Alfred C. Kinsey, Wendell B. Pomery, and Clyde E. Martin, *Sexual Behavior in the Human Male* (W. B. Saunders, Philadelphia, 1953).

Note the systematic character of the evidence—that is, how closely the nature and extent of the homosexual element depends upon the sheer timing of puberty. Much in this graph would already qualify as important if its only message were "the younger the start of sex, the higher the amount of homosexuality." But beyond this, early puberty also brings a marked upward *slant* of the curve at its start, indicating that those who arrive youngest at puberty begin their sexual experiments with a bang—a certain instant readiness, an especially high, ready-to-go initial enthusiasm—as reflected in the steep start and sharp convex shape of their curve. For Lincoln to have arrived at puberty before he was ten (more than a year sooner than even the youngest boys depicted here) means he was literally off the graph—even farther to the left on some still steeper curve. Beyond the biological "bang" of the early puberty male's immediate sexual readiness, Kinsey offered an insightful, largely social Plain Jane interpretation:

[T]he boy who becomes adolescent at 10 or 11 has not had as many years to build up inhibitions against sexual activity as the boy who does not mature until 15 or later; . . . the younger boy plunges into sexual activity with less restraint and with more enthusiasm than the boy who starts at a later date.[20]

Not that such earliness necessarily implies a homosexual result. Note that at its maximum—as with boys who reach puberty at the youngest ages—the homosexual component still occurs in less than half the subjects. This merely means what is already well known: A great variety of factors play into the origins of sexual orientation. True enough, and yet it still seems fair to conclude that the clustering of items that occur together—such as early puberty, having a higher than average sex drive, and more frequent homosexual experience— are likely to operate as an influential unit that may show up in quite distant contexts.

Lincoln's stream of jokes and yarns and one-liners ties into still another Kinsey finding regarding puberty. As he put it:

There is some reason for thinking that these early-adolescent males are more often the more alert, energetic, vivacious, spontaneous, physically active, socially extrovert, and/or aggressive individuals in the population.[21]

Lincoln was all this—athletic, adventuresome, jovial, provocative, the life of every party, and a legendary storyteller—with an added sexual twist. As his lawyer friend Henry Dummer noted, "Lincoln had two characteristics: one of purity, and the other, as it were, an insane love [of] telling dirty and smutty stories."[22] Plainly uninhibited in speech, Lincoln regaled his male listeners with sidesplitting off-color stories in a great variety of social settings. His risqué tales became part of the Lincoln legend. And while he never told these in mixed company or embarrassed any woman with them, he had a decidedly raunchy mind, a sexy, lusty curiosity that loved the lewd and that laced his thinking all the way from the political top right on down to the bottom of his earthy expressions. In mixed gatherings he could hardly contain himself: "at the very first opportunity he would have the men separated from their ladies and crowded close around him . . . listening to one of his characteristic stories."[23]

Some of Lincoln's ribald stories were brief—like one about an old Virginia gentleman who stropped his razor on a young negro's "member." (The underlying point more implied than spelled out: In order for the member, the penis, to be "stropped on," it has to be hard.)[24] Or in his better story recounted from Ethan Allen's visit to England: When his hosts teased him by hanging a picture of General Washington in the Back House, far from being offended, he said he fully understood, because there "is Nothing that Will Make an Englishman Shit So quick as the Sight of Genl Washington."[25]

At other times an occasional bit of Lincoln's doggerel or naughty poetry could be so complicated he would have to write it out to get it right. Once as he bounded into the Springfield courthouse, he simply handed over one such joke to a bailiff standing by. He called it *Bass-Akwards*:

He said he was riding *bass-ackwards* on a *jass-ack*, through a *potton-catch*, on a pair of *baddle-sags*, stuffed full of *binger-gred* when the animal *steered* at a *scump* and the *lirrup-steather* broke, and throwed him in the *forner* of the *kence* and broke his *pishing-fole*. He said he would not have minded it, much, but he fell right in a great *tow-curd*; in fact he said it gave him a right smart *sick of fitness*—he had the *molera-corbus* pretty bad—he said, about *bray dake* he come to himself, ran home, seized up a *stick of wood*, and split the ax to make a light, rushed into the house, and found the door sick abed and his wife standing open. But, thank goodness, she is getting right *hat* and *farty* again.[26]

Although Lincoln could be raunchy, this was not the general flavor of his wit. "He loved a good story however extravagant or vulgar if it had a good point. [But] if it was merely a ribald recital and had no sting in the end, that is, if it exposed no weakness or pointed no moral, he had no use for it." As Lincoln neared the punchline, his friend Ward Hill Lamon noted, "mirth seemed to diffuse itself all over him, like a spontaneous tickle." Others had said, "His laugh was striking [and his] awkward gestures belonged to no other man. They attracted universal attention, from the old sedate down to the schoolboy. Then in a few moments he was as calm and thoughtful as a judge on the bench, and as ready to give advice on the most important matters; fun and gravity grew on him alike."[27]

For better or worse, much of Lincoln's roughest material went unrecorded. His law colleague Henry C. Whitney lamented that Lincoln's salacious yarns were his best: "[T]he pity is that his funniest stories don't circulate in polite society or get embalmed in type."[28] Herndon realized that exposing the earthy side of the martyred president could offend Victorian sensibilities, but he rejected a cover-up. "Some writers would probably omit these songs and backwoods recitals as savoring too strongly of the Bacchanalian nature, but that would be a narrow view to take of history," he argued. "If we expect to know Lincoln thoroughly we must be prepared to take him as he really was."[29] Lincoln himself would undoubtedly have been shocked at just how much of his "Bacchanalia" and his devotion to it was destined to survive and be remembered as a basic part of his personality. In 1859, in a spate of telling yarns in the Supreme Court room of the States House, someone asked, "Why do you not write out your stories and put them in a book?" As Henry Dummer later described the moment, "Lincoln drew himself up—fixed his face, as if a thousand dead carcusses [sic] . . . were Shooting all their Stench into his nostrils, and Said 'Such a book would Stink like a thousand privies.' "[30] The point thus far is that all of Lincoln's sexy talk and thought, along with his pervasive sex jokes, are in line with Kinsey's early puberty model. Or to put it the other way around, for that much rampant raunchiness to prevail without the physical and psychological support imparted by the extra zest of early puberty would be almost unimaginable.

Even so, Lincoln's good humor did not erase a persistent moroseness. He was still, as Herndon said, "a sad-looking man; his melancholy dripped from him as he walked. His apparent gloom impressed his friends, and created sympathy for him—one means of his great success."[31] In fact, nearly every close friend of the adult Lincoln was well aware of his melancholia. Lincoln himself referred to his gloomy spells as his "hypo" (short for hypochondria, one definition of which in Victorian times was extreme melancholy—depression). "It is true that Lincoln told folksy anecdotes to illustrate his points," wrote Stephen B. Oates in *Abraham Lincoln: The Man Behind the Myths*. "But humor was also tremendous therapy for this depression—it was a device to 'whistle down sadness,' as Judge Davis put it." Lincoln agreed, saying of himself: "I laugh because I must not weep—that's all, that's all" and "I tell you the truth when I say that a funny story, if it has the element of genuine wit, has the same effect on me that I suppose a good square drink of whiskey has on an old toper; it puts new life into me."[32]

It is easy to see why various keepers of the flame have urgently wanted to guard Lincoln's image. Patriotic motives have proved ever ready to obscure the raw parts, in effect threatening to turn the real Lincoln into yet another cardboard character, as happened to George Washington; anything seems better than that. Better by far to trust the truth, wherever it leads, even to Lincoln's famous and infamous *First Chronicles of Reuben.* This little satire with its small poem at the end, perhaps unique in nineteenth-century American literature, amounts to the first fully loaded "smoking gun" in Lincoln's sex history. Charles Shively, in *Drum Beats*, has discussed it as a homosexual poem and helpfully traced its reception.

The story began simply enough. In 1826, Abraham Lincoln's sister, Sarah, married Aaron Grigsby. A year and a half later, she died in childbirth. Lincoln blamed the entire Grigsby family, which consisted of four brothers, named Reuben, Jr., Charles, Billy, and Nathaniel. "He was only awaiting the opportunity to 'even up' the score," wrote Herndon. This tragedy ignited an antagonism that had been slowly brewing and accumulating since Sarah's marriage.

Then in April 1829 two of Aaron's brothers, Reuben, Jr., and Charles, were both to be married. Lincoln was snubbed, invited neither to the weddings, which occurred on the same day in separate counties, nor to the joint celebration at the Grigsby mansion. Half in anger, but also in fun, Abe contrived through a confederate to cause a great confusion of brides and of grooms following the festivities—a practical joke in which the brides were directed to the wrong beds, where each would be approached in the dark by the other's new husband. "The transposition of beds produced a comedy of errors which gave Lincoln as much satisfaction and joy as the Grigsby household embarrassment and chagrin," wrote Herndon.[33]

Sweetening the revenge, Lincoln penned a satire of the event in mock biblical language. He titled his 713-word narrative *First Chron-*

icles of Reuben (full text in Appendix 1). "This he dropped at a place on the road 'carelessly, lost it as it were' and it was found by one of the Grigsby family. It was anonymous, of course, but everybody knew who wrote it—nobody in the neighborhood but Lincoln could have written it."[34] At the end he added a sixteen-line poem about a marriage between two boys that further amused and shocked people:

> *i will tell you a Joke about Jouel and mary*
> *it is neither a Joke nor a [s]tory*
> *for rubin and Charles has married two girles*
> *but biley has married a boy*
> *the girles he had tried on every Side*
> *but none could he get to agree*
> *all was in vain he went home again*
> *and sens that he is married to natty*
>
> *so biley and naty agreed very well*
>
> *and mamas well pleased at the matc[h]*
> *the egg it is laid but Natys afraid*
> *the Shell is So Soft that it never will hatc[h]*
> *but betsy She Said you Cursed ball [bald] head*
> *my Suiter you never Can be*
> *besids your low cro[t]ch proclaimes you a botch*
> *and that never Can answer for me*[35]

The above couplet:

> *the egg it is laid but Natys afraid,*
> *the Shell is So Soft that it never will hatc[h]*

suggests Abe was well aware of the term "jelly baby." Originally from Negro vernacular, the phrase soon came to be used by whites as well: slang denoting what uneducated folk imagined (and sometimes still imagine) as a "pregnancy" from homosexual intercourse.[36]

The *Chronicles* achieved instant notoriety. Everybody for miles around seems to have talked of it, rated which parts were morally worst, or cleverly the best. Some locals memorized the whole of it and could recite parts of it for life. As Lincoln's boyhood friend Joseph C. Richardson later said, "This poem is remembered here in Indiana in scraps better than the Bible, better than Wake's hymns. This was in 1829, and the first production that I know of that made us feel that Abe was truly and really *game*."[37]

Unable to purchase the only surviving copy in Lincoln's handwriting, which surfaced in 1865 and has since disappeared, Herndon acquired an oral version in the same year from old Mrs. Crawford, a former friend and employer of young Lincoln. "Abe was a moral and model boy. . . . He was the noblest specimen of man I ever saw," said Mrs. Crawford to Lincoln's biographer Herndon.[38] But as she began to recollect the bawdy poem, she became apprehensive and hesitant. She broke off her first recitation, saying: "The poem is smutty . . . I can't tell it to you, [but] will tell it to my daughter-in-law; she will tell her husband, and he shall send it to you"—all of which was done. Through it all, Mrs. Crawford lived up to her reputation for having "an uncommonly strong memory." In a letter of October 25, 1865, Nat Grigsby, who thirty years before had been a complaining "victim" of the poem, assured Herndon that his copy of the poem was indeed "correctly written."[39]

Oddly enough, the poem's remarkable boy-marries-boy theme stirred no particular comment at the time. It was as if the locals, who immediately identified Lincoln as the anonymous author, didn't "get it," or didn't care to admit they got it, or were simply too absorbed with other objections. But what does the poem say of Lincoln? The probability is near zero that any genuinely naive nineteen or twenty-year-old heterosexual male, living out on the American frontier, would have the savvy and the motivation first to dream up and then to spin out the tale of an overt, ongoing, homosexual "marriage." For all this to go on before such things were talked about, or indeed, before any regular language for it (this side of "jelly baby") had yet been invented, adds an extra measure of its reality for Lincoln.

As a poem, Lincoln's rhyme of course is a mere trifle, except that it is perhaps the most explicit literary reference to actual homosexual relations in nineteenth-century America—more explicit certainly than anything Walt Whitman ever wrote about the "love of comrades."

Under pressure from his inept Chicago publisher, Belford, Clark, Herndon bowdlerized the poem's next-to-last line, changing "Besides your low crotch [big penis] proclaims you a botch" to "Besides your ill shape proclaims you an ape." But this touch of censorship counted for little. As David Donald noted, "Nearly every reviewer pointed to the 'Chronicles' as uncouth, coarse, and vulgar."[40] Yet common folk thoroughly enjoyed it and found more room for laughter than lament, as if in agreement with Herndon himself, who proclaimed, "I admire the good tastes of life as well as any man or woman and cannot be made to defend the nasty, obscene, or vulgar under any circumstances, but I do fail to see why the episode causes a blush on any man's or woman's cheek."[41]

Not too surprisingly, the fiercest reactions came from "official" sources—from critics, editors, reviewers, and frightened publishers—whose caustic comments had their effects. In September 1889, two months after Herndon's book appeared, the *Chicago Journal*, in the tone of the times, printed a scathing attack:

> It is one of the most infamous books ever written. . . . It vilely distorts the image of an ideal statesman, patriot and martyr. . . . The obscenity of the work is surprising and shocking. Anthony Comstock should give it his attention. It is not fit for family reading. Its salacious narrative and implications . . . are simply outrageous. . . . In all its parts and aspects—if we are a judge, and we think we are, of the proprieties of literature and of human life—we declare that this book is so bad it could hardly have been worse.[42]

A few days later, Belford, Clark declared bankruptcy, toward which it had been headed for months. The mismanaged inaugural edition had been presented, as one Lincoln scholar said, "in its mutilated form, poorly printed, on poor paper, in three ridiculous little volumes."[43] Exactly fifteen hundred copies were printed and sold (Herndon's contract called for his royalties to begin only *after* that number, thus he received not a cent). For the next half century various publishers issued countless later editions of Herndon's *Life of Lincoln*, with *First Chronicles of Reuben* expurgated from them all—until 1942, when the editor Paul M. Angle reinserted them. Nor to this day is any part of the *Chronicles* included in either of the two classic reference works: Basler's ten-volume *Collected Works of Abra-*

ham Lincoln or the ten volumes of Nicolay and Hay's *Abraham Lincoln: A History*.

No doubt the usual explanation applies: Nothing overtly sexual, particularly if said by Lincoln himself, should be preserved; it might shock the reader and tarnish the image of a great man. The consequence was wide, indeed. Note that it took a half century before Paul Angle was to reinsert both the name of *First Chronicles of Reuben* and the poem itself into the classical biography, *Herndon's Life of Lincoln*. Nor do even these facts fully cover the breach; there are tendrils of connection between the wit of the *Chronicles* and the biology behind them.

Or to say it more simply: Something significant is gained from seeing the connections between Lincoln's basic biology, which drove him toward an especially early puberty, and a sex-mindedness that dominated his sense of humor and much of his life.

Likewise, as Lincoln's sense of humor rushed down roads of fewer than average guardrails (as early puberty is prone to prefer them), it drove much of his personality toward a naughtiness at the very edge of respectability. That touch of raunchiness apparent in the *Chronicles* was to appear in countless other samples of his wit. Little wonder Whitney felt "the pity is that his funniest stories don't circulate in polite society or get embalmed in type." In the end, all these spin-offs, bolstered by his early puberty—including many sober matters in the mix—were to have far-reaching importance.

THREE

The New Salem Years: Starting Afresh

New Faces, New Beginnings

Just when Lincoln chose to leave home and float down the Sangamon River for a fresh start in a new place, he was overtaken by a flood that caught him in its slow insistent swell. As Herndon was later to say of young Lincoln:

> He assured those with whom he came in contact that he was a piece of floating driftwood; that after the winter of deep snow, he had come down the river with the freshet; borne along by the swelling waters, and aimlessly floating about, he had accidentally lodged at New Salem. Looking back over his history we are forced to conclude that Providence or chance, or whatever power is responsible for it, could not have assigned him to a more favorable refuge.[1]

Indeed so, for Lincoln had hardly put his foot ashore that July day in 1831 when one remarkable opportunity after the other presented itself, as if preplanned. For lack of something better to do he was walking around, and he stopped by where a group of men had gathered and were discussing a state election to be held right away. One of the election clerks had suddenly taken ill, so as young Lincoln approached, another official, Mentor Graham, a schoolteacher, asked the tall stranger if he could write. When the answer came, "Yes—a little," another of the group asked, "Will you act as clerk of elections to-day?" Lincoln said, "I will try and do the best I can, if you so request." (Others later reported Lincoln's answer as simply, "I can try it.") He was then sworn in on the spot.[2]

In a way it was a test, for there were forty-nine candidates and quite a few tallies had to be made. None of this escaped the sharp eye of Mentor Graham, who was also impressed by young Lincoln's clear handwriting, and later by how he "performed the duties with great facility—with much fairness honesty, & impartially."[3] Thus, with nobody realizing it at the time, and fresh off his small boat,

> Lincoln . . . from the very beginning, took part in the politics of New Salem and Sangamon County. [Moreover], as the tiresome hours wore on, broken only by voters announcing their preferences, which the clerks recorded, Lincoln brightened the time by telling stories, and thus from the outset, pleased and entertained those among whom he had [accidentally] come to live.[4]

Graham was pleased, too, to find that Abe had heard of and even read a bit of Henry Clay, and gave other evidence of a certain "mental hunger." Before leaving Graham reportedly commented, "Drop in to see me, Lincoln, whenever you feel like it. Drop in to [my] school down at the church when you're not busy."[5] Historic words.

Abe accepted immediately, and the day was arranged. Graham also invited along his young cousin, eighteen-year-old Billy Greene (William G. Greene), to meet Abe and join them for supper and a social evening. As Graham reportedly said, "When Lincoln came into our house that first time, he walked straight to my book shelves and straight into my heart."[6]

That same evening Mentor Graham had a long talk with Abe over a drop-leaf table; he drew the youth out, eliciting from him details of his education such as it was, as well as his hopes and dreams, including his aspiration to some day become a "public man." By this time Graham had taken a great liking to Abe and, hoping to have him as a student, he made quite a case for the high prospects of New

Salem. Lincoln already liked the town and said he thought he had a "right smart chance" of becoming a clerk in Denton Offutt's new store, soon to open. And so it went.[7]

They talked on into the evening, with Abe invited to stay over; he and Billy Greene evidently shared the same bed or bunk on the floor. Nothing unusual in that, what with the crowded conditions in small frontier cabins. Yet as later became clear, it was from this first night that Abe and Billy developed an extensive, intimate relationship that was to be especially important throughout their New Salem years. And yes, based on evidence soon to be seen, they promptly fell into an overt homosexual relationship—most probably instigated by Billy. Just as there is reason to believe Abe was well into previous homosexual experience (his early puberty, later followed by his first *Chronicles of Reuben*), strong evidence of a different sort also exists for Billy before he had ever heard of Abe.

Although Billy and Abe had never met before they came together at Mentor Graham's house, this was not the first time Billy had seen him. Earlier in the year as "the winter of the deep snow" melted into a major long-lasting flood, a merchant, Denton Offutt, had hired Abe over in Sangamon town at twelve dollars a month, first to help build a flatboat and then sail with it to New Orleans to pick up merchandise.[8] When the boat became lodged on the New Salem mill dam, it was Lincoln who took over its rescue as the townsfolk came down to share the excitement. The crowd included Billy Greene who, as he later reported to Herndon, was much impressed by Abe's physique. If Billy had merely focused on standard male attributes such as Abe's broad shoulders, his strong muscles, and perhaps his air of self-possession, it would have amounted at most to a more or less conventional homosexual response. But without realizing it Billy revealed much more. As he later reported to Herndon:

> I Saw the boat soon after it landed . . . then and there for the first time I saw Abraham Lincoln. He had on a pair of mixed blue jeans pants—a hickory shirt and a Common Chip hat. He was at that time well and firmly built: his thighs were as perfect as a human being Could be.[9]

"Thighs" in this context mean considerably more than Billy was consciously aware of revealing. For him to see Lincoln as "well and firmly built [with] thighs as perfect as a human being could be" strongly suggests a sexual practice later named "femoral intercourse" (penis between tightly clasped *femora*, Latin for thighs). More than a hundred years later Alfred Kinsey inserted a question about femoral intercourse into the sex histories he took and reported on in the 1940s; it proved to be one of the most frequently used homosexual techniques.[10]

It was immediately clear from events at Mentor Graham's house that Abe and Billy were fascinated with each other. Not only did they manage to be together constantly, it was noticed in the household that nothing could separate them. Allegedly, Graham's wife, Sarah, specifically mentioned that Billy and Abe "had an awful hankerin', one for t'other," though it is by no means certain, even if the quote is correct, that she fully realized exactly what she was saying.[11] In any event, it was a fascination promptly turned to good use, with Abe daily visiting the Grahams to borrow books and have discussions, and with Billy making it his business to also be present, where he was soon part of what might be called the drilling of Abe.

From the moment Lincoln set his sights on becoming a "public man" he needed to improve his grammar, and with Graham's help, he needed to change his language too—an enormous task. For as is recognized in common folklore, "You can take a girl [or boy] out of the country, but you can't take the 'country' out of [them]." The adage itself warns that such things as speech reflect one's very being and background—earmarks that get stamped in like an indelible, telltale fingerprint. But fingerprint or not, Lincoln was soon to radically change it in a gigantic effort.

He had apparently long noticed a difference between the language he read in books and what he and his friends spoke. One day he mentioned to Mentor Graham his interest in studying grammar. And when Graham said something in support of this, Abe quickly added, "If I had a grammar, I would commence now." Graham suggested that a friend, a farmer named John Vance some six miles away, might have one he could get. Abe immediately got up, went on foot the twelve miles to and from Vance's, and soon returned with the book (it was *Samuel Kirkham's English Grammar . . . Accompanied by a*

Compendium Embracing A New Systematick Order.) As Graham reported, "He then turned his immediate & almost undivided attention to English grammar"—doing so in way staggering to this day.[12]

First, Abe set about to memorize and make second nature the hard formalities of grammar. For this he enlisted the ever present and more than willing aid of Billy Greene. Day after day Billy held the book and checked for accuracy as time and again Abe reeled off technical rules. When Billy asked what adverbs qualify, Abe gave back his bookish answers: "Adverbs qualify verbs, adjectives and other adverbs"; "verbs are qualified by adverbs"; and "so are adjectives qualified by adverbs . . . while verbs, adjectives, and other adverbs get qualified by adverbs," and so on and on it went in an endless parsing of parts against the whole. When Billy asked, "What is a phrase?" the rigorous answer came back, "A phrase is an assemblage of words, not constituting an entire proposition, but performing a distinct office in the structure of a sentence or of another phrase." Then he would write the whole of it down and read it back aloud, usually to Billy (who, enthralled with Lincoln, seems never to have been bored or expressed the slightest complaint). Did he have it right? Now from the top again. Now with the subparts interchanged once more. On and on it went, ad infinitum.[13]

A common college saying has it that the best way to learn a language is "in bed," meaning in bed with a sexual partner, where the hard work of tireless drill is bathed in the gentle stuff of unending patience—and affectionate reward. Never to a better use was put that "awful hankerin', one for t'other" that Abe and Billy reportedly felt for each other.

When Mentor Graham began to hear sounds of progress he seems to have upped the ante—going after countless errors he heard in the words themselves and wanted to correct. Kirkham had included a number of maxims and aphorisms in his book; these would do. "Ruthless waste makes woeful want." Say it right; *slower*; I want to hear the *words* clearly. Ruthless sounds better as two words, like *ruth less*. And *stress* that long *o* in "woeful." Get the *sense* of it; get the *sense!* And there's a *t* at the end of *want*. If you "are coming," then say *are*, not *air*—"*air*" is what you breathe—"*are*" is the second person singular of the verb *to be*. All this caught the eyes and ears of many observers. In fact, as Ida Tarbell found, "Lincoln's eagerness to learn was such that the whole neighborhood became interested."[14]

What Lincoln actually faced far exceeded what these few samples might suggest. Nor does a complete record exist as to which parts of his training were imposed by Graham versus those that were self-imposed by the superautodidact Lincoln himself.[15] Nevertheless, as the biographer Albert Beveridge has shown, the task per se was monumental. Lincoln came from the backwoods and spoke like everyone else there. They called themselves "pore" people. A man who read books was "eddicated." What was certain was "sartin." Joints were "j'ints" (not to be confused with "jines," meaning "joins"). Even after Lincoln rose from the likes of these—indeed, right up through his presidency—he would switch back to bits of his early speech, sometimes with great effect. Once, on hearing a legislator proclaim that the Mexican War was not aggressive, he commented, "That reminds me of the farmer who said, 'I ain't greedy 'bout land, I only jus' wants what jines mine.' "[16]

In the end most of the words and phrases of Lincoln's backwoods language were successfully obliterated, never to reappear. These included such things as saying fruit was "spilled" instead of spoiled, or that people who planted corn "drapped" the seeds (or if they broke a plate they "drapped" it). They went on errands and "brung" things back. Their dogs "follered" coons. Flannel was "flannen," a bandanna a "bandanner," a chimney a "chimbly," a shadow a "shadder," and a cover a "kiver." They asked, "Have ye et?" or "Kin ye?" "No, I cain't." As Carl Sandburg said, "They made their own words. Those who spoke otherwise didn't belong, were 'puttin' on.' This was their wilderness lingo; it had gnarled bones and gaunt hours of their lives in it."[17]

If a man was feeble he was "powerful weak," and when he grew better he was "fitter." The word "sot" could mean sit or set or sat. Nobody fought; they "fit." You didn't stay awhile, but "a spell." "How-do-you-do" was definitely for people who were putting on airs; for people who weren't, it was "Howdy" or "Howdy!" or "Howdy-do!"— the last being a first-word greeting Lincoln himself kept all his life. Other regionalisms disappeared: You come "outen," not out of, a house or a field. "A lot" or "a great many" was a "heap." Wages were "yearned," not earned; where was "whar"; came was "kum"; took was "tuck"; care was "keer"; and children were always "young-uns."

Through an especially intensive form of drill Lincoln managed to leave behind virtually all ignorant-sounding words. What he did not change, and never tried to change, were many of his idioms and early pronunciations. A scant year before he was president he began his famous Cooper Union speech with "Misteer Cheermun." (In fact, throughout his presidency he continued to address the head of every committee as "Misteer Cheerman."[18] And there appear to have been a handful of other words left in place, such as "sot" for sat, "kin" for can, "airth" for earth, and a few others. Some of the folksy forms he held to were technically incorrect, which he undoubtedly knew, but he kept them for flavor. Indeed, to this day they retain an earthy authentic ring: "I hain't been caught lyin' yet, and I don't mean to be."

So how did Lincoln finally do with his grammar? He learned his lesson well, very well indeed, enough to virtually never speak in outright error. And with his new education he sometimes greatly enjoyed the grammar errors of others, especially when his watchful eye saw them in print. He found it hugely amusing, a real knee-slapper, when he saw a showman's advertisement one day: "A Grate Sho Of Snaix."[19] Then, too, his new mastery of language laid before him rich and fresh experiences, since he somehow turned out to have an extraordinarily sensitive and poetic ear (clear even in his first speeches). Where *that* came from nobody knows. But much richness surrounding his grammar study is known and appears to have helped him.

Almost as if lifted by some magic hand more than a hundred years into the future, the ever more demanding sessions that Lincoln underwent sound to modern ears much like George Bernard Shaw's *Pygmalion* (and like its later incarnation, *My Fair Lady*). For young Lincoln—as lithe and limber as Eliza Doolittle—had to put up with all her trials, and more, as his Professor Higgins (Mentor Graham) bore down hard, and with fewer chocolates. The cast of characters even included a Colonel Pickering, in the person of Dr. John Allen, a neighbor of Graham's who often stopped in to check on Lincoln's drill and progress.[20] Little wonder that in the end the biographers of Mentor Graham (Kunigunde Duncan and D. F. Nickols), against the oft-repeated statement that Lincoln's education added up to less than a year, concluded to the contrary: "Actually, the man went to college and earned a high degree in the unflinching course of study provided by his guide and teacher [Mentor Graham]."[21]

As might have been anticipated, in later years Graham's work with Lincoln was frequently discounted, even denied, often with the admittedly exceptional talents of Lincoln himself given the entire credit. Other critics expressed doubt about Graham himself; Herndon called him "flighty at times and yet he was a good school master."[22] David Donald in his 1995 biography, *Lincoln*, speaks of Mentor Graham as "semi-literate," a rating sharply contradicted by others. R. B. Rutledge said at the time, "I know of my own knowledge that Mr. Graham contributed more to Mr. L.['s] Education whilst in New Salem than any other man."[23] Various naysayers might still want to diminish Graham, as Billy Greene later did (assigning special credit to himself). However, the counterargument is commanding. A full thirty years after those grammar sessions, when it came time for Lincoln to be sworn in as president, the one and only New Salem friend he invited to come sit on the platform at his inauguration was Mentor Graham—not exactly an unimportant or forgotten figure in Lincoln's eyes.[24]

Nor was Billy Greene forgotten. In later life on a visit to the White House Lincoln introduced him to his secretary of state, William Seward, saying that this friend of his, William Greene, was the man who taught him grammar. This embarrassed Greene, who knew little about grammar, so he remained silent for fear Seward would notice his deficiency. Lincoln later reminded Greene that he had helped Lincoln by quizzing him from a grammar book. Certainly the White House tribute was proof enough of Greene's help, and a salute as well to the reality of the grammar problem. But why, in fact, was Greene so embarrassed? One cannot know for sure, but a reasonable guess might be that those long ago grammar sessions, many of them in bed, ended with sexual contact. To now have these private events suddenly recalled within the formal surroundings of the White House by what may have seemed at the moment an all too free-speaking long-ago bed partner could have been a real jolt.

But enough of this distraction into the future. Time now to return to much else in Lincoln's early days at New Salem—along with considerably more about Billy Greene.

All his life Lincoln had a curious, orderly, step-by-step, seemingly slow way of proceeding from one situation to the next, even when events whirled around him with great rapidity. Not infrequently this came across as a kind of passivity on his part, even though he could never be rightly accused of shirking a duty or obligation. On the contrary, even when he moved at only a lumbering, leisurely pace he kept busy—busy taking any slack out of the rope, taking on the next logical task, and returning constantly to his favorite focus of reading, study, and self-improvement.

Lincoln's learning situation becomes more remarkable when one realizes the context in which it occurred, in particular his fluid, rootless, ever-changing lifestyle. Yet nothing swerved him off course. He took his meals at such a variety of boarding houses that no full record of them exists. And he frequently changed where he hung his hat as well, moving in with one set of friends after the other. Yet there was no sign of his ever wearing out his welcome; besides being very good company, he was always considerate and helpful with chores. Some of his living arrangements were especially fortunate, as in 1833 when he moved in with the Grahams. Mentor's wife, Sarah, reportedly said, "might as well, here all the time anyway," later commenting as before, that Abe "ate books up whole."

At other times his constantly changing circumstances seemed to depend mostly on where he found himself. When Denton Offutt opened his store in New Salem in September 1831 Lincoln was the only clerk. He was there all day, and also slept there at night—maintaining his closeness with Billy Greene, with whom he shared a narrow cot. (Reports to the effect that Billy was "hired" to help Lincoln or that he only "occasionally" stayed the night and other cover stories were simply untrue.) An interesting sidelight at the moment is that when Herndon heard of the sleeping arrangements from Billy Greene himself, he naively took the report at face value, mostly quoting Greene's own words: "so strong was the intimacy between them that 'when one turned over the other had to do likewise.' "[25] More on that later.

Although Lincoln was in a period of especially intense study while minding Offutt's store, he nevertheless always seemed to enjoy the customers rather than feel distracted by them. Mentor Graham commented, "He was among the best clerks I ever saw: he was attentive to his business . . . kind and considerate to his customers & friends and always treated them with great tenderness—kindness & honesty."[26]

Offutt's store started to fail within months, but Lincoln, having made much progress with his grammar, and also "encouraged by his great popularity among his immediate neighbors" as he himself later put it, began to make arrangements for a big step: to learn how to, and then actually run for, a seat in the state legislature, making his first political appeal with a kind of handbill dated March 9, 1832.[27] There is no record of his follow-up. But with the store already in collapse he and Billy soon enlisted together (April 21, 1832) for a three-month stint in the Black Hawk War—a militia's move against an Indian uprising. They were back in late July as planned, allowing a few days for Lincoln to campaign before election day, August 6, 1832. Lincoln lost, but not by much, and was greatly pleased that his own precinct cast 277 votes for him and only 7 for the other candidates. He was later to take pride, too, in the fact that "this was the only time [he] was ever beaten on a direct vote of the people."[28]

It must have been gratifying, or should have been, for Lincoln to have done so much and so well in New Salem so quickly; it was scarcely a year since he had accidentally arrived there as "a piece of floating driftwood." Like staccato events in fast succession, he made friends on every side, greatly improved both his speech and grammar, learned what it took to be a "public man" and what one had to do to run for office, and then had actually done so. Even the hiatus of the Black Hawk War was a chapter of notable success. On the very day of his enlistment he joined a volunteer company, and much to his own surprise was immediately elected captain of it. He described his tour of duty as involving "the ordinary hardships of such an expedition, but was in no battle." (It was a bit better than that; he attained great popularity with his whole company, and soon demonstrated notable leadership when he saved the life of an old Indian who, despite having valid papers, was on the verge of being shot as a spy by trigger-happy recruits before Lincoln stepped in to demand his safety.) Lincoln always seemed to revel in his Black Hawk War days, and decades later was to say: "[H]e has not since had any success in life which gave him so much satisfaction."[29]

But just how much satisfaction was Lincoln able to enjoy from the rest of that eventful, highly productive year in New Salem? Less than one might expect. As he said after his defeat at the polls, he "was without means [stone broke] and out of business, but was anxious to remain with his friends who had treated him with so much generosity, especially as he had nothing elsewhere to go to." It was a disturbing low point, low enough to threaten his return to manual labor, even down to thoughts of possibly "learning the black-smith trade."[30]

However, as often happened with Lincoln, events rushed forward to guide his fate. Out of nowhere came a man ready and willing to loan to Lincoln and to an equally destitute friend of his (William Berry) "an old stock of goods on credit"—sufficient for them to open a kind of general store, the Lincoln & Berry Store. As Lincoln himself later said, "Of course they did nothing but get deeper and deeper into debt," before the store finally "winked out."[31] Yet in that half year, between the store's distantly spaced customers, Lincoln strode forward faster in some ways than at any other period of his life. He began improving his education with a vengeance. He immediately obtained and read Rollin's *Ancient History* and a large volume on American military biography. He soon completed Edward Gibbon's massive six-volume *Decline and Fall of the Roman Empire*. Meanwhile, using the learning system he had devised as a boy, he took great pains to understand and remember everything he read. He wrote down whole pages of text, reciting them over and over, including not only the Rollin and Gibbon volumes, but most of the writings of Robert Burns and Shakespeare.[32]

No doubt this was very rewarding personally, but the store was failing, partly due to New Salem's declining population, and the rest to the ill-suitedness of Lincoln and Berry as businessmen. As Herndon observed: "[W]hile Lincoln at one end of the store was dispensing political information, Berry at the other was disposing of the firm's liquors" and ruining his health.[33] Indeed, Berry soon died, defaulting on his own and other notes he had signed at the start of the firm. Lincoln might well have walked away from these debts as he could legally have done. Or at most he might have acknowledged only claims for which he held direct responsibility. Instead, he paid what he could immediately, and slowly paid off the rest bit by bit, to the last cent, over the next fifteen years. But for now he was brought once again to the edge of rank poverty—barely able to pay his board bill.

Then, suddenly, a friend heard that John Calhoun had recently been appointed county surveyor and was looking for an assistant, and strongly recommended Lincoln. Lincoln gladly accepted the offer, but only after making sure that Calhoun (a prominent Democrat) would not try to bias his politics. Knowing next to nothing of surveying, Lincoln "secured copies of Abel Flint's *System of Geometry and Trigonometry, Together with a Treatise on Surveying,* as well as Robert Gibson's *Treatise of Practical Surveying,* then scraped together enough money to produce a compass and chain" and, as he said, "went at it." At least it "procured bread, and kept soul and body together."[34]

Still other friends of Lincoln who were much concerned over his poverty and his hand-to-mouth existence went out of their way to get him appointed postmaster of New Salem—"the office being too insignificant, to make his politics an objection."[35] Lincoln hesitated at first, not wanting to deprive anyone else, but his backers were adamant and insisted he have it. The appointment, which he was to keep for his remaining years in New Salem, began on May 7, 1833. The pay was indeed small, being a percentage of postal receipts, which in Lincoln's time averaged a little over four dollars a month; but Lincoln was overjoyed by the access it gave him to all sorts of newspapers, "his never yet being able to get half that he wanted before."[36]

In 1834 Lincoln again ran for the state legislature, this time winning by the highest vote cast for any candidate; it was an unparalleled boost. More than merely a gratifying win, its modest pay of four dollars a day (thirty times what the post office paid) was the largest income he had ever earned. Better still, during the canvass he was able to renew his friendship with John T. Stuart, formerly a comrade in the Black Hawk War, now a practicing lawyer who was also campaigning (and who also won). Stuart encouraged Lincoln's run for office in every way, even at the risk of sacrificing his own chances. And after the election Stuart greatly encouraged him to study law, lending him a stream of books; these Lincoln obtained by repeatedly traveling from New Salem to Stuart's office in Springfield, reportedly reading and reciting from the latest volume as he carried it open in hand. He studied with nobody, either at that time or later; he read and thought out such tomes as Blackstone's *Commentaries* entirely on his own.[37]

Whenever the legislature met the law books were temporarily dropped, but he took them up again at the end of each session. Through all this he kept up his surveying to pay his board and clothing bills. By the autumn of 1836 he had received his law license and won his second term in the legislature. Within months he would be moving to Springfield to become Stuart's law partner, and to begin a major new chapter in his life—with Joshua Fry Speed.

Looking back over Lincoln's New Salem years, a pressing question stands out. What about those remarkable friendships—some of them with hardly more than bystanders—that keep turning up in Lincoln's life? Any one of them, seen alone, might look like luck, or like some stroke of chance. What could be more natural than for a school-teacher, Mentor Graham, to detect the budding student in Lincoln, and to urgently want to help him? Denton Offutt had no such high motive, but he knew a bright and honest young man when he saw one, vowing then and there to open a store in New Salem and employ Abe; no doubt his aim was self-serving, but there was something generous in it, too.

In fact, trust and generosity were what Lincoln most often engendered in his friends, a level of trust much in evidence when he was offered that chance to open his own store, with both goods and credit freely offered to start him off. Herndon later asked his cousin Rowan Herndon "what induced him to make such liberal terms [to] Lincoln whom he had known for so short a time." Rowan's answer might later fit the feelings of countless others: "I believed that he was thoroughly honest and that impression was so strong in me I accepted his note in payment of the whole [and] would have advanced him still more had he asked for it."[38]

Then there were all those many generosities offered Lincoln immediately after his store "winked out." First was the friend (his name never recorded in history) who rushed forward to recommend him for that surveying job with John Calhoun. Then came those other friends who first thought up and then hurriedly followed through to arrange that postmaster appointment they knew Lincoln needed and would enjoy. The leftover store debts brought similar responses. Most creditors were happy enough to have Lincoln slowly pay off their loans; a few others, like James Rutledge, refused any payback. But not so with a man named Van Bergen, who brought suit against Lincoln, seizing by court order his personal effects, including his horse and surveying instruments along with the rest. But yet again, "a friend, one James Short . . . interposed; brought in the property [at auction] and restored it to the hopeless young surveyor."[39]

Herndon recognized the whole picture as a curious, repeating theme in Lincoln's life:

> The bonds he [made] were destined to stand the severest of tests. His case never became so desperate but [that] a friend came out of the darkness to relieve him. There was always something about Lincoln . . . to encourage his friends. He was not only grateful for whatever aid was given him, but he always longed to help someone else. He had an unfailing disposition to succor the weak and the unfortunate, and always, in his sympathy, struggling with the under dog in the fight.[40]

This is the way Herndon has it in his biography of Lincoln. But in a letter to his coauthor, Jesse Weik, he wrote more, as he struggled to account for what lay behind the essential mystery of Lincoln's powerful appeal:

> Men . . . everywhere saw that Lincoln was a sad, gloomy man . . . I have often and often heard men say: "That is a man of sorrow, and I really feel for him, I sympathize with him." This sadness on the part of Mr. Lincoln and sympathy on the part of the observer were a heart's magnetic tie between the two. This result gave Lincoln a power over men, rather it was self-inspired. . . . Men who do not know Mr. Lincoln, and never did, have paraded his hardships and struggles in his younger days in glowing words, or sad ones. Such an idea, such a description of the man, is not exactly true; he never saw the minute, the hour, nor the day that he did not have many friends to aid him, to assist him, and to help him in all ways. His friends vied with each other for the pleasure or the honor of assisting him. Lincoln deserved all this respect and confidence; he was all honor and integrity, spoke the whole truth, and acted it.[41]

Were these various qualities in Lincoln *all* that drew people toward him in his every crisis? Certainly his kindness and sympathy, along with his often noted sad melancholia, amounted to a powerful magnet. But that was not quite the whole of it. Lincoln, remember, was also very good company, a pleasure to be with; he had a quick and lively wit that drew people into whatever joy he found—and he found plenty of it in a bottomless supply of stories and often hilarious jokes. People love to laugh and be entertained, perhaps the more so in drab frontier environments. And for reasons too intricate to trace, wit and humor are much enlarged when drawn from a nearby melancholy. Then, too, enjoyment breeds gratitude, the bedrock of generosity.

Lastly, something is to be said for the sheer surprise of Lincoln's contradictions. From this angular and awkward figure, gloomy in repose, it must have been a matter of much amazement to find such abundant warmth and kindness on easy tap in Lincoln's highly independent, utterly private, do-it-yourself personality. In short, Lincoln was a warm and witty autodidact of the first water! But whoever heard of such a thing? Autodidacts, besides being rare, are usually too cool and remote and independent ever to be warm and witty, let alone the life of the party. Yet Lincoln was all of these in a fine good mix, with one glaring exception: "he froze in the presence of eligible girls."[42] And yet Lincoln readily showered his generosity on others—including the wives of all his friends. With them he was especially prone to express kindly concerns, and with more than mere words. Sarah Graham, for instance, found him nothing short of a treasure who quickly

> took the baby from her when the food was about to burn; who kept the woodpile higher than it had ever been before and never let the wood box get empty; who told the children stories to hush their crying; who took the heavy tub or bucket from her and carried it . . . and never had to be told to empty the wash water.[43]

Little wonder Lincoln was a prized visitor. And with his wit and all the rest, he was enormously surprising. This quality often left friends and observers feeling they never quite fathomed the whole man (a veritable disease among Lincoln scholars). It has not infrequently infected even casual friends and associates as well, causing them to admire Lincoln all the more, and to lean forward with uncommon bounty—which, just as Herndon said, poured in from the darkness whenever it was needed.

What remains unsolved at the moment are a number of small and not so small sexual puzzles. It would clearly be a mistake to search out and highlight every trace of homosexual response in Lincoln, which would not only risk serious errors and possibly take on the tone of a prosecuting attorney, but might also project false importance onto small events. Thus, the rule here has been to seriously consider and possibly accept for analysis only particular homosexual examples in Lincoln's life that are supported by at least two separate facts or pieces of evidence. This guards against what is called in probability theory a "type one error." But there have also been surprises in the other direction, where what started out as a promising source of some new revelation has suddenly vanished into nothingness.

One such example is especially interesting. The world of historians and Lincoln scholars, like other conclaves, is made up of persons holding differing views, and who also differ in how well known they are as experts. One such Lincoln scholar (whose name shall go unmentioned) is important enough to always be asked his opinion by the media every time a new report on Lincoln's homosexuality turns up in the news; he has consistently denied such reports, often adding that he knows of no evidence for any such thing. One day in a perfectly friendly way he offered his advice to the present study in approximately these words: "If you intend to stay with your investigation of Lincoln's homosexuality, then don't forget to have a careful look at [Charles] Maltby." This suggestion implied his own belief in such evidence, though it was not quite as contrary to his public stance as it may seem. Historians committed to one point of view often harbor private sympathies for a contradictory opinion. Maltby was perhaps a reasonable possibility, what with his being close to Lincoln for a time during their New Salem years. However, the search led to nothing more than a few overnight stays together, which even then held no indication of anything sexual, not even sharing the same bed. Even so, sexual implications can sometimes be missed if tucked away in unexpected places, or when couched in unlikely language. With this in mind, a sizable semibiography of Lincoln that Maltby wrote (*The Life And Public Services of Abraham*

Lincoln) was sent to India for retyping, with its 140,925 words fed into the largest Lincoln computerized database existent.[44] Careful analysis revealed nothing more substantial than the few overnight stays in shared quarters, including what Maltby called "pleasant memories of the days and nights spent with Lincoln."[45] Again, there was no indication of their sharing the same bed, let alone any sexual action; and even if there had been, it still would have amounted to merely one—rather than the minimum of two—pieces of evidence required to warrant serious consideration.

William Herndon, the champion Lincoln expert of them all, amounts to more of a puzzle. From the very day of Lincoln's funeral to the last day of his life more than a quarter century later, Herndon spent virtually his entire substance collecting, weighing, and checking as best he could every detail he found of Lincoln's life. As a result, despite a few errors, he clearly came to know Lincoln better than any other individual ever did. And yet a few of his blind spots were conspicuous. Not only did he fail to detect any of Lincoln's homosexual trends, he paid the usual price of completely misinterpreting nearly all of Lincoln's heterosexual life as well. Although Herndon correctly picked up on Lincoln's pervasive sex-mindedness (as constantly apparent in his jokes), he attributed Lincoln's near total lack of pursuit or even flirtatiousness with women entirely to various moral constraints. Although Herndon was well aware that Lincoln, rather than ever wanting to be, was plainly trapped into marrying Mary Todd, he nevertheless still saw Lincoln as "true as steel to his wife" while repeatedly fending off the temptation of other women.

The real problem with this lay where one might not think to look: in the unusual nature of Herndon's own heterosexuality. For while most people are heterosexual, few men ever come anywhere near matching Herndon's extremes—both in the intensity of his devotion to marriage, and his utter lack of fatigue with it. Herndon married early and soon had a houseful of children (six by his first wife and, after she died, two more by his second). With all these mouths to feed he often felt under a great and constant burden, but he never complained. On the contrary, unlike Lincoln, he hated to be away from home—a main reason for his mostly refusing to travel the circuit. However, whenever he did, he would rush home on weekends. Once when he had gone to Chicago on business and his employers urged him to stay over a day, he flatly refused, saying he had to get right back to Springfield, "to buss the old woman and the babies."[46] Even as an old man three months before he died, Herndon described his whole married life as "an eternal stream of happiness."[47]

Little wonder that with marriage glowing like a diamond in his own life Herndon was blind as a bat to other possibilities. Although he had clerked in Speed's store for some months and had slept in the same room across from the bed where Speed and Lincoln bundled together, he still did not catch the drift. Nor did he later, even after correctly reporting that at various times Billy Greene and A. Y. Ellis had gone out of their way (sometimes far out of their way) to land in Lincoln's bed. Alluding to Greene and Lincoln nestled in a cot, Herndon simply retold the tale he heard from Greene, that "so strong was the intimacy between them that when one turned over the other had to do likewise," but still no register, nor the slightest awareness, that the picture painted was itself a cover-up. What was *not* said was the part hidden. Anyone can see that with two adults in a short and narrow cot (as they all were back then), "when one turned over the other had to do likewise." But that is hardly half of it. When one of those adults happens to be six-feet-four, perhaps in summer he could sometimes fit by letting his feet hang over, but mostly he must stay jackknifed, with his knees sharply bent—a position his partner must match, forcing both into a very close intimacy indeed. Billy Greene was able to divert attention from this by only mentioning their moments of turnover.

Yet despite Herndon's oblivion—indeed, because of it—he constitutes a source all the richer for sex research. With wide-open eyes of innocence, he says of A. Y. Ellis that he had "come up from Springfield and taken quite a fancy to Lincoln. The two slept together and Lincoln frequently assisted him in the store." Here, as repeatedly, Herndon's naive openness inadvertently says more than he seems to realize, even though still more might have been obvious if Herndon had included some of the side details right there: A. Y. Ellis not only "took a fancy" to Lincoln and slept with him at the store in Springfield, but left home at his own expense to join Lincoln on his first political canvas, where one can be sure they continued to share the same bed at night. In the daytime Ellis was right there at Lincoln's side, and thrilled to be so, a vantage point that made him a witness of Lincoln's first political speech (at Pappsville in 1832). In correspondence with William Herndon many years later, Ellis helped to ensure that this speech went into the historical record.[48]

At other times Herndon's heterosexual bias was less fortunate. It allowed him to wonderfully compose various seduction struggles during which Lincoln had to hold himself back, like a team of wild horses, from one tempting conquest after the other. The true and entirely correct part of this was Lincoln's pervasive sex-mindedness (unmistakable, as mentioned before, from his more or less constant stream of sex jokes). Thus, he concluded as Judge Davis once did, that "Lincoln had terribly strong passions for woman, could scarcely keep his hands off them, and yet had honor and a strong will [enough] to put out the fires of his terrible passion."[49] In still another letter, this time to James H. Wilson, Herndon repeats the bit about Lincoln's purity: "Mr. Lincoln's honor saved many a woman from ruin. . . . This I knew from my own knowledge. I have seen Lincoln tempted and I have seen him regret the approach of women."[50] Not all biographers of Lincoln were this naive. The historian Richard N. Current quotes Lincoln's biographer Nathaniel W. Stephenson: "Lincoln lacked the wanton appetites of the average sensual man." Edgar Lee Masters, too, specifically responded to Lincoln's well-known disinterest in women—which, remarkably, he managed to see with clarity while remaining unaware of Lincoln's pervasive sexiness:

> Lincoln was an under sexed man. That is the simplest way to express it. He liked to be with men when he liked to be with anyone. . . . He was one of those manly men, whose mind made him seek masculine minds. Marriage with him had the slightest sexual aim. It was rather taken for social reasons, or other self-regarding motives, all apart from romantic impulses. If the story of Ann Rutledge, and Mary Owens and Mary Todd do not prove this, nothing could.[51]

Less funny by far was the fact that Herndon's heterosexual bias was probably entirely, or at least partly, responsible for his launching the Ann Rutledge story. The ins and outs of this legend will be examined in Chapter Four.

It has sometimes been suggested that Herndon reveled in the Ann Rutledge story to embarrass and goad Mary Lincoln, who it was said he "hated," a charge with two serious flaws in it. In the first place, this particular brand of small mean-spiritedness was not part of Herndon's makeup. Secondly, the irony was, and is, that far from mistreating Mary Lincoln or being overly harsh in his judgments of her, Herndon was arguably more evenhanded than many of her critics, and more generous than she deserved. More than once he went out of his way to give Lincoln a full share of blame for their exceedingly bad marriage, once insisting that

> [in order to] reconcile the strange course of his courtship and the tempestuous chapters in his married life, [one must await new] facts, long chained down [which] are gradually coming to the surface. When all is at last known, the world I believe will divide its censure between Lincoln and his wife.[52]

In recent times it has become fashionable for historians to put Herndon down, to belittle him for minor flaws, and even to disparage him as an unreliable source. What makes this harsh opinion especially unfair is the fact that nearly all we know of Lincoln's early personal life comes from Herndon's tireless spadework—and brain work—along with his mostly very carefully weighed opinions. He is due this much credit without question, but all the more so now that so many of his and other solid observations of Lincoln have been cast aside if not replaced by what purport to be "deeper" insights offered by a number of still quoted "psychohistorians"—along with a number of newer but very fashionable amateur psychologists.

Psychohistory, so-called, harks back to the 1930s, during which it became fashionable in some circles to employ psychoanalytic words and concepts (mostly Freudian) to supposedly explain various human motivations and actions. At first, the very language sounded rich and special, with phrases such as "sexual identity," "identity crisis," and "mother identification"—and just "identity" alone—a far cry from the Plain-Jane logic that Herndon used, and that mostly still holds up. Fortunately, the fad of psychohistory did not spread to all Lincoln scholars, or even to most. Moreover, many Lincoln experts have bravely called a spade a spade. Mark E. Neely, Jr., one of the most substantial and reliable Lincoln scholars, in his *Abraham Lincoln Encyclopedia* has characterized "psychobiographies of Lincoln" as "unmitigated disasters."[53] Despite a few hangers-on and what is left in print, conjectures of this ilk are now sharply on the wilt because the vine simply died at the root; Freudian psychology is all but dead, and largely a laughingstock to boot.[54] But it had quite a run while it lasted, and at its peak caught the fancy of clever and much quoted Lincoln specialists. Whether they themselves continue to believe in defunct psychoanalytic ideas or not, the mischief still lies very much around in libraries and in easy popularizations, where it greatly needs cleaning up.

As an example of special clarity, take the case of Professor Charles B. Strozier, who was not the first nor yet the last of distinguished historians to have latched onto the distortions of psychohistory. One of his revelations deals with a famous little event that Lincoln himself related from his boyhood in a short election autobiography written in 1860. As Lincoln put it, in the third person:

> A few days before the completion of his eighth year, in the absence of his father, a flock of wild turkeys approached the new log cabin, and A[braham] with a rifle gun, standing inside, shot through a crack, and killed one of them. He has never since pulled a trigger on any larger game.[55]

No surprise here, since Lincoln always felt great sympathy for animals—too much to ever enjoy hunting the rest of his life. Enter the psychohistorian Strozier. His analysis was that since the gun belonged to Abe's father, and may have been loaded by his mother, it is "apparent [that] Lincoln wished his father away [dead] because he wanted to [sexually] possess the mother." But since the gun "proved more deadly than anticipated [and] killed the helpless turkey . . . punishment must be extracted." This became all the more urgent, says Strozier, since Abe's mother soon died, leaving him with a double guilt, both for what he did to the turkey and "for his own earlier forbidden sexual wishes. [Therefore,] as punishment for his love, she died." This, it was said, left Lincoln with everlasting mental complications.[56] Beyond the stark improbability of such an interpretation, this homegrown turkey-gobbler version of an already moribund

Greek psychoanalytic Oedipal myth seems enough to have embarrassed even Freud.

Not that all of Strozier is so blatant and coarse. On the contrary, in one area he very nearly wins a garland or a laurel, and may deserve one anyway. When Strozier took the trouble to analyze a few lines of homosexual verse from Lincoln's *Chronicles of Reuben*, he brought the matter of Lincoln's homosexual side to the very edge of what would still be a creditable and correct interpretation, only to be sidetracked at the last moment into throwing it all away, casting it into the stereotypical conclusion that Lincoln had a "fragile sexual identity."[57]

There was, of course, very little in Lincoln that was in any sense "fragile," least of all his rock solid, autodidact persona, made all the more so by the certainty and independence that only a very early puberty affords. This puts us within a stone's throw of several new revelations. But these will have to wait for final analysis in Chapter 9, by which time enough new material should be on board to illustrate and to back up an entirely fresh view of Lincoln—both within and completely aside from the sexual side of his character and personality.

FOUR

Ann Rutledge

Then and Now

Nothing about Abraham Lincoln is more familiar than the Ann Rutledge legend: When he was a young man he fell in love with a beautiful girl by that name who, alas, soon sickened and died, leaving him heartbroken in the tiny village of New Salem, Illinois. Who would ever have dreamed that such a tale, hanging as it does on hardly more than a few gossamer threads of folk-say, could have lasted so long? Let alone that in the 1990s and on into the twenty first century it would evolve into ever new reincarnations? It is useful to recall the story's basic details, since a bit later some rarely cited evidence transforms virtually every aspect of it into quite a different picture.

The story got its start the year after the assassination, when William Herndon decided to cash in on his well-deserved reputation as an authority on Lincoln, with whom he had shared a law practice and a close friendship for years. He delivered a series of public lectures; the first three, filled with interesting details and mature assessments, were a great success. But then in his fourth and final lecture (November 16, 1866) Herndon told an all too sentimental story in which he declared that "Abraham Lincoln loved Miss Ann Rutledge with all his soul, mind, and strength," that "she loved him as dearly," and that "they seemed made in heaven for each other." Alas, within months she fell fatally ill, leaving the lovers only a few pathetic final moments together. Lincoln was devastated; Herndon described how he "sorrowed and grieved, rambled over the hills and through the forests, day and night. . . . He slept not, he ate not, joyed not. . . . His mind wandered from its throne [until] his reason . . . walked out of itself along the uncolumned air, and kissed and embraced the shadows and illusions of the heated brain."[1] So crushed was Lincoln that never again was he able to love another woman—which of course included his wife.

For decades to follow the story led a kind of double life. Most Lincoln biographies (including several Hollywood movies), simply repeated the Ann Rutledge romance, minus the part about his not loving his wife. But a few Lincolnists, more concerned with accuracy than with a hackneyed Victorian melodrama, became ever more disturbed by all the sentimental fantasy repeated on every side. Thus, in 1927 one offended scholar, Paul M. Angle, published a serious challenge, noting that the story was "entirely traditional"—a mere cliché lacking any true flavor of Lincoln. Angle pointed out, as is still true, "No reliable contemporary record has ever been discovered for it."[2] As the popular press continued to rehash the romance, nonbelievers could only seethe in frustration.

Then, in 1945, a world-class Lincoln scholar, J. G. Randall, took up the cudgel with a deservedly famous essay, "Sifting the Ann Rutledge Evidence," in which he carefully examined the pros and cons of the matter.[3] In making his many points Randall juxtaposed facts with legend, underscoring serious contradictions and demonstrating some of the pitfalls inherent in reminiscences called up from hazy, thirty-year-old memories.

It was to Herndon's credit that for two years following the assassination he made prodigious efforts to glean all he could from Lincoln's still living friends and associates on any and all topics. But once he arrived at the notion of Lincoln's having had a great romance with Ann, he pursued this theme to the hilt, sometimes squeezing it from subjects who had not mentioned it on their own; in more than a few instances he ignored conflicting evidence. Yet, for the most part, Herndon had the honesty to retain all his materials (including various negative and contrary reports) among his papers, which is where Randall found them nearly eight decades later.

Beyond ignoring major contradictions Herndon distorted his evidence in far more serious ways. His main Rutledge family informant, Robert B. Rutledge (a boy of seventeen when his sister Ann died), provided a terse, emotionally flat account of the romance that included very few specific memories. However, Robert invited Herndon to reshape and expand the story:

> I trust largely to your courtesy as a gentleman, to your honesty and integrity as a historian, and to your skill in writing for the public, to enlarge wherever my statements seem obscure, and to condense and remove whatever seems superfluous. . . . I beg of you to consider well the testimony in each case, and make up your history from those statements which may appear to you best fitted to remove all doubt as to their correctness.[4]

Herndon fully embraced that leeway in his lecture a month later, dressing up the Rutledges' scant reminiscences about Lincoln and Ann with a tearjerking saga of doomed romance, replete with a deathbed farewell scene that no Rutledge claimed to have remembered until well after Herndon's lecture had made it a nationally famous drama. In this fashion Herndon did, indeed, arrive at a history "best fitted to remove all doubt."

Short on details as Robert Rutledge's romance testimony was, it nonetheless was the product of apparently extensive consultations with his mother, elder brother, and a first cousin. Robert had written Herndon that this would help him fill in blanks in his own memory; but as Randall noted:

> In the law of evidence, however, it is insisted that testimony ought to come straight. If witnesses arrange their recollections so as to make them agree, or if they seek to build them up where they admit uncertainty, the result lacks the validity of statements obtained from witnesses separately and unretouched.[5]

No less serious, as Randall pointed out, were contradictions in and around the hard facts of the case. Ann Rutledge died in August 1835, supposedly leaving her betrothed Lincoln adrift and distraught. One complication was that Ann at that time was engaged to one John Mc-Namar, a friend of Lincoln's who had been away some two years attending to family business in New York. Leaving aside the extreme unlikelihood that Lincoln ever would have moved in on a friend (or on anyone else) in this way, the question arose: Did Ann blithely go ahead with an engagement to Lincoln, thus becoming engaged to both men simultaneously? Herndon himself privately struggled with the idea that Ann was indeed engaged to both men at once, as he wrote to his coauthor, Jesse Weik, on January 11, 1889, shortly before their Lincoln biography was published.[6] But of course the penalty for *not* believing in the double engagement would have been to admit that Lincoln and Ann were never engaged—which would have wiped away much of the romance Herndon had come to have such a stake in claiming.

A few weeks after Ann died McNamar arrived back in New Salem, bringing into the picture a host of new contradictions. More than thirty years later McNamar was asked how he had felt about Lincoln back then. Not quite getting the point he simply said, "Mr. Lincoln was not to my knowledge paying particular attention to any of the Young Ladies of my acquaintanc [sic] when I left [for New York]."[7] When then asked follow-up questions to elicit his possible jealousy, McNamar answered:

> I never heard an[y] person say that Mr. Lincoln addressed Miss Ann Rutledge in terms of courtship[,] neither [from] her own family nor my acquaintances otherwise [although] I heard . . . from two prominent Gentlemen of my acquaintance and Personal Friends that Lincoln was Grieved very much at her death.[8]

Nor did McNamar have any complaints. On the contrary, when he returned he resumed his friendship with Lincoln, who, as he proudly said, "wrote a deed for me which I still hold."[9]

Not only had McNamar been engaged to Ann for some time before he left for New York, he was also closely intertwined with the whole Rutledge family in what they termed a "family arrangement."[10] It amounted to McNamar having bought the Rutledge farm, with the Rutledges still allowed to live there. And of course New Salem was a small village, which meant that everyone shared the news and gossip. Years later this led Randall to observe amusingly: "If Lincoln did court Ann to the point of betrothal, and McNamar who was known to be engaged to her was not told of this fact when he returned to New Salem, human nature in country towns has radically changed!"[11] This was more than droll humor. The fact by itself was enough to cast huge doubt on the whole assemblage of romantic reminiscences from all sources. Or to put it sharper: For McNamar to have heard not a word of any such thing is a fact strong enough to blow the whole ship out of the water.

According to the Rutledge family tradition, McNamar corresponded with Ann for some time after leaving New Salem for New York but then stopped writing, a signal he had lost interest in the marriage.[12] There is no record of any correspondence between Lincoln and Ann, however, even when Lincoln himself departed New Salem to serve his first term in the state legislature at Vandalia from late 1834 to early 1835. This is curious, if the two were in fact romantically involved. Lincoln was a dutiful letter writer; moreover, letters from him would have provided a much needed reassurance to Ann, given her history with McNamar. Thus, one would think that in Rutledge family lore letters from Lincoln would have been fondly remembered. There is no such lore.[13]

Indeed, Ann Rutledge's name appears nowhere in any of Lincoln's writings, as Randall points out.[14] His paper as it sifts the evidence raised many other significant points of doubt as well, and consequently had a decidedly expurgatory effect. For while it did nothing to change the public popularity of the legend (any more than evidence against George Washington's cherry tree ever stopped the story of his chopping it down), what it *did* do was shake the house of Lincoln history to its foundations, causing it to "clean up its act" for almost half a century. As the noted scholar Benjamin P. Thomas put it in his *Abraham Lincoln: A Biography*, "most [Lincoln students now] regard it [the Ann Rutledge romance] as improbable, and reject utterly its supposed enduring influence upon Lincoln."[15] Wise words indeed, based on Randall's careful analysis of the legend. But then why did Randall's firm findings come under serious attack a half century later, in the 1990s? Answering this uncovers some less than savory maneuvers within Lincoln scholarship. But before opening that door, better to have at hand an up-close image of Lincoln himself.

LINCOLN AND WOMEN

Lincoln had a terrible record with women. As his kindly stepmother first noticed, "He was not very fond of girls as he seemed to me."[16] Later, many close friends made similar mentions. His cousin John Hanks complained, "I never Could get him in Company with women: he was not a timid man in this particular, but did not seek such Company."[17] Dennis Hanks, too, said Abe "Didn't love the Company of girls."[18] David Turnham (the lifelong friend whose dates and descriptions give us the exact timing of Lincoln's arrival at puberty) noted that "Abe did not much like the girls,"[19] later adding, "When in Company with Men & Women he was rather backward but with the Boys, he was always cheerful and talkative. He did not seem to seek the Company of the girls and [when abou]t them was rather backward."[20] When clerking for Abner Ellis, he "allways disliked to wait on the Ladies[;] he preferred trading with the Men & Boys as he used to Say."[21] Lincoln's friend Daniel Burner commented: "The four years I knew him in New Salem I never saw him with a girl. . . . Talking about girls, I want to say there is no truth in the story about Lincoln being engaged to Ann Rutledge."[22] As N. W. Branson too described Lincoln to Herndon, "He didn't go to see the girls much. He didn't appear bashful, but it seemed as if he cared but little for them. Wasn't apt to take liberties with them, but would sometimes. He always liked lively, jovial company, where there was plenty of fun & no drunkenness, and would just as lieve the company were all men as to have it a mixture of the sexes."[23] Nobody knows just when or where or how this early conditioning arose, merely that it seemed to be there from the start, like a fingerprint.

Yet this characteristic, so widely known and commented on by Lincoln's close friends, seems never to have been noticed by casual acquaintances, or registered in village gossip at any time. Why not? Probably because it was sharply contradicted in other ways. All his life Lincoln was wonderfully warm, friendly, helpful, and first-rate company not only with men but also with married women of all ages, especially the wives of friends. Nor did class seem to matter; he was as outgoing and congenial with the illiterate Hannah Armstrong as he was with the upper-crust Orville Brownings, Mrs. Browning being a special friend. In short, he was quick to lean forward toward women who were "already taken," yet any encounters with *eligible* girls and women (as David Donald was the first to notice), instantly stirred discomfort if not disdain.[24]

Thus, it is highly probable that from his first beginning to board at the Rutledge Tavern in 1832, Lincoln felt easy and friendly with Ann, who was known to be engaged to his friend, John McNamar. Nothing could have made her safer and more "already taken" than that. By all accounts Ann was amiable, bright, fun to be around, qualities that Lincoln, who saw her daily as she attended to guests at the tavern, no doubt found endearing. This attractiveness of Ann is a matter of probability rather than hard fact; none of Herndon's informants told an eyewitness story of an affectionate friendship between Lincoln and Ann, let alone gave any firsthand knowledge of their courtship or engagement. Only gossip and hearsay pictured Lincoln and Ann's relationship as romantic.

Not that the idea of a "romance" was embraced by everyone, or that the notion grew with much initial vigor. It took a quarter century for the first traces of the story to show up in a barely noticed newspaper article, and fully four more years for the legend of Lincoln and Ann to take shape in Herndon's lively imagination, as shown in his lecture. By then, of course, Lincoln was martyred and very famous—which in itself may have sparked wishful memories for old-timers. Even so, only a small minority of those who later became known as "Herndon's informants" spoke of or in any way alluded to any romance between Lincoln and Ann. Yet almost from the start of his Lincoln studies in 1865, Herndon closely questioned anyone who might know anything of Lincoln's private life. On December 1, he wrote to his father-in-law and helper G. U. Miles:

If you ever see Mrs [Hannah] Armstrong please get out of her all the facts in reference to Mr. Lincolns life when in Menard—what he did—what he said—when he said it where he said it—before whom—How he lived—his manners— customs—habits—sports, frolics—fun—his sadness—his wit; his humor. What he read—when he read it—How he read— and what and who he loved. etc. etc. and in short all she may know about him in mind—heart—soul—body.[25]

As it later turned out, Herndon himself interviewed Hannah, who remembered nothing of any Lincoln romance.[26]

Thus the mystery remains: If only a fraction of Herndon's informants remembered a romance between Lincoln and Ann, and *none*, including surviving members of the Rutledge family, could summon up a specific memory of having seen any love affair, what generated the story? The seeds likely were planted by the probable warmth of Lincoln and Ann, which the villagers no doubt imbued with increasing zest in the ever more protracted absence of McNamar. But the clincher—the single most powerful persuader in favor of the romance—seems to have been Lincoln's apparent reaction to Ann's death. About his sadness, grief, or depression there were, in fact, many comments and eyewitness accounts of what villagers had seen, or thought they had seen, in Lincoln's response to Ann's passing.

However, there was another quite remarkable set of factors, one not so much as hinted at in any standard telling of the tale: the actual physical situation at the time. To fill in this blank is interesting in its own right, not only because of certain seldom cited revelations about Lincoln, but for other details hidden within a number of twists and turns that tend to get bypassed in recounting Lincoln history.

THE ACTUAL SITUATION

The dire events of 1835 began simply enough. Central Illinois was hit by very unusual weather—heavy continuing rains in the spring and early summer, followed in late July by extreme heat, then more rain, exactly the right conditions for a rampant breeding of the *Anopheles* mosquito. People started suffering extreme chills and fever—"bilious fever" as malaria was then called. The whole Rutledge family came down with it, Ann one of the last to succumb. Her illness, however, was especially severe and fast moving; she had developed not only bilious fever, but soon "brain fever"—typhoid. The sanitary conditions were unspeakable. What with no toilet and no running water, most of the eleven people living in this impossibly overcrowded one-room cabin were too sick to get up and make it to the outhouse, or even just outside the door to a latrine of sorts. The situation was made worse, much worse, by nearly everyone being plagued either by an extreme diarrhea typical of malaria, or a variant of it, a form of constipation that would suddenly explode into it. Besides all this mayhem of misery amid wretchedly dirt-poor poverty during an era of no screens or sanitation, the air was filled not only with mosquitoes, but with swarms of noxious large black flies and poisonous yellow ones that flew in unhindered from feasting on dung heaps and human feces.[27]

Lincoln helped as hurriedly and as constantly as he could, first by coming over from New Salem every day with Dr. John Allen; often he would stay overnight or return with the doctor, who would stop by for him after visiting other patients. As conditions worsened, Lincoln stayed over more often to offer continual help with the nursing, and with the many other hard and dirty tasks at hand.[28]

Soon Lincoln's own health began to fail, as chills and fever hit him, at first only on alternate days. (The latter detail earmarks his specific first infection: *Plasmodium vivax*, one of the four basic protozoa of malaria.) Nevertheless, he kept up the nursing as best he could, taking heroic doses of jalap and calomel, the latter bringing him to the very edge of mercury poisoning. Greatly adding to Lincoln's depression over the illness on every side—his own and that of the others—were the deaths of several of his friends, who became part of a veritable stream of burials taking place in a rush despite the neighborly aid he and a few others could offer.* "There were no undertakers. No caskets were kept on hand. Coffins had to be made after the death; and in a few instances he [Lincoln] had assisted in making them for his friends," said Arminda Rankin.[29]

Meanwhile, Lincoln himself was becoming progressively worse, worn down to emaciation by his malarial infection and overwork. Then, suddenly, as a kind of last straw, Ann's condition declined sharply as she went into a final five days of crisis, during the last two of which she was supposedly delirious. She died on Tuesday, August 25, 1835, with no known funeral service, as was often the case in those days, especially under crisis conditions.

Dr. Allen was now fully alarmed over Lincoln's condition—his

---

*Although malaria is not as deadly as typhoid or tetanus, in that most of its victims do not die, the accompanying severe anemia, avitaminosis, and protracted diarrhea still made it a frequent killer before anything was known of germs or vitamins.

gaunt and haggard look, his by then constant chills and fever (*Plasmodium falciparum* had set in), along with still other ravages of his disease. Allen spoke of his concern to Squire Bowling Green and his wife, Nancy (with whom Allen boarded when he as in town). He then prevailed on Lincoln to go to the Greens' quiet home and remain there under a specific medical regimen—"until he passed three consecutive weeks without a chill."[30] Under this care, "cheerfully [and] gladly given by Mr. and Mrs. Green," Lincoln soon began to recover.[31] By September 17 (less than a month after Ann died) he had met the medical requirement and was back as postmaster; by September 24 he had completed his next surveying job.[32]

Most certainly this set of plain facts does not fit with those many reports of Lincoln being "desperately in love" with a "beautiful girl" named Ann, of his being called to her bedside for a last loving good-bye, of friends having to restrain him from suicide after her death—individuals as well as groups watching over him and going so far as to place knives and other sharp instruments out of his reach. One story had it that a group of friends forced or bodily carried him over to the Greens', another that Lincoln took Ann's death so hard that he "was locked up by his friends . . . to prevent his derangement or suicide."[33]

Most of these wild stories and outright fictions appear to have stemmed from exaggerations or slight word errors that caused accounts to veer off down one wrong track after the other. Take exaggeration. Ann was repeatedly said to be a beautiful, or even a wonderfully beautiful girl. In the service of this idea subtle changes crept into estimates of her height and weight, always toward making her slimmer. One exception was Mrs. Parthena Hill, wife of Samuel Hill, a leading New Salem figure. Mrs. Hill, as delicately as possible, laid it squarely on the line, describing Ann as "heavy set"[34]—a description David Donald accurately quoted—but then perhaps to detoxify it, he added that "in Lincoln's eyes this was no disadvantage, for all of the women he loved were plump."[35] That was true enough of the women, but not of Lincoln, who particularly disliked fatness in females. Fat was all right at a distance; for instance, Mrs. Browning, a special pal of his, was downright roly-poly. But when Mary Owens gained weight after their first meeting, he was to describe her to friends as "a fair match for Falstaff."[36]

Later with his wife, Mary Todd, there was the same problem. Never exactly a sylph herself, Mary, to his alarm, kept gaining weight. Once he tried to speak lightly of it in a letter, but within a sentence or two he could restrain himself no longer, flatly and none too gently requesting: "Get weighed, and write me how much you weigh."[37] As for Ann, Lincoln liked all the Rutledges, and he may well have liked Ann the best, perhaps much the best. But if that relationship had not been thwarted by numerous roadblocks diverting him from women—and had allowed him to get anywhere near romance, let alone high romance—it would definitely *not* have been in Ann's favor that she was "heavy set."

But were there not persistent reports of Lincoln's being broken-hearted both when Ann died and later? Indeed so. In fact, this observation is the only one having a certain eyewitness flavor: People actually saw it, or thought they did. (Quite unlike Lincoln's "courtship" and "romance" with Ann, where there were many reports, but all of them at second or third hand; nobody claimed to have actually witnessed any of it themselves.) Yet even more credible reports of Lincoln's depression stand as a curious blend of fact and fiction. Comments to the effect that Lincoln was pathologically depressed at the time Dr. Allen arranged for him to move in with the Greens might almost be true, as stated. Besides being seriously ill at the time, and profoundly downcast over the deaths of Ann and other friends whose loss right then was a serious lament, Lincoln also had a long history of falling into extreme depressions for lesser reasons, or indeed for no apparent reason at all. In fact, friends who had for years seen him in these states now warned others not to be overly alarmed; since he very often experienced deep depressions, the situation was probably less serious than it looked.[38]

The latter fact seems strangely understated (if not ignored entirely) by most tellers of the tale. Not hard to imagine why. Depression that exists on its own—or worse still, stems from unknown inner conflicts—does nothing for romantic drama, and even sharply competes with it. Combine this with the fact that nearly everything ever written about Lincoln and Ann had less to do with them, much less, than it did with the speakers, writers, and readers of those tales. Thus, one repeatedly finds a tendency to virtually "move the furniture around" in the telling of decidedly doubtful events occurring under conditions of dirt-poor poverty, recasting them to fit a scene of luxuriant romance. Take Herndon speaking of Ann on her deathbed:

> Lincoln was sent for and the poor girl felt his approach and heard his tread; on his quick and hasty arrival he was admitted to see Ann; the doors were closed, and no one knows but God what was felt, thought and said.[39]

Fiction crowds in on every side. Notice how far away Lincoln is pictured, not at all constantly present and sorely busy with bedpans, mopping up bodily excrescences from the soggy floor of this small, filthy, overcrowded hovel with Ann only steps away, moaning amid the miseries of most of the eleven Rutledges, many of them seriously sick at the same time. Yet the legend has it that Lincoln is off somewhere, oblivious to it all with no notion of Ann's dire circumstance, and thus had to be "sent for." In the Herndon account Lincoln comes quickly enough, but then the place has suddenly been transformed. Gone is the one-room hovel. The accommodations have now become downright luxurious, with space enough for Ann to have her own private room—apparently behind double doors through which Lincoln has to be "admitted." But once inside, there at last is Ann, who like Camille lies desperately ill and dying in romantic splendor. Even to be aware of the great sorrow and suffering that regularly prevailed on the American frontier fails to save the scene. As Herndon pictures it the sweep of histrionics makes it all come across as comic high romance—indeed, high camp.

So much for Herndon's pure fantasy and unintended humor. Nearby, however, serious issues abound. For instance, was Lincoln really thrown into a major depression when Ann died, one so severe that some people thought he went crazy? "Crazy with grief" was a standard phrase at the time.[40] Folk-say proclaimed it, a serious problem being that people are prone to copy and reiterate conventional opinion, especially when it is dramatic or juicy.

True, some reports of his depression were better. James Short, who saw Lincoln almost daily, said he "did not know of any . . . tender passages between Mr L and Miss R at the time[.] But after her death [Lincoln] seemed to be so much affected and grieved so hardly that I then supposed there must have been something of the kind."[41]

Although this is a classic instance of what Randall called a "must have been true" conclusion, still it is perhaps better than pure hearsay.[42] The same might be said of Elizabeth Abell's remark where, again, one hears a must-have-been-true assumption that Ann's death was the cause: "[H]e was not crazy but he was very disponding [sic] a long time."[43] From these and other reports it all has the look and sound of high romance gone tragic—but since there was not, in fact, any romance, what exactly was it?

Perhaps this is the place to remember that Lincoln was a very unknown character, and never obvious. Throughout his life he played all personal feelings close to the chest, fully confiding in nobody; yet this private policy of his never came across as fear, or caution, or any other form of standoffishness. Why not? Probably because in so many other ways he was utterly plain and genuine, though never simple in the usual sense. As his friend and colleague Leonard Swett once observed: "He told all that was unimportant with a gushing frankness."[44] Still, since he never lied, the net result came across in ways that tended to give others confidence in their own assessments of him. Even casual observers thought they could "read" him, especially in his tragic moods. In this perhaps they were right; Lincoln often felt despondent, and it showed. Years later Herndon put one of these images in a nutshell: "He was a sad-looking man; his melancholy dripped from him as he walked. His apparent gloom impressed his friends, and created sympathy for him—one means of his great success."[45]

At close range it often seemed easy to guess the source of his sadness, as in the case of Ann's death; but then still closer, an added detail or two could severely shake one's first impression, or even reverse it. Take the report of Lincoln's utter despair at Ann's death. Without benefit of knowing their relationship was something other than romantic, the whole image could suddenly collapse. As John Hill reported to Herndon, "Lincoln bore up under it [the shock of Ann's death] very well until some days afterwards [when] a heavy rain fell, which unnerved him."[46] A delay of "some days" before real sadness set in? Hardly the instant response of a brokenhearted lover.

No question about why and how the rain came as a huge shock, and why it "unnerved him"—though once again a rarely mentioned fact is needed to understand it. Lincoln always had an especially sharp reaction to death (more about that in a moment), particularly to what happens to the body of a friend or loved one as water seeps into the grave. Thus, it was the rain that brought on his poignant lament "I can never be reconciled to have the snow, rains and storms to leak on her grave"—or as Elizabeth Abell recalled, "he could not bare [sic] the idea of its raining on her Grave."[47] Not that this reaction was unique; no doubt countless people for eons have felt much the same on seeing a friend or loved one alive one moment, then lifeless and exposed to the ravages of nature the next. (To this day the shock sponsors an urge to delay funerals, and to fend off nature with embalming and waterproof caskets.) More here than meets the eye.

More broadly, too, Lincoln had a tendency to react very sharply to death; he never seemed able to accept it. When he tried to deliver a eulogy at the funeral of his friend Bowling Green, he broke down completely and left in tears.[48] When young Elmer Ellsworth was killed ("the first casualty of the Civil War") he sobbed profusely not only at the time and with official visitors standing close by, but also days and months later, often in public, and sometimes at the mere mention of Ellsworth's name.

At first glance Lincoln's extreme sadness at the sudden loss of his favorite son, Willie, who died in 1862, may look like that of any devoted father, yet it too was exceptional. Not only was Lincoln said to have never fully recovered, he seemed to keep reliving his loss— twice having Willie's body disinterred, just to see him again.[49] Was his extraordinary reaction to death due in part to his long ago having discarded most religion, including whatever consolation he might have had from believing in a life after death, as his friend Ward Lamon once suggested?[50] Undoubtedly so. But no need to guess; we have the main thrust from Lincoln himself. When Mrs. Parthena Hill once asked Lincoln, "Do you really believe there isn't any future state?" he replied: "I'm afraid there isn't. It isn't a pleasant thing to think that when we die, that is the last of us."[51]

In short, Lincoln's sharp reaction to death was but one more of his many routes into severe depression. Or, as was often the case, he could get there entirely on his own with no excuse, no trigger from the outside, no black horse to ride in on. Thus it is pure folly—an exercise in self-deception—to presume to know, or to guess, just why Lincoln was dejected at any particular time. This understanding, of course, was a caution shared mainly by close friends; most others were ready to rush right in to join the prevailing opinion that Lincoln was much disturbed, and that Ann's death was the cause (or as Herndon had it, the cause of his sadness for the rest of his life). Would this fiction have foundered if people had known Lincoln and Ann were friends rather than lovers, and that his anguish after her death came only after it rained, reminding him of impending events inside the grave? If such news had come late, the best guess is that it probably would not have changed the course of events. For while new and correct information may quickly gain ground in the eyes of discerning individuals, it stands little if any chance of prevailing—let alone of carrying public opinion along with it—unless and until it is widely held, or is thought to be.

Modern research on public opinion has shown that the opinion of most people, including that of most professionals, tends to go with the flow of popular sentiment—the bandwagon effect. This tendency to jump aboard what appears to be an agreed upon theme and thus "stay parallel" to popular sentiment seems especially evident in the Ann Rutledge story. For while Herndon's original audience for his lecture (November 16, 1866) was tiny, Herndon sent out hundreds of copies of his broadside, some of them beforehand, to key Lincoln friends and associates. Many of the recipients knew a very different Lincoln from the one pictured, and gave evidence of being surprised, such as B. F. Carpenter, Billy Greene, and Joshua Speed. Yet for whatever reason, most Lincoln friends chose to go along with Herndon's dramatic story rather than contradict it. Thus the Herndon theme became a study in successful bandwagonry, driven, as it were, from both sides: first by whatever appeal the story itself held, and then by the tendency of many joiners to accept Herndon's invitation to hop aboard.

Sometimes the joiners give us a jolt. Why should Arminda Rogers—a little-known Lincoln chronicler who was present in August 1835 as Ann lay dying, and remembered for history the whole scene of malarial misery, of flies and filth and vomit on the floor, and of Lincoln helping mop it up—why should she of all people later join the crowd in circulating the romantic myth, though it was far afield from facts she knew to be the case? Equally extreme in their way were those like Henry C. Whitney, who were young children or not yet born when Ann died, yet whose testimony and retelling of Herndon's tale could tease tears from a stone statue. As a young student Whitney first met Lincoln in 1853, observed him well for seven years on the circuit, but never knew a thing of his early life; yet years later in 1892 he used his known connection to Lincoln to strike a pompous pose: "To my mind the life and death of Ann Rutledge was not a misadventure, or in vain; . . . [it] will be hailed as one of the agents of Destiny in the salvation and regeneration of the nation."[52]

A continuing question in sex research is a puzzle here as well: Why and how does it happen that there should be so many places in and near sex where people believe, or claim to believe, the unbelievable? One is reminded of Joshua Speed saying of Herndon's story of Lincoln and Ann, "It is all new to me—But so true . . . of Lincoln's character . . . I would almost swear to it." Likewise with Billy Greene who, on reading Herndon's lecture, had only a mild complaint of his exaggerating the "Picturesk" of the New Salem countryside, raising not a single objection to Herndon's depiction of Lincoln, though he was bound to have known it was not true.[53] Why this incessant going along with a false image merely because others do?

Such feigned belief is quite familiar. One sees it at lower reaches in the readiness of readers to more or less unhesitatingly accept what they read in the likes of gossip magazines and grocery store tabloids (*The Enquirer*, etc.), where sex and sin play key roles. (Key roles, yes, though in a tone of moral righteousness, which probably provides a good deal of the reward as one savors sin and condemns the wicked.) Often the content of the stories is too extreme, too far-fetched, to be soberly believed, and yet it is not disbelieved. In this it shares a great deal with the unbelievability of the Lincoln and Ann story, especially its morality play side as Lincoln, pictured as helplessly overtaken by his own passion, steals away Ann, his friend McNamar's fiancée, while she, filled with guilt, wrenches mightily over the sin of it all. This version, too, is a spin-out and too silly to be believed, and yet in the minds of many it is not disbelieved.

Sometimes a few of the disbelievers did so loudly. Within days of Herndon's lecture his friend Judge T. L. Dickey wrote to complain,

Thank you for [the] copy of that fancy lecture—Romance is not your forte—The few grains of history stirred into that lecture—

in a plain narrative would be interesting—but I don't like the garnishments.[54]

Not that sentiments of this sort had any chance with Herndon, since by this time he was fully committed to the great romance, and there was no turning back.

At the opposite extreme—that is, at the highest levels of motive and reward—it is often insisted that avid readers and storytellers alike find a richness, a certain tragic catharsis, in a romance that develops with promise, only suddenly to collapse into failure for whatever reason. Perhaps so. But Lincoln and Ann, unlike Romeo and Juliet, were real-life figures, friends rather than lovers, and hardly archetypes of romance. No matter. Whether in high form or low, the melodrama to this day continues to exert strong appeal, even for many professional Lincolnists, who over the last decade have been lured aboard what turned out to be a new legend bandwagon.

Less than two years after Lincoln died a lawyer friend of his, one Isaac Cogdal, stepped forward to say that in 1861 Lincoln himself had invited him over to "reminisce" about old friends they had known back in New Salem, and that during the session he, Cogdal, had had a chance to query Lincoln and get specific answers to a few very personal questions about his relationship with Ann. According to Cogdal Lincoln affirmed the romantic nature of the relationship. This was precisely what the legend had long lacked: direct confirmation from Lincoln himself. Now that Lincoln had been martyred and instantly elevated to a man of the ages, it was all the more urgent to be able to fill in glaring gaps and hearsay with firm information. The urge would hold, too. More than a century later, in the 1990s, the revisionist Lincoln scholar Douglas L. Wilson cited the Cogdal interview to argue, contra Randall, that it did indeed provide conclusive evidence for the legend's reality.

But who was this Isaac Cogdal? According to T. G. Onstot, Isaac Cogdal "was a farmer and stone mason who operated a quarry. . . . He was eventually admitted to the Illinois bar in 1860, having been encouraged in the law by his old New Salem friend, Ab. Lincoln."[55]

Several unique features gave Cogdal's testimony far greater credibility than the statements of other legend informants. Not only did he claim to have interviewed Lincoln directly and to have asked specific very personal questions about his relationship with Ann Rutledge, he also chose to quote Lincoln's exact words, or claimed to. And since Cogdal's Lincoln interview was either during or shortly before February 1861, and he became one of Herndon's informants only four or five years later,[56] there was no question of his having to struggle with "dim and misty memories," as had been a complaint with other informants.

Then, too, both the situation and the feel of Cogdal's firsthand Lincoln quotations seem to place his evidence on a different plane from that of other informants. Not that Cogdal himself made any such claim; he simply said that after Lincoln was elected president (but before being sworn in), he suggested one day

"Ike Call at my office in the State house about an hour by sun down. The Company will then all be gone"—

Cogdal[57] went according to request & Sure Enough the Company dropt off one by one—his, Ls, Clerk included.

"I want to enquire about old times and old acquaintances," said Lincoln. He then said—"When we lived in Salem there were the Greens, Potters, Armstrongs—& Rutledges. These folks have got scattered all over the world—some are dead. Where are [the] Rutledges—Greens—&c."

After we had spoken over old times—persons—Circumstances—in which he showed wonderful memory I then dare[d] to ask him this question—

May I now in turn ask you one question Lincoln, said Cogdal.

"Most assuredly. I will answer your question if a fair one with all my heart," then it was that he answered, as follows:

Abe is it true that you fell in love with & courted Ann Rutledge, said Cogdal. Lincoln said, "It is true—true indeed I did. I have loved the name of Rutledge to this day. I have kept my mind on their movements ever since and love them dearly," said L[incoln].

Abe—is it true—said Cogdal, that you ran a little wild about the matter.

"I did really—I ran off the track: it was my first. I loved the woman dearly & sacredly: she was a handsome girl—

would have made a good loving wife—was natural and quite intellectual, though not highly Eduated—I did honestly—& truly love the girl & think often—often of her now."[58]

J. G. Randall, noting Cogdal's account, commented: "The most obvious thing about this effusive statement is its unLincolnian quality." Noting how disinclined Lincoln always was to express private feelings, Randall added, "In the face of such reticence, the Cogdal record seems artificial and made to order. It was given out after Lincoln's death; it presents him in an unlikely role; it puts in his mouth uncharacteristic sayings."[59]

Indeed so. In fact, hardly a phrase of it could pass as likely Lincoln language—either to those who accepted Randall's revisionism at the time, or to Lincoln students who might read it today.

Yet on the basis of Cogdal's account, some forty-five years after Randall's comments, the Lincoln scholar Douglas L. Wilson in a 1990 paper attacked the whole notion of questioning it, charging, "We have no more reason to doubt [Cogdal's] testimony than did Herndon, who knew Cogdal as a man highly regarded in his community and an old friend of Lincoln's."[60] Three years later, in a 1993 paper,[61] Wilson sharpened his attack, stating firmly that "Angle[62] and Randall had no more reason to doubt Cogdal's testimony than that of many other witnesses they chose not to question." And "Their disposition to treat Isaac Cogdal as untruthful is clearly the result of their disinclination to accept what he had to say."[63] In short, Wilson argues none too pleasantly that Angle and Randall arrived at their conclusions from personal bias, not evidence.

This serious accusation is notable for two reasons. First, it very aggressively defends Cogdal, leaving Wilson open to the same charge of bias he makes against Angle and Randall. Second, Wilson's quick dismissal of Randall's objections never seriously engages them.

The underlying reason for Wilson's aggressive defense of Cogdal is clear. Although he has some two dozen other informants whose statements he cites to bolster the believability of the legend, none of that testimony holds a candle to the power and seemingly irrefutable details of Cogdal's firsthand information. As Randall crisply made clear, most of the informants' memories were either too vague, secondhand, or in the case of the Rutledge family's memories, too "dim and misty" to be reliable. But in Cogdal's testimony Wilson could point to what seemed both recent and straightforward.

However, in touting Cogdal and rejecting Randall, Wilson at his own peril ignores a set of penetrating observations: the "unLincolnian quality" of the "Cogdal record"; that it "seems artificial and made to order"; and that "it puts in [Lincoln's] mouth uncharacteristic sayings." In fact, all of the opposition to Randall that has appeared in print in the 1990s—from the seminal article by J. Y. Simon[64] to later writers Douglas L. Wilson and Michael Burlingame[65]— have failed to answer or to honor Randall's case on Cogdal. In the meantime Cogdal has become the witness of choice for those who, for whatever reason, have chosen to go with the flow toward a rebirth of the great romance.

Sometimes the size of a changed posture is impressive. After a lifetime building a well-earned reputation as a top Lincoln scholar, David Donald suddenly does an about-face on his whole position toward Ann Rutledge. In his 1995 best-selling biography *Lincoln* he largely joins the crowd accepting Wilson, restating not a word of his previous ridicule and doubt concerning the legend. However, in the midst of quoting several "uncharacteristic sayings" attributed to Lincoln, Donald *does* hedge his bet; at a crucial turnaround point he wisely inserts the proviso, "if Cogdal's memory can be trusted."[66]

Indeed, the trusting of Cogdal is the nub of the matter. Not that there is anything fundamentally new here about the Cogdal/Lincoln interview; it has been in the literature since Herndon put it there well over a century ago. What *is* new, however, is to read it with a straight face in the twenty-first century. In fact, the problems with Cogdal's testimony that Randall pointed to in 1945 have become even more glaring in the light of certain computer-assisted observations that quickly expose the bottom line: *What in Lincoln is the real Lincoln?* versus *How to spot a counterfeit a mile away.*

Not so hard to do. Forgers and counterfeiters who try to invent language for Lincoln face a surprisingly tough and treacherous task. Handwriting experts know that in forging a signature it is *much* harder to convincingly reproduce writing that is full of straightforward lines and curves than it is to fake an elaborate autograph.[67] The same is true in speech, where at first glance it might seem that common words and phrases, by their very plainness, offer great leeway to the counterfeiter. But the fact is that he walks a slippery slope on which the slightest stumble leaves a faulty footprint.

Perhaps because Lincoln had great mental precision in both his speaking and writing he avoided using "paired duplicates" and "near duplicate" adjectives; it was as if he held to some inner rule to be direct, to express himself once and clearly, and then leave it there. He also had his well-known track record of warding off personal questions. If anyone had ever had the temerity to ask Lincoln if he had fallen in love with, and courted, Ann Rutledge—and was foolish enough to ask two questions at once in this way—*and* if Lincoln had chosen to answer such a question at all (a double if not a quadruple improbability), nothing in his style suggests that he would have stammered it out three or four times in one phrase after the other, with the likes of, "It is *true—true indeed I did* [love her]"; or that he "loved the woman *truly and sacredly;*" or that he "did *honestly and truly* love the girl"; or that he thinks "*often—often* of her now." Certainly nowhere else in Lincoln's language is there any such unctuous laying-on of empty duplicates, least of all in the service of persuading a listener to believe him. Nor for that matter is there evidence of his ever having said he loved any woman (or man), even where we have reason to believe he probably did.

Lincoln's alleged use of "sacredly" is another case in point (even if it weren't paired and weakened with "truly"). He often borrowed scriptural words to use in decidedly nonreligious ways, as in his first inaugural address where he spoke of "the better angels of our nature," and where his meaning is so powerful and instantly clear, one neither has to be religious nor to believe that angels actually exist in order to catch his cadence and be moved by it. Likewise it was often Lincoln's style to evoke the best and broadest meanings of "sacred" without implying religion in any sense, as in: "our sacred soil"; "the sacred name of democracy"; "the sacred cause of liberty"; and "our sacred right of self-government." Note that all his meanings have to do with principles, rights, and broad beliefs, not the narrow stuff of personal action and aggrandizement. Nevertheless, might these broad meanings sometimes have been extended to include adverbial possession, as in Cogdal's "I loved her truly and *sacredly*?" One might well suppose so, and yet it is not true. Not in his entire *Collected Works*, including the *Supplements*, does Lincoln use the word *sacredly* so much as a single time.

Not that the issue rests merely on the use of a few unlikely words. Much of Lincoln's personality and his basic style are contradicted in still other parts of this dubious interview. For instance, when Cogdal proposes asking a question, Lincoln is quoted as saying, "Most assuredly. I will answer your question if a fair one with all my heart." But nowhere else in the Lincoln style does one find guarantees in advance ("Most assuredly I will"), or a demand for fairness ("if it is a fair one"), nor was Lincoln ever known to gush out a promise ("with all my heart"). Trivial as such examples may seem they are the epitome of what Randall labeled as "unLincolnian" and as "uncharacteristic sayings."[68] In a sense they are as transparent as the "emperor's new clothes."

Clearly Cogdal and his entire testimony reeks of deliberate fraud, though major questions still remain. First and foremost: Did Cogdal ever interview Lincoln at all? If so, one wonders again what he was up to. Possibly he may have had some kind of interview with Lincoln, but if he did we are left without a single reliable word of what was said on either side. As for Cogdal's exact motive, we shall never know for sure; his particular brand of secrecy and fakery suggests it may share the drive of many another large and small forgery and fraud—from Piltdown man and crop circles on down to numerous forged Lincoln signatures, false documents, and fake bits of memorabilia—hoaxes often traceable to nothing more than some ego gain a hoaxer gets from teasing or tampering with history.

Much more than a mere fad, Randall's argument held sway unchallenged for almost half a century. But considering what fate tends to do to overwhelming success within the scheme of things, might this mean the Randall revolution was especially vulnerable to the onslaught from Simon and Wilson? Timewise, very probably. Forty-five to fifty years seems about par for the course of constancy in history, long enough for the very strongest evidence to come under attack, get cycled into disbelief, or as is often the case, reversed. The fact that no Randall opponent has yet grappled with several of his sharpest charges (let alone answered them) suggests that replacements for Randall are not yet quite ready, or as is more probable, simply do not hold. In any event, it is remarkable, and a tribute to Wilson in particular, that the energy and persuasion of his multiple papers have proved powerful enough to carry some of his arguments forward, even though they depend enough on Cogdal and on distant informants to falter under close examination.

FIVE

Lincoln, Mary Owens, and the Wilds of Lincoln Wit

Among the close friends Lincoln made in New Salem and often stopped by to see were Dr. Bennett Abell and his wife, Elizabeth. One day in 1833, when Lincoln came by on such a visit, he was introduced to Mrs. Abell's sister, Mary Owens, who had come for a month's stay. She and Lincoln got along well enough, though without much enthusiasm on either side. Perhaps their relationship was partly put off by the obvious matchmaking efforts of Mrs. Abell, nor was the match much helped by what Mary Owens later noted: "his training had been different from mine; hence there was not that congeniality which would otherwise have existed."[1] Although they had little contact that month, as Herndon said, "she lingered long enough to make an impression on Lincoln."[2] But what sort of impression? She was nice looking enough at that time, and was noted for her intellect as well. For Lincoln, the timing was also right. By 1833 he was headed toward being a "public man," and to be in politics virtually demanded that he marry. In fact, his mind was much more on the necessity of marriage than on its actual appeal, as evidenced by his less than ardent words, that he "saw no good objection to plodding life through hand in hand with her."[3]

Part of this loud note of nonromance (indeed, noninterest) may have stemmed from his sheer naiveté. He had never been in love, neither is there any evidence of his ever having been physically attracted to any girl. Nor had he tried his hand at courtship, least of all with a new girl in town (even one somewhat older than himself) as opposed, say, to a home-grown neighborhood lass. Not that any of this (or all of it) fully accounts for the degree of his cool standoffishness, indeed, his drab and mundane picture of marriage as "plodding life through" with whoever she turned out to be. Still, the urgency he felt to *be* married was such that soon after Mary's departure back to Kentucky, Lincoln tossed out a boast: "If Mary Owens ever returned to Illinois a second time he would marry her."[4]

Three years later, in the fall of 1836, Mary Owens did return to visit her sister. Here was his chance to start again. "True to his word, Lincoln called upon the young lady; [but] instead of the slender, blooming maiden of his former acquaintance, he found a mature woman with an over-abundance of adipose tissue."[5] Struggling to look past that fat for the moment, Lincoln did his best to "court" Mary Owens, both by joining her on social occasions and by writing her four very personal letters, three of which turned out to have a remarkable second life. For this history all credit is once again owed to the indefatigable Herndon who, more than thirty years after the fact, was able to document the entire contact between Lincoln and Mary Owens.

About a year after Lincoln's death, far away in the tiny town of Weston, Missouri, Herndon discovered Mary Owens, long married as Mrs. Vineyard. He extracted many details from her despite her sharp objections to being cross-examined ("Really, [Mr. Herndon,] you catechise me in true lawyer style.") Nevertheless, in the end she answered all his questions, and eventually handed over all her Lincoln letters that, amazing in itself, she had kept and preserved.[6] Better yet, Herndon was able to jog her memory, and with some difficulty, through repeated requests and persuasions, he got her to answer long lists of new questions, replete with details that turned out to be at least as important as the letters. Her revelations not only gave her side of the picture; they also managed to lift this whole period of Lincoln's life into new and unexpected territory.

In one of Mary Owens Vineyard's first letters back to Herndon she made her much quoted complaint, that "Mr. Lincoln was deficient in those little links which make up the chain of [a] woman's happiness."[7] Undoubtedly so. But two months later (July 22, 1866) she spelled out her objections and her feelings of neglect with examples that are of special interest:

> We never had any hard feelings towards each other that I know of. . . . [Yet] I thought him lacking in smaller attentions. One circumstance presents itself just now to my mind's eye. There was a company of us going to Uncle Billy Greene's. Mr. Lincoln was riding with me, and we had a very bad branch to cross. The other gentlemen were very officious in seeing that their partners got safely over. We were behind, he riding in, never looking back to see how I got along. When I rode up beside him, I remarked, "You are a nice fellow! I suppose you did not care whether my neck was broken or not." He laughingly replied (I suppose by way of compliment), that he knew I was plenty smart to take care of myself.
>
> In many things he was sensitive almost to a fault. He told me of an incident: that he was crossing a prairie one day and saw before him, "a hog mired down," to use his own language. He was rather "fixed up," and he resolved that he would pass on without looking at the shoat. After he had gone by, he said the feeling was irresistible; and he had to look back, and the poor thing seemed to say wistfully, "There now, my last hope is gone"; that he deliberately got down and relieved it from its difficulty.[8]

The part about the hog mired down is a reminder here, as it was to Mary Owens Vineyard, that ordinarily Lincoln was wonderfully sensitive and empathetic toward everyone and anyone, including any animal. So where was all his concern and sympathy as Mary risked her neck in crossing the dangerous stream? It was absent, of course—but why, and what was holding it back? Better for a moment to look at the other side of the question. How was it that those "other gentlemen" managed to be "very officious in seeing that their [ladies] got safely over" the dangerous stream, while Lincoln failed miserably?

The short answer is that those "gentlemen" had a large charge of heterosexual enthusiasm, enough to keep them *tuned in* and *turned on* to their partners. As with young men the world over, one can see how they welcomed the opportunity—indeed, reveled in it—to sweep in perhaps with dash and derring-do to save the dainty damsels from distress. Lincoln had many lovely qualities, but gallantry and chivalry were not among them—nor was any other form of polite formality or courtly machismo.

This situation and its interpretation are so full of obvious truth, one is tempted to leave it there and move on, but for the fact that it is also full of double motives, a sure indication that one should look again. How, for example, would Lincoln's courtship behavior look if reexamined with all machismo and posturing elements parsed out, to see what is left? Fortunately, exactly this possibility is supplied by an actual event, thanks to one more tableau provided by Herndon from Mary Owens Vineyard:

> One day Miss Owens and Mrs. Bowlin [sic] Green were making their way slowly and tediously up the hill to Able's [sic] house, when they were joined by Lincoln. Mrs. Green was carrying "a great big fat child, heavy, and crossly disposed." Although the woman bent pitiably under her burden, Lincoln offered no assistance, but, dropping behind Miss Owens, beguiled the way according to his wishes. When they reached the summit, Miss Owens said to Lincoln laughingly, "You would not make a good husband, Abe." They sat on the fence; and one word brought on another, till a split or breach ensued.[9]

It is clear that Lincoln's benevolence awaited no invitation to display high manners or machismo. Rather, the overflowing kindness he was famous for and which ordinarily was so quickly and easily forthcoming from him—even for a "hog mired down"—was here being turned off, clear off, by something else, but by what? Undoubtedly his usual empathy was being frozen or seriously blocked by some preoccupation that was absorbing all his attention; perhaps he was too intently focused on how his courtship efforts were faring or failing. To say the least he was rattled and uptight, perhaps from not knowing just what to do or say next. In any case, the uphill path he was on in his own mind was steeper than Mrs. Green's climb—and his load heavier by far than her fat baby.

Sometimes a young man can be discombobulated in this way from the sheer urgency of his own desire. But that was hardly Lincoln's problem. He was patently short on romantic desire, and far from champing at the bit for closer contact; he was sending out signals of a very different sort. As he lurched alone and ahead of Mary Owens over that difficult branch to cross, it is clear why he failed to look back; in a sense he *welcomed* the distance and had not the slightest desire to pursue courtship, let alone a gallant kind. She picked up the message all too clearly, while Lincoln was lucky enough to think of a compliment (her being plenty smart to take care of herself) to disguise his disinterest. Remarkably, she even bought it, or seemed to—though they both soon went their separate ways.

It was of course wonderful that some thirty years later Herndon was able both to discover Mrs. Vineyard (née Mary Owens), then living in that tiny town in Missouri, and to persuade her to hand over the several letters Lincoln had written while "courting" her back in New Salem. Besides reflecting a number of their interactions together, the letters show in detail Lincoln's overmodest and decidedly self-defeating proposal of marriage to Mary—a kind of reaching forward while sharply leaning back. Of course there was more to it than that. His ambivalence was evident in a balance of sorts between his urge to hurry up and become a married man, along with the fiercely repellent fact of how fat Mary had become—not to mention serious doubts about his minimal heterosexual motivation in the first place.

Soon after Lincoln and Mary Owens parted (she none too politely by simply not answering his last letter and proposal). He then wrote a long, amusing letter to his pal, Mrs. Orville Browning. He had first met the Brownings more than a year earlier (1836) while serving his second term in the legislature, when they were all in Vandalia. His letter was a kind of three-way caricature of himself, his courtship of Mary, and a long list of her most repelling traits. When the letter was first revealed (in Ward Lamon's biography of Lincoln in 1872) the comedy was largely lost on various Victorian killjoys who saw no humor but plenty of unwelcome sharp edges in the words of the by then martyred Lincoln, who, as a saintly symbol, was not supposed either to make jokes or have harsh thoughts, even privately. But Lincoln alive was far from tight and tedious:

To Mrs. Orville H. Browning

Springfield, April 1, 1838—

Dear Madam:

Without appologising for being egotistical, I shall make the history of so much of my own life, as has elapsed since I saw you, the subject of this letter— And by the way I now discover, that, in order to give a full and intelligible account of the things I have done and suffered *since* I saw you, I shall necessarily have to relate some that happened *before*—

It was, then, in the autumn of 1836, that a married lady of my acquaintance, and who was a great friend of mine, who being about to pay a visit to her father and other relatives residing in Kentucky, proposed to me, that on her return she would bring a sister of hers with her, upon condition that I would engage to become her brother-in-law with all convenient dispatch— I, of course, accepted the proposal; for you know I could not have done otherwise, had I really been averse to it; but privately between you and me, I was most confoundedly well pleased with the project— I had seen that said sister some three years before, thought her inteligent and agreeable, and saw no good objection to plodding life through hand in hand with her— Time passed on, the lady took her journey, and in due time returned, sister in company sure enough— This stomached me a little; for it appeared to me, that her coming so readily showed that she was a trifle too willing; but on reflection it occurred to me, that she might have been prevailed on by her married sister to come, without any thing concerning me ever having been mentioned to her; and so I concluded that if no other objection presented itself, I would consent to wave this— All this occurred upon my *hearing* of her arrival in the neighbourhood; for, be it remembered, I had not yet *seen* her, except about three years previous, as before mentioned—

In a few days we had an interview, and although I had seen her before, she did not look as my imagination had pictured her— I knew she was over-size, but she now appeared a fair match for Falstaff; I knew she was called an "old maid", and I felt no doubt of the truth of at least half of the appellation; but now, when I beheld her, I could not for my life avoid thinking of my mother, and this, not from withered features, for her skin was too full of fat to permit its contracting in to wrinkles; but from her want of teeth, and weather-beaten appearance in general, and from a kind of notion that ran in my head, that *nothing* could have commenced at the size of infancy, and reached her present bulk in less than thirtyfive or forty years; and, in short, I was not all pleased with her— But what could I do? I had told her sister that I would take her for better or for worse; and I made a point of honor and conscience in all things, to stick to my word, especially if others had been induced to act on it, which in this case, I doubted not they had, for I was now fairly convinced, that no other man on earth would have her, and hence the conclusion that they were bent on holding me to my bargain— Well, thought I, I have said it, and, be consequences what they may, it shall not be my fault if I fail to do it— At once I determined to consider her my wife; and this done, all my powers of discovery were put to the rack, in search of perfections in her, which might be fairly set-off against her defects— I tried to imagine she was handsome, which, but for her unfortunate corpulency, was actually true— Exclusive of this, no woman that I have seen, has a finer face— I also tried to convince myself, that the mind was much more to be valued than the person; and in this, she was not inferior, as I could discover, to any with whom I had been acquainted—

Shortly after this, without attempting to come to any positive understanding with her, I set out for Vandalia, where and when you first saw me— During my stay there, I had letters from her, which did not change my opinion of either her intelect or intention; but on the contrary, confirmed it in both—

All this while, although I was fixed "firm as the surge repelling rock," in my resolution, I found I was continually repenting the rashness, which had led me to make it— Through life I have been in no bondage, either real or immaginary from the thralldom of which I so much desired to be free—

After my return home, I saw nothing to change my opinion
of her in any particular— She was the same and so was I— I
now spent my time between planing how I might get along
through life after my contemplated change of circumstances
should have taken place; and how I might procrastinate the evil
day for a time, which I really dreaded as much—perhaps more,
than an Irishman does the halter—

After all my suffering upon this deeply interesting subject,
here I am, wholly unexpectedly, completely, out of the "scrape";
and I now want to know, if you can guess how I got out of it—
Out clear in every sense of the term; no violation of word,
honor or conscience— I dont believe you can guess, and so I
may as well tell you at once— As the lawyers say, it was done in
the manner following, towit— After I had delayed the matter as
long as I thought I could in honor do, which by the way had
brought me 'round into this last fall, I concluded I might as well
bring it to a consumation without further delay; and so I
mustered my resolution, and made the proposal to her direct;
but, shocking to relate, she answered, No— At first I supposed
she did it through an affectation of modesty, which I thought
but ill-became her, under the peculiar circumstances of her case;
but on my renewal of the charge, I found she repelled it with
greater firmness than before— I tried it again and again, but
with the same success, or rather with the same want of success—
I finally was forced to give it up, at which I verry unexpectedly
found myself mortified almost beyond endurance— I was
mortified, it seemed to me, in a hundred different ways— My
vanity was deeply wounded by the reflection, that I had so long
been too stupid to discover her intentions, and at the same time
never doubting that I understood them perfectly; and also, that
she whom I had taught myself to believe nobody else would
have, had actually rejected me with all my fancied greatness; and
to cap the whole, I then, for the first time, began to suspect that
I was really a little in love with her— But let it all go— I'll try
and out live it— Others have been made fools of by the girls;
but this can never be with truth said of me— I most
emphatically, in this instance, made a fool of myself— I have
now come to the conclusion never again to think of marrying;

and for this reason; I can never be satisfied with any one who would be block-head enough to have me—

When you receive this, write me a long yarn about something to amuse me— Give my respects to Mr. Browning—

Your sincere friend,

A. Lincoln

Comical as it is, the letter is made more so as one remembers Lincoln's assiduous avoidance of eligible women, and his near allergy to fat females. Here he finds his would-be wife, already "over-size," now ballooned to "a fair match for Falstaff" and whose "unfortunate corpulency" fills her skin too full of fat to show any wrinkles of age, for surely "*nothing* could have commenced at the size of infancy and reached her present bulk in less than thirtyfive or forty years." Having told her sister he would take her for better or worse, little wonder "all [his] powers of discovery were put to the rack in search of perfections in her which might be set-off against her defects" to help his resolve— "firm as the surge repelling rock"—to keep his promise as well as his willingness, perish the thought, to plod life through with her.

When the Brownings heard all this they thought it merely another of Lincoln's "funny stories"—perhaps by its date, an April fool fantasy. They had not the slightest idea until years later, when the whole story came out, that like so much else in Lincoln's life, it held hidden details.

By 1861 (twenty-three years later) Lincoln was president and Orville Browning was a senator, with him and his wife continuing their close political and social ties to Lincoln and to his administration. Then one day, as Senator Browning recalled:

[A] Boston gentleman who had been a publisher . . . came there to Washington . . . gathering material for a . . . book about Mr. Lincoln. He came to see Mrs. Browning and said he had understood she had in her possession a very amusing letter written at an early day by Mr. Lincoln, and asked her to let him have it. Mrs. Browning, however, refused. . . .

A few days after this interview she was at the White House, and mentioned the subject to Mr. Lincoln. He then, very much to her surprise told her that there was much more truth in that letter than she supposed, and told her he would rather she would not for the present give it to any one, as there were persons yet living who might be greatly pained by its publication.[10]

Little wonder the Brownings were greatly surprised. Not only did the letter turn out to contain "much more truth" than could be safely revealed nearly a quarter century later; it no doubt gave the Brownings second thoughts of their own.

What neither of the Brownings had understood was the personal duress Lincoln was under in his urge to get and to be married. Thus, as they read the letter it never dawned on them it could be anything other than a joke, least of all that he might really be spending his attentions on so unlikely a prospect as Mary Owens. But for Lincoln there were small as well as large advantages to marriage. Socially it would put a stop to endless, sometimes embarrassing questions of the sort people like to ask aging bachelors about when they are going to hurry up and "find a girl." (At age twenty-eight Lincoln was already beyond the average marriage age.) A larger if more obvious fact was that it would be virtually impossible for an unmarried man to have a career in politics. The Brownings were undoubtedly well aware of this, but what was evidently too far-fetched for them to have imagined was the utter improbability of Lincoln suddenly doing an about-face against his whole style and trying his hand at conventional courtship, *and* on some largely toothless, great big fat girl at that.

Quite a few other people came to be astonished as well, albeit for very different reasons. Ward Hill Lamon's 1872 biography of Lincoln, full of twisted interpretations as it was, was the first to carry Lincoln's letter to Mrs. Browning. Lamon offered not a word either to explain or to interpret the letter, although in front of it he inserted a moralistic and frankly self-serving apology of sorts:

For many reasons the publication of this letter is an extremely painful duty. If it could be withheld, and the act decently reconciled to the conscience of a biographer professing to be honest and candid, it should never see the light in these pages. Its grotesque humor, its coarse exaggerations in describing . . . a lady whom the writer was willing to marry, its imputation of toothless and weather-beaten old age to a woman really young and handsome, is [completely unacceptable].[11]

Such straight-faced posturings were expressed as well by Thomas P. Reep and numerous others, including Benjamin P. Thomas and even John E. Walsh as late as 1993, but this does not necessarily mean they were as square and humorless as they sound. The martyred Lincoln was largely seen as a saint. For many, halos and hilarity are an inappropriate mix (in the conventional iconography there are no depictions of Jesus Christ or even church fathers smiling, let alone laughing); likewise, somberness and a fixed face are what get painted into Lincoln's image, even when he is pulling one's leg unmercifully.

Among the more astonishing interpretations of Lincoln's letter are those that not only miss the whole point, but posit entirely new problems, and then proceed to answer these. In something of a triple travesty, Thomas Reep, author of *Lincoln At New Salem*, not only fails to catch the joke of the letter, but takes literally Lincoln's mention of Mary Owens's "want of teeth" and then proceeds to analyze why she lost them, how she might have avoided the vacuum, and perhaps why she was overweight as well. Her problem, says he, stemmed from "an excessive use of sweets."[12]

Nor are such journeys into creative phantasmagoria limited to lonely lost scholars of long ago. They are alive and well in the likes of Lincolnian luminaries close at hand. Take for instance Michael Burlingame, who, sounding as if he were too early back from an unfinished incarceration in a Viennese insane asylum, chooses to take literally Lincoln's being reminded of his mother from some of Mary Owens's traits. He sees Lincoln's mention of her unlovely physical features in the same breath with similar ones of his aging stepmother, plus Lincoln's supposed neglect of his birth mother's grave, as evidence of his "little filial devotion to the memory of a mother." Which mother? His reference to "a mother" is evidently supposed to be broad enough to cover whichever mother is meant from one moment to the next.[13] But by any measure it still amounts to a mighty mix-up of mothers. And quite beyond that near comedy of errors, it's an impossible stretch anyway, the sort of thing that Freud himself once called "wild psychoanalysis."

Plainly, Lincoln was joking and jostling in his depiction of Mary Owens, making her not as dried-up as his stepmother, but otherwise judging her looks as much the same: "not from withered features . . . but from her want of teeth, and weather-beaten appearance in general," plus her "bulk" being abundant enough to have taken years to grow to be "a fair match for Falstaff." His underlying message (not very far under) was how appallingly without sex appeal Mary Owen was—about equal to that of his ancient stepmother.

Quite a case could be made for bypassing all technical aspects of Lincoln's wit, and instead, simply going with his flow, enjoying the journey and the side trips he takes us on along the way. And yet much might be lost by it. Consider Lincoln's juxtaposing a number of Mary Owens's admirable qualities—her intellect, her agreeableness, and her pleasant fine face—stacked in a gesture of fair play against her "unfortunate corpulency" and other "defects." He walks both sides of this street with an open claim of justice and balance—and, indeed, there is something of that in it. But by the time he finishes his would-be even-handed portrait it looks a lot less like a lass well balanced-out than an image close-on to the bride of Frankenstein.

Is Lincoln's only defense going to be that "all is fair in love and war"? Not quite. Lincoln always steered clear of hurting people's feelings—first, as here, by not using Mary Owens's name, then years later by withholding the letter as there are "persons yet living who might be greatly pained by its publication." Not that such pebbles of politeness held much chance to check the onslaught of various Victorian vultures on the ready to vent their spleen at Lincoln's utter ungallantry, most especially his daring to conjure up images not literally true, as in his charge of her "want of teeth." Moreover, for the saintly Lincoln to dare do it in the first place was, in the eyes of many, approximately equivalent to catching Jesus with a rock in his hand.

Without doubt many outraged moralists would have been even more so (more moral and still more outraged) had they realized the underlying mechanism of the particular technique of wit Lincoln was using; it was what Sigmund Freud later labeled in his *Analysis of the Technique of Wit* as the use of a fake contrast in the name of justice and/or fairness. He cited the German philosopher Heinrich Heine, who said, on finding himself caught in a situation much like Lincoln's,

> This woman resembles the *Venus de Milo* in many points. Like her, she is extraordinarily old, has no teeth, and has white spots on the yellow surface of her body.[14]

But did Lincoln actually "know" what he was doing inside his own wit? No, and yes. Certainly he could not have formulated exactly what he was doing—nor could anyone else have done so before Freud first offered his fully worked-out analysis of wit in 1905.

Yet on another level it can be shown that Lincoln knew exactly what he was doing with his wit, and not just intuitively; in fact, he had parts of it well perfected by his early boyhood, and used it so adroitly and with such aplomb as to suggest he may well have inherited a great portion of these talents from somewhere within his gene pool. Remarkably, since more than a little of his levity was later to impinge on his relations with women—especially Mary Owens, but also others in far-reaching ways—one faces a certain obligation to open that door and to walk down at least a few of the passages soon to be seen.

It was Lincoln's kindly stepmother who first noticed that even as a child he would come home from church, repeat the preacher's sermon almost word for word, and mimic the hellfire and brimstone gestures he had seen—to the great delight of the children and everybody else. Years later Lincoln was to develop strong feelings against such religion, but what was driving this brand of wit when he was a boy? Certainly it was based on more than a mere chance to make jokes and amuse people, much as he enjoyed such antics himself.

In a letter to Mary Owens written a few weeks after moving to Springfield to begin his law practice, Lincoln mentioned he had not been to church yet: "I stay away because I am conscious I should not know how to behave myself." What *could* he have meant? Certainly not that. He had attended church for years and knew perfectly well that one need not speak, or even listen; the only firm requirement was to sit still, preferably with a somber face (a problem right there). But meeting new people before and after a sermon could hardly have been difficult; far from shy, Lincoln was a past master at this, especially at dealing with strangers in groups. However, there was a problem, one that was to take years for anyone to fully realize.

His old friend and colleague Henry C. Whitney pointed to part of it. After analyzing Lincoln's wit in great detail, showing how alert it was, how easily triggered, how carefully geared to an audience's sensibilities and all the rest, he spoke of how pervasive it was in Lincoln:

> In our walks about the little towns where courts were held, he saw ludicrous elements in everything, and could either narrate some story from his storehouse of jokes, else he could improvise one; he saw the ludicrous in an assemblage of fowls, in a man spading his garden, in a clothes-line full of clothes, in a group of boys, in a lot of pigs rooting at a mill door, in a mother duck learning her brood to swim; in anything and everything Lincoln saw some ludicrous incident.[15]

Most certainly it was a marvelous thing, a tease, a talent, a treasure in a hundred ways—among them a bottomless fountain to feed his funny bone, and ours. It could also be surprisingly expensive, sometimes in insidious ways soon to see. But for the moment other low-hanging fruit, suddenly made ripe and easy to reach by Whitney's comments, seem worth a moment.

That very quality of Lincoln's—to quickly grab a passing example, use it on the spot to make a point, to loudly underline its ludicrous side, or ride it into the wild blue yonder—were all parts of his style. Once, when it came time for the president to appoint a commissioner to the Sandwich Islands, there came a delegation suggesting the choice be their man:

> "They presented their case as earnestly as possible, and, besides his fitness for the place, they urged that he was in bad health, and a residence in that balmy climate would be of great benefit to him."[16]

Lincoln listened carefully, as he always did, then with a straight face closed the interview: "Gentlemen, I am sorry to say there are eight other applicants for that place, and they are all sicker than your man."[17] Thus, with a single supple phrase, Lincoln dispatched the mawkish notion that a candidate's health should be grounds for granting him a "balmy" posting.

But much else lies there, hidden behind several surprises. As Lincoln hears out the petitioners he never contradicts them or questions their motives in any way; to hear him tell it, it's just that their man loses due to two unlucky accidents: He got there late (after eight others had put in for the job) and then, as it turned out, all the early birds were even "sicker" than he. Of course it's a position frankly fake and fantastic, but then that's very much the way wit works, especially Lincoln's. He holds on to upside-down logic until the world looks level, loves nothing better than to "play straight" for fake facts, while with a sad and sober face he pretends to believe the totally unbelievable.

Moreover, wit is exceedingly efficient in that while it tends to let the teller of the tale get off scot-free, it manages to make the listener—victim or bystander—do all the heavy lifting, meaning sort out piles of details and submit them to some inner judge and jury. For this one might have to plow through stacks of sheer nonsense to salvage slivers of anything worth a second thought. Yet easily reaped rewards are close at hand; given a sense of humor, even victims can find witticisms very funny and enjoy the joke.

Here comes Mary Owens again—just in time to see how she looks through these binoculars. About a year after she went back to Kentucky, Mrs. Abell came for a visit, bringing along Lincoln's last message, word for word: "Tell your sister I think she was a great fool, because she did not stay here and marry me." Mary Owens only said, "Characteristic of the man!" Clearly, she did not see the joke; or if she glimpsed it at all, she was in no sense laughing. The best guess is that, as usual, she heard in the message a touch of criticism and/or a painful pang at not being catered to. (One cannot say for sure, since a classic penalty for having no sense of humor is to take oneself a bit too seriously, and to interpret as negative any personal comment that fails to reflect outright support.)

Lincoln's remark is no puzzle. One of his intentions was to tease and tickle her a little, no doubt hoping to bring a touch of lightness and air into the memory of their friendship, or relationship, or whatever it was—a boost they might both enjoy. At least his patent reversals suggest as much. The message is funny and light (his best idioms)—picturing himself as champing at the bit to marry her, and

she a "fool" for turning down his ardent bid—all with nary a note of
his thanking his lucky stars for his escape. ("Here I am, wholly unexpectedly, completely out of the 'scrape' . . . in every sense of the
term; no violation of word, honor or conscience.") Is he any less glad
to be out of it now? Certainly not; probably he was "gladder than
ever." Yet he still had a witty urge to smooth things over a bit, even
share his high spirits of joy and happy independence. Alas, the luxury
of his laugh and playfulness were entirely his own; he could hardly
have expected to hear back from her.

Remembering the sorts of situations where Lincoln had the most
trouble holding a straight face, the hardest were those where a certain forced solemnity caused him to see the situation as overdone,
and thus as a waiting target. Indeed, any part of a solemn sequence
might trigger off the rest, or a worry that it might. And yet, quite as
Whitney's many small examples suggest, nothing "reverent" need be
in the picture. It was both a talent and a trial for Lincoln that, willing
or not, his wit was all too ready to break the flow of ordinary events
when- or wherever they seemed in the least exaggerated.

One night on their way home from the office Herndon and Lincoln passed a public hall in which a benevolent society was giving an
entertainment. They decided to go in, where they found a very proper
lady elocutionist reciting a long wordy poem of more than three hundred lines. The story concerned "the perplexities that beset a Miss
Flora McFlimsey in her efforts to appear fashionable." This ultrafem-
inine talk on female fashions, titled "Nothing to Wear," was enough, of
course, to put it on the other side of the earth from Lincoln—precisely
what was hardest for his composure. Perhaps from the sheer shock he
held up awhile, until, "In the midst of one stanza, in which no effort is
made to say anything particularly amusing, and during the reading of
which the audience manifested the most respectful silence and attention, some one in the rear seats burst out into a loud, coarse laugh—a
sudden and explosive guffaw. It startled the speaker and audience, and
kindled a storm of unsuppressed laughter and applause. Everyone
looked back to ascertain the cause of the demonstration, and was
greatly surprised to find that it was Mr. Lincoln." As Herndon later recalled, with every eye focused on him, Lincoln "blushed and squirmed
with the awkward diffidence of a schoolboy."[18]

In the jokes and stories Lincoln himself told the level of hilarity easily distracts even careful observers from seeing certain sharply contradictory elements close at hand. Some of these are far from funny. For despite Lincoln's astonishing ability to exaggerate the minutiae of everyday life into mountains of amusement—sometimes with startling insights and leaps of fantasy full of surprise and invention—it turns out that these talents were often bought at the price of his *not* being very, or even reasonably sensitive at the next layer down.

Plainly put, Lincoln had a streak of being downright rigid, stiff, and concrete—frozen in a sense to see and value only what was tangible and "real." Time and again Herndon struggled to define this narrow line (nobody else even saw it). Quite as he observed,

[Lincoln] was not impulsive, fanciful, or imaginative, but cold, calm, precise, and exact; . . . Lincoln's fault if any was that he saw things less than they really were; . . . less beautiful and more frigid. In his mental view he crushed the unreal, the inexact, the hollow and the sham. . . .[19]

To some men the world of matter and of man comes ornamented with beauty, life, and action; and hence [is] more or less false and inexact.[20]

Indeed so, "ornamented . . . and hence more or less false and inexact" qualities are precisely those so useful for the bowing and scraping and gallantry of courtship, especially in the winning of women in Victorian times. Or to look at it from the other side: Lincoln's feet of clay were his most serious problem with Mary Owens. Where others might have soared into flights of fancy with wonderfully winning ways and with words to spell out sweet nothings against the sky, this was all an unknown world to Lincoln, a language he would never learn. No doubt it would have helped if he had felt the feelings to go with it, but they weren't there either. Thus, it is clear as day why Mary Owens "thought Mr. Lincoln was deficient in those little links which make up the chain of [a] woman's happiness."

Not that Mary Owens, so quick and sharp in her judgments of Lincoln, was entirely blameless herself. To the extent that common decency might be expected, her own behavior was badly out of

bounds. She often chose not to answer questions he posed in his letters, or even entire letters. In the first note to her of which we have a
record (December 13, 1836) Lincoln complains of unanswered matters, and of his "mortification" at "looking in the Post-Office [every
day] for your letter and not finding it."[21] Worse by far was another
habit of hers: to pass out failing report cards—complaints—after an
issue was past and nothing could be done about it. How much better
and smoother things might have gone, and how fleeting some of
their worst situations may well have been, had she leaned forward
with a helpful, kindly word where he was frozen or blocked for whatever reason: "Abe, Mrs. Green needs a hand," or with only a gesture,
"she needs a little help"; or, "Abe we need your strong arm." Most
any words would have worked toward lifting Lincoln out of himself,
probably fixing everyone's situation at once.

Granted, the value of such analysis is limited at most to a first-
level-down application, into the likes of Mary Owens's somewhat
lazy lassitude. (To extend it further risks many hazards of "improved"
revisions in retrospect.) If any changes had patched Lincoln's
courtship problems he might well have found it harder than he did to
escape that "bondage . . . the thralldom of which I so much desired to
be free." It puts one in mind of Oscar Wilde's warning, both funny
and deeply true: "Advice is bad, and good advice is absolutely lethal."
To the extent that well-intended good advice might well have facilitated Lincoln's courtship of a woman he could never have found attractive, indeed it may well have been lethal in its way.

It is hard to say what use, if any, Mary Owens was to Lincoln, but
her record, her letters, and even her faults add up to a rich and wonderful addition to what is known of him.

SIX

The Curious Case of Elmer Ellsworth

The death of Colonel Elmer Ellsworth, "the first casualty of the Civil War," inspired editorials, speeches, poems, and songs predicting that his name would never be forgotten. Yet it was forgotten, to the point that when historian Ruth Painter Randall embarked on her biography of Ellsworth (published in 1960) she discovered that "When I spoke of him the result was usually the question 'Who was Colonel Ellsworth?'"[1]

Indeed, most people might ask the same question today. But in the realm of Lincoln scholarship Ellsworth's story does live on, thanks to Randall, and only to her, because *Colonel Elmer Ellsworth: A Biography of Lincoln's Friend and First Hero of the Civil War* to this day remains the sole comprehensive account of his life. The result is that the present study owes Randall a particular debt. For while many of the interpretations drawn here were invisible to Randall, they would never have been discernible had she not put in exhaustive spadework, particularly her unearthing of obscure primary sources.

Lincoln knew Elmer Ellsworth for less than two years before this strikingly handsome young man came to his quick and tragic death. Yet Ellsworth's whole glowing presence was important for Lincoln—and highly instructive for us.

Ellsworth was a remarkable character from the outset, long before Lincoln ever knew him. From his early boyhood Ellsworth was fascinated—obsessed—with military matters, and bored with any and everything that distracted him from them. Even then, as Lincoln's secretary John Hay was to say, he "knew that God had made him a soldier."[2] And within a few years, at age fifteen, he was already doing a stint as drillmaster of the Black Plumed Riflemen of Stillwater. After he moved to Chicago at age seventeen—like so many other young men, to seek his destiny in the West—he won esteem as a trainer of volunteer military companies.

In those days most towns, large and small, had (or were about to have) some kind of volunteer quasi-military group vying for attention and trying to make a name for itself as a showy, parade-ground militia. Often adept at impressive-looking precision drills, these could be splendid—all the more so when decked out in bright uniforms and perhaps commanded by a stylish leader. Moreover, serious military types welcomed the trend, both as an advertisement for the stuff of military glory, and as backup ready-to-go militias capable of being called upon as a kind of National Guard in any emergency. As Randall observed:

> Naturally each of these companies needed someone to train it, a man who was an expert in military tactics and preferably one who was a magnetic leader. Ellsworth qualified eminently on both counts. In those years in Chicago his interest soon drew him into military circles. This explains why, as early as 1856 [age nineteen], he was attending the First Grand Military and Civic Ball of the Cadets of the National Guard. There was to be a mention in Ellsworth's *Manual of Arms* that he drilled these same cadets in July of the following year, 1857.
>
> His drawings of soldiers in his schoolbooks had revealed Ellsworth's love of uniforms. Furthermore, he liked uniforms that had style and color. It was part of the romantic approach to warfare; war was glamourized and poetized with such trappings as sweeping plumes, flowing sashes, golden spurs, and flashing sabers.[3]

Young Ellsworth was soon able to carry this stylish trend further as a result of an idea he got from reading newspaper accounts of the Crimean War. Here he first encountered the word zouave (zU-äv'), and learned about a showy, colorful, highly disciplined militia, the

Algerian Zouaves (*zU-ävs*'). He read of how French Zouave regiments were established and began to distinguish themselves with flamboyant military displays in the Crimea. Ellsworth vowed to learn more of these groups.

As luck would have it a Zouave authority happened to be travelling from Europe to Chicago right then: Charles A. DeVilliers, the former surgeon of a French Zouave regiment that had fought in the Crimean War. He and Ellsworth may have first met because of De-Villiers's mastery of swordplay, a skill the young man wanted to acquire. The two bonded; in time, DeVilliers transformed Ellsworth into one of Chicago's most accomplished fencers. Meanwhile, Ellsworth absorbed a wealth of information about the Zouaves. "Why were those scarlet trousers so loose and baggy and why did the dark blue and gold-trimmed jacket and blue shirt have no collar?" Fluid mobility was the reason: "no one could do the exacting Zouave drill in a stiff, tight uniform; a Zouave had to have complete freedom of motion to go through his maneuvers."[4]

DeVilliers suggested that Ellsworth acquire a number of French books about the Zouave system. Ellsworth promptly studied French well enough to read them, and with abounding energy and a fierce self-discipline he "budgeted his time almost to the minute," attaining a startling mastery of the most intricate drill ever seen at the time. One notable feature involved dividing companies into squads of four men each, positioned in such a way as to face out in all directions at once and maintaining the formation while quickly loading, firing on the run, and reloading from any position—be it lying down, kneeling, or rolling over—in short, carrying out their drill in exact unison with a machinelike perfection.[5]

This display would have been impressive enough by itself, but the effect was heightened by the squad's instantaneous, often staccato response to shouted commands from its leader, Major Ellsworth (a rank he was granted in 1857 at age twenty).[6] Young as he was Ellsworth's discipline and rigor were more than skin-deep. He had a history of placing exceedingly high demands on himself at all times, sometimes adopting arbitrary rules to live by, such as not accepting any favor (even an invitation for dinner), unless he was able to return it—a rule he stuck to even while starving on a diet of crackers and water.

When on tour with his Zouaves Ellsworth kept everyone at a

high pitch of readiness and gymnastic precision by straining against every looseness, training his men to revel in their hardiness by ignoring, even welcoming, physical discomforts and hardships. On the road the men weren't allowed to sleep in beds except by explicit permission. It was just this sort of rigor and discipline that led John Hay to note in his diary that he had followed Ellsworth into an armory,

> where a score of awkward youths were going sleepily through their manual, and [at] his first order, sharply and crisply given, would open every eye and straighten every spine. No matter how severe the drill, his men never thought of fatigue. His own indomitable spirit sustained them all.[7]

Certainly much of the joy and surprise of Ellsworth's Zouaves sprang from the whole image and bearing of Ellsworth himself. He was an unusually short, vibrant, very handsome young man with a deep, loud, resonant voice, which, as one of his corpsmen said, "could have been distinctly heard at a distance of four blocks away."[8] All this, plus a spirited vivaciousness seems to have captivated everyone.

As Ellsworth's first biographer, Charles Ingraham, said of him, quoting from a newspaper:

> A boyish figure, not exceeding five feet six inches in height, quick motioned, with well-formed, shapely limbs . . . a spirited well-balanced head crowned with a wealth of almost black hair that fell in careless, clinging curls about his neck, eyes of dark hazel that sparkled and flashed with excitement or melted with tenderness. . . . Add to this a magnetic and chivalrous personality which created a feeling of well-being, enthusiasm, and gaiety in those it touched; put this romantic figure in a dashing uniform, watch him put his company of Zouaves through the most intricate drills with perfect precision, and [who] could resist him?[9]

Lincoln couldn't resist him, and didn't.

In fact, the way Lincoln came to meet Ellsworth is itself interesting and significant. Even with no special intervention it is probable that Lincoln would eventually have become aware of Ellsworth and would have admired him greatly. The Zouaves and their dramatic leader with their showy exhibition drills and parades were quickly gaining celebrity in and around Chicago by 1858. Then, too, Ellsworth himself often received press attention on his own as he branched out to visit different towns, taking over the teaching and drilling of the local militia—and through it all, invariably winning enthusiastic support. It was in this vein that on December 18, 1859, Colonel Ellsworth took a train to Springfield, the burgeoning prairie town that was to shape his destiny, for it was where Lincoln lived.

Ellsworth had been invited by Col. John Cook, commander of the Springfield Greys to come train his Greys for an exhibition drill—and, as it turned out, just accidentally on purpose affording a chance for Lincoln to meet Ellsworth quietly. As John Cook described his own critical role, he was "in a position to know that Mr. Lincoln had a special interest in Ellsworth, and was making every effort to have him settle down in Springfield to study law in the Lincoln law office."[10] This suggests that Cook was acting as a procurer—as, indeed, it turned out he was.

Moreover, an air of surreptitiousness with which Cook handled all Lincoln approaches to Ellsworth—or, to put it softer, the delicate caution used—is further suggested by the fact that no notes from Cook to Lincoln seem ever to have been written, or vice versa. Nor, apparently, did Lincoln send any letters or notes to Ellsworth. Thus, when Ellsworth eventually turned up in Lincoln's office, he did so without a single written word of the arrangement (apart from letters from Cook to Ellsworth). The bidding came roundabout.

We happen to know all this and the whole pattern of events by the sheerest accident. Throughout the period Ellsworth was in love with a nineteen-year-old girl in Rockville, Illinois, named Carrie Spafford whom he was seldom able to visit, but to whom he often wrote details of his life. In his letter to Carrie of January 15, 1860, he told of John Cook urging him to come settle in Springfield and to study law in Lincoln's office. Ellsworth added, "I don't know what I shall decide in reference to Mr Lincolns proposition. . . . Mr Cook told me that Mr L—*especially desired him to leave no means unturned* [emphasis in original] to induce me to come to Springfield. I cannot but regard this as a very great compliment."[11]

Some two weeks later, on January 31, in a letter to Carrie's mother there was mention of still other high compliments and urg-ings: "I was offered very great inducements to <u>remain</u> at Springfield [emphasis in original], and still stronger ones, to go there in the spring & complete my studies with Hon Abram Lincoln. . . . What think you?"[12] Cook maintained close contact with Ellsworth through numerous letters and a stream of flattering incentives as Ellsworth pursued his career with his Zouaves, mainly in Chicago.

On March 11, 1860, Ellsworth wrote Carrie that Cook "spoke further about Mr. Lincoln's proposition. He had just received a letter from John Cook, emphasizing again Lincoln's extraordinary interest in him and the lawyer's earnest wish that Ellsworth would come to Springfield. John Cook had added, " 'My conviction that this is the place for you to commence life as a public man is unchanged.' "[13] Also in March 1860, Cook wrote:

> You ask me if I have seen our friend Lincoln. I answer yes repeatedly and never without the conversation turning upon you and his expressing an earnest desire that you should make this place your home & and his office your head quarters. He has taken in you a greater interest than I ever knew him to manifest in any one before.[14]

The latter wording again suggests that Col. Cook was very much an insider who well knew Lincoln's tastes in young men, and that Ellsworth was not the first whom he had known and approached for Lincoln.

Just when the decision and arrangements were made for Ellsworth to move into Lincoln's office to study law is not precisely known. However, it is clear that Lincoln admiringly observed Ellsworth for months. As Randall described one scene:

> It was hot in Springfield on that afternoon of August 13 [1860] and Mr. Lincoln watched the show [of Ellsworth and his Zouaves] as he stood in the shade of a cottonwood tree in a yard on Sixth Street. Few scenes could have blazed with more color than the one before him. In the bright sunshine stood some fifty fine young Americans dressed in gorgeous uniforms of red, blue, and gold. Each man wore loose scarlet

trousers, high gaiters, a collarless blue jacket trimmed with gold braid, a shirt of lighter blue, and a jaunty red cap with gold or orange decorations. . . . Mr. Lincoln watched the two-hour drill with kindling eyes. He too centered his attention upon the boyish-looking commander. Afterwards he said of Colonel Ellsworth, "He is the greatest little man I ever met."[15]

Lincoln tried never to miss any of Ellsworth's exhibition drills. On other occasions he was heard to comment that Ellsworth had "a power to command men" which was "surpassingly great," adding at still another time that he was "the best natural talent, in that department, I ever knew."[16]

How Lincoln was reacting was clear enough, but an interesting sidelight is a near parallel scenario—a daydream—that Ellsworth himself entertained during that hot August of 1860, and that he playfully confided to Carrie:

This is a very extensive world . . . and there are in it many people[,] among them undoubtedly is some aged and obese gentleman possessed of a fabulous fortune, in his own right, and a gold headed cane, who only awaits a convenient opportunity to pat me on the head and adopt me as his own. I expect to meet this individual about the same time my fortune changes and I can see in the future something else than *misfortune* and disappointment.[17]

That gentleman turned out to be Abraham Lincoln. A month later Lincoln won his long pursuit when Elmer Ellsworth returned to Springfield to join him as his student in law.

We know from Ellsworth that hardly any "law study" occurred in his Lincoln relationship; for one thing, the law bored him enormously. Rather, he soon became integrated into Lincoln's campaign plans, where he fit right in. "During these days in Springfield from September, 1860 to February, 1861, Ellsworth was seeing Lincoln constantly and their friendship had become, to use Lincoln's own word, 'intimate' "—an attachment much closer to successful courtship than to what many have sought comfort in calling *fatherly* love.[18]

At any rate, Lincoln's long pursuit of Ellsworth became decidedly personal, and indeed intimate, just as he said.

Does this mean that the Lincoln-Ellsworth relationship became overtly sexual? No evidence of it. For while Lincoln was greatly "turned on" by Ellsworth, and had been from the very beginning (which was what Cook's propositions, relayed messages, and planted lures were all about), at least one roadblock lay squarely in the way: Ellsworth was definitely and explicitly heterosexual. As a rigorously disciplined character he had early and firmly fallen in love with Carrie; his every mention and thought of her reflects a head-over-heels enthrallment of a kind that is fully in tune with robust ongoing heterosexual fantasies, very solid stuff indeed.

Most Lincoln scholars have gone out of their way to repeat or to re-invent the conventional notion that Lincoln's attraction to Ellsworth was merely a surrogate love—like what he might feel for a brother or son. Far from it. For, of course, where such common emotions prevail they are easily expressed smoothly and directly in affectionate ways, poles apart from using roundabout seductions such as those pursued first by procurer John Cook, and later by Lincoln himself.

Another observer of the Lincoln-Ellsworth affair was Lincoln's longtime friend Henry C. Whitney. When young he had had a similar relationship with Lincoln, but for whatever reason he was careful not to reveal too much of it. In speaking of the Ellsworth tie he found a semisexual analogy, noting, "A relation like that of knight and squire of the age of chivalry existed between the two."[19]

More to the point is the question of what, exactly, Lincoln found irresistible about Ellsworth: Perhaps, in part, it was his nimble, animated, quick reactions full of discipline and polish, with all that these traits imply. Then, too, something is to be said for sheer charm. Lizzie Grimsley (Mary Lincoln's cousin and an early visitor at the White House) put the whole flavor of Ellsworth in a single phrase: "a magnetic, brilliant young fellow, overflowing with dash and spirit," qualities that anyone could admire, to be sure, but which for Lincoln were more than that; they must have felt like wonderful complementation.[20] For despite Lincoln's rich character and his larder of lovely qualities, he completely lacked, and understandably greatly admired, the agile lightness, the high precision, as well as the flamboyant magic of Ellsworth. In any case, both during Lincoln's election and for the first days and weeks in the White House young Ellsworth had the run of the place and was everybody's pet, especially Lincoln's. In fact, a clearly personal element and a special intensity pervaded most of Lincoln's actions for Ellsworth.

Day after day Lincoln expressed his high regard, often in tangible actions. Hurriedly, on March 5, 1861 (within twenty-four hours of his inauguration), he sent a first, modest enough note to his secretary of war, Simon Cameron:

Executive Chamber

March 5, 1861

Dear Sir:

If the public service admits of a change, without injury, in the office of chief clerk of the War Department, I shall be pleased of [sic] my friend, E. Elmer Ellsworth . . . shall be appointed.

Yours truly
A. Lincoln[21]

Not wanting to leave it there, less than two weeks later Lincoln wrote Cameron again, this time in a tone of impatience requesting much more definitive action, along with a host of specific requests much to the advantage of Ellsworth:

Executive Mansion

To the Secretary of War:

March 18th 1861.

Sir: You will favor me by issuing an order detailing Lieut. Ephraim E. Ellsworth, of the First Dragoons, for special duty as Adjutant and Inspector General of Militia for the United States, and in so far as existing laws will admit, charge him with the transaction, under your direction, of all business pertaining to the Militia, to be conducted as a separate bureau, of which Lieut. Ellsworth will be chief, with instructions to take measures for promoting a uniform system of organization, drill, equipment, &c. &c. of the U.S. Militia, and to prepare a system of drill for Light troops, adapted for self-instruction, for distribution to the Militia of the several States. You will please assign him suitable office rooms, furniture &c. and provide him with a clerk and messenger, and furnish him such facilities in the way of printing, stationery, access to public records, &c. as he may desire for the successful prosecution of his duties; and also provide in such manner as may be most convenient and proper, for a monthly payment to Lieut Ellsworth, for this extra duty, sufficient to make his pay equal that of a Major of Cavalry.

Your obt. Servt.

A. Lincoln[22]

How Secretary of War Cameron felt on receiving this missive is not recorded, but he could hardly have missed its sharpness. In no other Lincoln directive during his five years as president does one find any-where near this degree of insistence and specificity.

Later, on April 15, three days after Fort Sumter was fired on, Lincoln issued his first call for troops. That same day he wrote Ellsworth an open letter, again displaying his extraordinary regard and establishing broad privileges:

To Elmer E. Ellsworth

Col. E. E. Ellsworth

Washington, April 15, 1861

My dear Sir:

Ever since the beginning of our acquaintance, I have valued you highly as a person[al] friend, and at the same time . . . have had a very high estimate of your military talent. Accordingly I have been, and still am anxious for you to have the best position in the military which can be given you, consistently with justice and proper courtesy towards the older officers of the army. I can not incur the risk of doing them injustice, or a discourtesy; but I do say they would personally oblige me, if they could, and would place you in some position, or in some service, satisfactory to yourself.

Your Obt. Servt.

A. Lincoln[23]

Ellsworth had very great empathy with Lincoln as well. Even his early death came about in no small measure from his concern for Lincoln's feelings. Ellsworth knew that the first weeks of the war were made worse for Lincoln by his having constantly to see a large Confederate flag waving over Marshall House, a hotel in Alexandria, across the Potomac but in full view of the White House. Ellsworth had vowed to take it down. Thus, while on a military mission nearby, at dawn on May 24, 1861, there came a moment when he faced a choice of leading his regiment directly toward the telegraph wires they were to cut or, since they were nearby, to storm the hotel and tear down the flag that had been such an irritant for weeks. After a moment's hesitation followed by a sudden decision, Ellsworth rushed with seven companions into the hotel; he and two of his men quickly climbed three flights of stairs to retrieve the flag from its stanchion on the roof. On the way down at the first landing a man later identified as the hotel manager suddenly stepped from the shadows and fired a double-barreled shotgun, the blast hitting Ellsworth squarely in the chest. One of his companions, a newspaper writer named House, later said that Ellsworth "dropped forward with that heavy, horrible, headlong weight which always comes of sudden death inflicted in this manner." Another member of the team, Corp. Brownell, killed the assassin with a single rifle shot to the face, and then for good measure jabbed him with his bayonet.[24]

Mr. House, Corp. Brownell, and the others examined Col. Ellsworth, filled with disbelief at the sight of him lying face down in his own blood. House and a corporal named Winser carefully lifted the still form and carried it into a nearby bedroom, where they laid it out. "They had nothing to cover him with but the rebel flag wet with his blood. They wanted to get a surgeon, but did not know where one could be found nor could they leave Ellsworth's body alone in that house of violence." Meanwhile, according to House, they tried to "remove some of the unsightly stains from the Colonel's features and compose his limbs. His expression in death was beautifully natural."[25]

Reinforcements finally arrived and a surgeon was summoned. Then Mr. House remembered Ellsworth's mission to cut telegraph wires. This task was assigned, with some effort to keep the news of Ellsworth's death quiet for a while longer. But the news was soon out and spread rapidly, plunging the Zouaves into grief. "One of them with tears running down his face said, 'Oh God bless him, God bless him! We'll never have another friend like him!' Another said to one who had just come up, 'Our noble laddie's dead, Jim,' and turned away weeping."[26] Back in Washington, the immediate consequences reveal a few rare images of Lincoln.

He was in the White House library when a courier came to inform him of Ellsworth's death. As the messenger left the room

> two visitors who had come on a pressing matter of public business entered the library. Mr. Lincoln, his back to them, stood looking out of a window toward the Potomac and did not move until they came quite close. Then, turning, he extended his hand and said, "Excuse me, but I cannot talk." The two gentlemen thought that perhaps a cold had affected his voice until suddenly they saw him burst into tears and cover his face with his handkerchief. "He walked up and down the room for some moments," said one of them, "and we stepped aside in silence, not a little moved at such an unusual spectacle, in such a man in such a place."
>
> After Lincoln had regained his self-control somewhat, he invited his visitors to sit down with him. "I will take no apology, gentlemen," he said, "for my weakness; but I knew poor Ellsworth well, and held him in great regard. Just as you entered the room, Captain Fox left me, after giving me the painful details of Ellsworth's unfortunate death. The event was so unexpected, and the recital so touching, that it quite unmanned me."
>
> Here Mr. Lincoln had to make another violent effort to control his feelings.[27]

Later in the day he drove with Mrs. Lincoln to the Navy yard to view Ellsworth's body. Several hours later Lincoln received a reporter and Senator Wilson at the White House, but excused himself again as unable to talk, sobbing profusely. Still later, well into the night (a fact seldom reported), Lincoln returned alone to the Navy yard to once again view and this time to sit with Ellsworth's body, no doubt full of reminiscence and sadness as he struggled to come to terms with his all too personal loss. He also arranged for the body to be moved to the White House; since the president had suffered a personal bereavement, the Ellsworth funeral services were to be held in the Executive Mansion. Thousands filed through the East Room to view the body as it lay in state.[28]

Strangely enough, something of the loss both for Lincoln and for the whole country became almost instantly realized and communicated. The San Francisco *Alta* not only ran a story on Ellsworth's death but caught the personal tragedy of it in its very title: THE TEARS OF LINCOLN.[29] Nor did all the distance and all the battle lines separating North and South block the news or its significance. When Robert E. Lee heard it he turned to his aide-de-camp, Major Barclay, and commented with much insight that "it was his belief if Ellsworth had lived, he would have become the commanding general of the Union Army."[30]

The next day, still distraught, Lincoln faced the obligation of writing something to Ellsworth's devastated parents, no easy task, certainly, for what of any value could anyone possibly say of a pointless loss? But true to form Lincoln poured out one of his truly great letters:

To the Father and Mother of Col. Elmer E. Ellsworth:
                    Washington D.C. May 25, 1861
    My dear Sir and Madam: In the untimely loss of your noble son, our affliction here, is scarcely less than your own. So much of promised usefulness to one's country, and of bright hopes for one's self and friends, have rarely been so suddenly dashed, as in his fall. In size, in years, and in youthful appearance, a boy only, his power to command men, was surpassingly great. This power, combined with a fine intellect, an indomitable energy, and a taste altogether military, constituted in him, as seemed to me, the best natural talent, in that department, I ever knew. And yet he was singularly modest and deferential in social intercourse. My acquaintance with him began less than two years ago; yet through the latter half of the intervening period, it was as intimate as the disparity of our ages, and my engrossing engagements, would permit. To me, he appeared to have no

indulgences or pastimes; and I never heard him utter a profane, or an intemperate word. What was conclusive of his good heart, he never forgot his parents. The honors he labored for so laudably, and, in the sad end, so gallantly gave his life, he meant for them, no less than for himself.

In the hope that it may be no intrusion upon the sacredness of your sorrow, I have ventured to address you this tribute to the memory of my young friend, and your brave and early fallen child.

May God give you that consolation which is beyond all earthly power.

> Sincerely your friend in a
> common affliction—
> A. Lincoln[31]

In retrospect, various traits of Lincoln and Ellsworth reflect a certain haunting similarity. Both were warm and witty autodidacts, self-reliant in the extreme, dubious of prayer, markedly superstitious, and possessed of a second sight that repeatedly proved downright clairvoyant. Moreover, they had the same kinds of superstition, the same kinds of forebodings in the face of signs and hunches and fatalistic attitudes. Ellsworth, like Lincoln, now and again viewed with crystal clarity what was about to happen. On the very eve of his death Ellsworth wrote two letters—one to his parents, the other to Carrie. They were found on his body in Alexandria:

> My dear Father and Mother
> The Regiment is ordered to move across the river tonight. . . . I am inclined to the opinion that our entrance to the City of Alexandria will be hotly contested. . . . Should this happen my dear parents it may be my lot to be injured in some manner. Whatever may happen cherish the consolation that I was engaged in the performance of a sacred duty—and tonight thinking over the probabilities of the morrow & the occurrences of the past I am perfectly content to accept whatever my fortune may be, confident that he who noteth even the fall of a sparrow will have some purpose even in the fate of one like me.

> My darling & ever loved parents, good bye. God bless, protect & care for you.
>
> > Elmer.[32]

And to Carrie Spafford, his fiancée:

> My own darling Kitty,
>
> My Regiment is ordered to cross the river & move on Alexandria Within six hours. We may meet with a warm reception & my darling among so many careless fellows one is some what likely to be hit.
>
> If anything should happen—Darling just accept this assurance, the only thing I can leave you—the highest happiness I looked for on earth was a union with you. You have more than realized the hopes I formed regarding your advancement—and I believe I love you with all the ardor I am capable of. You know my darling any attempt of mine to convey an adequate expression of my feelings must be simply futile. God bless you as you deserve and grant you a happy & usefull life & us a union hereafter.
>
> > Truly your own, Elmer.[33]

Nor was this quite all. One of Ellsworth's captains later recalled that in the early hours of the day of the expedition to Alexandria, Ellsworth spent time selecting his uniform and made "a remark about choosing the clothes in which he was to die." This captain also remembered Ellsworth saying he had a feeling that his country would require his blood immediately. In this mood he had fastened upon his breast "[a] gold badge with the Latin inscription which means 'Not for ourselves alone but for country' Non Solum Nobis, sed Pro Patria. When he was dressed and ready, he was again gay and full of jest."[34] Later in the day this medal was found driven into his flesh by the shot that killed him.

Now that the Ellsworth evidence is in, what new images of Lincoln does it offer? The sheer impact of this relationship suggests that in some ways it fully matched what he had felt for Speed. Yet here, as nowhere else, he was able safely to show and say what he felt. Was that because the drama of Ellsworth's death and what he called "the disparity of our ages" helped to disguise the force of what he felt as a personal loss? Perhaps that was part of it. Generations of Lincoln scholars have told the Ellsworth story without a hint of its sexual implications, an oversight easy to maintain in the absence of any mention or memory of notable courtship efforts, either those made by Lincoln himself or others via Colonel Cook.

Not that the will and the choices of the players in this play are the only determinants of how the story is told, and of the course of events. The very geometry of the situation touched a mainstream in the romantic tradition. In nearly all the great love affairs of history, whether fiction or fact—Romeo and Juliet, Daphnis and Chloe, Acis and Galatea, Tristan and Isolde, Paris and Helen of Troy, even the inexperienced stand-alone Greek beauty Narcissus, of whom it was said "many youths and many maidens sought his love"—in these as in most classic examples of romance, when death or some other barrier intrudes to stop sexual consummation, two main results are apparent: a sharp increase in the drama of the situation, and the liberty to lament it loudly. Had Lincoln gone as far in private with Ellsworth as he had with Joshua Speed (and as he later did with Derickson) it is doubtful indeed he would have felt the urge to quite so resoundingly lament his loss. Months later he was known to break into tears, even to sob aloud at the mere mention of Ellsworth.

No new revelations can be claimed here for Lincoln's empathy and sympathy; he was all his life a champion in these. However, what the Ellsworth experience did do to a remarkable degree was to draw back the curtains on the full extent of the shock and the loss Lincoln felt, allowing him to fully state and show these more clearly than perhaps anywhere else in his life.

"Yours Forever"

Early in 1837 Lincoln made a pivotal change in his life. With New Salem on the verge of vanishing, he decided to move to Springfield, some twenty miles away, where he would try his hand at a law practice. Some recent business losses (left over from that small store of his that "winked out") had left him completely broke and shackled with debt. Nevertheless, on a borrowed horse and with all he owned stashed in a pair of saddlebags, he arrived in Springfield on April 15, 1837. It was the halfway point of his life: Twenty-eight years old, he would live exactly twenty-eight years more, to the day.

Lincoln stopped at the general store, where he first met the owner and clerk, Joshua Fry Speed. He asked Speed what it would cost to get furnishings for a single bed. The price for a mattress, blankets, sheets, coverlid, and pillow came to seventeen dollars. As Speed recalled,

> He said that was perhaps cheap enough; but, small as the sum was, he was unable to pay it. But if I would credit him till Christmas, and his experiment as a lawyer was a success, he would pay then, saying, in the saddest tone, "If I fail in this, I do not know that I can ever pay you." As I looked up at him I thought then, and think now, that I never saw a sadder face.
>
> I said to him, "You seem to be so much pained at contracting so small a debt, I think I can suggest a plan by which you can avoid the debt and at the same time attain your end.

I have a large room with a double bed up-stairs, which you are very welcome to share with me."

"Where is your room?" said he.

"Up-stairs," said I, pointing to a pair of winding stairs which led from the store to my room.

He took his saddle-bags on his arm, went up stairs, set them down on the floor, and came down with the most changed countenance. Beaming with pleasure he exclaimed, "Well, Speed, I am moved!"[1]

This is the story as handed down by Joshua Speed and repeated ever since in numerous accounts of Speed's first meeting Lincoln when he moved to Springfield. Strangely enough, no Lincoln scholar except for Charles Shively seems ever to have questioned the story. But in the eyes of any sex researcher the tale is more than suspect; its details are questionable in the extreme. Most of the "sticking points" are up front in plain sight. Imagine, for instance, the improbability of anyone making an offer as generous as Speed's, but then suddenly, in the midst of it, turning so distant and unattentive as to virtually vacate the scene—merely point to some stairs to indicate that Lincoln should find his way up, alone and undirected. But never mind. One can be quite sure that no such series of events ever occurred in the first place. Speed probably simply invited Lincoln up and showed him around in a friendly and perfectly ordinary way. Yet in later telling the story he was apparently embarrassed by what might come through as erotic interest in his moves toward Lincoln and consequently felt it safer, more innocent sounding, to recast events by moving back, leaving Lincoln less well attended than he actually was. Thus, as in so many telltale events, it is not the facts themselves that give the game away, but precisely such distortions as Speed invented to hide behind. In short, what he removed from the picture only flags the probable reality and highlights what he most wanted to obscure.

In hindsight it is clear that their very first meeting began what was to become *the* major event in Lincoln's private life, an intense and ongoing homosexual relationship with Speed. Admittedly it was not recognized as such by anyone at the time, including the principals. The "H" word was itself still far away—more than a half century into the future—plus the fact that public opinion throughout the nineteenth century was remarkably naive about close male relationships. Yet what people *did* recognize at the time, as has every biographer since, is that Lincoln's relationship with Speed was by any measure unique—the "closest" as well as the "most intimate" relationship of his life. Even Lincoln's White House secretaries, as they wrote a biography of sorts under the close and wary eye of Lincoln's son Robert, labeled it as such.[2] But before exploring this side of the story it is necessary to make a few further corrections and additions to Speed's account of their first meeting.

To anyone alert to homosexual propositions it is perhaps obvious from the outset that this is very much what was involved here, as Speed quickly moved the situation from a sale on credit to a generous invitation for Lincoln to move right into his room and bed. On close examination the sexual implications become unmistakable. Note that the invitation lacked any of the usual qualifiers such as "for a few days" or "until you get settled." Instead, it was immediately warm, embracing, and open-ended, more geared to desire than to accommodation. Louder still is the additional fact that while Lincoln did not know Speed at all, Speed had been well aware of Lincoln for months and was filled with admiration for him, ever since having heard a speech he gave the previous summer (July 30, 1836) in which Lincoln had cleverly trounced a rude lawyer and adversary, George Forquer.[3]

Why did Speed not mention this, perhaps with a comment about how much he had enjoyed the speech, or his amusement at seeing Forquer get his comeuppance? The probable answer is clear enough. Within moments of Lincoln arriving on that borrowed horse Joshua Speed evidently targeted him as a desirable bed partner, and immediately began choosing his words carefully. Had he said anything about recognizing Lincoln, or expressed admiration for the speech, this would have immediately moved their contact toward a conventional, friendly familiarity—exactly appropriate for, say, the start of either an ordinary friendship or conventional courtship, be it heterosexual or homosexual—but enemy territory for any brand of rapid sexual conquest.

Enemy territory? This may sound topsy-turvy, since sexual motives are ordinarily preceded by many small steps of friendly familiarity, the friendlier the better. True enough. But in plenty of other situations the delays of courtship and a relatively slow step-by-step method of winning a partner are cast aside (especially in the absence of onlookers) in favor of a glance or a gesture suddenly indicating not only attraction but a sexual readiness that can trigger a quick, parallel response in a partner who may or may not have already had the same in mind. It is sometimes suggested that such rapid sexual response is more often a male than a female mode. Perhaps so, but there are a great many examples in which an individual man or woman instantly picks up a new partner's cue (or sends one out) implying not only sexual response, but leaving the door ajar for some immediate possibility.

It might be tempting to argue in the present case that Speed had not yet had time to decide exactly what he wanted or how he might proceed—and that even if he had, it was too early for Lincoln to yet recognize it. But both assumptions are highly unlikely here. It can hardly be an accident that from the outset Speed chose not to laud Lincoln for the cleverness of his Forquer speech; it was as if Speed somehow sensed that to do so would have granted a note of celebrity to Lincoln, slightly elevating him for the paltry pickings of paying him a compliment, but by this very rise in status making him that much harder to approach later in any sexual or surreptitious way. Plainly put, Speed seems decidedly more inclined to get on with the business at hand rather than to make lovely circles in the air.

In any case, Speed was clearly an expert at all this, as his first moves well show. Years later he would face the problem of how to report his initial encounter with Lincoln: which parts to state exactly, and which to leave out, plus precisely how they arrived at their roommate/bedmate arrangement. Being bedmates in those days did not usually imply anything sexual, especially if it were only for a short time. "Still," when it was protracted or not explained by circumstance, "it bordered on impropriety," as Mary Lincoln's biographer Jean Baker once put it.[4] But better to be safe than sorry; thus Speed's cover-up of claiming to send Lincoln upstairs alone.

If Speed's account sounds like some classic spider-and-fly situation, with Lincoln being the innocent fly, then beware. In the first place, seduction scenes between mature partners are seldom if ever single-pass situations; they involve many small backing-and-filling moves, a dance that requires two to tango. Although we have no way of knowing exactly when Lincoln "caught on" and began his side of the backing and filling, he could hardly have been naive or sexually inexperienced. Remember that he was an early-puberty male (with almost certainly more than the usual number of early homosexual contacts) who as a teenager had written homosexual poetry in his *Chronicles of Reuben,* made jokes suggesting his awareness of "jelly babies," and soon after that had developed more than casual relationships with at least Billy Greene and A. Y. Ellis back in New Salem. Thus, it is probable he was alert enough to know the score as he flew into Speed's web.

What cannot be known is the precise timing—that is, the moment at which their attraction became overtly sexual. Secondary evidence suggests it was very early, probably the first night. At any rate, it clearly began with genuine complementation on both sides. Speed's rich family background and something of what this might offer must have been apparent from the outset, while Lincoln's qualities and needs were patently clear on several levels. Speed's biographer Robert Kincaid put it precisely, and more knowingly than most: "Speed saw in Lincoln the rough-hewn product of the frontier . . ." and "In Joshua Fry Speed, Abraham Lincoln saw a youth who was truly a 'gentleman to the manor born.' "[5] In short, he was a polished young man from a rich and elegant Kentucky family, one that offered just the kind of upward mobility and chance for self-improvement that were always of much interest to Lincoln.

For four years they lived happily together with no known friction, quite as Shively and others have noted.[6] Lincoln took the lead as speaker in their discussion group—the Young Men's Lyceum—which regularly met at the back of Speed's store. And Speed led the way socially as he took Lincoln with him into society. Speed always managed to know and flirt with women without being "caught" or becoming attached to any of them. He was among the "birds of passage" Mary Todd spoke of at the time: "Mr. Speed's ever changing heart" was one of her comments, along with a note of complaint for his flitting toward and then past a number of her friends.[7] In this he was much like what the Japanese call a "butterfly" for tasting each blossom but quickly moving on to the next.

Yet Mary Todd clearly owed Speed a debt of gratitude for leading Lincoln to her, despite the pain of having him continue to hang around through many of Lincoln's visits, just to keep him comfortable and coming. In fact, she appears to have been fed up to the teeth with that part, but what could she do? Only bewail her fate; one can fairly hear the ambivalence and frustration in her words as she wrote to her friend Mercy Ann Levering in June 1841, complaining that Lincoln, alas, had managed to shake loose from her some months before, causing her to lose, mixed blessing as it was, his ever present sidekick: "Mr. Speed, our former most constant guest," she lamented, as indeed he had become.[8]

One truly major trauma of Lincoln's life suddenly came upon him on January 1, 1841—the "fatal first" as he ever afterward was to call it (See Appendix 2, Letter 8). A few days before, Speed had announced he was leaving and moving back to Kentucky. His father had died recently and his mother had asked him to return and help with problems at home, but the possibility that he might grant this request and actually move back home had apparently not been discussed. Lincoln was evidently crushed to learn of it that New Year's Day, and within hours, as if to complete his shake-up, he broke off with Mary Todd, whom he had been seeing for several months.

But exactly what kind of relationship was it that Lincoln broke with Mary Todd? In a tale that turned out to be untrue, Herndon heard from no less than Mary's sister, Elizabeth Edwards (wife of Ninian Edwards), who reported that Lincoln and Mary were engaged and due to be married on that very New Year's Day, with guests invited and cakes baked, but that Lincoln simply failed to show up.[9] Aside from anything of the kind being completely unlike Lincoln (and completely unlike Mary Todd not to have been furious over it had any such public humiliation occurred), no part of the story was true. No marriage was planned, nor had any license been issued. Learning this, later biographers (still romantically inclined) withdrew to the position that Lincoln only broke their "engagement" on that "fatal first." But neither is there any record of an engagement, though it might not be too much to say that in those days two people who were steadily seeing each other might well look, and seem, and be taken as actually engaged.[10]

If Lincoln's break with Mary Todd had been the focus of his depression over the fatal first, as many of his biographers have assumed, he could easily have reversed it simply by seeing her again, or even by writing a short note. Quite as Mary said to a friend six months later, she was more than ready to welcome him back, and if he returned "much much happiness would it afford me."[11] In fact, the full truth was still more remarkable. It was mainly for social and career reasons that Lincoln had considered getting married; certainly these motives were more important to him than any fascination he felt for Mary Todd. Indeed, so little was Lincoln committed to Mary that he had tried hard to break off from her before. During that separation he had halfheartedly asked a sixteen-year-old girl, Sarah Rickard (whom he had known since she was a young child), to marry him. In this he made the lighthearted case that because his name was Abraham and hers Sarah, they were plainly meant for each other.[12]

Do these examples mean he felt little drawn to Mary Todd? The short answer is, Yes. At least not enough to keep him from trying to get out of the affair in two major efforts. Yet Lincoln was always much concerned lest he contribute to anyone's unhappiness—as, indeed, he said he felt in this case.[13] (Let. 8.) However, in the same letter he also said, "Since then it seems to me I should have been entirely happy"—other than for that bit of guilt. His "fatal first" label fits the fact of more than a single shock, as was surely the case: his break with Mary, and his same-day realization that Speed had decided to break off from him.

Historians have repeatedly tried to turn Lincoln's split with Mary into a romantic tragedy, even blaming it for his severe depression weeks later. But that stance cannot be sustained given Lincoln's deliberate efforts to escape from Mary, not to mention how easy it would have been for him to change his mind. Conversely, Speed's leaving Lincoln behind is often quickly recounted as the loss of his closest friend. Even Jonathan Katz, coming at the matter from his own angle, lists "Lincoln's losing his closest male intimate" as a fact that upset him, although in a footnote Katz correctly says, "Lincoln's loss of Speed on January 1, 1841, has been consistently underrated by Lincoln scholars."[14] Indeed so, with the further complication of scholars ignoring the overtly homosexual elements and trying to make Mary the focus.

In any case, Lincoln's loss of Speed clearly belongs front and center. His anxiety over the Speed portion of this misfortune, and not seeing any way to recoup his loss, were what soon cast him into a major double-phase nervous breakdown (the worst kind). In the first phase he felt listless and shaken, yet he forced himself to attend several sessions of the legislature, during which he was preoccupied and could not keep his mind on the proceedings. Mostly he sat quietly, as if stunned, when he was able to attend at all; generally he contributed nothing. Sometimes he would only answer the roll call, or would disappear after an hour or two; once the only vote he joined in was "to adjourn."[15] His general debility was widely noticed , and was ready to snowball.

By January 13, 1841, the second phase of his nervous breakdown came on at full tilt. With no sign of fever or other physical sickness, he became totally incapacitated and was bedridden for six days in what sounds like a state of ongoing shock. It looked very serious to outsiders, too. Wrote James Conkling to his fiancée, Mercy Levering, on January 24, 1841:

> Poor L! how the mighty have fallen! He was confined about a week, but though he now appears again he is reduced and emaciated in appearance and seems scarcely to possess strength enough to speak above a whisper. His case at present is truly deplorable but what prospect there may be for ultimate relief I cannot pretend to say.[16]

Nor was Lincoln's description of himself much better. On the previous day (January 23, 1841) he had written to his law partner, John Stuart:

> I am now the most miserable man living. If what I feel were equally distributed to the whole human family, there would not be one cheerful face on the earth. Whether I shall ever be better I can not tell; I awfully forbode I shall not. To remain as I am is impossible; I must die or be better, it appears to me.[17]

Does this sound like the result of a broken heterosexual love affair that he could have repaired in one minute? Of course not. Moreover, to wonder "whether I shall ever be better" and to feel the despair of "I awfully forbode I shall not" are the feelings of desperation that come *not* when one has dropped a lover, but when one has himself *been dropped* in a love affair, and thus lacks the leverage to repair the situation—which is exactly what happened here as Lincoln confronted the desertion of his longtime bed partner and soul mate, Speed.

Nor did Lincoln recover any time soon. His changed demeanor and persona were still matters of comment two weeks later on March 7, when James Conkling again wrote Mercy Levering:

> And L, poor hapless simple swain . . . I suppose he will now endeavor to drown his cares among the intricacies and perplexities of the law. No more will the merry peal of laughter ascend *high in the air*, to greet his listening and delighted ears. . . . Alas! I fear his shrine will now be deserted and that he will withdraw himself from the society of us inferior mortals.[18]

It is not known just how long these rough seas lasted past this ninth week of Lincoln's breakdown, or just what eventually quieted them— nor shall we ever know, thanks to some adroit censorship by Speed himself.

Time for more light on Speed's cover-ups. As far as is known, Speed demonstrated reasonable veracity throughout his life—*except* where his homosexual relations with Lincoln threatened to surface. Here he could be as deliberately misleading as he was before in his account of meeting Lincoln and inviting him to share his room. His basic mode of defense was not only to act as if he and Lincoln were less close than they really were, but to send people like Herndon down the wrong path whenever possible, which was often. Soon after Lincoln was shot and Herndon began collecting materials for his biography, he asked Speed for his Lincoln correspondence. Speed at first refused on the grounds that the letters were too personal. But Herndon, as was his way, kept after him, sending him friendly notes and pleading the case for history, until Speed eventually relented and agreed to hand over his Lincoln letters—though not quite all of them.

On November 30, 1866, Speed wrote Herndon, "I enclose you copies of all the letters of any interest from Mr. Lincoln to me." The operative phrase, of course, was "of any interest." But the fact was then, as it is now, that every fragment of Lincolniana is of very great interest, especially personal letters written in his own hand. Yet strangely enough not a single Lincoln scholar over the years seems to have questioned Speed's gift of the letters, or of exactly what was withheld. For instance, Speed included only one letter from the pivotal year of 1841—the year that began with that "fatal first"—unquestionably the year of their most strained and turbulent times, and the year in which Lincoln had the only nervous breakdown of his life. In the sole letter Speed handed over from 1841, dated June 19, Lincoln mentions other recent correspondence—"yours of the 13th," and in another flashback, "I stick to my promise to come to Louisville"—details that point to other important correspondence.

That same June 19 letter reveals a few other notable details. It begins without a single personal item, but drones on in a 1,575-word account of a local murder trial. Hard to find anything less personal than that, yet it is precisely this kind of impersonal recounting of some irrelevant bit of news that is often resorted to by distraught lovers who are contending with some strain, and who thus choose to recount details from a neutral territory as they wait out a storm that swirls about them. Such letters often end, as does this one, on an especially warm note. Speed was, in fact, the one and only person in Lincoln's life on whom he repeatedly lavished his most personal and most endearing "Yours forever," in itself a major smoking gun and a salutation he never bestowed on any woman, including his wife.

Later on in his letter to Herndon Speed is able to combine truth with fiction for one of his more ingenious cover-ups. Regarding Herndon's newly contrived Lincoln and Ann Rutledge romance Speed writes, "Thank you for [sending] your last lecture. It is all new to me, but so true to my appreciation of Lincoln's character . . . I would almost swear to it." Thus, in a single stroke Speed both admits he never heard of Ann Rutledge (gaining the benefit of implied distance from Lincoln's private life), while at the same time encouraging Herndon to continue right on at full tilt down that fictional road. Most certainly it was not a choice without motive. By combining his ignorance of Ann with his readiness to "almost swear to" an alleged affair of Lincoln's he gains the safety and comfort of further "heterosexualizing" both himself and Lincoln—a handy move at just the moment he was handing over the Lincoln letters with their numerous edgy moments of togetherness.

Interestingly enough, both sides of Speed's duplicity have reverberated right down through the Lincoln literature, where one biographer after the other has found words within it to support his own belief. Some have specifically cited Speed's "It's all new to me" as prime evidence against the Ann Rutledge tale. Others, as if hungry for romance at any price, have aligned themselves with the other end of Speed's sentence, his readiness after reading Herndon's tale to "almost swear to it." The irony is that both arguments are wide of the mark. In his letter, as in his life, Speed was mainly concerned not with distant improbable heterosexual events, pro or con, but with his own long-standing homosexual relationship with Lincoln, and with what repeatedly stands out as his urgent need to deny it.

Most Lincoln scholars have ignored (or have simply not seen) the homosexual evidence for numerous and varied reasons. It was never familiar territory in the first place, and for many people, the very fact that both Lincoln and Speed eventually married was enough to certify their heterosexuality. Then, too, some of the premarital anxieties Speed expressed, and that Lincoln tried to reassure him against, were and still are commonplace concerns of men facing marriage. Likewise, much of the solace Lincoln offered him was entirely conventional. It involved reassurances about Speed having chosen the right girl, of his having loved Fanny Henning's "heavenly black eyes," of how his anxieties were sure to disappear in the future. It was just the kind of support one might expect and appreciate from a close friend or chum. Yet woven in among those reassurances were words and facts that went far beyond even the closest friendship.

In August 1841 Lincoln visited Speed at Farmington, his Kentucky home. As Kincaid rightly commented, "No incident in Lincoln's life was perhaps more enjoyable than his visit [with] Speed."[19] Indeed so, though the visit had both an inner and an outer reality. On the outside Speed had been trying to court Fanny Henning—an orphan girl whom "he was anxious that [Lincoln] should see"—but she lived with a talkative uncle, John Williamson, who intruded into every conversation to talk politics until Lincoln learned to distract him with one political argument after the other, giving Speed a chance to see Fanny alone, to court her, to eventually ask her to come meet his mother at Farmington, and to propose that she should marry him.[20] It all sounds a bit rushed and too condensed to be savored, but let us not quibble.

A few days later when it came time for Lincoln to leave, Speed was bedridden with a fever (probably the flu), but he insisted on getting up, packing, and going along with Lincoln on a protracted roundabout, vacationlike boat trip, returning via St. Louis. Eight days later they arrived in Springfield and took a room together at the home of William Butler (confirmed by Butler's son's mention of it decades later). Speed had no known business awaiting him in Springfield but nevertheless stayed on with Lincoln for months, finally leaving on January 3, 1842.

It is sometimes suggested that Lincoln and Speed spent much time during their Springfield stay discussing Speed's marriage anxieties. But this is not likely in view of the newness of the topic, as evident in one of Lincoln's parcels of advice included in a letter handed to Speed as he was ready to depart. (Let. 3) In fact, the evidence suggests that Speed himself kept at bay any worries about marriage until he was virtually out the door on his way home that January 3, 1842, echoing other indications that Fanny rated no more than a distant second when Lincoln was available. For instance, she had been invited to visit Speed and his mother at Farmington in late September. But this did not cause him to wait for her visit, or prevent him from quickly leaving his sickbed to join Lincoln for their boat trip back. (Only by a quick mention in Lincoln's second letter is it known that Fanny's visit was neither canceled nor honored by Speed.) Moreover, it is evident in the first few words of Lincoln's third letter—the one he wrote to Speed not at a distance, but handed to him on his departure—that they had not discussed his support of Speed to any extent. Lincoln wrote:

> I do not place what I am going to say on paper, because I can say it any better in that way than I could by word of mouth; but because, were I to say it orally, before we part, most likely you would forget it at the verry time when it might do you some good.[21]

The tone and tenderness of this is already at a level of intimacy and warm support well in excess of friendly advice. Or if that is not yet fully clear, it becomes so moments later as Lincoln lauds Speed for being a sensitive soul whose "painful difference [from] the mass of the world" sets him so apart from other men as to make him "one in a thousand." Once again these are not the words of even the closest chum; they are the language of love, and Lincoln seems fully aware of the risk here. Thus, in the next breath he is quick to gloss it over by loud expressions of support for Fanny and for Speed's whole heterosexual venture:

> But you say you reasoned yourself into [courting her]. What do you mean by that? Was it not that you found yourself unable to reason yourself out of it? Did you not think . . . of courting her the first time you ever saw or heard of her? What had reason to do with it at that early stage? (Let. 3)

All this and more argued in favor of Speed's heterosexual tryout. But it is typical, indeed a stereotype, of how bisexual men often support each other's heterosexual efforts in a spirit of being helpful, yet also as a way to stay close by and fully informed of every move. For Lincoln all these motives are crystal clear in his final sentence: "I shall be so anxious about you that I want you to write me every mail."[22]

Such sentiments, amounting to one affectionate embrace after the other, are apparent in every one of Lincoln's early letters to Speed. But they reach their peak, a kind of crescendo, in the sixth letter where, admittedly, the situation was exceptional. Speed married Fanny on February 15, 1842, and by prearrangement he had agreed to write Lincoln *immediately* the following day to report on how the wedding night had gone. For Speed and Lincoln to have been so anxious over Speed's "success"—a near panic over sex—certainly points to their huge worry over whether Speed would be able both to get an erection and vault the hurdle of achieving intercourse; but does it also mean Speed was a virgin with women? Not necessarily. (A famous problem among Victorian men—if informal reports are to be trusted—was that they were ravenously responsive to "bad" women but impotent or nearly so with their wives.)

As promised, Speed wrote back on the sixteenth, Lincoln waiting nervously for the letter to arrive. When it did, Lincoln wrote back (Let. 6):

"I opened the latter [letter] with intense anxiety and trepidation; so much, that although it turned out better than I expected, I have hardly yet, at the distance of ten hours, become calm."

This is perhaps the clearest "smoking gun" in the Lincoln-Speed correspondence. Had Lincoln been merely a close friend he would of course have reveled in the good news of a wedding night that "turned out better than I expected." Instead, he suffered a major anxiety attack that had hardly let up "at a distance of ten hours." One hears in this the loud bang of a traumatic blow, if not of an outright tragedy, not because Lincoln wished Speed any ill luck, but because he saw, or thought he saw, the crash of their own relationship.

While Lincoln's anxiety attack and his speaking right out about it loom very large indeed, other sources of strain are also apparent. To save face Speed undoubtedly put a better spin on his wedding night than it deserved. For although his morning-after report contained enough good news to make Lincoln feel it "turned out better than I expected," Speed also acknowledged alarm and disappointment. In answering Speed's letter Lincoln wrote: "You say that something indescribably horrible and alarming still haunts you." And further, "Again you say, you much fear that that Elysium of which you have dreamed so much is never to be realized." For once, Speed was ready to be more forthcoming and frank in dealing with his fears and failures than was Lincoln, who brushed past alarming details with his high spirits, offering his boundless support, and assuring Speed that "When your nerves once again get steady [three months from now], the whole trouble will be over forever."

But Speed's despair was more real and lasting than Lincoln then or ever realized. Evidence considered later suggests that from the outset Speed was sexually dysfunctional, indeed, completely impotent with his wife—and that he remained so for the rest of his life.

Lincoln, on the other hand, seems to have soon recovered from the shock of feeling he had lost Speed to what he construed as the "success" of his wedding night, and once again took on the role of confidant and supporter. In a way he became more a trusted colleague than ever, bringing a superintimacy into his ongoing affair with Speed. In the same envelope with his letter number six he enclosed number seven, a far less personal one for the eyes of Fanny, "which you can show her, if she desires it"—meaning that if she learns you have received this letter from me, you can show her this other one instead.

Speed answered these letters immediately, arousing in Lincoln his usual pleasant tone, yet accompanied by seemingly negative remarks about how little interest he has in Speed's farms and farming—almost certainly a ploy to mask the overflowing affection in his very next words:

> But on that other subject [of how you are], to me of the most intense interest whether in joy or in sorrow, I never had the power to withhold my sympathy from you. . . . [I]t now thrills me with joy to hear you say you are "far happier than you ever expected to be." . . . I am not going beyond the truth when I tell you that the short space it took me to read your last letter gave me more pleasure than the total sum of all I have enjoyed since the fatal first of Jany—'41. Since then it seems to me I should have been entirely happy, but for the never-absent idea that there is one [Mary Todd] still unhappy whom I have contributed to make so. (Let. 8)

He goes on to say how the latter fact "kills my soul." And yet how glad he was to hear "She accompanied a large party [on a rail trip] last Monday, and on her return spoke, so that I heard of it, of having enjoyed the trip exceedingly. God be praised for that"—meaning that, while he did not miss her, the fact that she could be happy without him freed him from feeling guilty over making her unhappy. (Let. 8)

On October 5, 1842, Lincoln sent Speed an urgent request. He was well aware that Speed had spoken of his marriage as a source of joy. But it was now eight months later and Lincoln had special reasons for wanting an update. Through the well-meaning efforts of a mutual friend, Mrs. Simeon Frances, he had again become entangled with Mary Todd. Should he struggle free, or move with the tide and marry her after all? The answer hinged on a number of factors (examined in Chapter 8), but some, he thought, were close to Speed's experience. He wrote:

That you are happier now than you ever were the day you married [Fanny] I well know, for [otherwise] you could not be living. But I have your word for it, too, and the returning elasticity of spirits which is manifested in your letters. But I want to ask a closer question, "Are you now in *feeling* as well as *judgment* glad that you are married as you are?" From anybody but me this would be an impudent question . . . but I know you will pardon it in me. Please answer it quickly, as I feel impatient to know.

> Yours forever,
> Lincoln. (Let. 10)

Speed's answer must have been encouraging. Within days Lincoln went ahead and married Mary Todd, on November 4, 1842.

For reasons to be examined later Speed's glad tidings mainly amount to a made-up fiction, and yet within limits, his famous statement made years later to Herndon about Lincoln was true: "One thing is plainly discernable [sic]—If I had not been married & happy—far more happy than I ever expected to be—He would not have married."[23]

From the time Lincoln married, on down through the months and years, Speed was the one person he would time and again reach out to in his continuing hunger for the intimacy he was loath to lose. Some two months into his marriage, at the end of a business letter to Speed, Lincoln wrote:

> Mary is very well and continues her old sentiments of friendship for you. How the marriage life goes with us I will tell you when I see you here, which I hope will be very soon. (Let. 11)

This mention of Mary and her "sentiments" was pure politeness, as it always was; she had never cared much for Speed, and even less so whenever she glimpsed his importance to Lincoln. But to discuss with Speed "how the marriage life goes" was a matter of special interest for Lincoln; at the very least it might have helped him figure out his own reactions. However, Speed resisted such meetings. Had this one ever taken place no doubt Lincoln would have said that his marital sex went all right (Mary apparently became pregnant on their wedding night), but that it felt strange and entirely new. He was remarkably frank about his surprise, and not just with Speed. At the end of a short letter to a not particularly close friend after his first week of marriage he wrote, "Nothing new here, except my marrying, which to me, is a matter of profound wonder."[24]

The unbounded intimacy between Lincoln and Speed was also reflected in a decidedly marriagelike pact agreed to in their early years: Lincoln's first son would be named Joshua. Speed loved the idea, and apparently sought to reconfirm it midway during Mary's first pregnancy. Lincoln wrote back, "About the prospects of your having a namesake at our house, can't say exactly yet." (Let. 12) Indeed not. Not only was the sex of the child still unknown, but Mary's assent was never to be taken for granted, least of all in honor of Joshua. In the end she voted it down emphatically, insisting the child should be named Robert T. Lincoln for her father. Nor was she amenable to "Joshua" for any later son, either.

Obvious throughout the Lincoln letters was his ongoing urgency to extend his intimacy with Speed—above all, to hold on to it. For this he needed to stay on good terms with Speed's wife, Fanny, who though friendly somehow kept her distance despite Lincoln's many leanings forward. As he says at the end of one letter, gently complaining about a lack of feedback from her: "I have sent my love to your Fanny so often, I fear she is getting tired of it. However, I venture to tender it again." (Let. 10)

Then a few months later:

> I most heartily wish you and your Fanny would not fail to come [visit]. Just let us know the time, a week in advance, and we will have a room provided for you at our house, and all be merry together for a while. . . . Mary joins in sending love to your Fanny and you. (Let. 14)

No such thing of course. Both women were standoffish, Mary in the extreme. Mary was notably hostile to everybody Lincoln ever liked, including each and every one of his relatives, especially those he most loved. Fanny was far kinder, but beyond a single short note (and a violet she dropped into one of Joshua's letters), she is not known ever to have either made or sent back any greeting. Not that being remote in this way was necessarily unusual for such women. The wives of bi-sexual men often resist what they see as a bit too much togetherness for comfort. Do they intuitively feel it as competition? Or are they simply reacting against more closeness than they feel themselves, or perhaps resist it for still other reasons? Sex researchers embrace var-ious of these explanations and often disagree with each other; how-ever, the reality of the stereotype is beyond question. In any case, Lincoln persisted with unfailing warmth at every turn. One high point of his affection came right before an impending disaster that nobody could have predicted: Speed's abrupt withdrawal from the friendship. Lincoln wrote: "We shall look with impatience for your visit this fall. Your Fanny can not be more anxious to see my Molly than the latter is to see her, nor as much so as I am—Don't fail to come." (Let. 15)

One hears in these few words Lincoln's celebration of a much anticipated reunion. But this meeting was never to take place, nor did Speed so much as acknowledge the letter. Instead, in what ap-pears to have been very painful for Lincoln, Speed simply backed away into silence, not just at that juncture, but for well over three years. When he finally did write it was mostly about small business matters, though in keeping with his views he also commented on their differences over slavery, and how this had served to drive a wedge between them. Lincoln sadly answered: "You, no doubt, as-sign the suspension of our correspondence to the true philosophical cause, though it must be confessed by both of us that this is rather a cold reason for allowing a friendship such as ours to die out by de-grees." (Let. 16)

Always the bridge-builder, Lincoln went on to say: "I propose now that, upon receipt of this, you shall be considered in my debt, and under obligations to pay soon, and that neither shall remain long in arrears hereafter. Are you agreed?" Speed's reaction was the ulti-mate coldness; he did not answer at all.

Never comfortable pushing himself on anybody, it had always been Lincoln's style to write Speed only in response to one of his let-ters. But in this case, after more than two additional years of silence, Lincoln had a pressing reason for writing at least a note. On a trip back to Springfield he had seen Herndon, who reported a certain legal difficulty regarding a debt collection for Speed. Lincoln dealt with this matter in a short letter, which ended: "Nothing of consequence new here, beyond what you see in the papers." (Let. 17) To anyone at all familiar with their painful estrangement for more than five years, Lincoln's uncharacteristic backing away from anything personal reflects a forlorn, poignant sadness—a starving for what had once been so intimate and personal.

The vein of unstated sorrow was to continue. This time Speed answered the legal details of Lincoln's letter soon enough, but included nothing at all personal beyond striking a spark, a very dim spark, of renewed hope. Lincoln in his quiet way and in a champion understatement, wrote back, "I like to open a letter of yours, and I therefore hope you will write me again on the receipt of this." (Let. 18) It was a sad commentary, indeed, and it brought the curtain down. Neither was to write the other for well over six more years.

During those years, twelve in all, the national debate over slavery was heating up fiercely—a matter of particular importance for Speed as well as Lincoln. As a prosperous Kentucky slave owner Speed had always defended the institution, a position that had often put him at odds with Lincoln. But now he was particularly feeling the strain with Lincoln's ever more prominent voice of opposition. Thus, on May 22, 1855, Speed broke his silence and wrote a long letter to Lincoln outlining their opposing views. Lincoln, who usually answered Speed's letters within a day or two, delayed his delicate and carefully balanced answer to this missile for three months. On August 24, 1855, he wrote Speed a 1,571-word issue-packed reply, one of the most interesting letters he ever wrote. (Let. 19)

While it can hardly be said that Lincoln ever lied, in phrasing delicate personal matters he could bend words and contexts in astonishing ways. His letter began:

> Dear Speed: You know what a poor correspondent I am. Ever since I received your very agreeable letter of the 22nd of May— I have been intending to write you in answer to it.

This, when neither Speed nor anybody else ever had a better or faster correspondent than Lincoln; nor could he have found anything "very agreeable" in Speed's letter other than perhaps his writing it at all. In any case, on issues of slavery, logic, and debate, Lincoln was exceedingly precise and subtle, quickly ready to correct an innuendo in Speed's letter to the effect that since Northern people did not own slaves they lacked any real interest in the matter. Lincoln's polite but sharp reply:

> It is hardly fair for you to assume, that I have no interest in a thing which has, and continually exercises, the power of making me miserable. You ought rather to appreciate how much the great body of the Northern people do crucify their feelings, in order to maintain their loyalty to the constitution and the Union.

Nor was he about to hold still for Speed's pretended Christianity:

> You say if Kansas fairly votes herself a free state, as a Christian you will rather rejoice at it. All decent slaveholders *talk* that way; and I do not doubt their candor. But they never *vote* that way. Although in a private letter, or conversation, you will express your preference that Kansas shall be free, you would vote for no man for Congress who would say the same thing publicly. No such man could be elected from any district in any slave-state. . . . The slave-breeders and slave-traders are a small, odious and detested class, [even] among you; and yet in politics, they dictate the course of all of you, and are as completely your masters, as you are the masters of your own Negroes. (Let. 19)

This was Lincoln at his most Lincoln-like: ready and able to launch a devastating frontal assault against the errors and the folly of even his closest, wayward friend—yet in the big picture to neither withdraw nor withhold the least bit of his highest affection. He ended with:

> My kindest regards to Mrs. Speed. On the leading subject of this letter, I have more of her sympathy than I have of yours. And yet let me say I am your friend forever.

Farther down the road Speed and Lincoln were to have a last very important set of contacts, but these came after Lincoln had become president, and thus to a great extent stand apart. Viewed right at this point—late August 1855—after all their main letters had been written and responded to (or pointedly not responded to, as the case might be), and before Lincoln and Speed had quite stepped into their final roles, it is time to say something perhaps less than obvious about Speed's personality.

In many ways he was a mixed bag. He could be warm and generous, or much less than that, as in some of his letters to Lincoln. Yet even Lincoln's two private secretaries, John G. Nicolay and John Hay, who knew him well, would later say in their ten-volume biography of Lincoln that "Speed was the only—as he was certainly the last—intimate friend that Lincoln ever had" and that "Speed and Lincoln poured out their souls to each other."[25] In the eyes of most Lincoln observers Speed was viewed merely as a very close friend or chum of Lincoln's over the years, an image that in part fits the figure if not the fact. But what kind of "close friend" or chum would suddenly break off without a word at the very moment he was enthusiastically expected to visit—or would inexplicably disappear for years, or otherwise go in and out of focus at crucial, intimate moments?

This is not to suggest that the Speed-Lincoln friendship was less intimate than was thought, but rather the opposite: It was much *more* intimate than was ever recognized at that time, or since. True, a close friend or chum would not have left Lincoln in the lurch (especially not repeatedly), and yet an erratic, tormented, conflicted, on-again-off-again lover—a man in some ways a failure in his private life—would have, and did, for this precisely describes Speed.

Nearby questions abound. How did Speed do in his marriage? Did his basic "response pattern" later stay the same? Or like many similar males did he eventually succeed in becoming more or less exclusively heterosexual at least in practice? In several ways Speed loudly suggested that he did. For while he had been frank enough about his numerous doubts and hesitations as he wended his way toward Fanny, soon after he was married he proclaimed his own transition complete, describing himself as "far happier than I ever expected to be." No doubt this loud claim was (and still is) convincing to conventional ears, but is less so to trained observers, who are more inclined to credit quieter evidence and to listen for nearby implications. Notice that what Speed is "far happier" about always concerns only himself—psychologists call it "self-reference"—since it speaks narrowly and only of his own feelings. Nor does one hear the usual triumphs of a new husband, or the settling in of one, such as the joy of having found the right girl or wondering how he could have managed so long without her. Here any focus on a living, breathing Fanny is curiously lacking. The interactions of Speed and Fanny will be easier to bring into focus later.

Beyond all yet said there were unaccountable bits of coldness in Speed that repeatedly expressed certain unsavory character traits. For instance, among the various small business dealings Speed had with Lincoln's law office—accounts to be collected and the processing of a few legal papers—Speed's disposition seems mostly on the edge of being irritable if not cantankerous, and decidedly short on generosity. One of his surviving letters to Lincoln (April 3, 1843) is all business; it contains not a single personal touch and ends with words to the effect that he expects Lincoln to retain a particular toll charge (a commission of perhaps ten dollars or less), yet: "Make it as light as you can." (Let. 13) Speed, remember, was part of a well-to-do family, and a member of the Kentucky landed gentry, while Lincoln, still paying off debts from his New Salem days, lived largely hand-to-mouth until fairly late in life.

Since Speed sounds so extreme in this example, could it have been only a local instance, a momentary blip in his behavior? Hardly. Time and again there were touches of temper and tightness that showed up in Speed's demand for Lincoln to explain a situation, or to correct some less than charitable interpretation Speed had hastily made on his own. Nor did it bode well that he so often had to be handled with kid gloves. Since Lincoln showed no tendency to put up with any other cantankerous and troublesome characters, why here? More astonishing still, how was he able to retain his admiration and full support ("Yours forever") toward Speed in the face of countless contradictions and unreturned kindnesses?

The answer in a nutshell is that an early and firmly established sexually validated attachment is phenomenally effective. It can lock one in a jail of enthrallment, overcoming violations of what is fair or reasonable or good judgment by any standard—and *still* remain firmly in place. There is nothing fair or reasonable about it. No sooner does one begin to shake loose from such a painful fascination than it can rise again like a phoenix at the slightest bidding—as was about to happen to Lincoln yet again.

. . .

After another long, six-year gap in their contact Speed seemed much surprised one day at what apparently struck him as Lincoln's sudden rise to public prominence, best reflected in Speed's own words of May 19, 1860:

> You can hardly imagine, and I can not describe my feelings when I saw by the papers this morning that you were a candidate for the Presidency. Allow a warm personal friend, though as you are perhaps aware, a political opponent, to congratulate you. Should you be elected and I think you have a fair chance for it—I am satisfied that you will honestly administer the government—and make a lasting reputation for yourself. . . . My wife is warmly for you. Cant [sic] you come and see us . . .[?][26]

It was a response of considerable dignity and feeling. Yet one can hardly avoid noticing that nothing so quickly warms the heart of a much cooled-off former lover than does the newfound celebrity Lincoln was just then entering. At least, Lincoln's suddenly expanded prominence was the horse Speed rode back in on. And while Lincoln was unable to accept that rare invitation just then, the lights came back on and the curtain went up again, as the stage was set for new and momentous events. These were to include a key role of historic proportions played by Speed, very much involving his special relationship with Lincoln.

Speed's Kentucky was a so-called border state, meaning that it shared many traditions of the South, although by a hairsbreadth it had not seceded into the Confederacy. But the situation was edgy, with much sentiment in favor of the South. Into this swirling cauldron came military obligations to serve the North and to fight for it—duties that were far from evenly felt. In fact, the war had hardly begun when Lincoln became concerned that a well-armed Kentucky militia under one Simon Buckner might defect to the Southern cause. To fend this off, and to do so with tact and secrecy, Lincoln privately asked a young lieutenant, William Nelson, to supply quiet aid and encouragement to loyal factions in Kentucky. Lincoln specifically directed him to approach Joshua Fry Speed for help, which Nelson proceeded to do, with sufficient cloak-and-dagger surreptitiousness to alarm Speed's wife.[27] Their first clandestine meeting occurred on the night of May 7, 1861, less than a month into the Civil War.[28]

Speed's continuing help kept him very much at the center of Kentucky affairs. Once, when General Sherman (William Tecumseh Sherman of later Atlanta and march-to-the-sea fame) became distraught and wild-eyed because his requests for additional supplies simply went unheeded in Washington, Speed interceded. As Kincaid reported:

> [Sherman] one day expounded his woes to Joshua Fry Speed. "What do you want?" Speed asked. "Everything," Sherman replied. "Arms, wagons, tents, bread and meat, money, and a competent staff."
>
> "Name what you want on paper and give it to me," Speed requested. Sherman hastily scrawled out his list. Speed took the train for Washington, submitted the request to President Lincoln, and within a few days was back in Sherman's office. He handed him copies of orders naming two important officers in the quartermaster corps to be assigned to his staff, with a drawing account for $100,000. One order, signed by Lincoln himself, directed the ordnance department to supply the Kentucky forces with 10,000 Springfield rifles of the latest design.
>
> Sherman was amazed. "How is this that more attention is paid to the requests of you, a citizen, than me, a general in the army?" he demanded. "You had better take command here."
>
> Quietly, Speed told Sherman of his friendship with Lincoln, and then said: "The only mistake you made, General, was not asking for more."[29]

From these and similar examples one might easily make the point that those first four years of close intimacy in the Lincoln-Speed relationship, along with all it ultimately led to, much influenced the rest of Lincoln's life, including a few major events in his presidency. If this sounds overdrawn it may seem less so when it is realized that Speed's visits to the White House were much more frequent than ever was entered into the formal record[30] and, in fact, that these extended for years, to within two weeks of Lincoln's death.[31]

Speculations as to the importance of these visits will not be pursued any further here for two reasons. By their very nature such conjectures invite a more extensive use of deduction than is used elsewhere in these pages. Second, for reasons that may not be instantly apparent, it would be an incongruous irony to "explain" Lincoln, of all people, by citing any one set of local events. Certainly he himself would have considered it folly. Lincoln, after all, was the ultimate dyed-in-the-wool fatalist.

Moreover, something is to be said for the remembered fact that Lincoln was all his life that unique autodidact—virtually impervious to suggestions and advice from others. Thus, while Speed was his ultimate confidant and trusted soul mate—and where Kentucky was concerned, even Lincoln's wheeler-dealer and mover-behind-the-throne—it would still be too much to say that Lincoln's choices were significantly changed by him. Or as Lincoln himself might have said, both his own choices and all of Speed's may have only been the tools of fate toiling and grinding away, their ends already predetermined.

As for Speed, from late in life we have one additional "take" on him, one that curiously enough knits together a last remaining set of loose ends. Years after Lincoln was gone, mainly as a contribution to the historical record, Speed wrote his own book, *Reminiscences of Abraham Lincoln*. In this, for reasons soon to see, he included a few last images of how happy his own marriage was, a highly suspect move in view of what is well understood in sex research. Why suspect? Mainly because loud claims of joy and happiness are hard to take at face value in the first place, and all the more so from one whose heterosexual commitment was shaky from the outset and oddly troubled in every subsequent image of it. Indeed, Speed seems never to have gotten over his dubious wedding night of long before. Long after Lincoln's death he was still portraying it as a glowing, saccharine fantasy, that is, trying to outshout its drab details with fairy-tale images and other romantic opposites. To wit, a sample letter Speed wrote his wife when she was away but a few days in Chautauqua:

Last evening, as I sat upon the porch watching the sun set, as we usually do, I thought of you and wished for you. Old Sol sank to rest in the arms of night so grandly, giving some new beauty with each expiring ray.

It seemed as though the clouds had more beautiful phantasms of every shape and form, like bridesmaids and bridegrooms, waiting in graceful attendance upon the wedding of day and night, than I ever saw before. Night, like the blushing bride, was coy and shy, and gave evidence of her modesty in her blushing cheeks, while day, like a gallant knight, who had won his spurs upon the bloody battle-field in the heady current of the fight, had done his duty, laid aside his helmet and his spear, and approached his bride in the rich and beautiful garb of a lover. The wedding over, the stars came out, like guests invited to the feast, and, I suppose, kept up the carousal till dawn of day. I retired, and give no further report.[32]

In all of literature one could hardly find a more glaring example of lush exuberance rushing in to fill the vacuum of what is lacking in hard reality, no pun intended. Like the glorious excesses of what can be afforded only in fantasy, this is the very model of the myriad hopes and images of an impotent male—a man who pours out his arousal not in bed but in word substitutes.

At what point does his impotence hark back to? Clearly to the very wedding night itself. The next morning Speed described to Lincoln not his enjoyment of the sex, or the pleasure of at least having successfully consummated his marriage, or even of a hurdle safely vaulted, but confesses—along with assurances that his wedding night had nevertheless been successful—elements of the very opposite: "that something indescribably horrible and alarming still haunts him." (Let. 6) That "something" was likely his fear of not ever being able to get an erection with his wife. It was a fear well-founded indeed, since years later he was still using all those vivid substitute images for solid sex in a plainly dysfunctional marriage—images of bridesmaids, bridegrooms, a blushing bride (twice), even a gallant knight who fresh from the bloody battlefield "lays aside his helmet and spear [to] approach his bride in the rich and beautiful garb of a lover."

With all these bits and pieces finally at hand many details of the Lincoln-Speed relationship now suddenly find their place in the total mosaic. No longer can there be serious doubt about Speed's ongoing impotence with his wife, an image that suggests in a flash why he shied away from comparing notes with Lincoln about their experiences in marriage, why he and Fanny steered clear of nearly every invitation to visit the Lincolns, or even to meet them briefly.

One also wonders how much and how often Speed regretted telling Lincoln as much as he did of his wedding night. Once made, his claim of success seems to have required repeated feedings with assurances that he was "happier than I ever expected to be." It sounds like a modest claim, yet it gave him an image to live up to, and was probably enough to cause some of Lincoln's casual comments to cut to the quick. When Lincoln wrote of his wife's first pregnancy his very next sentence forced an implicit comparison: "By the way, how do 'events' of the same sort come on in your family? Are you possessing houses and lands, and oxen and asses, and men-servants and maid-servants, and begetting sons and daughters?" (Let. 14) Little wonder that as Lincoln's family continued to grow, and with Joshua and Fanny looking quite barren with no children, the Speeds were even less inclined to visit and to face inevitable comparisons. These considerations remain, even if there were other reasons for staying away, such as Mary Lincoln's often dicey and unlovely personality.

Eventually it will be useful to compare these and other events with one another, particularly those that have been influenced if not wholly induced by homosexual factors. However, it is now time to examine Lincoln's heterosexual life on its own terms, his marriage to Mary Todd.

EIGHT

Marriage and Mary Todd

SCRAMBLED EGGS

From early in life Lincoln was famous for keeping his own counsel, for sharing few if any of his private problems and feelings with others. Herndon was not alone in finding Lincoln

> a profound mystery—an enigma—a sphinx—a riddle . . . incommunicative—silent—reticent—secretive—having profound policies—and well laid—deeply studied plans.[1]

Even as president, as David Donald has put it, "Nobody had his complete confidence. His loyal Secretary of the Navy was kept as much in the dark about Lincoln's views as the veriest outsider. 'Of the policy of the administration, if there be one,' Welles complained, 'I am not advised beyond what is published and known to all.' " Indeed, as Donald says, "Lincoln moved toward his objectives with muffled oars."[2]

In fact, muffled oars, with their implication of silence and secrecy, were a style, a method of approaching problems and dealing with conflict that pervaded every area of Lincoln's life. Thus, behind his affable front was a privacy prominent in his boyhood, a trait he developed into a fine art in his middle years, and that was widely evident in the Lincoln administration. Likewise, it is no surprise that Lincoln's marriage was also very much a backstage entity in which the main events were often dealt with behind the scenes—or left fallow to find their own solutions.

Over the years an ever-increasing accumulation of negative reports on Mary Todd from both biographers and bystanders have built her reputation to horrific proportions. Not too surprisingly, revisionist counterefforts along the way arose to deny or explain away most charges against her, sometimes repainting her in glowing colors. While many of these defenses were patently transparent, others were less so, and this contrast, too, has greatly scrambled the evidence.

Nevertheless, the fact is that neither Lincoln nor his marriage can be well understood without a reasonably accurate view of both Mary Todd and what their relationship was really like.

Nobody ever said it was a love affair—during Lincoln's lifetime. Soon after Joshua Speed brought Lincoln and Mary Todd together she apparently set her sights on Lincoln and began to care more and more for him. Lincoln was much less taken with her, though he continued to see her for several months (often with Speed at his side). They seem to have had few if any outright conflicts, although in disposition and temperament they were poles apart. The Edwardses (Ninian W. Edwards and his wife Elizabeth, Mary's sister) both

> told Mary & Lincoln they had better not Ever marry—that their natures, mind—Education—raising &c were So different they Could not live happy as husband & wife—had better never think of the Subject again.[3]

Lincoln, however, was less than enchanted with Mary anyway, and soon sought ways to slip out of the trap. He wrote her a letter saying he felt he did not love her enough to justify her marrying him, and tried to get Speed to deliver it. But Speed refused outright:

> I shall not deliver it now nor give it to you to be delivered; words are forgotten—misunderstood—passed by—not noticed in a private conversation—but once put your words in writing and they stand as a living and eternal monument against you.[4]

Thereupon I threw the unfortunate letter into the fire. . . . If you think you have the courage of manhood, go see Mary yourself; tell her, if you do not love her, the facts, and that you will not marry her. Be careful not to say too much, and then leave at your earliest opportunity.[5]

As Speed reports, "Thus admonished, [Lincoln] buttoned his coat, and with a rather determined look started out to perform the serious duty for which I had just given him explicit directions." That night Speed waited up for Lincoln's return. It was a long wait; not until after eleven o'clock did Lincoln come stalking in. From the late hour Speed suspected his directions had not been followed, and he was right:

"Well, old fellow, did you do as I told you and as you promised?" were Speed's first words.

"Yes, I did," responded Lincoln, thoughtfully, "and when I told Mary I did not love her, she burst into tears and almost springing from her chair and wringing her hands as if in agony, said something about the deceiver being himself deceived." Then he stopped.

"What else did you say?" inquired Speed, drawing the facts from him.

"To tell you the truth Speed, it was too much for me. I found the tears trickling down my own cheeks. I caught her in my arms and kissed her."

"And that's how you broke the engagement," sneered Speed. "You not only acted the fool, but your conduct was tantamount to a renewal of the engagement, and in decency you cannot back down now."

"Well," drawled Lincoln, "if I am in again, so be it. It's done, and I shall abide by it."[6]

And abide by it he did, with two remarkable changes in the near and not so near future.

Within a month or so came that "fatal first" of January 1841, when Lincoln politely but decisively pulled away from Mary Todd. It was a sharp change in his life occasioned by his urgent need to come to terms with losing Speed, as shown before (Chapter 7). But he was also greatly relieved to be away from Mary and out of the position of pretending to care for her. Fifteen months later he confided to Speed (Let. 8), "Since then it seems to me I should have been entirely happy, but for the never-absent idea that there is one [Mary Todd] who is still unhappy whom I have contributed to make so. That still kills my soul. I cannot but reproach myself for even wishing to be happy while she is otherwise," followed by saying how glad he was to have heard six days before that she very much enjoyed going with a large party to Jacksonville without him. Good; she could be happy without him.

Nevertheless, Lincoln's always easily triggered guilt feelings were to cost him more than he ever imagined. A few months later Mrs. Simeon Francis, the wife of Lincoln's good friend, the editor of the Sangamo *Journal*, decided to intervene. She invited both Lincoln and Mary to a social affair without telling either the other would be there; she brought them face-to-face, and enjoined: "Be friends again." The urging from this outer hand (perhaps made stronger by the social difficulty of going against any initiative offered by the powers behind the *Journal*, who had always been on Lincoln's side and published every word he ever wanted them to) was enough to restart the Lincoln and Mary affair. Both kept it a close secret, though for somewhat different reasons. The Edwardses were not to be told, certainly not right away, due to the news going squarely against their advice. Then, too, Mary had a kind of superstitious anxiety about it; she said it was best to keep the courtship from all eyes and ears since "Men and women and the whole world were uncertain and slippery." In this, she seemed well aware of Lincoln traveling that last mile much against his will.

Lincoln had specific hesitations. For while he had long felt he would have to marry, he was also clearly disinclined to choose Mary Todd as his wife. Was that because of the famous "difference in their natures," or was it sharper than that, perhaps a clear hunch that some fundamental philosophic contrast between their values would be a serious source of conflict? Probably it was the latter, but nobody will ever know for sure; sphinx that he was, Lincoln never confided his full thoughts to anyone. What we *do* know from the scrambled facts is that shortly after he had allowed himself to be maneuvered back onto the track of marrying Mary Todd he saw it as a dangerous compromise in which he felt no joy, yet hoped against hope that a "feeling" for it would come. Thus, the urgent last-minute question he posed to Speed (Let. 10): "Are you now in <u>feeling</u> as well as <u>judgment</u> glad you are married as you are?"

The answer he received must have been encouraging, though it went against a mountain of his own forebodings. Not until the very day of the wedding could he bring himself to actually go get the marriage license. And to the last moment he exuded an aura of unwilling gloom far worse than the well-known anxious knees of the ordinary bridegroom. Years later James Matheny recalled how Lincoln had come to him early on the day of his wedding lamenting with alarm, "Jim, I shall have to marry that girl." On the very evening of the marriage Matheny noted, "Lincoln looked and acted as if he was going to the Slaughter," adding that "Lincoln [had] often told him directly & indirectly that he was driven into the marriage."[7] Herndon's simpler statement is more to the point: "Lincoln married her for honor—feeling his honor bound to her."[8]

Unlike Speed, Lincoln had no trouble consummating his marriage ("tops" seldom do); nine months later to the day Robert Todd Lincoln was born. Yet soon after the wedding there was evidence of serious discord in which, for once, Mary comes across as less disturbed than Lincoln. He soon returned to his circuit court travels, his visits home few and far between. It was a pattern that became endemic in his married life. As Herndon observed:

> [Lincoln] spent over half the year following Judges Treat and Davis around on the circuit. On Saturdays the court and attorneys . . . would usually start for their homes. Some went for a fresh supply of clothing, but the greater number went simply to spend a day of rest with their families. The only exception was Lincoln, who usually spent his Sundays with the loungers at the country tavern, and only went home at the end of the circuit or term of court. "At first," said one of his colleagues [Judge Davis], "we wondered at it, but soon learned to account for his strange disinclination to go home. Lincoln himself never had much to say about home, and we

never felt free to comment on it. Most of us had pleasant, inviting homes, and as we struck out for them I'm sure each one of us down in our hearts had a mingled feeling of pity and sympathy for him."[9]

Perfectly true, with the added fillip about feeling sympathy for him, although Mrs. Davis "was a little critical of Lincoln, whom she adored, for staying out on the circuit when Mary was expecting."[10] Actually, the situation was worse than that, for as commonly observed even in Springfield, Lincoln frequently spent entire evenings away from home. While it would be easy to attribute this to qualities of personality in both partners, the simpler fact was that he did not enjoy being at home alone with his wife. It was boring, perhaps exactly the kind of married life situation Oscar Wilde once described as "Three is company, and two is none." How much of this can be attributed to the homosexual component? Hard to say; possibly very little if any of it, since escaping from wives is characteristic of a great variety of husbands.

What may have made Lincoln's marriage specifically depriving for him was his lifelong love of laughter and the festive social surroundings of small groups—not a whit of which Mary seems to have had the slightest feeling for. When young she "now and then indulged in sarcastic, witty remarks that cut,"[11] but with no trace of a gentle light touch anywhere, nor the kindly friendship that small groups thrive on. Who else close to Lincoln for a day—let alone half a lifetime—was so impervious to his wit and good humor? Poor Lincoln, really. "At bedtime, when he would go downstairs to fill a pitcher of water, he would often 'sit down on the steps of the porch and tell stories to whoever happened to be near.' His wife would cough to signal that she wanted him; sometimes he 'kept her coughing until midnight or after.'"[12] Still, as Herndon often said, some of his traits were no bargain either; when he was not in at least a small group he tended to be "abstracted" and refused to fight back even when challenged or under direct attack—all very laudable and sometimes lovable, but a great pain, too.

No doubt he was as unfortunate to have Mary Todd, and to have to live with her as his intuition had so loudly tried to warn him in advance—the whole of it made worse by comparing it with what might have been. Lincoln's colleague Henry C. Whitney wisely observed, "I think he would have been very fond of a wife had he had one to suit."[13] But that was fantasy. The reality was that Mary Todd dominated Lincoln's life in ways most men would have considered extraordinarily punishing. The one bright spot, an island of joy for him, were the children; never was there a more devoted father than Lincoln. Yet the mere tabulation of these separate sides of his life with Mary, let alone weighing them, has itself been a case of scrambled eggs. Sometimes family efforts to sweeten the brew have been far too contrived to be believable, as was her niece Katherine Helm's 1928 effort, *The True Story of Mary, Wife of Lincoln.* Much better, but still with entirely too much cover-up for comfort, was Ruth Painter Randall's 1953 contribution, *Mary Lincoln: Biography of a Marriage.*

Then came a very special article in 1994 by the counterrevisionist Michael Burlingame to "tell all" without fear of the sharp edges, namely his "Honest Abe, Dishonest Mary" (Historical Bulletin No. 50), a major effort to put the basic facts back into the Lincoln and Mary record. Not that even it is anywhere near complete. The Lincoln literature has become almost too massive to be mastered by a single mind or viewpoint. But since Mary Todd's "negatives" were so plentiful and unique, even when she was young and at her best, it seems useful and only fair first to be clear on her good qualities, especially those about which there is no question:

- She was undoubtedly well-intentioned toward Lincoln, especially his political career, which from the first she had always tried to advance and share.

- She loved her children and never did anything to deliberately harm or hurt any of them. And she shared Lincoln's own extreme overindulgence of them.

- Lincoln's biographer David Donald grants her special credit—as many others might—for her hard work in managing a busy household essentially alone, especially in view of her having grown up well-off and well-attended in the easy life of a slave state.[14]

- In searching for Mary's assets another Lincoln scholar, Margaret Leech, noted, "By the standards of the day, [Mary] received a good education, had a smattering of French and could turn a graceful phrase in writing a letter. Her manners were not vulgar [as some Washington matrons claimed], but genteel; the manners of the provinces."[15]

- Mary can be credited, too, with being consistently loyal both to husband and to country. Wartime rumors had it that since she was from the South and had brothers who fought for the Confederacy this, in either spirit or in fact, undermined her loyalty; but that was not true. On the contrary, her attitude toward even her best-loved family turncoats, as they one by one got killed in battle, was that it *served them right*.[16] This fact was not reduced by a certain private, sentimental suffering she felt at their loss. However, to place her loyalty entirely beyond question, she wisely arranged for every letter or package arriving for her during the war years to first be received and examined by White House staff.

- Mary deserves credit for a variety of small kindnesses and generosities. She was quick to send her condolences to friends who had lost loved ones. Better still, she once came to the aid of a sick mother next door, Mrs. Dallman, by nursing her new baby at her own breast.[17] Mary is also credited with visiting Washington hospitals (with and without Lincoln) to deliver flowers, food, and other gifts. Occasionally she helped soldiers write home.[18]

Perhaps she did not seek publicity for her hospital visits; in any case, to invite credit for it in 1862 would later have raised questions about why her visits did not continue as the war dragged on.[19] Newspapers again began to notice she was much out of town, and "shopping." In a way this demonstrates a problem much in evidence: Mary's "good" qualities did not have staying power.

It has been said that some people get better, and others worse, when fortune smiles and answers their prayers. Mary Lincoln was clearly disimproved by the good fortune of gaining what she had long wanted. For years she had looked forward to being the wife of a president, but no sooner had fate brought her this title with Lincoln's election on November 6, 1860, than she began to abuse and misuse it. Right away she insisted on being called "Madame President" or at least "Mrs. President Lincoln"; catching the spirit, the New York *Herald* took to calling her "The Presidentess." Virtually on arrival she began to intrude forceful opinions and suggestions as to who should be chosen not only for patronage jobs but even for some of the cabinet posts.

This might still only have fallen into the "bossy wife" category but for the fact that she bartered her influence for a great variety of financial and other gains—everything from sheer flattery and expensive gifts to outright kickbacks. Lincoln had barely won office—in fact, had not yet left Springfield for Washington—when she accepted expensive diamond jewelry from one Isaac Henderson on condition that she make sure Lincoln appoint him customs collector for New York ports.[20] Mary Lincoln often felt she was entitled to various kickbacks even without special favors rendered by herself, as she casually explained to her seamstress and confidante, Elizabeth Keckley:

> Hundreds of [appointees] are getting immensely rich off the patronage of my husband, and it is but fair that they should help me out of my embarrassment. I will make a demand of them and . . . they cannot refuse to advance whatever money I require.[21]

Kickbacks and embarrassment? Yes, Congress had voted twenty thousand dollars for White House refurbishments to be made over Lincoln's four-year term. But in a desire to flaunt an air of elegance, and to win flattery even from salespeople, Mary spent the entire amount in less than two months, with additional unpaid bills of more than $7,000 (a figure that grew to more than $70,000) at a time when the yearly salary of the governor of Illinois was $1,500.[22]

In an air of ostentation that was entirely out of keeping with the mood and constraints of wartime Washington, Mary Lincoln chose the most expensive furnishings imaginable—wallpaper at more than $7,500 for a single room. (The price included traveling expenses for sending her Philadelphia designer/dealer to Paris to exercise his regal taste in selecting it.) However, in ordinary purchases she became expert at padding household expenditures and presenting vouchers for nonexistent purchases. Not that all of her shenanigans worked. In one case she proposed to a New York merchant that he send a $500 chandelier to the White House, charge $1,000 for it, and extend a $500 credit toward jewelry for herself. This particular dealer refused, losing the sale, but that was unusual.[23] Another time, when ordering $800 worth of china from the Haughwout company "she evidently tried to hide other purchases [of] $1,400 by having the total bill of $2,200 applied to the china alone." When questions were raised by the skeptical secretary it came out that "the overcharge was made to disguise the unspecified items."[24] (The china she actually charged came to $3,195, including a separate set for herself.[25]) In yet another transaction, a bill for $3,000 was late enough among Mary's frauds to require Lincoln's specific approval. He refused on the grounds that the amount was exorbitant. The merchant's retort: "You forget, sir, . . . that I gave Mrs. Lincoln $1,500."[26] By this time Lincoln could not have been overly surprised, but was no doubt shocked at the dealer's considering it so routine as to have merely been "forgotten" by Lincoln. In still another case, silverware for her private quarters in New York was charged on a bill for repairing government plate.[27]

When an unpaid account was too large to pass by routinely, the president yet again had to be informed. Mary pleaded with Benjamin B. French, commissioner of public buildings, to come to her aid. In an effort to help, French informed Lincoln (with no mention of Mary) that a Mr. Carryl had presented a bill in excess of the congressional appropriation, and that he would have to have the president's approval before asking for the money.

Lincoln was furious: "It can never have my approval; I'll pay it out of my own pocket first—It would stink in the nostrils of the American people to have it said that the President of the United States had approved a bill over-running an appropriation of $20,000 for *flub dubs* for this damned old house, when the soldiers cannot have blankets." He asked how Carryl happened to be employed in the first place, and on hearing it was through Mrs. Lincoln said, "Yes, Mrs. Lincoln—well I suppose Mrs. Lincoln must bear the blame; let her bear it, I swear I won't!" Brave words; but in the end, French got the cost of the wallpaper tucked into an appropriation for sundry civil expenses.[28]

Lincoln's secretary John Nicolay was called, and he brought along

Carryl's bill; it read: "Elegant, grand carpet, $2,500." "I should like to know where a carpet worth $2,500 can be put." Major French suggested it was probably in the East Room. "No," said Lincoln, "that cost $10,000, a monstrous extravagance. It was all wrong to spend one cent at such a time; the house was furnished well enough, better than any one we ever lived in." He went on to say he had been overwhelmed with other business, and could not attend to everything.[29]

One wonders what Lincoln would have said and done had he ever realized the extent of Mary's extraordinary dishonesty. Among the least of her offenses, beyond the padding of government bills, was the issuing of fake work orders for special duties and jobs supposedly assigned to members of the household staff—but for which she collected. Even the French cook, Augustus Jullien, unbeknownst to himself, was listed for "work on the grounds," his payment going straight to Mary Lincoln.[30]

Most of her embezzlements were for more significant amounts. As John P. Usher reported, she tried to collect nine hundred dollars for a state dinner given for Prince Napoleon on August 3, and would have but for the fact that Interior Secretary Caleb B. Smith rejected her claim. Suspicious of the whole charge, Smith checked with Secretary of State William Seward, who, by chance, had shortly before also dined with the prince with the same number of guests at a dinner catered by the same restaurant. "For what Mr. Seward had paid $300, Mrs. Lincoln demanded $900." Not to be so easily thwarted by this refusal, "the First Lady then 'made her gardener make out a bill for plants, pots, etc. of the required amount, certified it herself and drew the money.'"[31]

Later, the gardener's account (often used to hide cost overruns) was described by White House gatekeeper James H. Upperman, "who complained to Interior Secretary Smith on October 21, 1861, about 'sundry petit, but flagrant frauds on the public treasury,' being the products of deliberate collusion." A truly staggering number of these frauds of seemingly every size soon turned up, including $700.75 for flowers and $107.50 for manure—plus an extra charge for a horse and cart to haul it. These various amounts stand out not alone for their variety, but for one other peculiarity: Most of the persons, the extra carts and horses, like the "services" they were supposed to have rendered, never existed at all.[32]

At the same time the First Lady railed against what she claimed to be the widespread dishonesty of others who, she insisted, fed their horses on government hay while she herself busily sold cast-off White House furniture, pocketing the money. And not just cast-offs. When she sold a White House rug to a photographer for money to pay a particular bill, the carpet was then replaced at government expense.[33] She allegedly even "appropriated the manure piles which had always been a perquisite of the gardener," taking this cash herself.[34] Later, as if generously, she gave up collecting for the manure on finding it only amounted to ten cents per wagonload.[35]

In a great many of her dealings with people Mary Lincoln was remarkably unpleasant. As people back in Springfield knew, she often "lost all control, picked quarrels, railed at servants and screamed like a fishwife."[36] Repeatedly she re-earned the names she had previously been given by Lincoln's secretaries. John Hay called her "the Hellcat," later complaining that she was getting "more Hellcattical day by day."[37] Nicolay sometimes spoke of "Her Satanic Majesty."[38] In addition to a personal unpleasantness, she indulged in forms of dishonesty both petty and monumental that were almost unimaginable. Twice she asked or arranged for a government employee to be fired on some pretext—with the salary continued, but piped back to her in cash. In one of these instances she established a nonexistent position, White House "steward," involving no duties and which nobody filled, the salary for which went to her.[39]

A curious detail is that all her life Mary had a reputation for being perspicacious, a sharp, good judge of people in general and of politicians in particular. Herndon and others gave her credit for this, as did Lincoln himself in the midst of defending a cabinet member, Salmon Chase, against one of her attacks: "I give you credit for sagacity, but you are disposed to magnify trifles."[40] It is tempting to believe she gained this reputation for correctly judging some individuals simply by being negative toward nearly everybody, and since many if not most public figures ultimately come under attack and lose credibility, Mary's mostly sharp negations later may have seemed correct from the start.

In any case, the irony was—and is—that perhaps nobody else in or near the Lincoln administration proved to be as consistently mistaken as she turned out to be in virtually all her judgments of people, especially those she herself chose to trust and deal with. From ordinary clerks to the high-ranking rakes with whom she shared her confidences, seemingly every fake and fool and four-flusher for miles around came running with their propositions; with few exceptions she chose the worst among them.

It was said at the time, and later repeated by many insiders, that soon after becoming First Lady Mary came under the influence of the White House gardener, John Watt, who taught her how to make money and cover her deficits by padding bills she submitted for household expenditures, and by presenting vouchers for nonexistent purchases. True, Watt had a long shady history extending over several White House administrations, and he may well have shown Mary new ways to fleece the government, but she was hardly new at the art. Back in February 1861, after Lincoln was elected but before he was sworn in (or the Lincolns had yet departed Springfield), she accepted that diamond jewelry from Henderson for demanding via one of her tantrums that Lincoln appoint him customs agent. This trend was much increased once Mary Lincoln became ensconced in the White House; thus, it was hardly surprising that these birds of a feather—Mary Lincoln and John Watt—became as thick as thieves and operated in full support of each other. In fact, their affiliation was to last not only through the exposure of many of Watt's misdeeds, but even survived Lincoln's effort to get rid of him by assigning him overseas to buy seeds for the agricultural division of the patent office.[41] Their relationship finally foundered only when Watt, with three of Mary's letters in hand, tried to blackmail the president for $120,000, and in part, actually succeeded.

Nobody ever found out the exact content of those letters, but Lincoln's biographer Michael Burlingame is probably correct in his surmise: "In those documents the First Lady evidently asked Watt 'to commit forgery and perjury for [the] purpose of defrauding the Government.' "[42] Certainly what she requested from Watt was illegal. And since blackmail itself was a serious offense, Lincoln could easily have seen to it that Watt was banished to prison for years, a threat Simeon Draper soon delivered with force. As Lincoln's secretary John Hay reported:

> Simeon Draper went to Watt in his greenhouse on 14th Street & told him he [had] come to take him to Fort

Lafayette, with much bluster and great oaths as [was] Simeon's wont; . . . Watt fell on his literal marrow bones & begged, & gave up the letters & the conspiracy[,] got demoralized & came down, down, to 1500 dollars which was paid, and the whole thing [was] settled.[43]

Another of Mary Lincoln's less than lovely misjudgments of people was epitomized by one Henry Wikoff. Wikoff's influence and importance were to spread far and wide, not only in the society of Mary's White House, but well into politics in ways that Lincoln himself would soon be forced to deal with. To make marks of this magnitude Wikoff required the practiced audacity of a polished confidence man—his main métier, though he was considerably more convincing to women than to men.

Presidential secretary John Hay very early "deemed" Wikoff an "unclean bird," a "vile creature," a "marked and branded social pariah, a monstrosity abhorred by men and women," and added that it was "an enduring disgrace to American society that it suffers such a thing to be at large."[44] But it was left to a respected news analyst of the day, Henry Villard, to leave in his memoirs the ultimate description of Mary Lincoln and Wikoff:

[S]he allowed herself to be approached and continuously surrounded by a common set of men and women who, through her susceptibility to even the most barefaced flattery, easily gained a controlling influence over her. Among the persons who thus won access to her graces was the so-called "Chevalier" Wikoff . . . who made pretension to the role of a sort of cosmopolitan knight-errant, and had the entree of society, but was, in fact, only a salaried social spy or informer of the New York *Herald*.

Wikoff was of middle age, an accomplished man of the world, a fine linguist, with graceful presence, elegant manners, and a conscious, condescending way—altogether, just such a man as would be looked upon as a superior being by a woman accustomed only to Western society. Wikoff showed the utmost assurance in his appeals to the vanity of the mistress of the White House. I myself heard him compliment her upon her looks and dress in so fulsome a way that she ought to have blushed and banished the impertinent fellow from her presence. She accepted Wikoff as a majordomo in general and in special, as a guide in matters of social etiquette, domestic arrangements, and personal requirements, including her toilette, and as always welcome company for visitors in her salon and on her drives.[45]

The entire facade soon crested to new heights, then came crashing down. A few days before Lincoln was to give his first State of the Union address, portions of his speech appeared in the New York *Herald*! The leak was quickly traced to Wikoff; desperate efforts were then made to hide Mary Lincoln's involvement. John Watt was persuaded to "confess" to having shown Lincoln's papers to Wikoff, but this turned out to have been impossible: Watt was asked how, in the quick look he claimed to have had at them, he was able to provide such a perfectly accurate rendering of the text. He at first tried to claim a marvelous memory for details. And in yet another desperate move the *Herald* tried to protect even Wikoff by claiming that the paper had received no help from anyone, and that its perfect rendition of portions of the text had been due to their own "shrewd surmise" as to what the president would say.[46] When this failed to wash, Wikoff was temporarily jailed, and a congressional committee set up to investigate the whole matter.

Where was Lincoln in all this? Behind the scenes and probably in much anxious discomfort. What is known exactly is that during the investigation Lincoln quietly visited Capitol Hill and "urged the Republicans on the investigating committee to spare him disgrace"[47] This request has the earmarks of having been very embarrassing for Lincoln to make, but it was undoubtedly easy to grant since reports of scandalous events tend to reflect badly on all party members.

When armed with specific information Lincoln often acted quickly and decisively. Early in February 1862, when Secretary of the Interior Caleb Smith on a White House visit showed him written proof of Wikoff's "purposes," Lincoln quickly said, "Give me those papers and sit here till I return." When he got back he "shook Smith's hand, and had Wikoff driven from the mansion that night."[48] What he said to Mary is not recorded, but it was probably an impressive moment of firmness, as similar face-offs had been. Years later, when Herndon interviewed Mary Todd Lincoln, one of her prominent memories of Lincoln was of his being "a terribly firm man when he set his foot down."[49]

In a few other instances as well, Lincoln pulled in the reins and refused to tolerate another moment of folly or foolishness, but these, too, were exceptional circumstances. For the most part his forbearance seemed bottomless, even where Mary's worst features were in full display—a matter for closer analysis later. Remarkable at the moment is why nearly every Lincoln scholar has chosen to either skip entirely, or at least greatly understate, the enormous punishment Mary managed to load onto Lincoln. When the likes of Watt and Wikoff are mentioned at all the tendency has been to keep the focus on *their* character defects and as far away as possible from Mary's considerable implication in their crimes. Even in discussing the "imbroglio" of Mary Lincoln's massive money madness the tendency has been to greatly abbreviate her record, or to imply it was only a laughable feminine flaw, like Imelda Marcos's collection of shoes.

The underlying assumption seems to be that to paint Mary Lincoln in her true colors might allow her black marks to rub off onto Lincoln, to dim his glow in some way. In the eyes of others it is downright unseemly to depict a president—let alone our best president—as being shackled with an embarrassing wife. Even chivalry lives on in the notion that unpleasant truths about Mary should be concealed: the first First Lady ever to be called that.

On the other hand, sheer brevity is one way around the problem. A great many people have a considerable interest in Lincoln without feeling a need to know "every little thing" about him—nor do they necessarily want to be reminded of how many rich dishes are left out of the box lunch they may find tasty enough. It is an audience of some size that many Lincolnists are ready to serve, one problem being how to sharply cut the content without letting the reduction look or seem too painfully obvious. By now an almost standard approach is to use what might be called "the insanity defense." That is, give a few quick instances of Mary Lincoln's bad behavior, perhaps of her extravagance or embezzlements or her brazen meddlings into politics—most any samples will do. From only a few of these it soon becomes apparent that Mary was plainly "insane" or something close to it.

Doubts about her mental state immediately permit a sharp cutback on details. This brevity can look and feel like gentle politeness expressed toward poor Mary, without the slightest indication that serious flaws have just been introduced into both the evidence, and the reader's mind. Certainly much is lost behind this screen of protecting Mary by rendering her portrait through a soft-focus lens that blurs the sharpness of unpleasant edges. The price is that it hides rather than reveals useful facts about the Lincoln marriage—and worst of all, it amounts to counterevidence that invites a dangerous pendulum effect.

This latter peril has become loudly apparent in recent times; notice a certain progression. In 1987 Jean H. Baker (the best and most recent biographer of Mary Todd Lincoln) noted early in her pages, "Today Mary Lincoln ranks among the most detested public women in American history."[50] True enough. Yet only three years later an important Lincoln scholar (John Y. Simon) noted that recent efforts to revamp Mary Lincoln's reputation have resulted in largely reversing yesterday's facts into "an alternate legend of Lincoln's happy marriage"—a trend still escalating. In 1999 David Donald published a sweet little thin book, *Lincoln At Home*—very thin indeed—that tells no outright lies by staying to a few written messages (letters and telegrams) that expose not a single drop of blood on the floor. Then, in 2001, a respected American television series, *American Experience*, ordinarily meticulous with its facts, produced a major six-hour documentary on the Lincolns: *A House Divided*.

The title suggests they started out on the right foot, if they didn't stay there long. The viewer is soon told of the Lincoln's happy marriage and the couple's close togetherness for years as they worked as a loving team toward his political aims. But, alas, when he became president and was taken up with the cares and worries of the Civil War "he had no time for her." This, in addition to the enormous loss of their favorite son, Willie (a genuine tragedy), left her all alone and otherwise "divided" the happy couple.

These and other emotional trappings seem borne out in the documentary by numerous scholars who were invited to comment on Lincoln and his times; as usual, they answered specific questions well before they knew how the producers intended to shape the not-yet-completed documentary. (Often their comments appear to have been "cherry picked" to fit the saga being told.) Conspicuous by his absence was the leading Lincoln scholar on the Lincoln and Mary marriage, Michael Burlingame, who was not invited.[51] The reason is not hard to guess. A comment or two from him could easily have blown the whole ship out of the water.

However, that was the *documentary's* insanity; what about Mary's? It does have a history of its own. In 1875 Mary's one remaining son, her firstborn, Robert T. Lincoln, brought evidence against her sufficient to result in her commitment for several months to an insane asylum in Batavia, Illinois. Some of his father's closest and most levelheaded friends, the lawyer Leonard Swett among them, supported the decision. True, there were a few new and alarming bits of evidence, such as Mary carrying around a sizable portion of the family assets on her person (fifty-six thousand dollars in securities, plus a considerable quantity of cash), sewn into pockets in her petticoats. And then there were her panicky telegrams concerning Robert's own immediate danger of death in Chicago (he was in perfect health). Although her symptoms varied greatly, many of them did sound patently paranoid, if not worse.

Trouble is: She was not insane (or psychotic or schizophrenic) by any formal definition. At least, she would not have been classed as such by any psychologic or psychiatric committee on which this observer ever served. Why not? Mainly because mental health professionals are exceedingly disinclined to label any craziness as psychotic when it "works." As Shakespeare had his Polonius say of some of Hamlet's crazy words: "Though this be madness, yet there is method in't." Likewise, much of Mary's madness was full of method. For one, she proved able to turn her craziness on and off at will. Moreover, she repeatedly came across as "crazy like a fox," able in one ploy after the other to land her lacerations accidentally on purpose with malice aforethought. True, all reasonably accurate portraits of her paint the epitome of a selfish, mean-spirited shrew, a termagant with arms akimbo spewing out hate and the kinds of appalling pain heedlessly inflicted by various psychopathic personalities.

Perhaps this is the place to remember that various outlaw types, from Hitler down to myriad petty criminals, are rightly classed as *"psychopathic personalities"* not because they fail to fathom the suffering of their victims, but because they have no empathy (no sympathy) for them. Like them, Mary Lincoln far from met the insanity requirement of poor reality testing; in fact, she might very well win that prize; Katie bar the door.

Not that distinctions between psychosis and psychopathology were known in the nineteenth century—or, for that matter, that those who ever found themselves caught in the crosshairs of Mary Lincoln's fierce temper would likely be in a mood to hear any sober academic opinion of it. Whether such a victim either chose to "forgive" her in a spirit of turning the other cheek, or to look past the pain for some other hair-shirt reason, it is only a personal choice. Still, it would have been helpful had both victims and onlookers refrained from bearing false witness. It has often been said, for instance, that after exercising her temper Mary was soon sorry for what she said or did to others, including Lincoln. Wrong again. At least in the present study not a single such example has yet been found. On the contrary, Mary Lincoln was prone to keep her tempers going for hours, sometimes days, with no sign of letup short of sheer exhaustion.

In any case, numerous examples of Mary's behavior point to a persistent stress she maintained in and around the marriage. And while Lincoln himself never knew many of the worst of her behaviors, he was continually "kept on edge" by what might happen next. As his close colleague O. H. Browning later reported, "He [Lincoln] several times [confided] he was constantly under great apprehension lest his wife should do something which would bring him into disgrace.[52] It was a worry painfully apparent.

In early drafts of the present chapter something remarkable kept happening. In what were felt to be full versions of the Lincoln and Mary Todd marriage much of the delicate detail needed to understand it kept losing impact in the telling; it was a loss common to other accounts as well. The one place this *does not* happen is in a striking first-person account written long ago by Adam Badeau, aide-de-camp to Gen. Ulysses S. Grant. Perhaps because Badeau's descriptions often depict himself caught with Lincoln in wonderfully up-close tableaus as Mary Lincoln launches her fierce attacks, the result is startling. The special value of Badeau's examples has, of course, been noticed before; quite a number of historians have borrowed words and phrases from him. But for reasons not immediately apparent none of those borrowings (nor the first ones tried here) succeeded. The songbird's melody is largely lost when one hears it only in snips and snatches. Better by far to let Badeau tell his own story of what he saw and felt up close in the last few days of Lincoln's life:

> The first time I saw Mrs. Lincoln was when I accompanied Mrs. Grant to the White House, for her first visit there as wife of the General-in-Chief. The next occasion that I recall was in March [1865], when Mrs. Lincoln, with the President, visited City Point. They went on a steamer, escorted by a naval vessel. . . . They slept and usually took their meals aboard, but sometimes both ascended the hill and were entertained at the mess of General Grant.
>
> On the 26th of March a distinguished party from Washington joined them. . . . It was proposed that an excursion should be made to the front of the Army of the Potomac, about ten or twelve miles off, and Mrs. Lincoln and Mrs. Grant were [part] of the company. A military railroad took the illustrious guests a portion of the way, and then the men were mounted, but Mrs. Grant and Mrs. Lincoln went on in an ambulance, as it was called—a sort of half-open carriage with two seats besides that for the driver. I was detailed to escort them, and of course sat on the front seat facing the ladies, with my back to the horses.
>
> In the course of conversation, I chanced to mention that all the wives of officers at the army front had been ordered to the rear—a sure sign that active operations were in contemplation. I said not a lady had been allowed to remain, except Mrs. Griffin, the wife of General Charles Griffin, who had obtained a special permit from the President. At this Mrs. Lincoln was up in arms, "What do you mean by that, sir?" she exclaimed. "Do you mean to say that she saw the President alone? Do you know that I never allow the President to see any woman alone?" She was absolutely jealous of poor, ugly Abraham Lincoln.
>
> I tried to pacify her and to palliate my remark, but she was fairly boiling over with rage. "That's a very equivocal

smile, sir," she exclaimed: "Let me out of this carriage at once. I will ask the President if he saw that woman alone." Mrs. Griffin, afterward the Countess Esterhazy, was one of the best known and most elegant women in Washington, a Carroll, and a personal acquaintance of Mrs. Grant, who strove to mollify the excited spouse, but all in vain. Mrs. Lincoln again bade me stop the driver, and when I hesitated to obey, she thrust her arms past me to the front of the carriage and held the driver fast. But Mrs. Grant finally prevailed upon her to wait till the whole party alighted, and then General Meade came up to pay his respects to the wife of the President. I had intended to offer Mrs. Lincoln my arm, and endeavor to prevent a scene, but Meade, of course, as my superior, had the right to escort her, and I had no chance to warn him. I saw them go off together, and remained in fear and trembling for what might occur in the presence of the foreign minister and other important strangers. But General Meade was very adroit, and when they returned Mrs. Lincoln looked at me significantly and said: "General Meade is a gentleman, sir. He says it was not the President who gave Mrs. Griffin the permit, but the Secretary of War." Meade was the son of a diplomatist, and had evidently inherited some of his father's skill.

At night, when we were back in camp, Mrs. Grant talked over the matter with me, and said the whole affair was so distressing and mortifying that neither of us must ever mention it; at least, I was to be absolutely silent, and she would disclose it only to the General. But the next day I was released from my pledge, for "worse remained behind."

The same party went in the morning to visit the Army of the James on the north side of the river, commanded by General Ord. The arrangements were somewhat similar to those of the day before. We went up the river in a steamer, and then the men again took horses and Mrs. Lincoln and Mrs. Grant proceeded in an ambulance. I was detailed as before to act as escort, but I asked for a companion in the duty; for after my experience, I did not wish to be the only officer in the carriage. So Colonel Horace Porter was ordered to join the party. Mrs. Ord accompanied her husband; as she was the wife of the commander of an army she was not subject to the order for return; though before that day was over she wished herself in Washington or anywhere else away from the army, I am sure. She was mounted, and as the ambulance was full, she remained on her horse and rode for a while by the side of the President, and thus preceded Mrs. Lincoln.

As soon as Mrs. Lincoln discovered this her rage was beyond all bounds. "What does the woman mean," she exclaimed, "by riding by the side of the President? And ahead of me? Does she suppose that _he_ wants _her_ by the side of _him_?" She was in a frenzy of excitement, and language and action both became more extravagant every moment. Mrs. Grant again endeavored to pacify her, but then Mrs. Lincoln got angry with Mrs. Grant; and all that Porter and I could do was to see that nothing worse than words occurred. We feared she might jump out of the vehicle and shout to the cavalcade. Once she said to Mrs. Grant in her transports: "I suppose you think you'll get to the White House yourself, don't you?" Mrs. Grant was very calm and dignified, and merely replied that she was quite satisfied with her present position; it was far greater than she had ever expected to attain. But Mrs. Lincoln exclaimed, "Oh! You had better take it if you can get it. 'Tis very nice." Then she reverted to Mrs. Ord, while Mrs. Grant defended her friend at the risk of arousing greater vehemence.

When there was a halt, Major Seward, a nephew of the Secretary of State, and an officer of General Ord's staff, rode up, and tried to say something jocular. "The President's horse is very gallant, Mrs. Lincoln," he remarked; "he insists on riding by the side of Mrs. Ord." This of course added fuel to the flame. "What do you mean by that, sir?" she cried. Seward discovered that he had made a huge mistake, and his horse at once developed a peculiarity that compelled him to ride behind, to get out of the way of the storm.

Finally the party arrived at its destination and Mrs. Ord

came up to the ambulance. Then Mrs. Lincoln positively insulted her, called her vile names in the presence of a crowd of officers, and asked what she meant by following up the President. The poor woman burst into tears and inquired what she had done, but Mrs. Lincoln refused to be appeased, and stormed till she was tired. Mrs. Grant still tried to stand by her friend, and everybody was shocked and horrified. But all things come to an end, and after a while we returned to City Point.

That night the President and Mrs. Lincoln entertained General and Mrs. Grant and the General's staff at dinner on the steamer, and before us all Mrs. Lincoln berated General Ord to the President, and urged that he should be removed. He was unfit for his place, she said, to say nothing of his wife. General Grant sat next and defended his officer bravely. Of course General Ord was not removed.

During all this visit similar scenes were occurring. Mrs. Lincoln repeatedly attacked her husband in the presence of officers because of Mrs. Griffin and Mrs. Ord, and I never suffered greater humiliation and pain on account of one not a near personal friend than when I saw the Head of the State, the man who carried all the cares of the nation at such a crisis—subjected to this inexpressible public mortification. He bore it as Christ might have done; with an expression of pain and sadness that cut one to the heart, but with supreme calmness and dignity. He called her "mother," with his old-time plainness; he pleaded with eyes and tones, and endeavored to explain or palliate the offenses of others, till she turned on him like a tigress; and then he walked away, hiding that noble, ugly face that we might not catch the full expression of its misery.

General Sherman was a witness of some of these episodes and mentioned them in his memoirs many years ago. Captain Barnes, of the navy, was a witness and a sufferer too. Barnes had accompanied Mrs. Ord on her unfortunate ride and refused afterward to say that the lady was to blame. Mrs. Lincoln never forgave him. A day or two afterward he went to speak to the President on some official matter when Mrs. Lincoln and several others were present. The President's wife said something to him unusually offensive that all the company could hear. Lincoln was silent, but after a moment he went up to the young officer, and taking him by the arm led him into his own cabin, to show him a map or a paper, he said. He made no remark, Barnes told me, upon what had occurred. He could not rebuke his wife; but he showed his regret, and his regard for the officer, with a touch of what seemed to me the most exquisite breeding imaginable.

Shortly before these occurrences Mrs. Stanton had visited City Point, and I chanced to ask her some questions about the President's wife. "I do not visit Mrs. Lincoln," was the reply. But I thought I must have been mistaken; the wife of the Secretary of War must visit the wife of the President; and I renewed my inquiry. "Understand me, sir?" she repeated; "I do not go to the White House; I do not visit Mrs. Lincoln." I was not at all intimate with Mrs. Stanton, and this remark was so extraordinary that I never forgot it; but I understood it afterward.

Mrs. Lincoln continued her conduct toward Mrs. Grant, who strove to placate her, and then Mrs. Lincoln became more outrageous still. She once rebuked Mrs. Grant for sitting in her presence. "How dare you be seated," she said, "until I invite you." Altogether it was a hateful experience at that tremendous crisis in the nations's history, for all of this was just before the army started on its last campaign.

But the war ended and the President and Mrs. Lincoln had already returned to Washington when General Grant arrived from Appomattox, bringing Mrs. Grant with him. On the 13th of April, Washington was illuminated in honor of the victories, and Mrs. Lincoln invited General Grant to drive about the streets with her and look at the demonstration; but she did not ask Mrs. Grant. The next night, April 14th, was the saddest in American history. Not only General and Mrs. Grant, but the Secretary of War and Mrs. Stanton, were invited to accompany the President and his wife to the theatre. No answer had yet been sent when Mrs. Stanton called on Mrs. Grant to inquire if she meant to be of the party. "For," said Mrs. Stanton, "unless you accept the invitation, I shall refuse. I will not sit without you in the box with Mrs. Lincoln." Mrs. Grant also was tired out with what she had endured, and decided not to go to the play, little dreaming of the terrible experience she was thus escaping. She determined to return that night to Burlington, New Jersey, where her children were at school, and requested the General to accompany her. Accordingly a note of apology was sent to Mrs. Lincoln, and Mrs. Stanton also declined the invitation. These ladies thus may both have saved their husband's lives.[53]

One complaint raised against Adam Badeau's remarkably detailed picture of Mary Lincoln at her worst has been just that—that by being perhaps the worst example of her behavior this very singularity sets it apart, making it atypical, something that ought to be ignored as exceptional. But the facts are otherwise. Every brand of insult and invective Mary Lincoln displayed at City Point came straight out of her regular repertoire. Certainly she invented nothing new for City Point. Yet a serious question remains: Why did Lincoln hold still for so much embarrassment and abuse rather than find a way to demonstrate that he could be "a terribly firm man when he set his foot down?" A very valid question it is—but better to hold it open a few moments longer than to rush in with half-right answers.

In fact, the question becomes all the more curious when one examines nearby events and details. Those embarrassments at City Point occurred on March 26, 27, and 28, the last of them overlapping hugely pressing events such as the arrival of Gen. Sherman; numerous visits to and from Gen. Grant, with Lincoln sometimes accompanying him to the front; a stream of important dispatches between Lincoln and Secretary of War Stanton; and still other urgent matters concerning the last battles of the war and Lee's surrender at Appomattox. The last mention of Mary at City Point was that she sailed back to Washington on April 1, leaving Tad with his father, and by chance meeting on the boat back an old friend from Springfield, Congressman Carl Schurz. On his arrival the next day Schurz wrote his wife how kind Mrs. Lincoln was to offer him a ride in her carriage, during which "I learned more state secrets in a few hours than I could otherwise in a year"—evidence enough of her returning to politeness and her penchant for cashing in on her insider status.[54]

More revealing were the immediate exchanges between Mary and Lincoln. On arriving back in Washington the morning of April 2, Mary sent Lincoln a short wire:

> Arrived here safely this morning, found all well—Miss, Taddie & yourself very much—perhaps, may return with a little party on Wednesday—Give me all the news.
>
> Mary Lincoln[55]

Later that same April 2, Lincoln responded:

> At 4:30 p.m. to-day General Grant telegraphs that he has Petersburg completely enveloped from river below to river above, and has captured, since he started last Wednesday, about 12,000 prisoners and 50 guns. He suggests that I shall go out and see him in the morning, which I think I will do. Tad and I are both well, and will be glad to see you and your party here at the time you name.
>
> A. Lincoln[56]

Still later that day, April 2 (7:45 P.M.) Lincoln wired:

> Last night Gen. Grant telegraphed that Sheridan with his Cavalry and the 5th. Corps had captured three brigades of Infantry, a train of wagons, and several batteries, prisoners amounting to several thousands. This morning Gen. Grant, having ordered an attack along the whole line telegraphs as follows:
>
> "Both Wright and Parke got through the enemies lines. The battle now rages furiously. Sheridan with his Cavalry, the 5th. Corps & Miles Division of the 2nd. Corps, which was sent to him since 1. this A.M. is now sweeping down from the West. All now looks highly favorable. Ord is engaged, but I have not yet heard the result in his front."

Robert yesterday wrote a little cheerful note to Capt. Penrose, which is all I have heard of him since you left. Copy to Secretary of War

A. Lincoln[57]

These two telegrams from Lincoln gave Mary "all the news" he had at the moment, the nuts and bolts of warfare, particulars that were of little interest to her then, or ever. As far as is known she neither commented on any of it, nor asked for more—nor, apparently, did Lincoln ever offer any more. The double question is: Why did she say "Give me all the news" in the first place; and why did he so quickly do just that? One can never know for sure, but the whole situation very much suggests that after days of Mary's outrageous social behavior, they both welcomed a chance to focus on tangible details as a way of returning to normalcy.

But what exactly was normalcy for the Lincoln marriage? In the White House as Mary's seamstress Elizabeth Keckley well described it, it might be a stream of time—hours or days—in which routine matters might fill the calendar with no dramatics to disturb the peace, although behind the scenes, peace and quietude were seldom felt. For while there were periods of no crisis, Mary's meddlesome and intrusive qualities were pervasive enough to maintain a tone of strain in the domestic atmosphere. True, as she would launch into one of her character assassinations of, say, his favorite general or a respected colleague in his cabinet, Lincoln might try to make light of her acid tongue, as if it hardly mattered. Thus, near the end of one of Mary's long harangues in which she several times bared her teeth at Grant, she added, "General Grant, I repeat, is an obstinate fool and a butcher." Lincoln replied mildly: "Well, mother, supposing that we give you command of the army. No doubt you would do much better than any general that has been tried." Elizabeth Keckley described Lincoln as having "a twinkle in the eyes, and a ring of irony in the voice"—a pleasant enough light touch that might even be convincing if it stood alone. But, alas, it was far from alone. The whole scene was typical of the more or less constant hectoring carried on by Mary— exactly the opposite of the quiet, supportive tranquillity a tired and overworked president so needed.[58]

Viewed from this angle Mary Lincoln fully lived up to her well-deserved reputation as an unremitting termagant, a shrew bent on forcing herself forward in intolerable ways—and yet in the eyes of modern psychotherapy she turns out to be nearly as much a victim as a villain. To see this clearly one needs to run a certain thought experiment. Suppose Lincoln and Mary had married other partners rather than each other; it is clear that neither would have ended up with the particular problems they had together. Why not? Simply because none of matchings or the "locks" would have been the same. Mary was able to build her intrusiveness to the sky in ways that allowed it to fit and lock into Lincoln's lifelong "passive" streak. Had Mary married someone else she would no doubt have tested the limits with him, as was her nature, albeit with next to no chance of finding the large leeway Lincoln accorded her. Likewise it is inconceivable that any other wife Lincoln could possibly have had would have turned out to be quite that aggressive—and such a fool.

This interlocking cooperative mismatch is by itself enough to rank the Lincoln and Mary Todd match as one of the worst marital misfortunes in recorded history. Even Mary's overly lenient biographer, Jean Baker, hovering as she did at the very edge of radical women's liberation, compared Lincoln in his marriage to Socrates' travails with Xanthippe. Why so few complaints from Lincoln? Mainly because there was exactly one aspect of his marriage that Lincoln adored beyond all measure: the utter infatuation he had for his children, as he watched and coddled them and catered to their every whim, spoiling them beyond all reason. One can well feel both Herndon's horror and Lincoln's love when he brought them to the office:

> If they pulled down all the books from the shelves, bent the points of all the pens, overturned inkstands, scattered law-papers over the floor, or threw the pencils into the spittoon, it never disturbed the serenity of their father's good-nature. . . . Had they shit in Lincoln's hat and rubbed it on his boots, he would have laughed and thought it smart. . . . Frequently absorbed in thought, he never observed their mischievous and destructive pranks . . . and, even if brought to his attention, he virtually encouraged their repetition by declining to show any substantial evidence of parental disapproval.[59]

But for the most part there was nothing amusing or lighthearted in what Lincoln had to contend with in his marriage; he was on edge a good deal of the time, and rightly so, since major social embarrassments—the "disgrace" he worried about to Browning—often did occur. And yet there was a veritable stream of smaller pains and mortifications that probably cost him more. He never felt free, for instance, to invite a visiting friend for dinner. When Billy Greene—let alone uneducated cousins such as Dennis Hanks or others who peopled his past—would stop by to say "hello" or renew their acquaintance, he could never so much as introduce them to Mary, much less have them to lunch or dinner. She was too elegant and high-toned to lower her standards for the likes of his coarse friends and relatives. Thus, Lincoln never felt free to invite his dearly beloved stepmother to the White House for so much as a single day (she probably would not have come anyway); her speech and social manners were enough to rule her out.

Even particular friends of Lincoln who could not be looked down upon were rejected for being more his friends than hers. An early law partner, John T. Stuart, said "he had been at L's house a hundred times [and] never was asked to dinner." And Judge David Davis, too, complained "that [as] often as he had been in Springfield, Lincoln had never entertained him, nor, so far as he could learn, any other visiting lawyer at his home." From this Davis rightly concluded not only that "Lincoln was not happy domestically" but correctly saw it as in line with Lincoln's habit long before on the circuit of making up excuses not to go home on weekends. "The next Monday, when the other lawyers returned, they would invariably find Lincoln still there anxiously awaiting their reappearance."[60] Thus, Lincoln's lack of liberty in his own home had deep and distant roots.

When one suddenly realizes the *range* of Lincoln's personal problem—that is, his difficulty in feeling free and comfortable at home, extending from the very earliest days of his marriage right on up through daily life in the White House—the magnitude of his marital mismatch becomes all too starkly apparent. It was his cross to bear.

Perhaps because Lincoln was so uncomplaining about Mary and his marriage casual observers and even a few historians have found it easy to claim—even act as if they really believe—Lincoln had a smoother domestic life than he ever did. Hardest to hide in this false stance are numerous small but screamingly loud reflections of serious turmoil underneath. Once at the White House when Mary's sister, Elizabeth Edwards, came to stay awhile, and it neared the time for her to depart, with tears in his eyes Lincoln pleaded in desperation for her to extend her visit: "do Stay with me—you have such a power & control, Such an influence over Mary—Come, do Stay and Console me."[61] Possibly due to duties back home Elizabeth felt she could not stay—a choice that quickly led to a torrent of consequences that alienated the sisters for years and removed Elizabeth still further from helping Lincoln. As she later summed it up:

> Mary Lincoln has had much to bear, though she don't bear it well: she has acted foolishly—unwisely and made the world hate her: She opened a private letter of mine after I left Washington because in that letter my Daughter gave me her opinion of Mrs. L. She became Enraged at me. I tried to Explain—She would Send back my letters with insulting remarks.[62]

This rift lasted for years, though not quite permanently. Eighteen years later Mary moved back into her original room at the home of Elizabeth and Ninian Edwards for the last months of her life. As the Lincoln scholar Margaret Leech once put it, "Greed and jealousy and rage leave their marks on the face of a woman of forty-three"; at the age of sixty-three she was *much* the worse for wear, and as with Dorian Gray's picture in the attic, it was all plainly there in her face.

NINE

Lincoln, Sex, and Religion

Lincoln's honesty was such that he was never known to have lied or misrepresented himself about anything, yet even this is an understatement. As his kindly old stepmother Sarah Bush Lincoln put it, besides never telling lies even as a child, Abe "never evaded—never equivocated—never dodged nor turned a corner to avoid any chastisement or other responsibility."[1] These traits were apparent from boyhood and right on up through his presidency. Still, with regard to religion, some of his statements and actions seem so self-contradictory—so not of one piece with each other—as to stir sharp arguments to this day among Lincolnists and other historians over just what he did believe.

A few observers attribute at least part of this contrast to a "change of heart" Lincoln had during the course of the war—perhaps something of a religious conversion—from the shock of seeing the enormous suffering and bloodshed on both sides, as well as his longing to find some purpose a Providence might have in the war. While this argument has its strong points—especially the part about seeking purpose in a Providence—powerful evidence stands against any increase in Lincoln's religiousness. Numerous of Lincoln's close associates saw no change in this aspect of him, including Leonard Swett, Orville Browning, and Jesse Fell, along with his secretaries and later biographers, John Hay and John Nicolay. Worth remembering too is that, as a young man, Lincoln thought deeply about—and then embraced—quite a number of decidedly antireligious arguments that he eventually wrote in his little "infidel" book, which his friend Samuel Hill threw into a fire to save Lincoln's career. In this, as well as in conversations that startled some of his friends, Lincoln "denied the miraculous conception of Christ, ridiculed the Trinity, and denied that the Bible was the divine special revelation of God"—a position that managed in a single stroke to disenfranchise Christ's miracles as well.[2] Although Lincoln's book did not survive, the memory of its ideas did, largely because he freely discussed them with his friends at the time. As his later law partner John T. Stuart remembered, "Lincoln went further against Christian belief—& doctrines & principles than any man I ever heard; he shocked me."[3]

However, Lincoln held these positions not as an antireligious stance, but as something close to the opposite: his effort to discover and work out the logic and fairness of a Supreme Being he was trying to envision for himself. Early on, he had pointed out to Herndon that it made no sense to believe in Hell and "eternal punishment" for trivial sins, or for any sins. As Herndon put it:

> [Lincoln] could never bring himself to believe in eternal punishment; that men lived but a little while here; and that if eternal punishment were man's doom, he should spend that little life in vigilant and ceaseless preparation by never-ending prayer.[4]

And speaking of prayer, the Lincoln White House saw very little of it. Not only did family insiders, Julia Taft Bayne among them,[5] notice and mention this, but close colleagues did as well. Orville Browning and his wife were at the White House during a particularly stressful period—late February 1862—from the very day that Lincoln's favorite son, Willie, died. The Brownings remained about a week, consoling the stricken Lincolns. As the days passed Browning sat up with Lincoln late into the night keeping a bedside vigil over Tad, also gravely ill. It was an excruciating time, with intense worry about the possibility of losing Tad as well.

Through an accident of history Browning left a record of his own thoughts and the prevailing atmosphere that week. In a reply to questions from Isaac N. Arnold (soon to publish an early Lincoln biography) Browning filled in the whole picture:

He [Lincoln] held a pew in the Presbyterian Church, of which Rev Dr Gurley was pastor, and often attended service there. He not infrequently sent his carriage, of Sunday mornings with a request that I would accompany him and Mrs Lincoln to church. Sometimes, after services were over, I would return with them to the White House to dinner, and spend the afternoon with him in the library. On such occasions I have seen him reading the bible but never knew of his engaging in any other act of devotion. He did not invoke a blessing at table, nor did he have family prayers. . . .

At the time of his little son Willie's death, Mrs Browning and I were out of the city, but returned to Washington on the evening of the same day of his death. The President and Mrs Lincoln sent their carriage for us immediately upon learning that we were in the city, and we went to the White House, and remained with them about a week. His son Tad was also very ill at the time, and I watched with him several consecutive nights. The President was in the room with me a portion of each night.

He was in very deep distress at the loss of Willie, and agitated with apprehensions of a fatal termination of Tad's illness; but what his religious views and feelings were I do not know. I heard no expression of them. My impression is that, during the time I remained at the White House on this occasion, he had several interviews with the Rev. Dr Gurley but what occurred between them never came to my knowledge.[6]

This firsthand account from so reliable a Lincoln observer as Orville Browning is perhaps enough by itself to establish the great distance that both the Lincolns felt from formal religion; certainly neither placed any reliance on a never mentioned Almighty. Nor did Mary's seamstress and close confidante, Elizabeth Keckley, in her long and intimate *Behind The Scenes* account of life at the White House ever mention any prayers or praying for help from Heaven, not even for Willie.[7] This was certainly not for any lack of feeling. At Willie's death Mary appears to have been virtually "out of it"—in a state of total shock. But Lincoln sustained the full brunt of his "deep distress" as he watched Willie die slowly and felt the attendant strains of both Tad and Mary. Surely it speaks volumes that he faced his anguish without, so far as we know, ever turning to prayer or in any sense pleading with the fates or with God to intercede in these dire events. True, in other ways Lincoln clearly did demonstrate his own brand of reverence—what Mary described to Herndon as "a kind of poetry in his nature."[8] It was something others, too, could easily see and appreciate, something at once both highly original and poles apart from the stereotypes of religion.

In fact, it was considerably more original than that. As the Lincoln scholar Allen Guelzo has shown, Lincoln had a way in the plainness of his language of soaring to magnificent heights, as in his first inaugural, where one hears of "[t]he mystic chords of memory stretching . . . all over this broad land" like some celestial harp. Even then, Guelzo nicely notes, "the better angels of our nature" are clearly the messengers of *our* nature, not of God's.[9]

However firmly this latter Lincoln language bestows its magic onto man rather than tracing it to some supernatural source, in other ways, too, the soft generality of it largely understates the depth of Lincoln's religious doubt. Or to say it differently, nothing one finds in Lincoln's speeches quite equals or denies the sharp edge of doubt he displayed with special clarity in his early infidel days. Back in New Salem Parthena Hill asked Lincoln, "Do you really believe there isn't any future state?" He replied, "I'm afraid there isn't [though] it isn't a pleasant thing to think that when we die that is the last of us."[10] This, while squarely direct, was at least still polite. At other times, Lincoln could be both candid and surprisingly blunt in his disbelief. In 1840, when a colleague in the legislature made a motion to adjourn from Christmas Eve, December 24, a Thursday, until the following Monday, Lincoln not only voted against it, he said something to the effect that since the legislators were being paid for those days, including Christmas Day, they ought to come in and do their work.[11] Of course his argument went over like a lead balloon and he lost the vote, but his point came through sharp and clear to his colleagues at the time, and now to us as well.

There were earlier indications of Lincoln's loud independence of mind, a nonreligious, downright irreverent bent; but where in the world could this have come from? At first glance it seems particularly surprising to find any brand of social protest in a backwoods Bible-

C. M. DERICKSON, SON OF CAPTAIN DAVID DERICKSON

Picture History

LINCOLN IN 1846

Library of Congress

RUTLEDGE TOMBSTONE

Library of Congress

MARY OWENS

Courtesy of Illinois State Historical Library

ELMER ELLSWORTH

Picture History

JOSHUA FRY SPEED

The Filson Historical Society, Louisville, Kentucky

JOSHUA AND FANNY SPEED

The Filson Historical Society, Louisville, Kentucky

MARY LINCOLN

Library of Congress

reading boy. On the contrary, Lincoln was always notably smooth with people, greatly disliked discord, and was all his life a peace-maker, a smoother-outer of conflict wherever possible. True, he had that "infidel" streak in which he held opinions far off the beaten track, but even in this he took no pleasure in picking fights or con-tradicting others. This much might well have been expected from his gentle and modest nature; but the pressing question at the moment is, Where and how did Lincoln find the freedom, and indeed the daring, to so firmly step away from convention and follow his own lights?

It is tempting to see both these trends—his quick, free step-back from conventionality, along with his bold self-reliance in forming his own opinions on matters of God and religion—as merely fresh ex-amples of Lincoln the autodidact. But careful here. Strange as it may seem, both "autodidactness" and its blood brother, great indepen-dence in matters of morals, are issues on which sex research offers specific and highly definitive pointers from its own pool of observa-tions. At least it offers grounds for believing that an independent morality system is one well-known effect of early puberty, as was partly shown before (Chapter 2). A Kinsey observation is worth re-peating and bearing in mind:

> [T]he boy who becomes adolescent at 10 or 11 has not had as many years to build up inhibitions against sexual activity as the boy who does not mature until 15 or later; . . . the younger boy plunges into sexual activity with less restraint and with more enthusiasm than the boy who starts at a later date.[12]

Such a boy is able to "plunge in," by the way, due to an interesting side fact: early puberty males easily tend to discover masturbation on their own, as opposed to late maturers who, perhaps feeling less ur-gency, more often wait until they hear of it, or are shown how by other boys. To discover for oneself the intense pleasure of full or-gasm when very young is by itself an impressive surprise; and for the experience to predate the standard warnings can be definitive indeed. True, a fraction of early-puberty males start out fully enjoying what-ever they have discovered in sex only to become inhibited or neurotic about it after later learning that society has strict rules against such things. Yet the great majority of early-maturing boys not only remain unconflicted by their own rule-breaking, but seem to like it all the more for that very fact (as Lincoln apparently did), and thus are virtually vaccinated from the outset against being victimized by the standard fears and warnings about sex they may later hear. In a sense, such a boy is doubly blessed, both by his early discovery of an easy, joyful pleasure and by a lowered likelihood of being twisted out of shape by false fears. Most certainly he knows that masturbation will not make him go blind or crazy, or give him facial pimples, or shorten his sex life, or make his penis drop off; nor will it ruin him for marriage, mangle his mind with moral mishaps, or otherwise threaten him.

Lincoln seems an especially good example. For while he later took on a heavy load of moral and ethical concerns, he never let these interfere with—or even slow up—his fascination with sex. Thus, he developed and retained his lifelong love of sex jokes, including all those "funniest ones" that Whitney lamented never got embalmed in type. Nor is there the slightest indication that his fascination with sex was limited merely to verbal or fantasy forms; Lincoln carried a fresh and nimble uninhibited quality over into most of his homosexual experiences that we know anything about.[13] Conversely, Lincoln left no reliable evidence of any overt heterosexual experience he may have had other than in his marriage. But given Lincoln's quick readiness to try things out when he was young, he may well have had at least a touch of early heterosexual experience.

However, more important by far than anything Lincoln's religion ever did to his sex life was the reverse—namely, the impact his sexual discoveries had on his religion. It is known he read the Bible from early times (though as his kindly stepmother put it, "less than is said"). And while the Bible is replete with a wide variety of antisexual statements both implied and specific, one cannot know how many of these young Lincoln understood, or even recognized as being sexual taboos. Probably at a time well after he began enjoying masturbation he became aware of both the "Fall of Man" in the Garden of Eden—including the "shame" of nudity and other "sex is bad" messages preachers so like to deliver—and soon after that, the sin of Onan with its dire warnings against "spilling the seed." But since Lincoln had already arrived on his own at the powerful pleasures of orgasm, loved it, and found that the sky did not fall, one can be sure that like most precocious youngsters he was in no mood to give it all up for bookish or Bible reasons. In any case, some combination of his coming to realize the full antisexual tilt of most religious doctrine along with his thinking it over in the light of his own enjoyments appear to have all worked in the same direction. Together it was as if they wound his pendulum for those forceful counterblows he landed in his Infidel book and readily discussed at the time. These were charges that for him disenfranchised much of the Bible as the word of God, along with the divinity of Jesus, the magic of the miracles, and much else that stirred his deepest doubts.

On the other hand, later as president he was known to read the Bible (rather more than before) and would not infrequently quote words and phrases from it.[14] Both these images—his Bible reading and borrowings from it—caused a few casual observers to believe he had become a convert, or at least that he came to lean more than he ever had before toward conventional beliefs. Far from it. Consistently through life—ever since those impressive events of early puberty—Lincoln was greatly disinclined toward prayers or praying or preachers; least of all was he ever prone to believe in, or to petition help from, any personal God. One remembers again that if Willie's slow and painful death could solicit no appeals from a desperately anguished Lincoln to some heavenly father for help, *nothing* could—or ever did.

During the war numerous occasions arose when it was felt appropriate for Lincoln to issue various formal orders for a "Day of Thanksgiving" (including his 1863 proclamation of our present "Thanksgiving Day," the last Thursday of November). The very word suggests a prayerlike thanking of God for a bounty of benefits. For Lincoln, however, this ground against his grain for several reasons. First, it was squarely out of kilter with his disbelief in a personal God. And it sharply contradicted his Calvinist-like belief in a brand of fatalism that could not be bought off or changed in any way by even the most heartfelt wishes and prayers, least of all by placations of fate or mere gratitudes of thanksgiving. His solution to this dilemma was to quickly agree to sign nearly every proposed proclamation for any Day of Thanksgiving after having carefully arranged for others, usually Secretary of State Seward (well known for his lordly language), to supply the needed words—especially any and all rhetoric of reverence and homage to the Almighty.

By the time he became president Lincoln had long since given up discussing his religious beliefs with even his closest friends and colleagues. (Some, such as Judge Davis, later insisted that nobody could possibly know what Lincoln's religious beliefs were, since he "never spoke of them.") Yet something of his cool standoffishness toward conventional religion glared out from between the lines. It was clear that his guiding light was not the usually envisioned God. Particularly conspicuous by its absence was any notion of a personal savior. Consequently, not in the entire *Collected Works*, including the *Supplements*, does Lincoln so much as mention Jesus. With such diffidence all too evident Lincoln ran the risk of frustrating sizable segments of his religiously devout admirers who repeatedly made known their complaints. Church leaders in particular were quick to suggest that Lincoln might improve himself and/or his administration in the eyes of God by citing this or that expression of the divine will. In fact, hardly a preacher he came across—and there were many—failed to offer him gleanings from God. These, in turn, stirred Lincoln to some of his most amusing rejoinders. During one of the almost daily visits he had from delegations of clergymen who brought him urgent pointers Lincoln replied, "I hope it will not be irreverent for me to say that if it is probable that God would reveal his will to others, on a point so connected with my duty, it might be supposed he would reveal it directly to me."[15]

Less amusing by far were the beliefs that Lincoln himself firmly held. These included, as Herndon often noted, Lincoln's fatalism, his conviction that conditions make the man and not man the conditions. Events result, cold as it may seem, from cause and effect, yet providence and predestination still steer the course, wherever it may lead. Holding these positions often led Lincoln to ponder and reponder the wisdom of Hamlet's "There's a Divinity that shapes our ends, / Rough-hew them as we will"—and how much he agreed with it. From this alone it is perhaps clear how Lincoln's philosophy helped keep him at arm's length from both the illusion—and the self-delusion—of trying to change fate by praying for heavenly intervention.

A near contradiction to the fatalism and predestination of Lincoln's philosophy were his own huge efforts; he worked himself to constant exhaustion in a vastly demanding presidency. If he had ever been challenged on the core discrepancy—Why work so hard if the outcome has already been preordained?—he would no doubt have answered that his own efforts were merely part of the picture, that they too had been predestined, and consequently were but one more cog in the wheels of some giant machine of fate that grinds out every event in history, good or bad. Hard to catch him at that.

Moreover, Lincoln was a past master at walking both sides of any street. He could picture himself as a helpless feather in the breeze, straight-facedly professing to a journalist, "I claim not to have controlled events, but confess plainly that events have controlled me."[16] This, while at the same time conducting one of the most hands-on, exceedingly demanding presidencies anyone could imagine. He was adroit at both cutting through red tape and anticipating and avoiding great hazards ahead. It amounted to masterminding myriad details of some hugely complicated game in which, as Leonard Swett once observed, he busily "handled and moved men remotely as we do pieces upon a chess-board"; more on that later.

In his public expressions Lincoln always came across as entirely honest, as indeed he was. Yet perhaps because of his simple and straightforward words neither of two dangerous cats ever got out of the bag, escaped into full view. He virtually never put on display the very great complexity of his mind and his methods, which consequently were understood by few. Nor were casual observers ever fully aware of the huge gulf that lay between Lincoln's cool, complicated philosophy and their own. Since this latter contrast contains several more surprises, one of which developed only late in his life, the transition is worth examining. First, a look at the remarkable stability of Lincoln's tone. In a note scribbled out to himself in 1862 he noted what later came to be called his *Meditation on the Divine Will*:

The will of God prevails. In great contests each party claims to act in accordance with the will of God. Both *may* be, and one *must* be wrong. God can not be *for*, and *against* the same thing at the same time. In the present civil war it is quite possible that God's purpose is something different from the purpose of either party—and yet the human instrumentalities, working just as they do, are of the best adaptation to effect His purpose. I am almost ready to say this is probably true— that God wills this contest, and wills that it shall not end yet. By his mere quiet power, on the minds of the now contestants, He could have either *saved* or *destroyed* the Union without a human contest. Yet the contest began. And having begun He could give the final victory to either side any day. Yet the contest proceeds.[17]

Less than three years later these ideas along with startling new ones concerning slavery and the motives of God were woven by Lincoln into his second Inaugural Address:

[Fellow Countrymen:] At this second appearing to take the oath of the presidential office, there is less occasion for an extended address than there was at the first. Then a statement, somewhat in detail, of a course to be pursued, seemed fitting and proper. Now, at the expiration of four years, during which public declarations have been constantly called forth on every point and phase of the great contest which still absorbs the attention, and engrosses the enerergies [sic] of the nation, little that is new could be presented. The progress of our arms, upon which all else chiefly depends, is as well known to the public as to myself; and it is, I trust, reasonably satisfactory and encouraging to all. With high hope for the future, no prediction in regard to it is ventured.

On the occasion corresponding to this four years ago, all thoughts were anxiously directed to an impending civil-war. All dreaded it—all sought to avert it. While the inaugural address was being delivered from this place, devoted altogether to *saving* the Union without war, insurgent agents were in the city seeking to *destroy* it without war—seeking to dissolve the Union, and divide effects, by negotiation. Both parties deprecated war; but one of them would *make* war rather than let the nation survive; and the other would *accept* war rather than let it perish. And the war came.

One eighth of the whole population were colored slaves, not distributed generally over the Union, but localized in the Southern part of it. These slaves constituted a peculiar and powerful interest. All knew that this interest was, somehow, the cause of the war. To strengthen, perpetuate, and extend this interest was the object for which the insurgents would rend the Union, even by war; while the government claimed no right to do more than to restrict the territorial enlargement of it. Neither party expected for the war, the magnitude, or the duration, which it has already attained. Neither anticipated that the *cause* of the conflict might cease with, or even before, the conflict itself should cease. Each looked for an easier triumph, and a result less fundamental and astounding. Both read the same Bible, and pray to the same God; and each invokes His aid against the other. It may seem strange that any men should dare to ask a just God's assistance in wringing their bread from the sweat of other men's faces; but let us judge not that we be not judged. The prayers of both could not be answered; that of neither has been answered fully. The Almighty has His own purposes. "Woe unto the world because of offences! for it must needs be that offences come; but woe to that man by whom the offence cometh!" If we shall suppose that American Slavery is one of those offenses which, in the providence of God, must needs come, but which, having continued through His appointed time, He now wills to remove, and that He gives to both North and South, this terrible war, as the woe due to those by whom the offence came, shall we discern therein any departure from those divine attributes which the believers in a Living God always ascribe to Him? Fondly do we hope—fervently do we pray—that this mighty scourge of war may speedily pass away. Yet, if God wills that it continue, until all the wealth piled by the bond-man's two hundred and fifty years of unrequited toil shall be sunk, and until every drop of blood drawn with the lash, shall be paid by another drawn with the sword, as was said three thousand years ago, so still it must be said "the judgments of the Lord, are true and righteous altogether." [Psalms 19:9]

    With malice toward none; with charity for all; with firmness in the right, as God gives us to see the right, let us strive on to finish the work we are in; to bind up the nation's wounds; to care for him who shall have borne the battle, and for his widow, and his orphan—to do all which may achieve and cherish a just, and a lasting peace, among ourselves, and with all nations.

How kindly and good-hearted the last paragraph genuinely is. Several earlier comments, however, rest on questionable logic that requires examination, particularly since most Lincoln scholars shy away from it. Lincoln was no doubt well aware of making several kinds of word compromises for the sake of clarity and public understanding. However, some of what he said to help his audience (and himself) deal with the war was entirely new and far more serious. First, the simple part. After pointing out that both North and South pray to the same God, as the Lincoln scholar David Donald has well summarized the situation:

> Lincoln then sought, both for himself and for the American people, an explanation of why the war was so protracted. His answer showed no trace of any late-at-night anguish over his own responsibility for the conflict. If there was guilt, the burden had been shifted from his shoulders to those of a Higher Power. The war continued because "the Almighty has His own purposes," which are different from men's purposes. This, Lincoln said later, was "a truth which I thought needed to be told," because to deny it was "to deny that there is a God governing the world."[18]
>
>   He might have put his argument in terms of the doctrine of necessity [fatalism], in which he had long believed; but that was not a dogma accepted by most Americans. In an earlier private meditation he had concluded that it was "probably true—that God wills this contest, and wills that it shall not end," thinking it "quite possible that God's purpose is something different from the purpose of either party" to the

conflict. But that was too gnostic a doctrine to gain general credence. Addressing a devout, Bible-reading public, Lincoln knew he would be understood when he invoked the familiar doctrine of exact retribution, the belief that the punishment for a violation of God's law would equal the offense itself.[19]

This is perhaps as insightful a summary of the second Inaugural Address as could be made. It is also notable for its peacemaking—in that it smoothly bypasses several sharp differences between Lincoln's thinking and that of his listeners, while at the same time gliding past a few potent land mines having to do with religion and the war without setting off any of them. Yes, quite as Donald said, in Lincoln's *Meditation* almost three years earlier, he had said to himself that God has his own (unknown) purposes, that He "wills this contest, and wills that it shall not end yet." Back then Lincoln had noted that God could easily have ended the war—"or He could have either *saved* or *destroyed* the Union without a human contest." If God had any complaints Lincoln made no mention of them in his mild 1862 *Meditation*. At that time one heard not a word of any guilt over slavery, let alone any "exact retribution" for the heavy sin of it. Yet the second Inaugural Address fairly bristles with guilt and recompense. From the first buzz of this one can hear the freight train coming loud and clear—the punishment of man, big time. But what in the world could have made such a change in Lincoln's mind and outlook—including his greatly altered new picture of God—from the mildness of His image in 1862 to this angry Almighty less than three year later in the second Inaugural Address?

None of the toughness is this Inaugural Address is at all Lincoln-like in character. Moreover, it is extremely low-level stuff: a fiendish story of a wrathful God straight out of that old-time religion, if not worse. True, Lincoln begins his fantasy verdict with a Bible phrase ("Woe unto the world because of offences . . ."), and softens it with a tentative, downright iffy beginning—"If we shall suppose that American Slavery is one of those offenses which [God intends to punish . . .]." Yet even from this maybe/might starting position that fierce God is promptly conjured up, complete with ringing retribution and righteous retaliation: "until every drop of blood drawn with the lash, shall be paid by another drawn with the sword."

It amounts to a masochistic exercise of sorts—a bathing in tragedy that the human spirit is heir to when long subjected to the blockage of inescapable pain and frustration—a brand of blockage that is the very mother of masochism. Although the point cannot be proved it is highly probable that the more or less constant blocks, hindrances, and extreme frustrations that Lincoln sustained through the war years increased his vulnerability toward more than mildly masochistic indulgences of this sort. Certainly his front-row-center seat for this bloodiest of wars was unspeakably hard for him to bear. As Lincoln himself put it, "If there is a worse place than Hell, I am in it." No doubt his pain was made still worse, if that was possible, by the knowledge that every decision he made, made him partly responsible for its outcome, replete as it always was with tragedy, even in victory. If Lincoln at his inaugural had had enough like-minded souls in his audience who, from their own sufferings, were ready to bask in the sacrifice he cited—ready to "enjoy" the sadness of it—he would have had more support than he found.

But who in his audience believed or felt enough of any such thing to find it reasonable and satisfying? Next to nobody. The public, primed at this inaugural moment to celebrate an all but consummated victory was certainly in no mood to eat crow and bathe in self-blame for sins they rightly saw as mainly the South's. Lincoln may have thought his Bible-reading public was ripe for receiving the image of a fierce and angry God venting his venom against both sides for four long years, and in the end, even being praised for it ("the judgments of the Lord are true and righteous altogether"), yet remarkable to say, for once in his life Lincoln was badly mistaken, and he evidently sensed it right away.

On March 15, 1865, Lincoln wrote to his friend and sometime political ally, Thurlow Weed:

> Every one likes a compliment. Thank you for yours on my little notification speech, and on the recent Inaugural Address. I expect the latter to wear as well as—perhaps better than—any thing I have produced; but I believe it is not immediately popular. Men are not flattered by being shown that there has been a difference of purpose between the Almighty and them.[20]

Despite having slightly misread Weed's note (as indicated in the reference) this letter of Lincoln's is important for several reasons: (1) It affirms his awareness of the less than enthusiastic public reception of his address; (2) It reflects his all too human urge to explain away the reason for people's coolness toward it; and, (3) It offers another "take" on Lincoln's strange detour into heavy religious guilt in his address, a position so out of sync not only with his own much gentler beliefs but also wide of the mark in matching the mood of the moment.

Public reactions to Lincoln's second Inaugural Address varied at the time from sheer bafflement to a kind of reverence for its Christian gentleness at the end. Leaving aside a handful of Copperhead journals that never approved of Lincoln or anything he said, most but not all responses were decidedly undramatic—somewhere between mild and bland. Again, as David Donald well put it:

> [M]ost newspapers gave Lincoln's second inaugural address a respectful if somewhat puzzled reception. In general, English editors praised it more highly than did the Americans. But the Washington *National Intelligencer* felt the President's final words, "equally distinguished for patriotism, statesmanship, and benevolence," deserved "to be printed in gold."[21]

Printed in gold or not, its ending was vintage Lincoln and could not have disappointed or much surprised anyone with its broad compassion and the gentle kindness of his "malice toward none; charity for all" position. Easy to see why. This emphasis quite correctly reflected his great concern for the wounded, for the widows, for the orphaned children, and others who had suffered special hardship. In a way, however, this turned out to be part of the problem in later interpretations. It is so easy to bask in Lincoln's poetic benevolence that it becomes virtually impossible to stay with him through such exactly opposite moments as his major mismove—his venture into a borrowed religious guilt and its image of that unforgiving God.

Thus, among the countless comments the second Inaugural Address has stirred in well over a century it is rare to find so much as a single mention—let alone a sorting out and analysis—of the harsh retribution Lincoln laced into his fiendish fantasy. Have historians hesitated to scratch that surface because they detected problems underneath? That may sometimes have been the case. Yet some of the largest problems in interpreting Lincoln stare out from contradictions in plain sight. How, for instance, could such a self-made man as this—one whom we have every reason to believe never prayed, never personally asked for Heavenly intervention even in the most dire circumstances—how could he of all people suddenly suggest that others credit that most ungodly God of all? And to top off even that, to do so in such an exceedingly high-profile situation as the second Inaugural.

As to why, exactly, Lincoln made this and several lesser choices we shall never know. This is not so much because details are lacking, but rather the opposite: Many factors in plain sight are known to have shared in Lincoln's thinking. What is not known is the relative weight of each. Is that important? Not necessarily. One must remember how thoroughly disbelieving Lincoln always was toward religious notions of Heavenly punishment; it was intimately tied to his earliest rejection of most religion, and to much else that motivated his deepest doubts, a stance he would have been much better off to stay to. In the end what left him most in the lurch was his effort to reenfranchise that ancient god of old.

No need to refight the battle for Lincoln, however, or to speak of other alternatives he might have chosen. Any agnostic or atheist could easily have resolved his whole dilemma with a few well-chosen words, just as many preachers and pundits might have offered endless debate. But in nothing else that Lincoln ever said or wrote are virtually all eyes focused so entirely on his benevolent words—and so assiduously avoid the others. It is this huge disparity, this one-eyed view of the second Inaugural Address, that caused it to be—and to remain—one of the most peculiar events in the entire life of Lincoln.

TEN

Morals, Ethics, and Leonard Swett's Lincoln

Lincoln led his entire life without a single known example of any violation of ethics. Not so in the case of morals. Here he was often at the edge—or over the edge—of what was commonly recognized as moral behavior, as in his penchant for ribald stories and sex jokes. Granted, to tell "immoral" tales or jokes is hardly equivalent to taking the actions, though in fantasy they are much the same. In any case there are reminders here of one of Lincoln's most remarkable traits: In both his witty and sober judgments, he saw and made sharp distinctions between morals and ethics, and lived by his own definitions of each. But whether conventionally or individually defined, exactly what is the difference between them?

The *sameness* of morals and ethics is mentioned in virtually every dictionary, but not the difference. On the surface they may well seem the same, since "morals" is from the Latin *mores*, meaning "customs," while "ethics" is from the Greek *ethos*, also meaning "customs." This seeming sameness is no doubt responsible for the terms being used almost interchangeably in popular or casual speech. Nevertheless there are sharp differences. "Morals" and "morality" are largely the language of local standards and values, often upheld by religion and religion-based judgments, while "ethics" and "ethical" imply less emotion and are more often the language of law. In the 1920s and 1930s a very much sharper difference began to be recognized by anthropologists, a contrast that was later elaborated even further in the 1940s by the sex research of Alfred Kinsey.

Today there is basic agreement on a few key characteristics of ethics. Or perhaps it is better stated the other way around. No society grants general approval to murder and mayhem, or to a great many lesser ethics violations—lying, cheating, stealing, and the like. By comparison, morals and morality vary enormously. They can differ sharply not only from one country to the next, but from town to town, and from town to farm, with some of the sharpest differences occurring in very close proximity, such as opposite sides of the railroad tracks. In each group popular belief tends to assume that people at *every other* social level than their own have "lower" social standards than theirs, and hence practice "looser morals" than their own. Thus, what George Bernard Shaw so amusingly spoke of as "middle-class morality" has tended for decades to lead its members to make a great fuss over the dos and don'ts of sex behavior and to look down on the "looser" standards of lower-social-level (meaning less educated) individuals. Yet those lower-level morals, while freer in some respects, can be a hundred times tighter in other ways—as, for instance, in matters of nudity.

When Lincoln for the first time saw his wife decked out in her full evening finery in preparation for a formal White House event, he found her in a low-cut dress with a long train. From his reaction one can fairly feel his moral shock as he suddenly came face-to-face with what, in fact, was merely a sharp difference in the social level of their upbringings. As he glanced at her half-nude breasts bulging forward with much bare skin above, Lincoln commented in outright chagrin, "Whew, our cat has a long tail to-night . . . it is my opinion, if some of that tail were nearer the head, it would be a better style."[1]

Lincoln's own social level gives evidence of having gradually increased from boyhood, no doubt as a result of his extensive reading and the contact this gave him with the ways and standards of people much better educated than himself. But, of course, what Lincoln read of other worlds was at some distance from what he was accustomed to seeing daily with his own eyes; thus, it is understandable that vision and nudity were particular areas where his log-cabin background held fast. Yet at the moment this hardly amounts to more than a peripheral fact; the central observation is that unlike his always rigorous stand in policing his own ethics, when it came to mere morals and moralistic matters Lincoln felt as free as a bird. He loved nothing better than to walk the very edge of the risqué and the raucous.

Yet a puzzle is apparent here. Since Lincoln lived almost a century before any modern definition of the difference between morals and ethics came into focus, how was he able to arrive on his own at a sharp distinction between them—sharp, that is, since he rigorously obeyed the rules of ethics, while with ease and joy overstepped the line on morals? Not that the whole of it is a mystery. Since boyhood he displayed a marked capacity to see the big picture in life and to not be swerved aside by smaller considerations. This already sounds much like ethics, based as it always is on widely shared values, ones poles apart from the petty differences honored on opposite sides of those railroad tracks. Thus, Lincoln may well have gained his abiding respect for the breadth and integrity of ethics from deep within his own disposition—and in the same sweep, discovered to his delight how to make jokes at the expense of morals.

Still, if Lincoln was rigorous in maintaining his own ethics, yet loose and limber and often licentious in at least bending morality, what does this say about his dealings with others? By itself, nothing whatever. But it begins to mean more when we learn from Judge Davis—and not only from him—that in courtroom situations during Lincoln's middle years he could be "hurtful in denunciation and merciless in castigation." While such examples may retain their rank as ethical, their tone and timbre reflect the righteous indignation of low-level moralism.[2] At least it can be said that Lincoln never tried to defend himself with any such moralistic ploys. On the contrary, when under attack he consistently managed to look past—indeed, to completely disregard—virtually every ethics or morals charge that outsiders ever could, or did, or might hurl *at him*.

Not that this latter observation is at all new. One of Lincoln's first biographers, Isaac Arnold, put it exactly:

> Personal abuse, injustice, and indignity offered to himself did not disturb him, but gross injustice and bad faith towards others made him indignant, and when brought to his knowledge, his eyes would blaze with indignation, and [a] denunciation few could endure.[3]

No doubt part of Lincoln's remarkable personal security that so reliably allowed him to look past attacks against himself stemmed, as did much else, from his autodidactic talents. A man who all his life was ready to tackle every task entirely on his own—seldom seeking any word of advice—was understandably disinclined to take personal attacks seriously.

Yet there was more to Lincoln's sure-footedness than that. And it was not new. From as far back as we have relevant records Lincoln was seen by close friends as utterly secretive. He was also complex—a layered, many-sided man somehow full of mystery and obscurity. Yet he was also honest, straightforward, and original, adding to the irony that both his actions and his words poured out smoothly and simply; they were also fresh. Long before anyone else mentioned it and before the Republican party had yet chosen its candidate to run for president, one minor party member wrote of Lincoln to an associate:

> What he does & says is all his own. What Seward and others do you feel you have read in books or speeches, or that it is a sort of deduction from what the world is full of. But What Lincoln does you feel to be something newly mined out—something above the ordinary[.] Don't be surprised at any result—in reference to him.[4]

Strangely enough, no Lincoln associate of substance ever noticed any such far-reaching characteristic until years later, when Herndon acquired from Leonard Swett a unique summary view of Lincoln.

Not long after Lincoln's death, when Herndon was collecting remembrances from close friends and colleagues of the great man, he wrote to the lawyer Leonard Swett. The letter arrived at a busy moment for Swett, who nevertheless hurriedly answered it the same day (January 17, 1866), with apologies for writing "only" an off-the-cuff reply. Rapid though it may have been it turned out to be one of the most thoughtful and remarkable documents in the entire Lincoln literature. Not that this judgment has ever been widely shared. For while Leonard Swett is well-known to every Lincoln scholar, only Herndon himself seems to have recognized the sweep and penetration of Swett's composite picture. The entire letter (Appendix 3) is replete with interesting detail. Yet even considered alone Swett's final paragraph on Lincoln is extraordinary:

> One great public mistake of his character as generally received and acquiesced in:—he is considered by the people of this country as a frank, guileless, unsophisticated man. There never was a greater mistake. Beneath a smooth surface of candor and an apparent declaration of all his thoughts and feelings, he exercised the most exalted tact and the wisest discrimination. He handled and moved man *remotely* as we do pieces upon a chessboard. He retained through life, all the friends he ever had, and he made the wrath of his enemies to praise him. This was not by cunning, or intrigue in the low acceptation of the term, but by far seeing, reason and discernment. He always told enough only, of his plans and purposes, to induce the belief that he had communicated all; yet he reserved enough, in fact, to have communicated nothing. He told all that was unimportant with a gushing frankness; yet no man ever kept his real purposes more closely, or penetrated the future further with his deep designs.[5]

One's first reaction has got to be sincere gratitude that Lincoln was an honest man; imagine what could have resulted had he been dishonest with all those talents of double-think and obfuscation! Notice, too, how hard it is to fully comprehend the row upon row of mystery and magic that are implied behind each of those Lincolnian traits. Take the matter that "He retained through life, all the friends he ever had." Who other than Lincoln, ever managed to do that— and do it, by the way, irrespective of whether some angry or forgetful friend *wanted* to be retained? In this one gets a whiff of the ire and ill-will that even in small amounts often causes one to relinquish a less than fully satisfying friendship. But not so with Lincoln—who, indeed, kept "all the friends he ever had"—a reminder again that for him, moral judgments and the many small hostilities that hide behind them simply went unweighted.

The remainder of Swett's sentence points out the still more remarkable fact that Lincoln "made the wrath of his enemies to praise him." This would be an astonishing accomplishment under any circumstance, but is made more so by being an accident of Lincoln's style, rather than a deliberate aim of his. It is memorable that Lincoln won his party's nomination for president over contenders such as Salmon Chase and William Seward, who began with far better prospects than he, understandably leaving the losers feeling wounded and resentful. Yet the entire situation was instantly revamped by Lincoln's immediately asking each loser (Chase, Seward, Cameron, and Bates) to come join his cabinet. All did so, though in the case of Chase, with jealousy and hurt feelings still aboil.[6] Nevertheless, each accepted the offer and soon, even to his own astonishment, found great respect for Lincoln who, just as Swett said, "made the wrath of his enemies to praise him."

Swett tells us that Lincoln managed this miraculous result not by any kind of low cunning or intrigue, but by far-seeing reason and discernment. Undoubtedly so. But how, exactly, did Lincoln apply his wisdom and acumen—and toward what end? His own view of the matter might help. At another place in Swett's letter he relates a small scene:

> One time, about the middle of the war, I left his house about eleven o'clock at night, at the Soldiers' Home [sic]. We had been discussing the discords in the country, and particularly the States of Missouri and Kentucky. As we separated at the door he said, "I may not have made as great a President as some other men, but I believe I have kept these discordant elements together as well as anyone could."

There was far more to it than that; all his life Lincoln greatly enjoyed standing next to conflict, often wiping it out by freely giving each side its due. It was what made him, even as a boy, a much sought after judge of sporting competitions. Later, in any battle of ideas he was quick to acknowledge valid points within any notion opposed to his own. No doubt this was part of what allowed him as president to keep wildly "discordant elements together," as he put it. Did he also welcome these contrasts as an aid in finding a middle course? That may have been part of it; but judging from an amusing image, involving pumpkins, which Lincoln used to describe his resolution of a cabinet crisis, his main motive lay elsewhere.

The Union defeat at Fredericksburg on December 13, 1862,

outraged the North and roiled Congress, in which the radical Abolitionist faction for some time had been restive with Lincoln's leadership in general and his cabinet in particular. Secretary of State
Seward, whose abolitionism had moderated as the war progressed,
took the brunt of the criticism. Secretary of the Treasury Chase,
himself privately a radical Abolitionist, saw in this an opportunity
to advance both his personal standing and his political agenda; if he
could engineer Seward's removal from the cabinet, he would hold
greater sway over the administration. In a behind-closed-doors
whispering campaign he convinced key Abolitionist senators that
the cabinet was fatally split, that Lincoln never consulted it, and
that Seward, exercising a sinister influence behind the scenes at the
White House, was to blame.

Chase almost prevailed. Seward, apprehensive that the controversy
would damage the administration, on December 16 sent Lincoln a letter of resignation. That would not do, from Lincoln's viewpoint, for he
had come to regard Seward as a valuable adviser. On December 18 he
received a committee of senators who echoed Chase's complaints
about Seward, and early the next day he convened the cabinet to assess
the situation (Seward did not attend); during these meetings he mostly
listened, without tipping his hand about his intentions. On the evening
of the nineteenth he called back to the White House both the senato-
rial committee and the cabinet. Neither group knew that the other had
been invited. But they sensed that Lincoln had laid the groundwork for
some kind of showdown, and they were not mistaken.

One by one Lincoln asked his cabinet members to assess for the
senators the state of the cabinet. This put Chase in an extremely
awkward predicament. If he were to repeat what he had told the senators behind closed doors he would reveal himself as disloyal to the
administration. On the other hand, if he pulled his punches—kept
his mouth shut about the alleged problems or changed his tone—he
would look weak and two-faced, and his maneuvers would fizzle.
Chase bristled but backed down, and said that the administration was
more or less fine.

Hours later the senators left the meeting with a deflated sense of
having been outwitted. Chase's standing with them plummeted cor-
respondingly. The ambitious treasury secretary, far from having
wrested dominance over the cabinet, instead had strengthened the

status quo: Radical Abolitionism would not hold sway in the Lincoln presidency.

The next morning, on December 20, Chase went to the White House with his own letter of resignation. Secretary of War Stanton and other officials witnessed what happened next. Chase didn't expect Lincoln to accept the letter, for he knew that the president needed him and on other occasions had offered to resign merely as a ploy to have it turned down and get his way. However, "The President stepped forward and took it with an alacrity that surprised and, it must be said, disappointed Mr. Chase." Lincoln now held two resignation letters: one from Seward, one from Chase.

He saw this as a crucial balance. "When the Cabinet had retired, and the President remained with the resignation of Mr. Chase in his hands," he spoke with his friend, Senator Harris, who had just entered the room, of how as a boy he had found a way to carry pumpkins on horseback. Using this analogy he told Harris, "Now I can ride; I have got a pumpkin in each end of my bag."[7]

As it turned out, Lincoln asked Chase and Seward to stay on for the good of the country, and both secretaries did. But Lincoln had not only maintained balance in his cabinet and rebuffed congressional meddling with it; he also had preserved the consensus that sustained his leadership. Almost a year later he looked back and summarized what he thought of the whole situation:

> I do not see how it could have been done better. I am sure it was right. If I had yielded to that storm and dismissed Seward the thing would all have slumped over one way, and we should have been left with a scanty handful of supporters. When Chase gave in his resignation I saw that the game was in my hands, and I put it through.[8]

In short, by first accepting the resignations of both his secretary of the treasury and of state, then immediately asking both to rejoin the fold "in the public interest," the conflict between them was much reduced. Quite as Nicolay and Hay wrote:

> The untrained diplomatist of Illinois had thus met and conjured away, with unsurpassed courage and skill, one of the

severest crises that ever threatened the integrity of his Administration, [and it] left the President seated more firmly than ever in the saddle.[9]

It would be hard to find another set of examples that better illustrates what Leonard Swett noticed in Lincoln's handling of such situations: "[H]e exercised the most exalted tact and the wisest discrimination [as] he handled and moved man remotely as we do pieces upon a chess-board." Nor could a better example be found of what he meant by Lincoln's exalted tact—which fully met the formal definition of the word itself: "a keen sense of what to say and do to avoid giving offense; skill in dealing with difficult or delicate situations."[10]

Yet, careful here. When one realizes the complexity of such examples along with the many-sidedness of the problems Lincoln faced and solved, it is tempting to weigh only his large moves and look past more modest marvels that were also at work. At least it appears to this observer that a major help to Lincoln throughout his life was that astonishing capacity of his to find and keep the big picture in focus—as he did in the case of ethics. His initial wide-angle view of a situation held several not always obvious advantages. It gave him a chance to put his chips in order and to hear a freight train coming if there was one. Better yet, it allowed him to exploit two other of his talents: on the one hand, to see and to set in motion whatever complicated plan seemed best, and on the other, to stay alert to serendipity—his readiness to quickly grasp the happenstance of a moment, as in that lightning Lincoln liftoff of the written resignation Chase held in his hand.

Neither the order nor the wording of these details is meant to take anything away from Leonard Swett's astute perception of Lincoln's lively capacity to cloak his real purposes, and to outdo any and all others as he "penetrated the future . . . with his deep designs." This propensity of his was marvelously well shown in the delicate maneuvers he devised in the "severest crises that ever threatened the integrity of his Administration." But there was also in Lincoln a simplicity, a surface logic, and a remarkable degree of straightforwardness, particularly in his initial approach to problems of any kind. It helps to keep this part of him in focus, as well as all the complications, in reaching for a final image of the man.

ELEVEN

On Lincoln's Sexuality, with Extensions

Let there be no mistake: From any point of view Lincoln was highly peculiar from the start. His homosexual side, while not unusual in itself, was connected with an early puberty of such extremity—fully four years sooner than average—as to make even it extraordinary. In terms of talents he was off the charts as well. Perhaps it was not particularly uncommon that he learned to read "on his own" without instruction at some very early age he remembered nothing about, since remarkable learning often took place in those haphazardly attended one-room schoolhouses. Nor were Lincoln's exceptional autodidactic talents enough alone to "make him a genius"—at least not until one merges his unmatched memory into the picture. His apparently life-long capacity to recall anything he ever saw in print—be it long speeches from Shakespeare or trivial bits of doggerel from common folktales—amounted to a near bottomless supply of parallel images and analogies that endlessly enlivened both his thinking and his constant glide from one story to the next.

To Lincoln's list of recognized talents several others could be added from his homosexual side. Some of these are impressive, yet it cannot be said with certainty how much weight they deserve in gauging his genius. In fact, genius stands unique, and appears to depend on a quite different set of assets, one quickly made evident in a simple parlor game anyone can play. One only need ask a few friends to jot down a list of, say, ten names of individuals who are remembered as geniuses, being careful not to show their choices to anyone else for the moment. When these lists are finally in hand, simply subtract the names of those persons known to be either homosexual or Jewish or both—and see how many are left. Very few, if any, will remain. The meaning of this is not quite what it may seem. For while both homosexual and Jewish apologists of the past have understandably felt a certain pride in what they saw, or thought they saw, as characteristic of their own group, they were mostly mistaken.

No, the glint of pure gold that shines forth from genius cannot be a group product. The mathematics of the matter carry the day: The "base rate" of genius is so shatteringly small—one in millions at most—as to make it an extreme rarity, certainly nothing anywhere near a group trait. Thus, the basic source of genius is clearly elsewhere. It appears to be most facilitated by its sheer placement, that is, from the inputs and opportunities that occur at the periphery of a society, rather than from anything found near its core. Or to say it the other way around, the uniformity that every society struggles to maintain for smoothness and easy communication (and in no small measure to defend its dogmas) is precisely the opposite of what genius requires for expression—that is, a freedom from constraint and a degree of wildness that lives at the very edge, or well over the edge, of social conformity.

This latter detail is well illustrated in Lincoln. Both on the surface and in no small part of his thinking he was quick to support conventional values. Time and again he spoke of the virtue and necessity of everyone strictly "obeying the laws" of the land. But when it came to his personal judgments he was quite ready to make a mockery of morals, as he often did in his wit; and in serious matters he virtually always came down on the side of comfort and kindness as he placed the personal desires of individuals well ahead of formal regulations of any kind. On Speed's last visit to the White House he was much alarmed both by Lincoln's health and a scene he observed of the sort that often rankled military authorities. After granting the request of two women for the release of their men, who had been imprisoned for resisting the draft, Lincoln said, "Now, ladies, you can go. Your son, madam, and your husband, madam, is free." Seeing how tired Lincoln looked, Speed commented, "Such a scene as I have just witnessed is enough to make you nervous." Lincoln replied, "How much you are mistaken. I have made two people happy to-day; I have given a mother her son, and a wife her husband. That young woman is a counterfeit, but the old woman is a true mother."[1]

In short, Lincoln was ready to cut through government regulations, and further irritate law enforcement officials, by granting kind personal concessions to ordinary people, even where half of his generosity was bestowed on a "counterfeit."

Lincoln's public reputation in such instances was entirely correct, as far as it went. He was, indeed, everything he seemed on that surface: kind, empathetic, and sympathetic to a fault, with a quick readiness to side with plain folk, whatever their problems. With good reason this quality has often been attributed to his great and generous sympathy for the helpless, particularly when they faced the crunch and formality of laws and regulations. This two-sidedness, his readiness to switch from one to the other, from strict ethics to an easy set-aside of morals, from chief officer of the land to such a loose bypasser of them as to unhesitatingly break rules, even for that counterfeit wife he wanted to help: Such contrasts are evident in countless examples on every side. In the light of certain insights from sex research they also qualify as remarkable examples of "inversion," about which much is yet to be said. Even Lincoln's generosity was inverted in several ways. For while it always rode in on a white horse of benevolence, pure and unambiguous in itself, it divided the world as Lincoln saw it between the Establishment and its victims, between formal statutes and private concerns, between the sharp edge of the law and whatever kind personal permissions he wanted to grant.

Tempting as it is to extend these observations right here, it seems more useful to first examine a few hovering questions not yet mentioned. For instance, was Mary Lincoln at all aware of her husband's homosexual side—and in any case, what relevance did it have in their marriage? Tangibly aware of it she certainly was not. In fact, she both correctly and yet mistakenly took pride in one of Lincoln's repeated reassurances. Shortly after his death, she wrote a friend:

> It was always, music in my ears, both before & after our
> marriage, when my husband, told me, that I was the only one,
> he had ever thought of, or cared for. It will solace me to the
> grace.[2]

That this was always such "music" attests to her urgent need for reassurance, and to her awareness on some level that she was getting something less than all of Lincoln's response. Yet Lincoln's meticulousness in never telling a lie offered her, and now us, further assurance that no other *women* in his life were ever of any importance. Even his very words—that he never "thought of, or cared for" instead of "loved" or was "devoted to"—seem sculpted to fit the facts of Mary's main value to him: more as the mother of his adored children rather than as a beloved wife.

Lincoln's fundamentally homosexual response appears to have played itself out in a variety of other ways. Immediately after Lincoln's inauguration Mary viewed herself as "Madam President," urged others to call her that, and quickly became her most impossible, embarrassing, and deliberately hurtful self in scores of ways. These included a great variety of abuses previously mentioned, from rude social behavior and cheating on accounts, to the selling of presidential favors she would then demand Lincoln grant. Often the facts were even worse than her reputation, as when her actions caused Lincoln to be blackmailed into buying back several of her most incriminating letters. And while Lincoln was never aware of the full extent of Mary's shenanigans, he knew enough of them often to be shocked—but not brokenhearted. A few historians have suggested that Lincoln held still for Mary's bad behavior because he considered her mentally unbalanced. Perhaps. But whether this was part of the picture or not, it is worth bearing in mind that the largely homosexual husband runs a far less than average risk of becoming either brokenhearted or crestfallen at wifely disappointments. These, after all, are emotions that require a previous closeness, even idealization, that in Lincoln were lacking from the outset.

For Lincoln this was a trend of long-standing duration. Since the early days of his marriage a main problem had been that he could hardly tolerate the high contact of daily life with Mary. Would he have been better off with a simple, more compliant girl as close friends often said? Probably so, although this can never be known. The fact is that he quickly ran off to life on the circuit—and still preferred it, remember, even when left alone there by other circuit riders as they returned home for weekends.

Does this mean Lincoln's great disinterest in his home life was largely due to his insufficient heterosexual response? Most probably so. No man with ordinary heterosexual appetites would elect to leave a new marriage within a week or two, and to stay away as long as possible at every opportunity. A few historians have made excuses for Lincoln's long absences from home, attributing them to inadequate railroads at that time. But of course this argument is made moot by the fact that his colleagues had no trouble regularly getting back to Springfield, and felt sorry for poor Lincoln as they left him behind in shabby roadside taverns. Mary may have been relatively blameless in this, but she was also short on humor, and tended to see the world entirely from her female point of view; it was a stance more foreign than fascinating to him.

As for his own part in this, not all the distance he felt can be blithely charged to his sexual orientation. As Kinsey and Freud both observed, a great many entirely heterosexual males quickly tire of time spent with their wives and seek escape, often to more compatible male company in bars and clubs. But for Lincoln, two factors intensified this trend. Beyond the fact that he was never comfortable with eligible girls and women, he almost exclusively keyed his wit and his entire way of life to men and to male audiences. Moreover, humorless Mary was most certainly a poor audience; she was never known to have slapped her knee at any of his knee-slappers, not to mention a host of other incompatibilities. Nearby lay still other problems.

Mary was a relatively highly sexed female, as evidenced by many small cues over the years, including comments of her own and others. And while Lincoln cannot be said to have exactly failed in his conjugal duties, he clearly offered less than she longed for; as a neighbor, James Gourley, put it:

> She always said that if her husband had stayed at home as he ought to that she could love him better; she is no prostitute, a good woman. She dared me once or twice to kiss her, as I thought, [I] refused [but] wouldn't now.[3]

Mary often recalled, as a widow, "my husband was my *all*"; but for years she seems to have realized she was never *his* all, as was made clear by her hanging onto him at every turn and her fierce jealousy of women he might see for only a moment in casual social contact or dance with at a party. Extreme examples such as the shocks she gave Adam Badeau at City Point—among them, "Do you know that I never allow the President to see any woman alone?"—attest well enough to her feeling that she was getting less than Lincoln had to offer, though she had the wrong kind of competition in mind.

Thus stacked, the cards suggest several ways in which Lincoln's homosexual side may well have played its part in his marriage. Even so, this does *not* mean it was the key to every item it touched; Mary's jealousy, for instance, was the sort likely to have far more than a single feed. Nor is the opposite side of the coin entirely safe. Lincoln's great privacy and standoffishness was of a kind often increased if not sponsored by a homosexual component. Yet this, too, like Mary's jealousy, is likely to have had multiple inputs rather than a single source.

With these several qualifications in mind, one might well ask: If the homosexual element is so tenuous and tentative, too silent to be a clear-cut culprit, why mention it at all? Of course the same might be asked of other Lincoln characteristics; neither his wit nor all he suffered from Mary can be said to have left any specific historic traces in his judgments. But if one cares to really know the man and feel something of what he felt from the inside, then all these seemingly side factors loom large. They include much from his homosexual side, from the qualities of his genius, and from what can be seen as a special brand of inversion in his life.

Early in 1947 during various statistical rechecks at the Kinsey Institute for Sex Research at Indiana University, one starkly apparent finding (Chapter 2) was: "[T]he earlier a boy's puberty, the higher his probability of making homosexual contacts." As this evidence poured from the computer a young staff member, Clyde Martin, remarked: "That makes sense; a boy who sexually matures way ahead of being old enough to go with girls has only other boys to turn to." Kinsey was not in the room at that moment, but Frank Beach, a noted experimental psychologist, was; he heard the remark and immediately responded, "Watch out! That's just the sort of thing one has to be especially careful about; I'll have it checked at Yale."[4]

Only a few months before Beach had accepted the prestigious

chair at Yale's department of experimental psychology. He had largely won this post as a result of his outstanding early work on the nature of inversion—that is, the conditions under which mammals tend to reverse their usual sex roles and display homosexual behavior. Why had Martin's remark about a young boy's lack of access to girls given Beach a moment of alarm and aroused his quick offer to "have it checked at Yale"; what, exactly, had to be checked? In a word: the gaping gap through which even well-established physical facts can lead to explanations that fall back toward low-level psychology. It was a concern Beach and Kinsey had often expressed and been on guard against; here the danger rose again, however fleetingly, even from a member of the Kinsey staff!

What does this have to do with Abraham Lincoln? Rather more than one might suppose. As was shown before, Kinsey was able to graph the age at puberty of his thousands of males against the incidence of their homosexual contacts, indicating that the younger the age at puberty, the "steeper the start" and the higher the actual number of such contacts. On this scale Lincoln was off the chart toward both a phenomenally higher than average sexual arousability (his lifelong sex-mindedness), plus what appears from the start to have been an especially high homosexual inclination, at least in the sense of avoiding girls. (This latter fact is by itself remarkable for someone like Lincoln, who had grown up with a close and beloved sister; usually boys with this background, regardless of their sexual orientation, turn out to be easy and comfortable with girls.)

Granted, a statistical probability of what one feels and wants does not become a fact until events in personal history validate it, which appears to have been what happened with Lincoln. Yet here again was that gaping gap between hard-won physical facts on the one hand versus the ease with which these are forgotten at a time when psychological theories are in vogue. Or to put it another way: Is one to be left merely to social and psychological explanations as to why Lincoln chose same-sex targets, as he almost certainly did in his earliest masturbation fantasies? It is no stretch to assume that Lincoln—like 99 percent of early-puberty males—managed to discover masturbation at or before he was able to ejaculate; had he employed heterosexual images, these might well have led to his wanting rather than avoiding contact with eligible women in later life.

Yet better not be overconfident of any of this until hearing again from Beach who, at Martin's remark, had immediately recognized both the "gap problem" and that it was testable. At Yale, new tests were run on rats, and later on dogs. The results not only confirmed previous findings that the higher the level of naturally occurring testosterone, the more prone a male is to invert his usual sex role; the new wrinkle was that both the testosterone level and its offshoot, inversion-readiness, run parallel to an animal's earliness of puberty, neatly eliminating the need for any psychological explanations. Translation: While bits of social or psychological biases may wend their ways into the human picture, none of these are required to either trigger or sustain inversion. Rather, inversion has major ties to the intensity of sexual arousability, a connection evident in both animal and human examples.[5]

But what, exactly, is inversion? At the simplest level it is what the word itself suggests: a reversal of commonly expected behavior. Unlike homosexuality, inversion implies nothing about the sex of the partner but keeps to role reversal. When a female dog mounts males, or other females, or even the leg of her owner, she is inverting her behavior from her more usual submissive-receptive mode into the specific, much more assertive behavior characteristic of males. In human examples inversion often extends far beyond any notion of sexual intercourse, and beyond sex itself. A person has not only an expected usual role in sex, but a whole socially defined gender role to live up to. Men and women are expected to express their gender in their attitudes, their body movements, in the clothes they wear, and in a variety of other ways. When any of these trends or styles are reversed even for a moment it constitutes a measure of inversion, whether the individual or a casual observer recognizes it or not.

Let it be remembered here that Lincoln's inversion had two notable attributes: (1) Its many-sidedness was widely evident in his wit, his philosophy, even in his sense of justice; and (2) its upside-down quality was a brand of variance loudly evident in diverse personalities, some of them quite unLincolnian in other respects.

Take the case of Winston Churchill. During World War II one of his closest friends and collaborators was Franklin D. Roosevelt. They had many similarities and differences. FDR was completely heterosexual all his life, while Churchill had a homosexual history in his youth, which his mother much gossiped about. (Years later, when Somerset Maugham had Churchill to dinner, he asked him point-blank if this was true. Churchill confessed to only one overt experience, with Ivor Novello. Maugham asked, "How was it?" Churchill replied, "Musical.")[6] As with most patricians, prudery held little sway with either of them, yet Churchill and FDR both held a lifelong interest in the private lives of others that bordered on utter fascination.[7]

However, the effect of their differing sex histories soon became apparent. For while each had a track record of saving and protecting friends and colleagues caught in compromising situations (heterosexual or homosexual), they differed greatly in what might be called their approach to gaining and handling secret information. From early in life Roosevelt was fascinated by (and hungry for) secret information, and yet he repeatedly demonstrated a certain simplemindedness about it. As late as Pearl Harbor he went along with routine recommendations for how secret information was sorted and sent to him, until abuses in the system actually threatened American safety.

For his part in England Churchill immediately jumped into the fray of code-breaking with great intensity and a hands-on sophistication. He not only revved up and greatly expanded the operations at Bletchley Park, the world's top-notch code-breaking center, but opened its doors still wider to a collection of wild characters, many of whom would have been rejected in a moment by the regular military: eccentric mathematicians and chess players, homosexuals, offbeat crossword puzzle addicts, and other strangers to convention; one can already see inversion at work. Among them was a handsome homosexual man in his twenties, Alan Turing, who soon proved to be the genius of the lot. Almost alone, especially in his approach and mathematical concepts, he broke the "unbreakable" German Enigma, a device of staggering complexity in which every letter typed into it was immediately transformed into a pair of other letters. These in turn were fed into first three, then four, and eventually twelve rotors where the results were reshuffled still again at every level, each change altering the internal circuitry of the device. The odds of making any headway from the surface of this maze of complexity were estimated by officials at Bletchley as less than one in 150 million, million, million.[8]

In retrospect, Turing appeared almost tailor-made for his wartime task. Like Lincoln, he was a pleasant although fiercely independent autodidact; as one of his earliest teachers put it, "He has his own furrow to plough." Once, years before, when his mother was leaving for India to join his father and continue their official duties, Mrs. Turing said, "You'll be a good boy, won't you?" Three-year-old Alan replied, "Yes, but sometimes I shall forget!" And "forget" he often did, especially in school. Before he was quite fourteen one of his teachers complained that he blithely "did algebra during religious instruction" and that it was hard to forgive "the stupidity of his attitude towards sane discussion of the New Testament." A few months later "Alan showed his mathematics teacher, a certain Randolph, some work he had done for himself. He had found the infinite series for the 'inverse tangent function' starting from the trigonometric formula for tan[gent] ½x. [A]ppropriately amazed, [Randolph] told Alan's form master that he was 'a genius' "— particularly for doing this without knowing calculus. Moreover, "the most remarkable thing was his seeing that such a series should exist at all."[9]

Yet even Randolph later reported unfavorably: "Not very good. He spends a great deal of time apparently in investigations in advanced mathematics to the neglect of elementary work; a second groundwork is essential in any subject. His work is dirty" (meaning that his pages filled with ink blotches and cross-outs). In 1928, at age sixteen, another of Alan's math teachers, "Eperson, just a year down from Oxford and a gentle, cultured person," commented:

> All that I can claim is that my deliberate policy of leaving him largely to his own devices and standing by to assist when necessary, allowed his natural mathematical genius to progress uninhibited.

As Turing's biographer Hodges observed, Eperson and others had found that "Alan always preferred his own methods to those supplied by the text book, and indeed Alan had gone his own way all the time."[10]

At Bletchley Park one of Alan Turing's first innovations—a veritable triumph of inversion by itself—was to design a computerlike device to search, *not* for any of the many unknowns, but rather the opposite: to search through and discard hundreds of millions of possibilities that the answer *could not possibly be*, and to do so after each and every keystroke. At first, this upside-down approach greatly astonished his cohorts, who were filled with admiration when it quickly proved to zero in on a sharply reduced number of possibilities requiring analysis. Soon, to unscramble and decode an entire message became so efficient that sometimes when German headquarters submarine commander Karl Döenitz would relay attack information to his submarine wolf pack about a convoy bound for Britain, before the pack had had time to decipher and read Döenitz's message, it was already being used by British Naval Intelligence to reroute the convoy. By war's end Bletchley Park was decoding more than eighty-four thousand secret messages a month, including all of Hitler's own communications. It was a feat stemming back to a handful of geniuses, Turing at the top, with a staff of ten thousand attached to the processing unit at Bletchley.[11]

American code breakers were not exactly pikers, either. Before Pearl Harbor they had broken the top Japanese code Purple, but due to military bureaucratic rivalries much was either lost or late, with the Army and Navy each month alternating as to which would deliver summaries of secret transcripts to Roosevelt (until he finally "woke up" and demanded direct reports). Churchill was just the opposite. Like Lincoln, he could hardly wait for new information and never trusted any bureau to get it to him. In fact, Churchill demanded to see so much of the traffic (not just what others might think would interest him) that he had a Mrs. Owens of the Women's Auxiliary Air Force assigned full time exclusively to oversee his deliveries from Bletchley. And he was extraordinarily hands-on in other ways, being especially alert to the value of special talents. When he received a private letter from Alan Turing (October 21, 1941) stating a need for extra materials and office help, Turing's biographer Hodges described the effect of Churchill's response as "electric"; he immediately ordered General Hastings Ismay, his top aide, to "Make sure they have all they want on extreme priority and report to me that this [has] been done."[12]

In the end, what did it all mean for the world, and for the individuals involved? The work traceable directly to Alan Turing saved hundreds of ships and well over a million lives. According to Bletchley's executive, Tony Sale, British military authorities later estimated that the phenomenal code breaking shortened the war by no less than two years. A look behind the scenes reveals that even these estimates are minimal compared to what they could and indeed should have been, were it not for the exercise of one of the worst wartime corruptions: bits of military macho on both sides of the Atlantic.

In August 1942, Churchill arrived in North Africa to revamp British forces, which had been losing badly to Rommel's Africa Corps in one desert defeat after the other. Churchill fired his generals and put Field Marshal Bernard Montgomery in charge. Bletchley's Enigma findings, called Ultra for short, had warned of an imminent attack "somewhere in Egypt." After assessing the terrain Montgomery predicted and prepared for an attack at Allum Ridge. When this turned out to be precisely where Rommel made his move and was handily defeated by Montgomery, the latter was so filled with himself and with self-confidence, he refused from then on to heed any outside information, even from Ultra. As Ralph Bennett, a code breaker at Bletchley, put it: "We told Monty how few tanks Rommel had [down to eleven at one point] and how little gas, so he could have wiped Rommel off the face of the earth. Why he didn't do so I simply do not know and nobody else does." Montgomery paraded his victory and polished his ego instead, with disastrous long-term consequences.[13]

On the other side of the Atlantic a worse corruption was about to occur. Bletchley warned that on December 23, 1941, Nazi submarines were ordered to the American northeast coast to begin a concerted attack on U.S. shipping, to start January 13, 1942. The Nazis were delighted to find ships and the shorelines behind them ablaze with lights, and no defenses in place. Picking their targets at will, it was a turkey shoot. As reports of sinkings came in and ship wreckage began to pile up on American coasts, "The U.S. Navy chose to repeatedly dissemble"; it announced it had been tracking and had successfully sunk many submarines. The truth was that under orders from Admiral Ernest L. King—an Anglophobe who hated everything English, including the people, their navy, its crews, and even a stream of warnings he received from Ultra—no destroyer or any air cover was ordered (then or ever), though the newspapers continued to banner the official line of successful submarine sinkings. No submarines were ever sighted, let alone sunk. In the first six months alone 397 American ships were downed, some of them large liners, with virtually no survivors. Behind the scenes an unknown number of officials knew at least part of the truth; General Eisenhower confided to his diary, "The best way to win the war is to shoot Admiral King." British protests became ever louder; so did undeniable evidence from newsreels showing German submarine crews being awarded iron crosses for inflicting so many American losses. Gradually the slow wheels of bureaucracy began to grind against the core corruptions that lay behind the whole debacle (though by then the Nazis had withdrawn their submarines to the mid-Atlantic).[14]

It is crucial to search out those "core corruptions" lest calamity of this ilk be attributed only to the individuals involved, or to local defects in human character. But they are not so local, and soon lead back both to the opposite of centerline Lincoln traits, and to much else learned via his example. First, a word about Lincoln himself. Most certainly he never did or tolerated anything approaching the fakery and egocentricity (let alone violations of loyalty) implicit in the General Montgomery and Admiral King instances—but that may simply have been from his honesty and character. Beyond that, however, Lincoln had what might be called intuitive guardian powers he may never have recognized as such—Churchill and Turing had them, too—buried in the very nature of an ever-ready inversion readiness. It gave each of them the capacity to turn on a dime, sometimes at the first whiff of an advantage or blockage, and often invited them to reverse an initial impulse. The consequences could be remarkable and extended far beyond what one might suppose.

Leaving aside the less than laudable personal side of the Montgomery and King examples, they displayed damaging dangers made the more so by unsuspected drawbacks in their conventional setting. Other examples abound, for instance in and around the Pearl Harbor disaster. As Joseph Persico found:

> On Sunday morning, December 7, [one last warning remained.] Navy cryptographers were decrypting the last piece of the fourteen-part Japanese message, the so-called Final Memorandum, which declared that Tokyo was breaking off negotiations. At the same time, Army cryptographers were breaking a separate instruction to Ambassador Nomura to

submit the long message to the State Department at 1 p.m. Washington time. Colonel Rufus Bratton, the astute head of the Far East section of Army intelligence, was struck by the preciseness of the hour and its unusual Sunday afternoon delivery. To Bratton, this timing signaled a Japanese attack. . . . Precious time was lost while Bratton tried desperately to locate General Marshall, who was off on his regular Sunday horseback ride. Two and a half hours later, Bratton was finally explaining his interpretation of the 1 p.m. delivery to Marshall. The Army Chief of Staff immediately fired off to commanders in the Pacific a warning that the Japanese had, in effect, presented an ultimatum and "to be on the alert accordingly." The message went first to Manila, next to the Panama Canal, and last to Hawaii. "Fired off" is perhaps not the right phrase regarding the Hawaii delivery since the signalman could not get through on their military circuits, and Marshall's warning of imminent hostilities had to be sent by commercial cable. By the time the warning reached General Short's headquarters, the skies over Pearl Harbor were dotted with Japanese planes. The church bells announcing Sunday services were being drowned out by torpedoes exploding against Kimmel's clustered warships and by bombs destroying Short's bunched-up planes.[15]

Could such a series of blunders have occurred under Lincoln or Churchill? Absolutely not; both would have demanded to be the first informed of such a message—not have it sent to anyone else—least of all to await the whereabouts of a missing general, nor handed to brainless signalmen for casual relay. Lincoln barely trusted his reliable telegrapher, whom he hovered over as the Morse code was sent. Both he and Churchill were innately distrustful of protocol or of anything else that could reduce their hands-on "feel" of a situation. This is obvious enough to raise serious questions at the other side of the issue.

What is it in the comfortable garden of conventional manners and morals that makes it rich pickings for character defects, for messages that go astray, and corruptions of authority like those of Montgomery and King? Worse yet, why does it prevent so many from blowing the whistle, with incensed insiders saying nothing or confiding only to their diaries? Not that it would help much if there were perfect answers to these questions; primary loyalties tend to stay with the Establishment ("my country right or wrong"). Yet there remain two warnings for the wise to worry about and never forget: (1) The smooth surface of apparent conformity is replete with hidden pitfalls and potholes that can and regularly do swallow up alarming counter-evidence, and (2) The opposite: Rejection of small variances such as homosexuality can rob and even ruin broad areas of government.

Thus, had the British and American governments known or even suspected the sexual tastes of Alan Turing, routine policies would have quickly shunted him aside—at the price of the millions of lives he saved and many more months of war. As it turned out, after the war police did discover his homosexuality and arrested him, which brought serious consequences.[16] He was charged on a morals violation. Had this been wartime, "blackmail" would have been the usual excuse. What an irony, since there exists not a single known instance of government-related sexual blackmail, heterosexual or homosexual.[17] If all this sounds a bit passé for modern America, it is not; a few weeks before the second Gulf War, at a time of great need, nine linguists, six of them Arabic speakers, two who spoke Korean, and another Chinese, were fired by the Bush administration's language institute for being homosexual. Could this have been the mere foolishness of some low-level federal functionary? Not quite; the action sparked loud ridicule in the press, plus legal protests, but to no effect.[18]

What net is broad enough to catch and unify not only such details, but the broad territory traversed by such divergent characters as Abraham Lincoln and Alan Turing? Most certainly each went his own way and followed his inner compass rather than local social dictates. In that sense, both were essentially nonmoral in ignoring the moral mainstream. Lincoln, in particular, often took joy in defying conventional standards; Turing ignored them as if by default. When policemen finally confronted him in 1954 with a charge of homosexuality he not only answered every question fully and unhesitatingly, he also startled them by stopping to play for them favorite tunes on his violin, as if entertaining honored guests. One can call this openness to the enemy "crazy," as indeed his friends and his mother later did, but one must remember he was a guileless and straightforward follower of his own lights, who, like Lincoln, measured his actions by strictly ethical standards. Whether one looks at Lincoln virtually flaunting Derickson to the many who saw them together, or listens to Turing's tunes on his violin, the message is essentially the same.

Reactions and Comments

_____

I. A RESPECTFUL DISSENT

by Michael Burlingame, Professor Emeritus,
Connecticut College

In the interest of full disclosure I should state that I knew and liked Dr. Tripp, who several years ago very generously gave me a copy of his remarkable Lincoln database in return for a digital copy of my book, *The Inner World of Lincoln*. At that time I was using an Apple computer, which could not read the disk containing that database; Dr. Tripp kindly lent me an IBM machine, which I picked up at his home in Nyack. I think fondly of Dr. Tripp whenever I consult that database, which is virtually every day as I work on my multivolume biography of Lincoln. We spoke on the phone occasionally, discussing various aspects of Lincoln's life and respectfully disagreed on many subjects.

One topic on which we emphatically did agree was the Lincolns' marriage, which was more woe-filled than even its bleak portrayal in this volume suggests. I welcome the publication of *The Intimate World of Abraham Lincoln* as a useful antidote to what John Y. Simon (dean of documentary editing in American history, editor of the monumental *Papers of U. S. Grant*, and cowinner of the Lincoln prize) aptly called "the legend of Lincoln's happy marriage."[1] That legend began half a century ago when Ruth Painter Randall began publishing books about Mary Lincoln. The premier Lincoln scholar of our time, Douglas L. Wilson (winner of the Lincoln prize for *Honor's Voice: The Transformation of Abraham Lincoln;* author of *Lincoln before Washington: New Perspectives on the Illinois Years;* coeditor of the invaluable *Herndon's Informants: Letters, Interviews, and Statements about Abraham Lincoln*, which won the Abraham Lincoln Institute book prize; and codirector of the project to transcribe, annotate, and mount on the Internet the Library of Congress's collection of Abraham Lincoln papers) justly deems Mrs. Randall's writings on Mary Lincoln "a highly partisan and self-conscious effort to rescue the character and reputation" of her subject.[2] David Herbert Donald, chief protégé of Mrs. Randall's husband, James, has in his various writings on the sixteenth president helped perpetuate the myth of the happy marriage.[3]

The most recent incarnation of the "happy marriage legend" is David Grubin's six-hour documentary, *A House Divided* (PBS, 2001), which makes some passing references to trouble in the marriage but which ignores a mountain of evidence showing that Lincoln's married life was, in Herndon's words, "a domestic hell on earth," a "burning, scorching hell," "as terrible as death and as gloomy as the grave."[4] Carl Schurz, the eminent German-American reformer who knew the Lincolns and championed the Republican cause, called the marriage "the greatest tragedy of Mr. Lincoln's existence."[5] Those who dealt with Mary Lincoln in the White House had little good to say about her. The president's chief personal secretary, John G. Nicolay, referred to the First Lady as "her Satanic majesty."[6] Nicolay's assistant, John Hay, called her "the Hellcat."[7] The White House physician, Dr. Robert K. Stone, used similar imagery, terming her "a perfect devil."[8] Benjamin Brown French, the commissioner of public buildings who worked with her often, likened Mary Lincoln to a hyena.[9]

Dr. Tripp dwells on Mrs. Lincoln's unethical conduct as First Lady, but curiously he says little about her deplorable conduct before her husband became president.[10] She physically abused Lincoln, striking him with firewood, chasing him out of the house with a knife, cursing and ridiculing him in public, flinging hot coffee in his face, and hurling potatoes, books, and other objects at him. Her ungovernable temper also led her to strike her children as well as her servants. Overwhelming evidence documenting such behavior can be found in *The Inner World of Abraham Lincoln*. Since that volume appeared in 1994 more such evidence has turned up and is incorporated in my forthcoming multivolume life of Lincoln.

Insofar as Dr. Tripp's book helps disabuse the reading public of the "legend of Lincoln's happy marriage" it serves a valuable function, but insofar as it leads people to think that Lincoln was gay, it does a disservice to history, for the evidence Dr. Tripp adduced fails to support the case. This is also the view of David Herbert Donald, author of *Lincoln, Lincoln's Herndon, Lincoln Reconsidered*, and two-time winner of the Pulitzer prize. (More full disclosure: Professor Donald was my mentor in my undergraduate years at Princeton and in my graduate studies at Johns Hopkins, and though we disagree about Lincoln, I will be eternally grateful for all he did for me throughout the 1960s.) In his 2003 book, *"We Are Lincoln Men": Abraham Lincoln and His Friends*, Professor Donald addresses the two cases—Joshua Speed and David Derickson—that Dr. Tripp dwells on at greatest length and which provide the strongest evidence for his thesis that Lincoln was "primarily homosexual."

Professor Donald rightly points out that Lincoln's letters to Speed in the 1840s, while the most intimate that he ever penned, lack a homoerotic tone, and "unlike the letters between other enamored males that have been preserved, are totally lacking in expressions of warm affection." Tellingly, Professor Donald observes that Lincoln's use of "yours forever" in letters to Speed, a phrase that Dr. Tripp finds significant, also appears in his letters to others, including William Herndon, Samuel D. Marshall, Richard S. Thomas, Andrew Johnston, Elihu B. Washburne, and John Todd Stuart. It is possible that Speed's letters to Lincoln in the 1840s may contain "expressions of warm affection," but they are not now available. Someday they may surface, but until then it must be said that the Speed-Lincoln correspondence does not sustain Dr. Tripp's contention that they were homosexual lovers.

The most convincing objection to that thesis, Professor Donald argues, is Lincoln's 1864 statement to Assistant Attorney General Titian J. Coffey about James Speed, whom the president called "a man I know well, though not so well as I know his brother Joshua.

That, however, is not strange, for I slept with Joshua for four years, and I suppose I ought to know him."[11] Professor Donald comments: "I simply cannot believe that, if the early relationship between Joshua Speed and Lincoln had been sexual, the President of the United States would so freely and publicly speak of it." And so Professor Donald concludes that, in his judgment, "these two young men were simply close, warm friends, who came close to achieving Montaigne's definition of complete comradeship, a relationship in which 'all things being by effect common between them: wills, thoughts, judgments, goods. . . . honour, and life."[12]

Lincoln also acknowledged that he had slept with Charles Maltby over a long period. In 1863, the journalist James W. Simonton reported that Maltby, with whom Lincoln had served as a clerk at a New Salem store three decades earlier, testified in Washington about corruption among government officials. Commenting on the veracity of that testimony, Lincoln said (according to Simonton): "I know Maltby, for I slept with him six months, and he used to be an honest man." (I called Dr. Tripp's attention to Maltby, but he failed to find this reference, which appears in a 1998 book which I edited, *Lincoln Observed: Civil War Dispatches of Noah Brooks.)*[13]

Professor Donald's argument could apply as well to Speed, who told a friend that "he and Lincoln slept together about four years." This friend gave a variation on the story of Lincoln's first meeting with Speed. The latter allegedly told the former, "my partner [James Bell] and I have been sleeping in the same bed for some time. He is gone now, and if you wish, you can take his place."[14] It seems unlikely that Speed would have been so open about that sleeping arrangement if he and Lincoln (or he and Bell) had been homosexual lovers. Between 1837 and 1841 Lincoln bunked with Speed in the room above the store, where Speed's clerks, William H. Herndon and Charles R. Hurst, also slept.[15] There was no partition and hence no privacy for those four men sharing that upstairs dormitory.[16]

Professor Donald also doubts that Lincoln and Captain Derickson were homosexual lovers and suggests that the president "developed what Aristotle would call an enjoyable friendship with Derickson, who was an amiable, undemanding companion." He notes that the president, when afflicted with insomnia, occasionally "talked with Derickson until late into the night. I think it is hardly surprising that he may on occasion have asked the congenial captain to share his bed; in those days, it was not unusual for men to sleep together. And it is possible–though neither man ever mentioned it–that he offered his guest a nightshirt. That their relationship was friendly, not sexual, is suggested by the ease with which their association ended when Derickson returned to Pennsylvania. They never saw each other again."[17] Indeed, it is striking that Derickson's Company K of the 150th Pennsylvania Volunteers stayed on as a presidential guard throughout the Civil War, but the captain left to become a provost marshal in April 1863.[18]

Another historian, Professor Charles B. Strozier, author of *Lincoln's Quest for Union: A Psychological Portrait*, shares Professor Donald's skepticism: "It is highly unlikely, it seems to me (though it cannot be decisively excluded as a possibility), that Lincoln had a sexual relationship with Joshua Speed. Had Lincoln been homosexual, his relationship with Speed would have been less complicated—and he would not have become the Lincoln we know in history."[19]

There is evidence above and beyond Lincoln's marriage and fatherhood indicating that he was sexually and romantically attracted to some women. He was "a Man of strong passions for woman," according to his good friend David Davis, who said that Lincoln's "Conscience Kept him from seduction" and "saved many a woman."[20] (As president, Lincoln allegedly told a friend: "I believe there is even a system of female brokerage in offices here in Washington, for I am constantly beset by women of all sorts, high and low, pretty and ugly, modest and the other sort. Here, yesterday, a very handsome young lady called; she would not take a denial, was admitted, and went straight to work soliciting a certain office for somebody supposed to be her husband. She pled her cause dexterously, eloquently, and at times was almost successful by her importunate entreaties. By degrees she came closer and closer to me as I sat in my chair, until really her face was so near my own that I thought she wanted me to kiss her; when my indignation came to my relief, and drawing myself back and straightening myself up, I gave her the proper sort of a look and said: 'Mrs. —, you are very pretty, and it's very tempting, BUT I WON'T.'" Bill Clinton might have profited from his example.)[21]

Herndon also recollected that Lincoln was "a man of terribly strong passions for women" and "could scarcely keep his hands off them." Lincoln once confessed to Herndon that in the mid-1830s he had succumbed to "a devilish passion" for a girl in Beardstown.[22] Long after his wedding, Lincoln, while riding the legal circuit in central Illinois, made improper advances to a young woman sleeping in a bed near his. Lincoln told Milton Hay, James H. Matheny, and Herndon that while spending the night at the home of a friend, he was awakened by the foot of his host's grown daughter, which inadvertently "fell on Lincoln's pillow. This put the *devil* into Lincoln at once, thinking that the girl did this of a purpose. Lincoln reached up his hand and put it where it ought not to be. The girl awoke, got up, and went to her mother's bed and told what had happened." Fortunately for Lincoln, who hurriedly departed the next morning, the mother urged her daughter to keep quiet.[23]

Lincoln reportedly told a similar tale to James Short: While surveying in Sangamon County, "he was put to bed in the same room with two girls, the head of his bed being next to the foot of the girls' bed. In the night he commenced tickling the feet of one of the girls with his fingers. As she seemed to enjoy it as much as he did he then tickled a little higher up; and as he would tickle higher the girl would shove down lower and the higher he tickled the lower she moved." Lincoln "would tell the story with evident enjoyment" but "never told how the thing ended."[24]

In early adulthood, Lincoln may have availed himself of the services of prostitutes. During the Black Hawk War he and other militiamen visited a whorehouse in Galena.[25] Herndon told Caroline Dall that "Up to the time of Anne Rutledge's death Lincoln was a pure perfectly chaste man. Afterwards in his misery—he fell into the habits of his neighborhood."[26] Herndon alleged that from 1837 to 1842, Lincoln and Joshua Speed, "a lady's man," were "quite *familiar*—to go no further [—] with the women."[27] On at least one occasion Lincoln shared Speed's taste in fancy women—in fact, the very same woman. Speed said that around 1839 or 1840, he "was keeping a pretty woman" in Springfield, and Lincoln, "desirous to have *a little*," asked his bunkmate, "do you know where I can get *some*." Speed replied, "Yes I do, & if you will wait a moment or so I'll send you to the place with a note. You cant get *it* without a note or by my appearance."

Armed with Speed's note, Lincoln "went to see the girl—handed her the note after a short 'how do you do &c.' Lincoln told his business and the girl, after some protestations, agreed to satisfy him. Things went on right—Lincoln and the girl stript off and went to bed. Before any thing was done Lincoln said to the girl—'How much do you charge'. 'Five dollars, Mr. Lincoln'. Mr. Lincoln said—'I've only got $3.' Well said the girl—'I'll trust you, Mr Lincoln, for $2. Lincoln thought a moment or so and said—'I do not wish to go on credit—I'm poor & I don't know where my next dollar will come from and I cannot afford to cheat you.' Lincoln after some words of encouragement from the girl got up out of bed,—buttoned up his pants and offered the girl the $3.00, which she would not take, saying—Mr Lincoln— 'You are the most conscientious man I ever saw.'"[28] If Speed was homosexual and impotent with women, as Dr. Tripp argues, why did he keep this "pretty woman" in Springfield? If Lincoln was having sex with Speed, why would he ask him where he could "get some"?

There is good evidence, as Herndon remarked, that Speed was a "lady's man" and highly susceptible to Cupid's arrows, falling in love with women regularly.[29] In March 1841, he wrote his sister about his latest romantic scrape. "I endeavor to persuade myself that there is more pleasure in pursuit of an object, than there is in its possession. This general rule I wish *now* most particularly to apply to women. I have been most anxiously in pursuit of one—and from all present appearances, if my philosophy be true I am to be most enviably felicitous, for I may have as much of the anticipation and pursuit as I please, but the possession I can hardly even hope to realize." He then describes the object of his desire: "her hair hangs loosely in curls about her neck like the wind at play with sunbeams. Three dimples she has upon her face one upon each of her rosy cheeks and one upon her chin each the grave of some unfortunate lover—and your poor illfated and susceptible brother lies entombed in the one that is darkest and deepest. I never expect to see the light of the sun again or any other light than that of the two stars that ever beam just over the dimple in which my heart lies buried."[30]

The beauty described by Speed was Matilda Edwards, a gorgeous eighteen-year-old from Alton, Illinois, who had spent the winter in Springfield capturing the hearts of many men, including Lincoln.

Dr. Tripp does not mention her in his book, and when I brought her up in a phone conversation, he pooh-poohed the idea that Lincoln cared for her. But there is ample evidence, both reminiscent and contemporary, indicating that he fell deeply in love with Matilda Edwards and broke his engagement to Mary Todd because his heart belonged to Miss Edwards, even though she cared not for him. Matilda, the cousin of Ninian Edwards, had come to Springfield from Alton and stayed with Mary Todd at the Edwards home. (Mary's eldest sister Elizabeth was married to Ninian Edwards.)[31] Like many other young women, she visited the capital during the legislative session to attend the numerous parties given at that time. A "legislative winter was as eagerly looked forward to by the ladies of the State as the politicians because it promised a season of constant gaiety and entertainment. An invitation to spend such a time in Springfield was a coveted honor. The pretty girls from all over the State flocked [t]here under the care of fathers, uncles, brothers, cousins, any relation, however remote who could be induced to bring them."[32]

The "very bright" Matilda Edwards was "something of a coquette" and "a most fascinating and handsome girl, tall, graceful, and rather reserved," who "moved at ease among the social and refined classes at Alton."[33] Her "gentle temper, her conciliatory manners, and the sweetness of her heart made her dear to all who knew her."[34] Lincoln was among the many young men who held her dear. In the winter of 1840–1841, she and Mary Todd "seemed to form the grand centre of attraction. Swarms of strangers who had little else to engage their attention hovered around them, to catch a *passing smile.*"[35] (She received twenty-two offers of marriage before wedding Newton D. Strong in 1843.)[36] In January 1841, Jane Bell reported from Springfield that Lincoln had declared "if he had it in his power he would not have one feature in her face altered, he thinks she is so perfect." Mrs. Bell added that Lincoln and Joshua Speed "spent the most of their time at [the] Edwards [home] this winter" and that "Lincoln could never bear to leave Miss Edward's side in company" because "he fell desperately in love with her."[37] Mrs. Nicholas H. Ridgely, a leader of Springfield society in Lincoln's day, told her granddaughter "that it was common report that Lincoln had fallen in love with Matilda Edwards."[38] According to Matilda Edwards's niece,

Virginia Quigley, "It is an undisputed fact that Lincoln was in love with her. She never cared for him."[39] In 1875, Lincoln's close friend Orville H. Browning told an interviewer that "Lincoln became very much attached to her (Miss Matilda Edwards) and finally fell desperately in love with her."[40] Mrs. Benjamin S. Edwards recalled that Lincoln "was deeply in love with Matilda Edwards."[41] Lincoln informed James Matheny, who served as a groomsman at his wedding in 1842, "[t]hat he loved Miss Matilda Edwards."[42] Joshua Speed told Herndon that "Lincoln did love Miss Edwards."[43] Herndon said Lincoln was determined "to marry Miss Edwards if he could."[44] Mary Todd's brother-in-law, Ninian Edwards, informed Herndon "That during Lincoln's Courtship with Miss Todd—afterwards Lincoln's wife—that he, Lincoln, fell in Love with a Miss [Matilda] Edwards—daughter of Cyrus Edwards."[45]

Evidently Lincoln was too shy to approach the young beauty, who confided to Elizabeth Edwards that he "never mentioned Such a Subject to me: he never even Stooped to pay me a Compliment."[46] (She may not have been entirely truthful with Elizabeth Edwards. A niece of one of Mary Todd's sisters said it "was always known in our family . . . that Mr. Lincoln courted Matilda Edwards, a fact which for many reasons she divulged only to her nearest and dearest.")[47] After becoming enamored of Matilda Edwards, Lincoln told John J. Hardin "that he thought he did not love" Mary Todd "as he should and that he would do her a great wrong if he married her."[48] Hardin shared this story with his sister Lucy Jane, whose son-in-law informed a journalist that "some have questioned whether he [Lincoln] ever wanted to marry Mary Todd. He was in love with her cousin," Matilda Edwards.[49]

Dr. Tripp's failure to deal with the Matilda Edwards story is hardly unique. Professor Donald states flatly: "There is no credible evidence that Lincoln was in love with Matilda Edwards."[50] As Douglas Wilson sensibly remarks, in assessing the validity of this judgment "each reader must judge for himself" but it "is difficult to understand why Speed, Matheny, Browning, and the others should all lack credibility."[51] Moreover, Professor Donald alleges that "Those who blamed Matilda Edwards for the rupture [of Lincoln's engagement to Mary Todd] seem to have their information from Mary Todd, who was looking for a face-saving reason for Lincoln's actions."[52] That may have been true of the testimony of Ninian Edwards and Mrs. Benjamin S. Edwards, but it is probably not true of the testimony of James Matheny, Orville Browning, William Herndon, Joshua Speed, Jane D. Bell, Mrs. Nicholas H. Ridgely, Matilda Edwards's niece, and the son-in-law of John J. Hardin's sister. Professor Donald's dismissal of the testimony of Browning is especially puzzling, for in his book on Lincoln's friendships, he devotes an entire chapter to the close relationship between Browning and Lincoln.[53]

Charles B. Strozier also dismisses Browning's testimony, saying: "Browning not only hedges his statement with a crucial 'perhaps' but also was not at this point particularly close to Lincoln nor was ever an intimate part of the Todd family circle."[54] Professor Strozier is wrong on all three counts. In 1875, Browning did not use "a crucial 'perhaps'" when describing Lincoln's passion for Matilda Edwards: "Mr. Lincoln became very attached to her, (Miss Matilda Edwards) and finally fell desperately in love with her." Lincoln, Browning insisted, "was engaged to Miss Todd, and in love with Miss Edwards." Professor Strozier is also wrong in suggesting that Lincoln and Browning were not close in 1840–41. Both were then Whig leaders in the Illinois General Assembly. Browning recalled that as legislators they had become good friends. "At that time," he said, "Lincoln had seen but very little of what might be called society and was very awkward, and very much embarrassed in the presence of ladies. Mrs. Browning very soon discovered his great merits, and treated him with a certain frank cordiality which put Lincoln entirely at his ease. On this account he became very much attached to her. He used to come to our room, and spend his evenings with Mrs. Browning. As I now remember, most of his spare time was occupied in this way." In 1872, Browning described to Isaac N. Arnold his friendship with Lincoln: from the mid-1830s until 1865, "our relations were very intimate: I think more so than is usual. Our friendship was close, warm, and, I believe, sincere. I know mine for him was, and I never had reason to distrust his for me. Our relations, to my knowledge, were never interrupted for a moment." Professor Strozier is also wrong in suggesting that Browning was not close to the Todd circle. Browning said that in the winter of 1840–41 "I was at Mr. Edwards' a great deal, and Miss

Todd used to sit down with me, and talk to me sometimes till midnight, about this affair of hers with Mr. Lincoln."[55]

In assessing the Matilda Edwards story, it should be noted that as an adolescent, Lincoln had been similarly smitten by a beautiful girl. In August 1827, he reportedly was captivated by the beauty of Julia Evans in Princeton, Indiana.[56]

Months after Matilda Edwards left Springfield, Lincoln courted Sarah Rickard, the sister of Mrs. William Butler (née Elizabeth Rickard). To his credit, Dr. Tripp does not dismiss that story as some historians have done.[57] Between 1837 and 1842, when Lincoln boarded at the Butlers' house, he often saw Sarah, who lived there. She was only twelve years old when they first met; four years later he seriously paid her court and proposed marriage, remarking that since her name was Sarah, she was destined to marry Abraham. She rejected the offer because, as she later explained, "his peculiar manner and his General deportment would not be likely to fascinate a young girl just entering the society world."[58] She "liked him as a big brother," not as a potential mate.[59]

Lincoln also proposed to Mary Owens. Dr. Tripp suggests that Lincoln did not really love her, but there is good reason to believe otherwise. Lincoln's mocking account of the courtship, written to Mrs. Orville H. Browning, is misleading, for his correspondence with Mary Owens indicates that he "had grown very fond" of her and backed away only after she wounded him severely.[60] Herndon plausibly maintained that a letter he wrote her in December 1836 "shows that Lincoln was in love—deeply in love."[61] In that missive, Lincoln complained of "the mortification of looking in the Post Office for your letter and not finding it." He scolded her: "You see, I am mad about that *old letter* yet. I don't like verry well to risk you again. I'll try you once more anyhow." The prospect of spending ten weeks with the legislature in Vandalia was intolerable, he lamented, for he missed her. "Write back as soon as you get this, and if possible say something that will please me, for really I have not [been] pleased since I left you."[62] Such language, hardly that of an indifferent suitor, tends to confirm Parthena Hill's statement that "Lincoln thought a great deal" of Mary Owens.[63]

. . .

Much more evidence shows that Lincoln loved Ann Rutledge. Dr. Tripp's chapter on her is the weakest part of his book. Herndon interviewed two dozen people who had knowledge of Ann. Twenty-two of them testified that Lincoln courted her or loved her or both; two expressed no opinion on that matter. Seventeen of the twenty-four testified that Lincoln grieved at her death; seven expressed no opinion. Seventeen also said that Lincoln and Ann were engaged; two denied it; and five expressed no opinion.[64] Of those twenty-four, two (Mentor Graham and Isaac Cogdal) said they heard about the romance from Lincoln himself. Another (Mrs. Nancy Green) was so close to Lincoln that her testimony in all likelihood was based on what he had confided to her. At least two other informants heard the story of the romance from Ann (her brother, Robert B. Rutledge, and her cousin, James McGrady Rutledge.) In addition, others gave testimony about the romance, including two of Ann's sisters, a cousin, and a close friend.[65]

In dismissing this mountain of evidence Dr. Tripp misguidedly argues from authority, citing an appendix in a multivolume study of Lincoln's presidency by James G. Randall, the most celebrated academic Lincoln scholar of two generations ago. Dr. Tripp makes an understandable error in ascribing that appendix, titled "Sifting the Ann Rutledge Evidence," to Randall himself, whereas in fact, it was largely written by his wife, Ruth Painter Randall. Mrs. Randall, the highly partisan biographer of Mary Todd Lincoln, deplored "the shabby manner in which the image of Ann [Rutledge] has tended to obscure the years of Lincoln's love and devotion to Mary, his wife, and to belittle her love and devotion for him."[66] Mrs. Randall wanted this curious appendix to form part of the main text. (In fact, it was inserted as an early chapter in the original manuscript, now at Lincoln Memorial University, Harrogate, Tennessee.) She undertook the project at the suggestion of her husband, James G. Randall, who told a friend that his wife "helped me handsomely with the Ann Rutledge chapter. It is very largely her work."[67] Since Mrs. Randall was not a trained historian but rather an aggressive special pleader for Mary Lincoln, the argument from authority loses much of its force.

In 1990, John Y. Simon showed how badly Mrs. Randall had misread the evidence; later that year, Douglas L. Wilson corroborated Simon's findings.[68] Three years thereafter their interpretations were fleshed out in John Evangelist Walsh, *The Shadows Rise: Abraham Lincoln and the Ann Rutledge Legend.*[69] Readers interested in knowing the true story of Lincoln's relationship with Ann Rutledge should consult those sources, along with Wilson's *Honor's Voice.*

Dr. Tripp makes an egregious error in handling the testimony of Isaac Cogdal, a friend of Lincoln who in the winter of 1860–61 asked him about Ann Rutledge. In 1866, Cogdal recounted their conversation to Herndon, quoting Lincoln directly. Dr. Tripp dismisses Cogdal's testimony on stylistic grounds, arguing that Lincoln did not use words and syntax like those which Cogdal ascribed to him. Far be it from me to belittle close textual analysis (using that technique, along with other evidence, I have tried to show that John Hay wrote Lincoln's beloved letter of condolence to the Widow Bixby.)[70] But it is unreasonable to discredit Cogdal just because he reproduced Lincoln's remarks in a prose style different from Lincoln's written work. Don E. Fehrenbacher, an eminent Lincoln authority, offered sensible advice about direct quotations of Lincoln's recollected words, recalled years after the event: "[M]uch recorded utterance, and especially the lengthy remark recalled over a long span of time, should probably be treated as, at best, *indirect* rather than *direct* quotation."[71] Indeed, Cogdal's version of Lincoln's words should be regarded as paraphrases and not subjected to the kind of rigorous stylistic scrutiny that would be appropriate when trying to determine the authenticity of a Lincoln letter. Everything about Cogdal's testimony seems plausible except the exact phraseology allegedly used by Lincoln.[72]

Dr. Tripp's dismissal of the testimony of more than two dozen informants in the case of Ann Rutledge contrasts sharply with his willingness to accept extremely scanty evidence to prove that Lincoln had homosexual relations with William G. Greene, Abner Y. Ellis, Horace White, Henry C. Whitney, and Elmer Ellsworth. Those highly conjectural cases do not pass the test that Dr. Tripp says he used to establish the validity of a claim: namely, at least two independent sources. That test is met in the case of Derickson, which is the strongest argument made for a homosexual relationship in this volume. But it is far from conclusive.

. . .

Since it is virtually impossible to prove a negative, Dr. Tripp's thesis cannot be rejected outright. But given the paucity of hard evidence adduced by him, and given the abundance of contrary evidence indicating that Lincoln was drawn romantically and sexually to some women, a reasonable conclusion, it seems to me, would be that it is possible but highly unlikely that Abraham Lincoln was "predominantly homosexual."

II. AN ENTHUSIASTIC ENDORSEMENT

by Michael B. Chesson, Department of History,
University of Massachusetts, Boston

Was Abraham Lincoln gay? That is Tripp's question, premise, and conclusion. The stale objection that the word "homosexual" was not coined until after the Civil War is pointless. Skeptics may cite the dating of terms as long as they do not pretend that sex between men did not occur until after certain words appeared in print. The delightful "gay" was ripped out of other contexts by activists, and is more modern as applied to men.[1] That Lincoln did not and could not have thought of himself as either "homosexual" or "gay" (Lincoln was seldom truly gay) hardly detracts from the substance of Tripp's argument.

The Intimate World finally takes this topic out of the closet, where it has long been sequestered by the Lincoln establishment, despite the increasing curiosity of the general public about the rail splitter's sexual orientation, as noted by his preeminent biographer, David Herbert Donald.[2] Until now it has been mostly gay activists who have discussed it. I hasten to add that I am not now, nor have I ever been, either gay or an activist. As someone who cares about our past, particularly the Civil War era, I am indebted to those who are, lonely pioneers like my emeritus colleague Charles Shively. I did chair a session at the annual convention of the American Historical Association in 1990, "Gay American Presidents?," with papers on Washington, Buchanan, Lincoln, and Garfield. Tripp was present, and got the Lincoln bug. Must we now think of "Gabe" as the great gay emancipator, the homosexual martyred captain of the Union ship of state?

Was Lincoln engaging in civil unions even during our most uncivil war?

Donald has said that "the subject deserves careful and cautious consideration."³ That is wise advice from a meticulous scholar, a two-time Pulitzer Prize winner and author of the finest life of Lincoln. What to make of Tripp's evidence, arguments, and conclusions? As scholars, we are called on to follow the truth wherever it may lead, even if we find that a president had a child by a slave woman or oral sex with an intern. Yet professional historians, particularly the lords of the Lincoln establishment, have advanced with less than deliberate speed, and often obfuscation—if not howls of rage and denial—at the merest suggestion that their hero and mine might have been anything less than a robust, masculine, "normal," exclusively heterosexual American male in the mainstream of nineteenth-century American culture, as found in the northern states, specifically the Indiana and Illinois frontier. Their unspoken credo is "don't ask, don't tell, don't pursue." The truth, that is, whatever it may be. All agree that Lincoln was robust. He was certainly masculine, meaning that he was a man's man, attracted to other men, as they were certainly drawn to him. He was also a freak, a very odd-looking human, as William H. Herndon, who knew him best, and others who knew him well, have testified.⁴ But that Lincoln was "normal" in almost any sense or meaning of that much abused word will not bear even the most casual scrutiny. Tripp has demonstrated, at the very least, that in his orientation Lincoln was not exclusively heterosexual.

Orthodox Lincolnistas point to his marriage with Mary Todd, a union that produced four sons, though only one survived into adulthood. That a married man who sired children could not have been a homosexual seems to be their proposition. Yet how many of us know or have heard of happily married couples, often with children, one of whom after some years or even decades of presumed domestic bliss, discovers their true identity, divorces their partner, and has a same-sex relationship? Whether Lincoln's marriage was happy or hellish or somewhere in between remains a subject of bitter debate among specialists, largely along gender lines, from Jean Baker to Michael Burlingame and Douglas Wilson, but there is abundant evidence of marital discord and dissatisfaction on the part of both partners, before and during the Civil War.⁵

Lincoln's courtship, if that is what it can be called, of Mary Owens is usually presented as an early sign of the future president's sexuality. This comic episode is both an example of his incredible awkwardness with women and of a streak of cruelty best seen in his letter about the affair to Mrs. Orville H. Browning, a close friend and the wife of a Whig ally, in which he ridiculed the fat, wrinkled, and toothless Kentuckian.[6] Whether Miss Owens (who married another man) looked that way before she rejected Lincoln's ambivalently offered hand has been questioned, by the notably critical Edgar Lee Masters, among others.[7]

More often pulled out of the shadows in recent years is the legend of an earlier, doomed love affair. Ann Rutledge and Abe fell in love, but she died tragically. Lincoln never recovered. That at least is the story. It is rather like that of another Ann, in Lancaster, Pennsylvania. James Buchanan fell in love with Ann Coleman, but something drove them apart. Ann went to Philadelphia, where she soon died. Buchanan never recovered, and was a bachelor until his death. But his warm and affectionate relationship and years of rooming with fellow congressman and future vice president William R. King was the talk of Washington gossips for decades.[8]

In the several generations of scholarship following Herndon's launch of the Rutledge affair in 1866 the pendulum first swung far to the right in the early twentieth century against there being any factual basis for it. In the past two decades it has begun to swing back to, if not a consensus, a growing belief that the two were more than casual friends. Though the great majority of Herndon's informants supported the story after Lincoln's death, and decades after Ann's, there is no contemporary factual basis for anything more than ordinary friendship between them, a much weaker foundation than the evidence for Lincoln's attraction to males.[9]

This poor young woman would have been forgotten, little noted nor long remembered, had it not been for her tie to Lincoln. She has been made to bear a far heavier weight than she can support. Ann has returned to prominence as proof that Lincoln did not love Mary Todd, or that he was normal, because he was romantically linked with not one, but three women (sufficient evidence of a conventional sexual orientation)—or both. Ann was his first (perhaps only?) love, before Mary Todd, and a more appealing figure (as described by her rejected suitor) than Mary Owens. Mrs. Lincoln was understandably hostile to the Rutledge story, and so have been most biographers until quite recently. Other women have even been suggested as Lincoln crushes, including teenagers Matilda Edwards and Sarah Rickard.[10] Whatever may be the truth about Ann, Mary, Abe, and the younger damsels, far more scholarly energy has been spent on the matter than on the possibility that his sexual orientation was something other than exclusively straight. It is a classic case of the assumption of heterosexuality. For those averse to homoerotic relationships, why not focus on Lincoln's only documented sexual relationship with a woman, and the nature and quality of that marriage?[11]

It is often said that William Herndon and Mary Todd had a mutual hatred. They were clearly jealous of each other. Both loved the same man, and resented having to share him. But Herndon's biography at times is quite sympathetic to her. He realized that being Mrs. Lincoln was not easy, anymore than being married to her was. For her part, the grieving widow unbent enough to give Herndon details about married life with the late President. Lincoln did not seem interested in other women (despite Mary's occasional tantrums), but Tripp gives us a case in which he may have been unfaithful, sleeping with Captain Derickson during his wife's absences. What of Mary's fidelity? Donald in his masterful *Lincoln* comments on her low-cut gowns and scandalous décolletage. Using the same evidence, Baker, one of Donald's most prominent students, feels that the president was proud of his wife's assets, and of her display of them.[12] The evidence for Mary's infidelity is no more than circumstantial, whether with the slimy Henry Wikoff or her acting commissioner of public buildings, the mysterious William S. Wood. At best, she showed a serious lack of judgment, in the eyes of her many critics. At worst, she was accused of infidelity, by Illinois governor Richard Yates, one of Lincoln's strongest supporters, among others.[13]

Deborah Hayden has reexamined Herndon's story that Lincoln had, or thought he had, syphilis.[14] Most authorities doubt it. They claim to know Lincoln's body, his sexual experience or lack thereof, and his symptoms, real or imagined, better than he did himself. It is unlikely that he would have married knowing he would pass a social disease on to Mary Todd. But it is even less likely that *she* had it to pass on to him. The real question is why Lincoln would have said such a thing to Herndon—unless he felt guilt or concern about something he had done. Can Herndon be trusted? Ranking officers in the Abraham Lincoln brigade believe Herndon when he supports their thesis, and accuse him of various scholarly crimes, even alcoholism, when he does not. What this story suggests is that Lincoln had premarital sex; it is not the only such story. Whether it was with a woman (always assumed) is a mystery; as is his possible venereal infection.

By far the most documented of Lincoln's male affairs is that with Joshua Speed. Every serious Lincoln scholar has discussed their friendship, often at some length and in considerable detail. I continue to be struck by their first encounter, as described by biographers from Browne to Donald, and a host of lesser authors.[15] Lincoln arrived in Springfield in 1837 without even the money to rent a room. Speed sized up the stranger, whom he knew by reputation, and invited him upstairs to inspect the double bed where he had been sleeping alone. Is it not possible that Lincoln appraised the friendly merchant as well? Abe went up, and soon came down to say that he had moved in. It was lust at first sight. But what developed over the next few years was true love, beyond platonic friendship.

Donald in his recent work goes so far as to ask if it was a homoerotic albeit chaste relationship, similar to those of Emerson and Webster with male friends.[16] But there was no sex between Speed and Lincoln, no spilling of seed. How does Donald know? He cannot know with certainty, but gives it as his considered judgment, having spent a lifetime studying Lincoln. Just as the burden of proof is on Tripp to make his case, so it is on anyone making a positive denial about the mere possibility of a sexual relationship.

These two young men slept together in the same bed for nearly four years, and despite having married and separated, had a tie that bound them for life. Speed went back to the slave state of Kentucky. His politics increasingly diverged from Lincoln's, especially in the 1850s after the latter's political rebirth. Yet when President Lincoln needed help in the early months of his administration he reached out to Speed. What is even more surprising, given their recent political differences, is that Speed responded, quickly, warmly, fervently.[17] The best part of what they once enjoyed had not been destroyed by marriage, slavery, politics, time, or distance. How many men have had a friendship that survived such pitfalls?

Jean H. Baker's reaction to their bed-sharing is commonsensical and feminine. Of course they had sex. How could they not have, given their close physical proximity for several years? What is the evidence? In part, that the arrangement continued for so long. Once Lincoln got his bearings in Springfield he could have found other accommodations, but chose not to. Readers unversed in the Lincoln literature will not realize how rare Baker's reaction is among top rank scholars. Most biographers have treated the matter as if the two men were in a bundling bed, with a board between them.[18] Straight males who have to sleep together, at least in our own time, and from my own knowledge, are careful to stay as far on "their own" side of the bed as possible, and they make other arrangements immediately, unless it is a one-night stand. Rather than share a bed, most straights will flip a coin. The loser gets the sofa or the floor.

But anyone with a little knowledge about American popular culture and public lodgings in the early republic will immediately object to a claim of homosexuality based on sleeping arrangements. Tripp's critics will say that men often slept together, in boarding houses or while traveling and staying at inns. Quite true. Tucked in the Charles Sumner papers at Harvard's Houghton Library is the story of a Scot on the road at night who finally manages to find lodging. An innkeeper tells him there is but one space left, in a bed already occupied by two men. The Scot climbs in between an Englishman and an Irishman. Early in the morning the Englishman is awakened by a wet warmth on the sheets. Realizing what has happened, and the culprit, he shakes him awake. The Scot, unperturbed, tells the Englishman to relax, because "I have done worse to him behind me," meaning the poor Irishman. Lincoln would have liked the joke and told it far better than I have (with three different accents) to an all-male audience, perhaps adding some sexually suggestive details. Lincoln's humor was smutty, with a strong anal fixation. I am skeptical that it was the joke, and not the smut, that attracted him. Anyone can tell a dirty joke, some better than others. The trick is to tell a good joke that is not off-color. Most of Lincoln's could not be told in mixed company, or printed for later generations to enjoy, thanks to the censorship of his friends, though a few can be dredged out of Sandburg.

This joke shows at least two things. Yes, men did sleep together, at various times and places, without being homosexual (since the word had not been invented). Civil War soldiers slept together, sometimes in spoon fashion in groups, to keep warm and survive, without being gay (not invented then). Second, and more surprising, Senator Sumner had a sense of humor, unlike some of the distinguished members of the Lincoln establishment, and academics generally. Yet how many American males in any age have voluntarily, cheerfully, even joyously slept with another man in the same bed for three or four years without having been involved sexually? Surely this question will attract the scholar squirrels (Gore Vidal's phrase) of the historical profession. Just in the free states before the Civil War there must have been hundreds, even thousands, of men, either prominent or soon to be, who shared a bed for one or more years with another man yet carefully avoided any touching under the blankets. Go find them.

Lincoln did not marry until the age of thirty-three, in 1842, seven years older than the typical man of the era (though most Springfield bachelors married by twenty-four, according to Baker). Even outsiders coming to the capital, like Lincoln, usually married by thirty-one.[19] Speed, five years younger, preceded him to the altar. Why did Lincoln wait so long? Ann Rutledge or no, Mary Owens or not, let alone nubile teens, Lincoln married reluctantly and, like Speed, with great trepidation. Most young men married eagerly and expectantly.[20]

Lincoln was clearly attracted to the charismatic drillmaster Elmer Ellsworth. He installed him in his Springfield law office and arranged an army commission for him in 1861 under dubious circumstances. Tripp presents evidence about Lincoln's feelings for the young man that have somehow been left out of most biographies of the president. It is all rather queer, so to speak, that careful, methodical biographers have failed either to find, or present, such material.[21] It amounts to a conspiracy of silence.

Even odder is Lincoln's friendship with a soldier, David V. Derickson of the 150th Pennsylvania Volunteers.[22] Washington women talked about them sleeping together, it was mentioned in the unit's regimental history decades later, and noted by historians Ida Tarbell (who never married) and Margaret Leech generations ago. Yet among a dozen major male biographers only Sandburg mentions the subject.[23] Captain Derickson led two hundred Bucktails to march in Lincoln's funeral procession at Cleveland.[24] If it walks like a duck and quacks like a duck, whether mallard or Muscovy, it might really be a duck. Do straight male presidential birders need their Pentax 7x50s to spot a sexual orientation different from their own? As Baker notes, women are more alert to or sensitive about such matters than men, especially if like Herndon and so many others they are unable, or unwilling, to see the tree for the forest. Carl Sandburg, a rude man, still sensed Lincoln (and Speed's) nature, as quoted by Tripp and Baker.

Tripp, for all his research, sophistication, and insight, has not proved his case conclusively. There is no smoking gun that we can link to Long Abe. Unlike the exposers of Jefferson, Tripp could not call upon DNA evidence or other scientific proof, though Lincoln's bone fragments at the Armed Forces Institute of Pathology await analysis, which might reveal the presence of the Marfan syndrome (unlikely) or venereal disease (possible). Unless some scholar finds previously unknown love letters by Lincoln or another man, or a diary kept by someone like Speed, this case will never be proven to the satisfaction of the Union army of Lincoln idolaters and homophobes everywhere.

Nor, perhaps, has Tripp proven his case even beyond a reasonable doubt. But any open-minded reader who has reached this point may well have a reasonable doubt about the nature of Lincoln's sexuality. The "Tall Sucker" was a very strange man, one of the strangest in American history, and certainly the oddest to reach a position of national prominence, let alone the presidency. If Lincoln was a homosexual, or primarily so inclined, then suddenly our image of this mysterious man gains some clarity. Not everything falls into place, but many things do, including some important, even essential, elements of who Lincoln was, why he acted in the way he did, and a possible reason for his sadness, loneliness, and secretive nature. Lincoln was different from other men, and he knew it. More telling, virtually every man who knew him at all well, long before he rose to prominence, recognized it. In fact, the men who claimed to know him best, if honest, usually admitted that they did not understand him. Women did not know him as intimately, but many commented on his awkwardness around young, available females.

In our age of gay-bashing, AIDS, and rampant priestly pe-
dophilia, the governor of Massachusetts blocks gay marriage with a
1913 antimiscegenation law. Other politicians invoke God to protect
the sanctity of matrimony (in a society where half of all marriages
fail) or waffle on the issue. In the midst of the 2004 election-year
twaddle, Tripp's book is far more than a breath of fresh air. Like *The
Homosexual Matrix*, it is a hurricane of revelation. Its flaws can and
will be corrected in the debate that has now begun. It has been
thirty-five years since Stonewall. In the words of a recent ad, "Your
sister is getting married. Her fiancé's name is Jill. Let the discussion
begin." And so it should, and must. If not now, when? If not by historians, who? Will scholars, Civil War buffs, and fans of Honest Abe
be content to let the Moral Majority and the self-annointed Lincoln
establishment set the agenda for research on our greatest president?

III. A PSYCHOLOGIST'S PERSPECTIVE

by Alice Fennessey, Ph.D.

This book is a vivid, detailed, and invaluable addition to the existing
literature on Lincoln.

I knew C. A. Tripp for many years, and watched him combine his
immense technical expertise with an abiding interest in history, particularly in Abraham Lincoln, to create a massive database of all
things Lincoln. He included both published and unpublished writings by and about Lincoln to make the totality of existing Lincolnia
more accurate, easily analyzed, and accessible to all who are interested.

The computer database allowed him to make detailed and un-
precedented analyses of the Lincoln literature, thereby revealing errors and fraudulent stories about Lincoln that had been accepted for
generations. Tripp's analysis has changed the opinions of many leading Lincoln scholars on a variety of topics.

This book is also, to my knowledge, the first book on Lincoln by
a prominent psychologist with a background in sexuality. Dr. Tripp
was the author of a scholarly book on homosexuality that became a
college textbook and is printed in fourteen languages.

As his friend, I can attest that the point of this book is not to make the case that Lincoln was a homosexual or, in effect, to "out" him. First, the facts about Lincoln's relationships with men have been widely known for a long time; second, according to the Kinsey criteria which Dr. Tripp uses, Lincoln was definitionally bisexual. Sexuality, like every variable in nature, when measured carefully reflects a bell curve. Lincoln, like every other human being, was at a certain point on that curve. The aim of this book is to define Lincoln's true identity as nearly as possible, not merely on a sexual curve, but as a whole man. Obscuring any part of his personality creates a barrier to this understanding.

When biographers—through ignorance, prejudices, or romantic notions—tamper with reality they can obscure the truth and create an image which stands in the way of seeing the real man. The interesting question psychologically—about Lincoln's biographers—is why no amount of irrefutable evidence has dislodged it. One obvious explanation is Lincoln's status as an American icon, imbued with virtues revered by viewers, a picture of perfection that resists change. A man who does and says unexpected or inexplicable things, as Lincoln did, is unnerving. Icons are not allowed that liberty.

Ultimately, the Tripp I knew wished to present the truth, a concept that was closer to Lincoln's heart than any other.

[F]irst Chronicles of [R]uben

[N]ow thair was a man in those days whose name was ruben and the Same was very grate in substance in horses and Cattle and Swine and avery grate house hold and it Came to pass that when the Sons of ruben grew up that thay ware desirus of taking to them Selves wives and being too well known as to onor in ther own Country So thay took to them Selves a Journey in to a far Country and procured to them Selves wives   and it Came to pass that when thay ware about to make the return home that thay Sent a messenger before them to bare the tidines to there parents So thay inquired of the mesengers what time there Sones and there wives wood Come   So thay made a grate feast and Cald all ther kinsmen and neighbors in and maid grate preperations   So when the time drew near thay sent out two men to meet the grooms and ther brids with a treet to welcome them and to acompny them So when thay Came near to the house of ruben there father the mesengers Came on before them and gave a Shout and the whole multitude ran out with Sho[uts of] Joy and mu-sick playing on all kinds of instruments of musick Some playing on harps and Some on vials and Some blowing on rams hornes Some Casten dust and ashes tourd heaven and amongst the rest Josiah blo-ing his buble making Sound So grate that it maid the neighborin hills and valys eco with the resonding aclamation So when they had played and harped Sounded tell the grooms and brides approached the gate the father ruben met them and welcomed them in to his house and the weding dinner being now ready thay ware all invited to Set down to dinner placing the bridegroomes and ther wives at each end of the table waters ware then apointed to Carve and wate on the guests So when thay had all eaten and ware ful and mary thay went out and Sang and played tell evening and when thay had made an end of feasting and rejoising the multitude dispersed each to his one home the family then took Seat with

ther waters to Converse awhile which time preperations ware being maid in an upper Chamber for the brids to be first Convayed by the waters to ther beds this being done the waters took the two brids up stares to ther beds placing one in a bed at the rite hand of the Stares and the other on the left   the waters Come down and nancy the mther inquired of the waters which of the brids was paced on the rite hand and thay told her   So She gave directions to the waters of the bridegrooms and thair thay took the bridegrooms and placed them in the rong beds and Came down Stares but the mother being fearful that thair mite be a mistake inquired again of the waters and learning the fact took the light and Sprang up tares and runing to one of the beds exclaimed ruben you are in bed with Charleses wife   the young men both being alarmed Sprang out of bed and ran with such violence against each other that thay Came very near nocking each other down which gave evidence to those below that the mistake was Ceartain   thay all Came down and had a Conversation about who had maid the mistake but it Could not be decided

So ended the Chapter

i will tell you a Joke about Jouel and mary
it is neither a Joke nor a [s]tory
for rubin and Charles has married two girles
but biley has married a boy
the girles he had tried on every Side
but none could he get to agree
all was in vain he went home again
and sens that he is maried to natty

so biley and naty agreed very well
and mamas well pleased at the matc[h]

the egg it is laid but Natys afraid
the Shell is So Soft that it never will hatc[h]
but betsy She Said you Cursed ball [bald] head
my Suiter you never Can be
besids your low Cro[t]ch proclaimes you a botch
and that never Can anser for me

From Douglas L. Wilson and Rodney O. Davis, eds., *Herndon's Informants: Letters, Interviews, and Statements about Abraham Lincoln* (University of Illinois Press, Chicago, 1998).

The Speed Letters

LETTER NO. 1

Springfield, June 19, 1841

Dear Speed:

We have had the highest state of excitement here for a week past that our community has ever witnessed; and although the public feeling is somewhat allayed, the curious affair which aroused it is very far from being even yet cleared of mystery. It would take a quire of paper to give you anything like a full account of it, and I therefore only propose a brief outline. The chief personages in the drama are Archibald Fisher, supposed to be murdered, and Archibald Trailor, Henry Trailor, and William Trailor, supposed to have murdered him. The three Trailors are brothers; the first, Arch., as you know, lives in town; the second, Henry, in Clary's Grove; and the third, William, in Warren County; and Fisher, the supposed murderee, being without a family, had made his home with William. On Saturday evening, being the 29th of May, Fisher and William came to Henry's in a one-horse dearborn, and there stayed over Sunday; and on Monday all three came to Springfield (Henry on horseback), and joined Archibald at Myers's, the Dutch carpenter. That evening at supper Fisher was missing, and so next morning some ineffectual search was made for him; and on Tuesday, at one o'clock P.M., William and Henry started home without him.

In a day or so Henry and one or two of his Clary Grove neighbors came back and searched for him again, and advertised his disappearance in the paper. The knowledge of the matter thus far had not been general, and here it dropped entirely, till about the 10th instant, when Keys received a letter from the postmaster in Warren County, stating that William had arrived at home, and was telling a very mysterious and improbable story about the disappearance of Fisher, which induced the community there to suppose he had been disposed of unfairly. Keys made this letter public, which immediately set the whole town and adjoining county agog, and so it has continued until yesterday. The mass of the people commenced a systematic search for the dead body, while Wickersham was despatched to arrest Henry Trailor at the Grove, and Jim Maxcy to Warren to arrest William. On Monday last, Henry was brought in, and showed an evident inclination to insinuate that he knew Fisher to be dead, and that Arch. and William had killed him. He said he guessed the body could be found in Spring Creek, between the Beardstown road and Hickox's mill. Away the people swept like a herd of buffalo, and cut down Hickox's mill-dam *nolens volens*, to draw the water out of the pond, and then went up and down and down and up the creek, fishing and raking, and ducking and diving for two days, and, after all, no dead body found.

In the meantime a sort of scuffling-ground had been found in the brush in the angle, or point, where the road leading into the woods past the brewery and the one leading in past the brick-yard join. From the scuffle-ground was the sign of something about the size of a man having been dragged to the edge of the thicket, where it joined the track of some small wheeled carriage which was drawn by one horse, as shown by the horse tracks. The carriage-track led off toward Spring Creek. Near this drag-trail Dr. Merryman found *two hairs*, which, after a long scientific examination, he pronounced to be triangular human hairs, which term, he says, includes within it the whiskers, the hair growing under the arms and on other parts of the body; and he judged that these two were of the whiskers, because the ends were cut, showing that they had flourished in the neighborhood of the razor's operations. On Thursday last Jim Maxcy brought in William Trailor from Warren. On the same day Arch. was arrested and put in jail. Yesterday (Friday) William was put upon his examining trial before May and Lavely. Archibald and Henry were both present. Lamborn prosecuted, and Logan, Baker, and your humble servant defended. A great many witnesses were introduced and examined, but I shall only mention those whose testimony seemed to be the most important. The first of these was Captain Ransdell. He swore that when William and Henry left Springfield for home on Tuesday before mentioned, they did not take the direct route,—which, you know, leads by the butcher shop,—but that they followed the street north until they got opposite, or nearly opposite, May's new house, after which he could not see them from where he stood; and it was afterward proven that in about an hour after they started, they came into the street by the butcher shop from toward the brick-yard. Dr. Merryman and others swore to what is stated about the scuffle-ground, drag-trail, whiskers, and carriage-tracks. Henry was then introduced by the prosecution. He swore that when they started for home, they went out north, as Ransdell stated, and turned down west by the brick-yard into the woods, and there met Archibald; that they proceeded a small distance farther, where he was placed as a sentinel to watch for and announce the approach of any one that might happen that way; that William and Arch. took the dearborn out of the road a small distance to the edge of the thicket, where they stopped, and he saw them lift the body of a man into it; that they then moved off with the carriage in the direction of Hickox's mill, and he loitered about for something like an hour, when William returned with the carriage, but without Arch., and said they had put *him* in a safe place; that they went somehow—he did not know exactly how—into the road close to the brewery, and proceeded on to Clary's Grove. He also stated that some time during the day William told him that he and Arch. had killed Fisher the evening before; that the way they did it was by him (William) knocking him down with a club, and Arch. then choking him to death.

An old man from Warren, called Dr. Gilmore, was then introduced on the part of the defence. He swore that he had known Fisher for several years; that Fisher had resided at his house a long time at each of two different spells—once while he built a barn for him, and once while he was doctored for some chronic disease; that two or three years ago Fisher had a serious hurt in his head by the bursting of a gun, since which he had been subject to continued bad health and occasional aberration of mind. He also stated that on last Tuesday, being the same day that Maxcy arrested William Trailor, he (the doctor) was from home in the early part of the day, and on his return, about eleven o'clock, found Fisher at his house in bed, and apparently very unwell; that he asked him how he came from Springfield; that Fisher said he had come by Peoria, and also told several other places he had been at not in the direction of Peoria, which showed that he at the time of speaking did not know where he had been wandering about in a state of derangement. He further stated that in about two hours he received a note from one of Trailor's friends, advising him of his arrest, and requesting him to go on to Springfield as a witness, to testify to the state of Fisher's health in former times; that he immediately set off, calling up two of his neighbors as company, and, riding all evening and all night, overtook Maxcy and William at Lewiston in Fulton County; that Maxcy refusing to discharge Trailor upon his statement, his two neighbors returned and he came on to Springfield. Some question being made as to whether the doctor's story was not fabrication, several acquaintances of his (among whom was the same postmaster who wrote Keys, as before mentioned) were introduced as sort of compurgators, who swore that they knew the doctor to be of good character for truth and veracity, and generally of good character in every way. Here the testimony ended, and the Trailors were discharged, Arch. and William expressing both in word and manner their entire confidence that Fisher would be found alive at the doctor's by Galloway, Mallory, and Myers, who a day before had been despatched for that purpose; while Henry still protested that no power on earth could ever show Fisher alive. Thus stands this curious affair now. When the doctor's story was first made public, it was amusing to scan and contemplate the countenances and hear the remarks of those who had been actively engaged in the search for the dead body. Some looked quizzical, some melancholy, and some furiously angry. Porter, who had been very active, swore he always knew the man was not dead, and that *he* had not stirred an inch to hunt for him; Langford, who had taken the lead in cutting down Hickox's milldam, and wanted to hang Hickox for objecting, looked most awfully woebegone: he seemed the *"wictim of hunrequited haffections,"* as represented in the comic almanacs we used to laugh over; and Hart, the little drayman that hauled Molly home once, said it was too *damned* bad to have so much trouble, and no hanging after all.

I commenced this letter on yesterday, since which I received yours of the 13th. I stick to my promise to come to Louisville. Nothing new here except what I have written. I have not seen Sarah since my long trip, and I am going out there as soon as I mail this letter.

Yours forever,
Lincoln

LETTER NO. 2

Bloomington, Illinois, Sept. 27th 1841

Miss Mary Speed,
Louisville, Ky.

My Friend:

Having resolved to write to some of your Mother's family, and not having the express permission of any one of them [to] do so, I have had some little difficulty in determining on which to inflict the task of reading what I now feel must be a most dull and silly letter; but when I remembered that you and I were something of cronies while I was at Farmington, and that, while there, I once was under the necessity of shutting you up in a room to prevent your committing an assault and battery upon me, I instantly decided that you should be the devoted one.

I assume that you have not heard from Joshua & myself since we left, because I think it doubtful whether he has written—

You remember there was some uneasiness about Joshua's health when we left. That little indisposition of his turned out to be nothing serious; and it was pretty nearly forgotten when we reached Springfield. We got on board the Steam Boat Lebanon, in the locks of the Canal about 12 o'clock M. of the day we left, and reached St. Louis the next Monday at 8 P.M.—Nothing of interest happened during the passage, except the vexatious delays occasioned by the sand bars he thought interesting.—By the way, a fine example was presented on board the boat for contemplating the effect of *condition* upon human happiness. A gentleman had purchased twelve negroes in diferent parts of Kentucky and was taking them to a farm in the South. They were chained six and six together—A small iron clevis was around the left wrist of each, and this fastened to the main chain by a shorter one at a convenient distance from the others; so that the negroes were strung together precisely like so many fish upon a trot-line—In this condition they were being separated forever from the scenes of their childhood, their friends, their fathers and mothers, and brothers and sisters, and many of them, from their wives and children, and going into perpetual slavery where the lash of the master is proverbially more ruthless and unrelenting than any other where; and yet amid all these distressing circumstances, as we would think them, they were the most cheerful and apparently happy creatures on board. One, whose offence for which he had been sold was an over-fondness for his wife, played the fiddle almost continually; and the others danced, sung, cracked jokes, and played various games with cards from day to day.—How true it is that "God tempers the wind to the shorn lamb," or in other words, that He renders the worst of human conditions tolerable, while He permits the best, to be nothing better than tolerable.—

To return to the narrative. When we reached Springfield, I staid but one day when I started on this tedious circuit where I now am. Do you remember my going to the city while I was in Kentucky, to have a tooth extracted, and making a failure of it? Well, that same old tooth got to paining me so much, that about a week since I had it torn out, bringing with it a bit of the jawbone; the consequence of which is that my mouth is now so sore that I can neither talk nor eat—I am litterally "subsisting on savoury remembrances"—that is, being unable to eat, I am living upon the remembrance of the delicious dishes of peaches and cream we used to have at your house—

When we left, Miss Fanny Henning was owing you a visit, as I understood—Has she paid it yet? If she has, are you not convinced that she is one of the sweetest girls in the world? There is but one thing about her, so far as I could perceive, that I would have otherwise than as it is—That is something of a tendency to melancholly—This, let it be observed, is a misfortune, not a fault—Give her an assurance of my verry highest regard, when you see her—

Is little Siss Eliza Davis at your house yet? If she is, kiss her "o'er and o'er again" for me—Tell your Mother that I have not got her "present" with me; but that I intend to read it regularly when I return home. I doubt not that it is really, as she says, the best cure for the "blues" could one but take it according to the truth—Give my respects to all your sisters (including "Aunt Emma") and brothers—Tell Mrs. Peay, of whose happy face I shall long retain a pleasant remembrance, that I have been trying to think of a name for her homestead, but, as yet, can not satisfy myself with one—I shall be verry happy to receive a line from you, soon after you receive this; and, in case you choose to favour me with one, address it to Charleston, Coles Co., Ill, as I shall be there about the time to receive it.—

Your sincere friend
A. Lincoln

LETTER No. 3

[January 3, 1842.]

My dear Speed:

Feeling, as you know I do, the deepest solicitude for the success of the enterprise you are engaged in, I adopt this as the last method I can invent to aid you, in case (which God forbid!) you shall need any aid. I do not place what I am going to say on paper, because I can say it any better in that way than I could by word of mouth, but, were I to say it orally before we part, most likely you would forget it at the very time when it might do you some good. As I think it reasonable that you will feel very badly some time between this and the final consummation of your purpose, it is intended that you shall read this just at such a time.

Why I say it is reasonable that you will feel very badly yet, is because of three special causes added to the general one which I shall mention.

The general cause is, that you are naturally of a nervous temperament; and this I say from what I have seen of you personally, and what you have told me concerning your mother at various times, and concerning your brother William at the time his wife died.

The first special cause is your exposure to bad weather on your journey, which my experience clearly proves to be very severe on defective nerves.

The second is the absence of all business and conversation of friends, which might divert your mind, give it occasional rest from the intensity of thought which will sometimes wear the sweetest idea threadbare and turn it to the bitterness of death.

The third is the rapid and near approach of that crisis on which all your thoughts and feelings concentrate.

If, on the contrary, you shall, as I expect you will at some time, be agonized and distressed, let me, who have some reason to speak with judgment on such a subject, beseech you to ascribe it to the causes I have mentioned, and not to some false and ruinous suggestion of the Devil.

"But," you will say, "do not your causes apply to every one engaged in a like undertaking?" By no means. The particular causes, to a greater or less extent perhaps, do apply in all cases; but the general one,—nervous debility, which is the key and conductor of all the particular ones, and without which they would be utterly harmless,—though it does pertain to you, does not pertain to one in a thousand. It is out of this that the painful difference between you and the mass of the world springs.

I know what the painful point with you is at all times when you are unhappy. It is an apprehension that you do not love her as you should. What nonsense! How came you to court her? Was it because you thought she desired it, and that you had given her reason to expect it? If it was for that, why did not the same reason make you court Ann Todd, and at least twenty others of whom you can think, and to whom it would apply with greater force than to her? Did you court her for her wealth? Why, you know she had none. But you say you reasoned yourself into it. What do you mean by that? Was it not that you found yourself unable to reason yourself out of it? Did you not think, and partly form the purpose, of courting her the first time you ever saw or heard of her? What had reason to do with it at that early stage? There was nothing at that time for reason to work upon. Whether she was moral, amiable, sensible, or even of good character, you did not, nor could then know, except, perhaps, you might infer the last from the company you found her in. All you then did or could know of her was her personal appearance and deportment; and these, if they impress at all, impress the heart, and not the head.

Say candidly, were not those heavenly *black eyes* the whole basis of all your early *reasoning* on the subject? After you and I had once been at her residence, did you not go and take me all the way to Lexington and back, for no other purpose but to get to see her again, on our return in that seeming to take a trip for that express object?

What earthly consideration would you take to find her scouting and despising you, and giving herself up to another? But of this you have no apprehension; and therefore you cannot bring it home to your feelings.

I shall be so anxious about you that I want you to write every mail.

Your friend,
LINCOLN.

Letter No. 4

Springfield, Illinois, February 3, 1842

Dear Speed:

Your letter of the 25th Jany came to hand today. You well know that I do not feel my own sorrows much more keenly than I do yours, when I know of them; and yet I assure you I was not much hurt by what you wrote me of your excessively bad feeling at the time you wrote. Not that I am less capable of sympathizing with you now than ever, not that I am less your friend than ever, but because I hope and believe, that your present anxiety and distress about *her* health and *her* life must and will forever banish those horrid doubts, which I know you sometimes felt, as to the truth of your affection for her. If they can once and forever be removed (and I almost feel a presentiment that the Almighty has sent your present affliction expressly for that object) surely, nothing can come in their stead, to fill their immeasurable measure of misery. The death scenes of those we love, are surely painful enough; but these we are prepared to and expect to see. They happen to all, and all know they must happen. Painful as they are, they are not an unlooked-for-sorrow. Should she, as you fear, be destined to an early grave, it is indeed, a great consolation to know that she is so well prepared to meet it. Her religion, which you once disliked so much, I will venture you now prize most highly.

But I hope your melancholly bodings as to her early death, are not well founded. I even hope, that ere this reaches you, she will have returned with improved and still improving health; and that you will have met her, and forgotten the sorrows of the past, in the enjoyment of the present.

I would say more if I could but it seems I have said enough. It really appears to me that you yourself ought to rejoice, and not sorrow, at this indubitable evidence of your undying affection for her. Why Speed, if you did not love her, although you might not wish her death, you would most calmly be resigned to it. Perhaps this point is no longer a question with you, and my pertenacious dwelling upon it, is a rude intrusion upon your feelings. If so, you must pardon me. You, know the Hell I have suffered on that point, and how tender I am upon it. You know I do not mean wrong.

I have been quite clear of hypo since you left; even better than I was along in the fall.

I have seen Sarah but once. She seemed very cheerful, and so I said nothing to her about what we spoke of.

Old Uncle Billy Herndon is dead; and it is said this evening that Uncle Ben Ferguson will not live. This I believe is all the news, and enough at that unless it were better.

Write me immediately on the receipt of this.

> Your friend as ever
> Lincoln.

Letter No. 5

Springfield, Illinois, February 13, 1842.

Dear Speed:

Yours of the 1st instant came to hand three or four days ago. When this shall reach you, you will have been Fanny's husband several days. You know my desire to befriend you is everlasting; that I will never cease while I know how to do anything. But you will always hereafter be on ground that I have never occupied, and consequently, if advice were needed, I might advise wrong.

I do fondly hope, however, that you will never again need any comfort from abroad. But should I be mistaken in this, should excessive pleasure still be accompanied with a painful counterpart at times, and even the agony of despondency, that very shortly you are to feel well again. I am now fully convinced that you love her as ardently as you are capable of loving. Your ever being happy in her presence, and your intense anxiety about her health, if there were nothing else, would place this beyond all dispute in my mind. I incline to think it probable that your nerves will fail you occasionally for a while; but once you get them fairly graded now, that trouble is over forever.

I think, if I were you, in case my mind were not exactly right, I would avoid being idle. I would immediately engage in some business, or go to making preparations for it, which would be the same thing. —If you went through the ceremony calmly, or even with sufficient composure not to excite alarm in any present, you are safe beyond question, and in two or three months, to say the most, will be the happiest of men.

I would desire you to give my particular respects to Fanny; but perhaps you will not wish her to know you have received this, lest she should desire to see it. Make her write me an answer to my last letter to her at any rate. I would set great value upon another letter from her. Write me whenever you have leisure.

Yours forever,
A. Lincoln.

P. S. I have been quite a man since you left.

LETTER NO. 6

Springfield, February 25, 1842.

Dear Speed:

I received yours of the 12th written the day you went down to William's place, some days since, but delayed answering it till I should receive the promised one of the 16th, which came last night. I opened the latter with intense anxiety and trepidation; so much, that although it turned out better than I expected, I have hardly yet, at the distance of ten hours, become calm.

I tell you, Speed, our *forebodings* (for which you and I are rather peculiar) are all the worst sort of nonsense. I fancied, from the time I received your letter of Saturday, that the one of Wednesday was never to come, and yet it *did* come, and what is more, it is perfectly clear, both from its tone and handwriting, that you were much happier, or, if you think the term preferable, less miserable, when you wrote it than when you wrote the last one before. You had so obviously improved at the very time I so much feared you would have grown worse. You say that something indescribably horrible and alarming still haunts you. You will not say that three months from now, I will venture. When your nerves once get steady now, the whole trouble will be over forever. Nor should you become impatient at their being even very slow in becoming steady. Again you say, you much fear that that Elysium of which you have dreamed so much is never to be realized. Well, if it shall not, I dare swear it will not be the fault of her who is now your wife. I now have no doubt that it is the peculiar misfortune of both you and me to dream dreams of Elysium far exceeding all that anything earthly can realize. Far short of your dreams as black-eyed Fanny. If you could but contemplate her through my imagination, it would appear ridiculous to you that any one should for a moment think of being unhappy with her. My old father used to have a saying that "If you make a bad bargain, hug it all the tighter"; and it occurs to me that if the bargain you have just closed can possibly be called a bad one, it is certainly the most pleasant one for applying that maxim to which my fancy can by any effort picture.

I write another letter, inclosing this, which you can show her, if she desires it. I do this because she would think strangely, perhaps, should you tell her that you received no letters from me, or, telling her you do, should refuse to let her see them. I close this, entertaining the confident hope that every successive letter I shall have from you (which I here pray may not be few, nor far between) may show you possessing a more steady hand and cheerful heart than the last preceding it.

As ever, your friend,
Lincoln.

Letter No. 7

Springfield, February 25, 1842

Dear Speed:

Yours of the 16th instant, announcing that Miss Fanny and you are "no more twain, but one flesh," reached me this morning. I have no way of telling you how much happiness I wish you both, though I believe you both can conceive it. I feel somewhat jealous of both of you now; you will be so exclusively concerned for one another, that I shall be forgotten entirely. My acquaintance with Miss Fanny (I call her this, lest you should think I am speaking of your mother) was too short for me to reasonably hope to long be remembered by her; and still I am sure I shall not forget her soon. Try if you cannot remind her of that debt she owes me—and be sure you do not interfere to prevent her paying it.

I regret to learn that you have resolved to not return to Illinois. I shall be very lonesome without you. How miserably things seem to be arranged in this world! If we have no friends, we have no pleasure; and if we have them, we are sure to lose them, and be doubly pained by the loss. I did hope she and you would make your home here; but I own I have no right to insist. You owe obligations to her ten thousand times more sacred than any you can owe to others; and in that light let them be respected and observed. It is natural that she should desire to remain with her relatives and friends. As to friends, however, she could not need them anywhere; she would have them in abundance here.

Give my kind remembrance to Mr. Williamson and his family, particularly Miss Elizabeth; also to your Mother, brothers, and sisters. Ask little Eliza Davis if she will ride to town with me if I come there again. And finally, give Fanny a double reciprocation of all the love she sent me. Write me often, and believe me.

Yours forever,
Lincoln.

P. S. Poor Eastham is gone at last. He died awhile before day this morning. They say he was very loath to die.

No clerk is appointed yet.

L.

LETTER No. 8

SPRINGFIELD, MARCH 27, 1842.

Dear Speed:

Yours of the 10th instant was received three or four days since. You know I am sincere when I tell you the pleasure its contents gave me was, and is, inexpressible. As to your farm matter, I have no sympathy with you. I have no farm, nor ever expect to have, and consequently have not studied the subject enough to be much interested in it. I can only say that I am glad you are satisfied and pleased with it. But on that other subject, to me of the most intense interest whether in joy or in sorrow, I never had the power to withhold my sympathy from you. It cannot be told how it now thrills me with joy to hear you say you are "far happier than you ever expected to be." That much I know is enough. I know you too well to suppose your expectations were not, at least, sometimes extravagant, and if the reality exceeds them all, I say, enough, dear Lord. I am not going beyond the truth when I tell you that the short space it took me to read your last letter gave me more pleasure than the total sum of all I have enjoyed since the fatal first of Jany—'41. Since then it seems to me I should have been entirely happy, but for the never-absent idea that there is one still unhappy whom I have contributed to make so. That still kills my soul. I cannot but reproach myself for even wishing to be happy while she is otherwise. She accompanied a large party on the railroad cars to Jacksonville last Monday, and on her return spoke, so that I heard of it, of having enjoyed the trip exceedingly. God be praised for that.

You know with what sleepless vigilance I have watched you ever since the commencement of your affair; and although I am almost confident it is useless, I cannot forbear once more to say that I think it is even yet possible for your spirits to flag down and leave you miserable. If they should, don't fail to remember that they cannot long remain so. One thing I can tell you which I know you will be glad to hear, and that is that I have seen Sarah and scrutinized her feelings as well as I could, and am fully convinced she is far happier now than she has been for the last fifteen months past.

You will see by the last Sangamon Journal that I made a temperance speech on the 22nd of February, which I claim that Fanny and you shall read as an act of charity to me; for I cannot learn that anybody else has read it, or is likely to. Fortunately it is not very long, and I shall deem it a sufficient compliance with my request if one of you listens while the other reads it.

As to your Lockridge matter, it is only necessary to say that there has been no court since you left, and that the next commences to-morrow morning, during which I suppose we cannot fail to get a judgment.

I wish you would learn of Everett what he would take, over and above a discharge for all the trouble we have been at, to take his business out of our hands and give it to somebody else. It is impossible to collect money on that or any other claim here now; and although you know I am not a very petulant man, I declare I am almost out of patience with Mr. Everett's importunity. It seems like he not only writes all the letters he can himself, but gets everybody else in Louisville and vicinity to be constantly writing to us about his claim. I have always said that Mr. Everett is a very clever fellow, and I am very sorry he cannot be obliged; but it does seem to me he ought to know we are interested to collect his money, and therefore *would* do it if we could.

I am neither joking nor in a pet when I say we would thank him to transfer his business to some other, without any compensation for what we have done, provided he will see the court cost paid, for which we are security.

The sweet violet you inclosed came safely to hand, but it was so dry, and mashed so flat, that it crumbled to dust at the first attempt to handle it. The juice that mashed out of it stained a place in the letter, which I mean to preserve and cherish for the sake of her who procured it to be sent. My renewed good wishes to her in particular, and generally to all such of your relatives who know me.

> As ever,
> Lincoln.

Letter No. 9

Springfield, Illinois, July 4, 1842.

Dear Speed:

Yours of the 16th June was received only a day or two since. It was not mailed at Louisville till the 25th. You speak of the great time that has elapsed since I wrote you. Let me explain that. Your letter reached here a day or two after I had started on the circuit. I was gone five or six weeks, so that I got the letter only a few weeks before Butler started to your country. I thought it scarcely worth while to write you the news which he could and would tell you more in detail. On his return he told me you would write me soon, and so I waited for your letter. As to my having been displeased with your advice, surely you know better than that. I know you do, and therefore I will not labor to convince you. True, that subject is painful to me; but it is not your silence, or the silence of all the world, that can make me forget it. I acknowledge the correctness of your advice too; but before I resolve to do the one thing or the other, I must regain my confidence in my own ability to keep my resolves when they are made. In that ability you know I once prided myself as the only or at least the chief gem of my character; that gem I lost—how and where, too well you know. I have not yet regained it; and until I do, I cannot trust myself in any matter of much importance. I believe now that had you understood my case at the time as well as I understood yours afterward, by the aid you would have given me sufficient confidence to begin that or the like of that again.

You make a kind acknowledgment of your obligations to me for your present happiness. I am pleased with that acknowledgment; but a thousand times more am I pleased to know that you enjoy a degree of happiness worthy of an acknowledgment. The truth is, I am not sure that there was any merit with me in the part I took in your difficulty; I was drawn to it as by fate; if I would I could not have done less than I did. I was always superstitious; and as part of my superstition I believe God made me one of the instruments of bringing your Fanny and you together, which union I have no doubt He had foreordained. Whatever he designs he will do for *me* yet. "Stand *still*, and see the salvation of the Lord" is my text just now. If, as you say, you have told Fanny *all*, I should have no objection to her seeing this letter, but for its reference to our friend here. Let her seeing it depend upon whether she has ever known anything of my affair; and if she has not, do not let her.

I do not think I can come to Kentucky this season. I am so poor and make so little headway in the world, that I drop back in a month of idleness as much as I gain in a year's rowing. I should like to visit you again. I should like to see that "sis" of yours that was absent when I was there, though I suppose she would run away again if she were to hear I was coming.

About your collecting business—We have sued Branson; and will sue the others to the next court, unless they give deeds of trust as you require.—Col. Allen happened in the office since I commenced this letter, and promises to give a deed of trust—He says he had made the arrangement to pay you, and would have done it, but for the going down of the Shawnee money—We did not get the note in time to sue Hall at the last Tazewell court— Lockridge's property is levied on for you. John Irwin has done nothing with that Baker & Van Bergen matter—we will not fail to bring the suite for your use, where they are in the name of James Bell & Co. I have made you a subscriber to the Journal, and also sent the number containing the temperance speech.

My respects and esteem to all your friends there, and, by your permission, my love to your Fanny.

Ever yours—LINCOLN.

Letter No. 10

Springfield, October 5, 1842.

Dear Speed:

You have heard of my duel with Shields, and I have now to inform you that the dueling business still rages in this city. Day before
yesterday Shields challenged Butler, who accepted, and proposed
fighting next morning at sunrising in Bob Allen's meadow, one hundred yards' distance, with rifles. To this Whitesides, Shield's second,
said "No," because of the law. Thus ended duel No. 2. Yesterday
Whitesides chose to consider himself insulted by Dr. Merryman,
and so sent him a kind of quasi-challenge, inviting him to meet him
at the Planter's House in St. Louis on the next Friday, to settle their
difficulty. Merryman made me his friend, and sent Whitesides a
note, inquiring to know if he meant his note as a challenge, and if
so, that he would, according to the law in such case made and provided, prescribe the terms of the meeting. Whitesides returned for
answer that if Merryman would meet him at the Planter's House as
desired, he would challenge him. Merryman replied in a note that
he denied Whiteside's right to dictate time and place, but that he
(Merryman) would waive the question of time, and meet him at
Louisiana, Missouri. Upon my presenting this note to Whitesides
and stating verbally its contents, he declined receiving it, saying he
had business in St. Louis, and it was as near as Louisiana. Merryman
then directed me to notify Whitesides that he should publish the
correspondence between them, with such comments as he thought
fit. This I did. Thus it stood at bedtime last night. This morning
Whitesides, by his friend Shields, is praying for a new trial, on the
ground that he was mistaken in Merryman's proposition to meet
him at Louisiana, Missouri, thinking it was the State of Louisiana.
This Merryman hoots at, and is preparing his publication; while the
town is in a ferment, and a street fight somewhat anticipated.

But I began this letter not for what I have been writing, but to
say something on that subject which you know to be of such infinite
solicitude to me. The immense sufferings you endured from the
first days of September till the middle of February you never tried

to conceal from me, and I well understood. You have now been the husband of a lovely woman nearly eight months. That you are happier now than you ever were the day you married her I well know, for without you could not be living. But I have your word for it, too, and the returning elasticity of spirits which is manifested in your letters. But I want to ask a closer question, "Are you now in *feeling* as well as *judgment* glad that you are married as you are?" From anybody but me this would be an impudent question, not to be tolerated; but I know you will pardon it in me. Please answer it quickly, as I feel impatient to know. I have sent my love to your Fanny so often, I fear she is getting tired of it. However, I venture to tender it again.

> Yours forever,
> Lincoln.

LETTER No. 11

Springfield, Ill., Jan. 18, 1843.

Dear Speed:

It has been a long time since I wrote you last, but you have not been forgotten nevertheless. Hurst called on me yesterday and as he said by your directions paid me $74 State Bank paper, $42 Shawneetown paper and $2.59 cents silver. What shall I do with it? The Nesbitts have let the time of redemption run out on the land you bought on their execution, so that the land falls to you, and the cost is to be paid to the officers' somehow. Van Bergen placed his debt on Walters in our hands to collect and pay you. We foreclosed on Walter's house and lots and sold them and bought them in your name. This sale, owing to the peculiarity of the case, was made without valuation or redemption, so that the property is now yours absolutely. But we suppose you would still prefer the money, and that Walters, (as he is re-elected Public Printer) will wish to redeem it. We therefore suggest the propriety of your signing the blank document at the end of this sheet, authorizing Col. Elkin to deed the property to Walters in case he shall redeem it. If he shall not so redeem it, there will be the cost to pay in that case too. It was sold for about $1200, the amount of Van's debt, but although you are the ostensible purchaser, we have a secret contract with Van that he is purchaser for so much of the purchase money as is over and above what will pay you.

I have just called on Judge Browne and find that he will pay nothing but Auditor's warrants, which of course I can not receive. I wish you would direct me to bring a suit against him at once.

Your brother James sent us a note on Bell Boice which you had assigned to your brother William. Ask James to write me whether we shall sue Boice now that Bell is dead.

Mary is very well and continues her old sentiments of friendship for you. How the marriage life goes with us I will tell you when I see you here, which I hope will be very soon.

Ever your friend
A. Lincoln.

Of course the order below is not to be used unless Walters pays the money.

Whereas at a sale of Lots 14, 15, and 16 in Block 7 in E. Iles addition to the late town now city of Springfield, Illinois, made by William F. Elkin as commissioner under a decree of the Sangamon Circuit Court I became the purchaser of said lots now therefore for value received of William Walters, I authorize and direct said Elkin to convey said lots by deed to said Walters, or to any other person that said Walters may direct. Witness my hand and seal this——day of——A.D. 1843.

LETTER NO. 12

Springfield, March 24, 1843.

Dear Speed:

Hurst tells me that Lockridge has redeemed the land in your case, & paid him the money; and that he has written you about it. I now have the pleasure of informing you that Walters has paid me $703.25 (in gold) for you. There is something still due you from him—I think near a hundred dollars, for which I promised him a little additional time—The gold, (except the toll) we hold subject to your order.

We had a meeting of the Whigs of the county here on last Monday to appoint delegates to a district convention, and Baker beat me, & got the delegation instructed to go for him. The meeting, in spite of my attempt to decline it, appointed me one of the delegates; so that in getting Baker the nomination, I shall be "fixed" a good deal like a fellow who is made a groomsman to the man what has cut him out, and is marrying his own dear "gal." About the prospects of your having a namesake at our house, can't say exactly yet.

[A. LINCOLN.]

LETTER NO. 13 — SPEED TO LINCOLN

LOUISVILLE 3 APRIL 1843

Dear Lincoln:

I received yours of 23 March a few days ago, and now write in a hurry to ask that if Mr. Leight a merchant of this place should call on you or the Judge that you will send by him all the money you may have for me—and please get from Moffett the money in his hands for which I gave Lincoln an order also see Hurst and ask him to send by Leight what he may have.

Please send me a calculation of the amt of interest and principle due by Van—how much is due upon the note of 572 32/100 Dolls and how much on the judgment assigned by Baker of 219.80 a separate calculation of each is what I want.

If you get this before Leight calls please endeavour to get the balance of Walters if you can and say to Hurst that he will be so good to collect if he can of Lockridge the 66 dolls due by him. Your *toll* you will keep of course. Make it as light as you can—and believe me as ever.

Yours
J. F. SPEED

LETTER No. 14

Springfield, May 18, 1843.

Dear Speed:

Yours of the 9th instant is duly received, which I do not meet as a "bore," but as a most welcome visitor. I will answer the business part of it first.

The note you enclosed on Cannon & Harlan, I have placed in Moffett's hands according to your directions—Harvey is the constable to have it—I have called three times to get the note, you mention, on B. C. Webster & Co; but did not find Hurst. I will yet get it, and do with it, as you bid. At the April court at Tazewell, I saw Hall, and he then gave me an order on Jewett to draw of him, all rent which may fall due, after the 12th day of Jany. last till your debit shall be paid. The rent is for the house Ransom did live in just above the Globe; and is $222 per year payable quarterly, so that one quarter fell due the 12th April. I presented the order to Jewett since the 12th and he said it was right, and he would accept it, which, however, was not done in writing for want of pen & ink at the time & place. He acknowledged that the quarter's rent was due, and said he would pay it in a short time but could not at the moment. He also said that he thought, by some former arrangement, a portion of that quarter would have to be paid to the Irwins—Thus stands the Hall matter—I think we will get the money on it, in the course of this year. You ask for the amount of interest on your Van Bergen note of $572.32, and also upon the judgment against Van assigned by Baker. The note drew 12 per cent from date, and bore date Oct. 1st 1841. I suppose the 12 per cent ceased at the time we bought in Walters' house which was on the 23rd Dec. 1842. If I count right, the interest up to that time was $78.69 cents, which added to the principal makes $651.01. On this aggregate sum you are entitled to interest at 6 per cent only, from the said 23rd Dec. 1842 until paid. What that will amount to you can calculate for yourself. The judgment assigned by Baker to you for $219.80 was so assigned on the 2nd of April, 1841, and of course draws 6 per cent from that time until paid. This too you can calculate for yourself. About the 25th of March 1843 (the precise date I don't now remember) Walters paid $703.25. This, of course must be remembered in counting interest. According to my count, there was due you of principal & interest on both claims on the 25th of March, 1843—$906.70. Walters then paid $703.25 which leaves still due you, $203.45, drawing 6 per cent from that date. Walters is promising to pay the balance every day, but still has not done it. I think he will do it soon. Allen has gone to nothing, as Butler tells you. There are 200 acres of the tract I took the deed of trust on. The improvements I should suppose you remember as well as I. It is the stage stand on the Shelbyville road, where you always said I wouldn't pay Baker's tavern bill. It seems to me it must be worth much more than the debt; but whether any body will redeem it in these hard times, I cannot say.

In relation to our Congress matter here, you were right in supposing I would support the nominee. Neither Baker nor I, however, is the man, but Hardin, so far as I can judge from present appearances. We shall have no split or trouble about the matter; all will be harmony. In relation to the "coming events" about which Butler wrote you, I had not heard one word before I got your letter; but I have so much confidence in the judgment of a Butler on such a subject that I incline to think there may be some reality in it. What day does Butler appoint? By the way, how do "events" of the same sort come on in your family? Are you possessing houses and lands, and oxen and asses, and men-servants and maid-servants, and begetting sons and daughters? We are not keeping house, but boarding at the Globe Tavern, which is very well kept now by a widow lady of the name of Beck. Our room (the same Dr. Wallace occupied there) and boarding only costs four dollars a week. Ann Todd was married something more than a year since to a fellow by the name of Campbell, and who, Mary says, is pretty much of a "dunce," though he has a little money and property. They live in Boonville, Missouri, and have not been heard from lately enough to enable me to say anything about her health. I reckon it will scarcely be in our power to visit Kentucky this year. Besides poverty and necessity of attending to business, those "coming events," I suspect, would be somewhat in the way. I most heartily wish you and your Fanny would not fail to come. Just let us know the time, a week in advance, and we will have a room provided for you at our house, and all be merry together for a while. Be sure to give my respects to your mother and family. Assure her that if I ever come near her, I will not fail to call and see her. Mary joins in sending love to your Fanny and you.

Yours as ever,
A. Lincoln

Letter No. 15

Springfield, July 26th, 1843

Dear Speed:

Yours of the 17th inst. is received. Your former letter of the 9th of June was also received. The note on Butler I did not wish to collect for reasons well understood by you; and I therefore handed it to Hurst. Butler has not been at home since it was received. He is, I suppose, this moment in New York City.

The B. C. Webster & Co. money you have got, as I see by a letter of yours to Hurst. We received the balance of the Walters money three or four days ago. We received an over-plus for Van at the same time and we take out of the gross sum for you, what, according to our calculation, is your due—That we make to be $212.95. We retain the $12.95 as you see, and send you enclosed two one hundred dollar Missouri bills. You often direct us and Hurst to deposit for you in St. Louis; but this is more difficult than it would be to deposit for you at Knob View, because, every other thing being equal, we do not know who to deposit with in St. Louis whereas we do at Knob View. We therefore enclose the present remittance to you direct.

I was talking with Allen a few days ago, and he said he would like still to try to sell the farm for something more than your debt; but that he would deed to you outright at any time, you desire it, provided you would take it and discharge his debt. You know that under the deed of trust you may sell it for what it will bring, and hold him bound for the balance provided it does not sell for enough to pay the whole debt. I told him I would write you.

We shall look with impatience for your visit this fall. Your Fanny can not be more anxious to see my Molly than the latter is to see her, nor as much so as I am—Don't fail to come—We are but two, as yet—

Your friend as ever,
A. Lincoln.

P.S. Since I wrote the above, I have seen John Irwin, who starts to the East within a week from now, and by whom I have concluded to send the money in preference to enclosing it. He will leave it with your brother James in the city.

A. L.

LETTER No. 16

Springfield, October 22, 1846.

Dear Speed:

Owing to my absence yours of the 10th inst. was not received until yesterday. Since then I have been devoting myself to arrive at a correct conclusion upon your matter of business. It may be that you do not precisely understand the nature and result of the suit against you and Bell's estate. It is a chancery suit, and has been brought to a final decree, in which you are treated as a nominal party only. The decree is that Bell's administration pay the Nelson Fry debt out of the proceeds of Bell's half of the store. So far you are not injured; because you are released from the debt, without having paid any-thing, and Hurst is in no way left liable to you, because the debt he and Bell undertook to pay, is, or will be, paid without your paying it, or any part of it. The question then is, "How are you injured?" By diverting so much of the assets of Bell's estate, to the payment of the Fry debt, the general assets are lessened, and so, will pay a smaller dividend to general creditors; one of which creditors I suppose you are, in effect, as assignor of the note to W. P. Speed. It incidentally enlarges your liability to W. P. Speed, and to that extent, you are injured. How much will this be? I think, $100 or $120—being the dividend of 25 or 30 per cent, that Hurst's half of the Fry debt would pay on the W. P. S. debt. Hurst's undertaking was, in effect, that he would pay the *whole* of the Fry debt, if Bell did not pay any part of it; but it was not his undertaking that if Bell should pay the whole of it, he would refund the whole, so that Bell should be the better able to pay his other debts. You are not losing on the Fry debt, because that is, or will be paid; but your loss will be on the W. P. S. debt,—a debt that Hurst is under no obligation to indemnify you against. Hurst is bound to account to Bell's estate for one half of the Fry debt; because he owed half and Bell's estate pays all; and if, upon such accounting anything is due the estate from Hurst, it will swell the estate, and so far enlarge the dividend to the W. P. S. debt. But when Bell's estate shall call Hurst to account, he will I am informed show that the estate, after paying the whole of the Fry debt is still indebted to him. If so, not much, if anything can come from that quarter—nothing, unless it can be so turned as to compel him [to] pay *all* he owes the estate, and take a *dividend* only, upon what the estate owes him. If you had paid the Fry debt yourself, you could then turn on Hurst and make him refund you; but this would only bring [you] where you started from, excepting it would leave Bell's estate able to pay a larger dividend and Hurst could then turn upon the estate to contribute one half, which would enlarge the indebtedness of the estate in the same proportion, and so reduce the dividend again. I believe the only thing that can be done for your advantage in the matter, is for Bell's administrator to call Hurst to account for one half the Fry debt, and then fight off, the best he can, Hurst's claim of indebtedness against the estate.

I should be much pleased to see [you] here again; but I must, in candour, say I do not perceive how your personal presence would do any good in the business matter.

You, no doubt, assign the suspension of our correspondence to the true philosophical cause, though it must be confessed by both of us that this is rather a cold reason for allowing a friendship such as ours to die out by degrees. I propose now that, upon receipt of this, you shall be considered in my debt, and under obligations to pay soon, and that neither shall remain long in arrears hereafter. Are you agreed?

Being elected to Congress, though I am very grateful to our friends for having done it, has not pleased me as much as I expected.

We have another boy, born the 10th of March last. He is very much such a child as Bob was at his age, rather of a longer order. Bob is "short and low," and I expect always will be. He talks very plainly,—almost as plainly as anybody. He is quite smart enough. I sometimes fear that he is one of the little rare-ripe sort that are smarter at about five than ever after. He has a great deal of that sort of mischief that is the offspring of such animal spirits. Since I began this letter, a messenger came to tell me Bob was lost; but by the time I reached the house his mother had found him and had him whipped, and by now, very likely, he is run away again. —Mary has read your letter, and wishes to be remembered to Mrs. S. and you, in which I most sincerely join her.

As ever yours,
A. Lincoln.

LETTER NO. 17

Washington, Dec. 25, 1848

Dear Speed:

While I was at Springfield last fall, Wm. Herndon showed me a couple of letters of yours concerning your note against Judge Browne. I suppose you and we (Logan and I) feel alike about the matter; that is, neither side likes to lose the money. You think the loss comes of our fault, and that therefore we should bear it; but we do not think it comes of our fault. We do not remember ever having had the note after you received the Auditor's warrant; and, after the most thorough search, we can no where find it. We *know* we have never received anything on it. In what you say, as to the note being left with us, we do not question your veracity, but we think you may be mistaken, because we do not remember it ourselves, and because we can not find it. We, like you, would rather lose it, than have any hard thoughts. Now, whatever you are short of your due upon the note Judge Browne still owes, and he must be made to pay it. You mention in your letter that you have our receipt for the note. I wish you would, at once, send a copy of the receipt to Logan. Browne will most likely be at Springfield this winter, and I wish Logan to see by the receipt, whether he or I could, by reference to it, sufficiently describe the note, on oath, to recover on it as a lost instrument. If he decides we can, he will have a writ served on him while he is there, unless he will voluntarily pay it. Dont neglect to do this at once.

Nothing of consequence new here, beyond what you see in the papers. Present my kind regards to Mrs. Speed.

Yours as ever
A. Lincoln.

LETTER No. 18

Washington, Feb. 20, 1849

Dear Speed:

Your letter of the 13th was received yesterday. I showed it to Baker. I did this because he knew I had written you, and was expecting an answer; and he still enquired what I had received; so that I could not well keep it a secret. Besides this, I knew the contents of the letter would not affect him as you seemed to think it would. He knows he did not make a favorable impression while in Congress, and he and I had talked it over frequently. He tells me to write you that he has too much self-esteem to be put out of humor with himself by the opinion of any man who does not know him better than Mr. Crittenden does; and that he thinks you ought to have known it. The letter will not affect him the least in regard to either Mr. Crittenden or you. He understands you to have acted the part of a discreet friend; and he intends to make Mr. Crittenden think better of him hereafter. I am flattered to learn that Mr. Crittenden has any recollection of me which is not unfavorable; and for the manifestation of your kindness toward me, I sincerely thank you. Still there is nothing about me which would authorize me to think of a firstclass office; and a secondclass one would not compensate my being snarled at by others who want it for themselves. I believe that, so far as the whigs in Congress, are concerned, I could have the Genl. Land Office almost by common consent; but then Sweet, and Don. Morrison, and Browning, and Cyrus Edwards all want it. And what is worse, while I think I could easily take it myself, I fear I shall have trouble to get it for any other man in Illinois. The reason is that McGaughey, an Indiana ex-member of Congress, is there after it, and being personally known, he will be hard to beat by any one who is not.

Baker showed me your letter, in which you make a passing allusion to the Louisville Post-Office. I have told Garnett Duncan I am for you. I like to open a letter of yours, and I therefore hope you will write me again on the receipt of this.

Give my love to Mrs. Speed.

Yours as ever
A. Lincoln.

LETTER No. 19

Springfield, Aug: 24, 1855

Dear Speed:

You know what a poor correspondent I am. Ever since I received your very agreeable letter of the 22nd of May—I have been intending to write you in answer to it— You suggest that in political action now, you and I would differ. I suppose we would; not quite as much, however, as you may think. You know I dislike slavery; and you fully admit the abstract wrong of it. So far there is no cause of difference. But you say that sooner than yield your legal right to the slave—especially at the bidding of those who are not themselves interested, you would see the Union dissolved. I am not aware that *any one* is bidding you to yield that right; very certainly I am not. I leave that matter entirely to yourself. I also acknowledge *your* rights and *my* obligations, under the constitution, in regard to your slaves. I confess I hate to see the poor creatures hunted down and caught, and carried back to their stripes, and unrewarded toils; but I bite my lip and keep quiet. In 1841 you and I had together a tedious low-water trip, on a Steam Boat from Louisville to St. Louis. You may remember, as I well do, that from Louisville to the mouth of the Ohio, there were, on board, ten or a dozen slaves, shackled together with irons. That sight was a continued torment to me; and I see something like it every time I touch the Ohio, or any other slave border. It is hardly fair for you to assume, that I have no interest in a thing which has, and continually exercises, the power of making me miserable. You ought rather to appreciate how much the great body of the Northern people do crucify their feelings, in order to maintain their loyalty to the constitution and the Union.

I do oppose the extension of slavery, because my judgment and feelings so prompt me; and I am under no obligation to the contrary. If for this you and I must differ, differ we must. You say, if you were President, you would send an army and hang the leaders of the Missouri outrages upon the Kansas elections; still, if Kansas fairly votes herself a slave state, she must be admitted, or the Union must be dissolved. But how if she votes herself a slave state *unfairly*—that is, by the very means for which you say you would hang men? Must she still be admitted, or the Union dissolved? That will be the phase of the question when it first becomes a practical one. In your assumption that there may be a *fair* decision of the slavery question in Kansas, I plainly see you and I would differ about the Nebraska law. I look upon that enactment not as a *law*, but as a *violence* from the beginning. It was conceived in violence, passed in violence, is maintained in violence, and is being executed in violence. I say it was *conceived* in violence, because the destruction of the Missouri Compromise, under the circumstances, was nothing less than violence. It was *passed* in violence, because it could not have passed at all but for the votes of many members, in violent disregard of the known will of their constituents. It is *maintained* in violence because the elections since, clearly demand its repeal, and this demand is openly disregarded. *you* say men ought to be hung for the way they are executing that law; and I say the way it is being executed is quite as good as any of its antecedents. It is being executed in the precise way which was intended from the first; else why does no Nebraska man express astonishment or condemnation? Poor Reeder is the only public man who has been silly enough to believe that anything like fairness was ever intended; and he has been bravely undeceived.

That Kansas will form a Slave constitution, and, with it, will ask to be admitted into the Union, I take to be already a settled question; and so settled by the very means you so pointedly condemn— By every principle of law, ever held by any court North or South, every negro taken to Kansas is free; yet, in utter disregard of this— in the spirit of violence merely—that beautiful Legislature gravely passes a law to hang men who shall venture to inform a negro of his legal rights. This is the substance, and real object of the law. If, like Haman, they should hang upon the gallows of their own building, I shall not be among the mourners for their fate.

In my humble sphere, I shall advocate the restoration of the Missouri Compromise so long as Kansas remains a Territory; and when, by all these foul means, it seeks to come into the Union as a Slave-state, I shall oppose it. I am very loth, in any case, to withhold my assent to the enjoyment of property *acquired*, or *located*, in good faith; but I do not admit that *good faith*, in taking a negro to Kansas, to be held in slavery, is a possibility with any man. Any man who has sense enough to be the controller of his own property, has too much sense to misunderstand the outrageous character of this whole Nebraska business. But I digress. In my opposition to the admission of Kansas I shall have some company; but we may be beaten. If we are, I shall not, on that account, attempt to dissolve the Union. On the contrary, if we succeed, there will be enough of us to take care of the Union. I think it probable, however, we shall be beaten. Standing as a unit among yourselves, you can, directly, and indirectly, bribe enough of our men to carry the day—as you could on an open proposition to establish monarchy. Get hold of some man in the North, whose position and ability is such, that he can make the support of your measure—whatever it may be—a *democratic party necessity*, and the thing is done. *appropos* of this, let me tell you an anecdote. Douglas introduced the Nebraska bill in January. In February afterwards, there was a call session of the Illinois Legislature. Of the one hundred members composing the two branches of that body, about seventy were democrats. These latter held a caucus, in which the Nebraska bill was talked of, if not formally discussed. It was thereby discovered that just three, and no more, were in favor of the measure. In a day or two Douglas's orders came on to have resolutions passed approving the bill; and they were passed by large majorities !!! The truth of this is vouched for by a bolting democratic member. The masses too, democratic as well as whig, were even, nearer unanimous against it; but, as soon as the party necessity of supporting it, became apparent, the way the democracy began to see the *wisdom* and *justice* of it, was perfectly astonishing.

You say if Kansas fairly votes herself a free state, as a Christian you will rather rejoice at it. All decent slaveholders *talk* that way; and I do not doubt their candor. But they never *vote* that way. Although in a private letter, or conversation, you will express your preference that Kansas shall be free, you would vote for no man for Congress who would say the same thing publicly. No such man could be elected from any district in any slave-state. You think Stringfellow & Co ought to be hung; and yet, at the next presidential election you will vote for the exact type and representative of Stringfellow. The slave-breeders and slave-traders are a small, odious and detested class, among you; and yet in politics, they dictate the course of all of you, and are as completely your masters, as you are the masters of your own negroes.—You inquire where I now stand. That is a disputed point. I think I am a whig; but others say there are no whigs, and that I am an abolitionist. When I was at Washington I voted for the Wilmot proviso as good as forty times, and I never heard of any one attempting to unwhig me for that. I now do no more than oppose the *extension* of slavery.

I am not a Know-Nothing. That is certain. How could I be? How can any one who abhors the oppression of negroes, be in favor of degrading classes of white people? Our progress in degeneracy appears to me to be pretty rapid. As a nation, we began by declaring that *"All men are created equal."* We now practically read it "all men are created equal, *except negroes."* When the Know-Nothings get control, it will read "all men are created equal, except negroes, *and foreigners, and Catholics."* When it comes to this I shall prefer emigrating to some country where they make no pretence of loving liberty—to Russia, for instance, where despotism can be taken pure, and without the base alloy of hypocrisy.

Mary will probably pass a day or two in Louisville in October. My kindest regards to Mrs. Speed. On the leading subject of this letter, I have more of her sympathy than I have of yours.—And yet let me say I am your friend forever

A. LINCOLN

Letter No. 20

Springfield, Dec. 12. 1855

Dear Speed:

Yours of the 7th accompanied by the deed of P. S. Loughbor-ough, to Lawrence Young, is this day received; and I answer in haste to say, that I am engaged for James M. Loughborough, and it might not be consistent with my duty to him, for me to to [sic] attend to the business for Mr. Young. I shall therefore hold the deed subject to your order; suggesting that the land is in Champaign county, and that I think H. C. Whitney, of Urbana, would be a very proper per-son to entrust the business to.

All well. Kindest regards to Mrs. S.

Your friend as ever
A. Lincoln

Letter No. 21

Springfield, Ills. Nov. 19, 1860

Dear Speed:

Yours of the 14th is received. I shall be at Chicago Thursday the 22nd. Inst. and one or two succeeding days. Could you not meet me there?

Mary thinks of going with me; and therefore I suggest that Mrs. S. accompany you.

Please let this be private, as I prefer a very great crowd should not gather at Chicago.

Respects to Mrs. S.

Your friend, as ever
A. Lincoln.

LETTER NO. 22

Confidential
Executive Mansion, Washington, March 17, 1863

My dear Speed

    I understand a Danville, Illinoisian, by the name of Lyman
Guinnipp is under an indictment at Louisville, something about
slaves. I know him slightly. He was not of bad character at home,
and I scarcely think he is guilty of any real crime. Please try if you
can not slip him through.

Yours as ever
A. Lincoln

From Robert L. Kincaid, *Joshua Fry Speed: Lincoln's Most Intimate Friend* (Department of Lincolniana, Lincoln Memorial University, Harrogate, Tenn.), letters no. 1 through 22 (pp. 38–69).

Letter from Leonard Swett to William H. Herndon

Chicago. Jan'y 17*th* 1866.

Dear Sir:

I received your letter today, asking me to write you by Freaday. Fearing if I delay, you will not get it done in time, I will give you such hasty thoughts as may occour to me to night. I have mislaid your second lecture, so that I have not read it at all, and have not read your first one since about the time it was published. What I shall say therefore, will be based upon my own ideas, rather than a review of the lectures.

Lincoln's whole life was a calculation of the law of forces, and ultimate results. The world to him was a question of cause and effect. He believed the results to which certain causes tended, would surely follow; he did not believe that those results could be materially hastened, or impeded. His whole political history, especially since the agitation of the Slavery question, has been based upon this theory. He believed from the first, I think, that the agitation of Slavery would produce its overthrow, and he acted upon the result as though it was present from the beginning. His tactics were, to get himself in the right place and remain there still, until events would find him in that place. His course of action led him to say and do things which could not be understood, when considered in reference to the immediate surroundings in which they were done, or said. You will remember in his campaign against Douglas in 1858, the first ten lines of the first speech he made defeated him. The sentiments of the "house divided against itself," seemed wholly inappropriate. It was a speech made at the commencement of a campaign, and apparently made for the campaign, and apparently made for the campaign. Viewing it in this light alone, nothing could have been more unfortunate, or unappropriate; it was saying first the wrong thing, yet he saw it was an abstract truth, but standing by the speech would ultimately find him in the right place. I was inclined at the time to believe these words were hastily and inconsiderately uttered, but subsequent facts have convinced me they were deliberate and had been matured. Judge T.L Dickey says that at Bloomington at the first Republican Convention, in 1856, he uttered the same sentences in a Speech delivered there, and that after the meeting was over, he (Dickey) called his attention to these remarks. Lincoln justified himself in making them, by stating they were true; but finally at Dickey's urgent request, he pronounced that for his sake, or upon his advice, he would not repeat them. In the Summer of 1859 when he was dining with a party of his intimate friends at Bloomington the subject of his Springfield speech was discussed. We all insisted it was a great mistake, but he justified himself, and finally said, "Well Gentlemen, you may think that Speech was a mistake, but I never have believed it was, and you will see the day when you will consider it was the wisest thing I ever said."

He never believed in political combinations; he never believed any Class of men could accomplish in politics any particular given purpose and consequently whether an individual man, or class of men supported or opposed him, never made any difference in his feelings, or his opinions of his own success. If he was elected, he seemed to believe that no person, or class of persons could ever have defeated him; and if defeated, he believed nothing could ever have elected him. Hence, when he was a candidate, he never wanted any thing done for him. He seemed to want to let the whole question alone, and for everybody else to do the same. I remember after the Chicago Convention when a great portion of the East were known to be dissatisfied at his nomination—. When fierce conflicts were going on in New York and Pennsylvania and when great exertions seemed requisite to harmonize and mold in concert the action of our friends. Lincoln always seemed to oppose all efforts made in that direction. I arranged with Mr. Thurlow Weed afther the Chicago Convention to meet him at Springfield. (I was present at the interview, but he said nothing. It was proposed that Judge Davis should go to New York and Pennsylvania to survey the field, and see what was necessary to be done.) Lincoln consented, but it was always my opinion that he consented reluctantly. He saw that the pressure of a campaign was an external force, coercing the party into unity. If it failed to produce that result, he believed any individual effort would also fail. If the desired result followed, he considered it attributable to the great cause, and not aided by the lesser ones. He sat down in his chair at Springfield and made himself the Mecca to which all politicians made pilgrimages. He told them all a story, said nothing, and sent them away. All his efforts to procure a second nomination were in the same direction. I believe he earnestly desired that nomination. He was much more eager for it, than he was for the first one, and yet from the first he discouraged all efforts on the part of his friends to obtain it. From the middle of his first term, all his adversaries were busily at work for themselves. Chase had three, or four secret societies, and an immense patronage extending all over the country; Fremont was constantly at work; yet Lincoln would never do anything either to hinder them, or to help himself.

He was considered too conservative, and his adversaries were trying to outstrip him in satisfying the radical element. I had a conversation with him upon this subject in October in 1863, and tried to induce him tc recommend in his annual message, the consitutional amendment abolishing slavery. I told him was not very radical, but I believed the result of this war would be the extermination of slavery; that Congress would pass the resolution; and that it was proper at that time to be done. I told him if he took that stand, it was an outside position and no one could maintain himself upon any measure more radical, and if he failed to take the position, his rivals would. Turning to me suddenly he said, "Is not that question doing well enough now?" I replied that it was. "Well," said he, "I have never done an official act with a view to promote my own personal aggrandizement, and I don't like to begin now, I can see that time coming; whoever can wait for it, will see it—whoever stands in its way, will be run over by it."

His rivals were using money profusely; Journals and influences were being subsidized against him. I accidentally learned that a Washington newspaper through a purchase of the establishment was to be turned against him, and consulted him about taking steps to prevent it. The only thing I could get him to say, was, that he would regret to see the paper turned against him. Whatever was done had to be done without his knowledge. Bennett with his paper you know is a power. The old fellow wanted to be noticed by Lincoln, and he wanted to support him. A friend of his who was certainly in his secrets (it came out through a woman when a Frenchman would say, "Who is she?") came over to Washington and intimated if Lincoln would invite Bennett to come over and chat with him, his paper would be all right. Bennett wanted nothing, He simply wanted to be noticed. Lincoln in talking about N. said, "I understand N. Bennett has made a great deal of money, some say not very properly; now he wants me to make him respectable. I have never invited Mr. Bennett or Mr. Greely here—I shall not therefore, especially Mr. Bennett."

All Lincoln would say was, that he was receiving everybody and he should receive Mr. Bennett if he came. Notwithstanding his entire inaction, he never for a moment doubted his second nomination. One time in his room disputing with him as to who his real friends were; he told me if I would not show it, he would make a list of how the Senate stood. When he got through, I pointed out some five, or six that I told him I knew he was mistaken in. Said he, "You may think so, but you keep that until the Convention and tell me then whether I was right." He was right to a man. He kept a kind of account book of how things were progressing for three, or four months, and whenever I would get nervous and think things were going wrong, he would get out his estimates and show how everything on the great scale of action—the resolutions of Legislatures, the instructions of delegates, and things of that character, was going exactly—as he expected. These facts with many others of a kindred nature have convinced me that he managed his politics upon a plan entirely different from any other man the country has ever produced. It was by ignoring men, and ignoring all small causes, but by closely calculating the tendencies of events and the great forces which were producing logical results.

In his conduct of the war he acted upon the theory that but one thing was necessary, and that was a united North. He had all shades of sentiments and opinions to deal with, and the consideration was always presented to his mind, How can I hold these discordant elements together? Hence in dealing with men he was a trimmer, and such a trimmer the world had never seen. Halifax who was great in his day as a trimmer, would blush by the side of Lincoln. Yet Lincoln never trimmed in principles—it was only in his conduct with men. He used the patronage of his office to feed the hunger of these various factions. Weed always declared that he kept a regular account book of his appointments in New York, dividing the various tit-bits of favor so as to give each faction more than it could get from any other source; yet never enough to satisfy its appetite. They all had access to him; they all received favors from him; and they all complained of ill-treatment; but while unsatisfied, they all had "large expectations," and saw in him the chance of getting more than from any one else—they were sure of getting in his place. He used every force to the best possible advantages. He never wasted anything, and would always give more to his enemies than he would to his friends, and the reason was, because he never had anything to spare, and in the close calculation of attaching the factions to him; he counted upon the abstract affection of his friends as an element to be offset against some gift with which he must appease his enemies. Hence, there was always some truth in the charge of his friends that he failed to reciprocate their devotion with his favors. The reason was that he had only just so much to give away—"He always had more horses than oats." An adhesion of all forces was indispensable to his success and the success of the country; hence, he husbanded his means with a nicety of calculation. Adhesion was what he wanted; if he got it gratuitously, he never wasted his substance paying for it.

His love of the ludicrous was not the least peculiar of his characteristics. His love of fun made him overlook everything else but the point of the joke sought after. If he told a good story that was refined and had a sharp point, he did not like it any the better because it was refined. If it was outrageously low and dirty, he never seemed to see that part of it. If it had the sharp ring of wit, nothing ever reached him but the wit. Almost any man that will tell a very vulgar story, has got in a degree a vulgar mind, but it was not so with him. With all his purity of character and exalted morality and sensibility, which no man can doubt, when hunting for wit, he had no ability to discriminate between the vulgar and the refined—substances from which he extricated it. It was the wit he was after—the pure jewel, and he would pick it up out of the mud, or dirt just as readily as he would from a parlor table.

He had very great kindness of heart. His mind was full of tender sensibilities; he was extremely humane, yet while these attributes were fully developed in his character and unless intercepted by his judgment controlled him, they never did control him contrary to his judgment. He would strain a point to be kind, but he never strained to breaking. Most of men of much kindly feeling are controlled by this sentiment against their judgment, or rather that sentiment beclouds their judgment. It was never so with him. He would be just as kind and generous as his judgment would let him be—no more. If he ever deviated from this rule, it was to save life. He would sometimes I think, do things he knew to be impolitic and wrong to save some poor fellow's neck. I remember one day being in his room when he was sitting at his table with a large pile of papers before him. After a pleasant talk, he turned quite abruptly and said, "Get out of the way, Swett; to morrow is butcher-day, and I must go through these papers and see if I cannot find *some excuse* to let these poor fellows off."

The pile of papers he had were the records of Courts Martial of men who on the following day were to be shot. He was not examining the Records to see whether the evidence sustained the findings. He was purposely in search of occasions to evade the law in favor of life. I was one time begging for the life of a poor devil. It was an outrageously bad case—I confessed I was simply begging. After sitting with his head down while I was talking, he interrupted me saying—"Grant never executed a man did he?" "I have been watching that thing." Some of Mr. Lincoln's friends insisted that he lacked the strong attributes of personal affection which he ought to have exhibited. I think this is a mistake. Lincoln had too much justice to run a great government for a few favorites, and the complaints against him in this regard when properly digested amount to this, and no more: that he would not abuse the privileges of his situation.

He was certainly a very poor hater. He never judged men by his like, or dislike for them. If any given act was to be performed, he could understand that his enemy could do it just as well as any one. If a man had maligned him, or been guilty of personal ill-treatment and abuse, and was the fittest man for the place, he would put him in his Cabinet just as soon as he would his friend. I do not think he ever removed a man because he was his enemy, or because he disliked him.

The great secret of his power as an orator, in my judgment, lay in the clearness and perspicuity of his statements. When Lincoln had stated a case, it was always more than half argued and the point more than half won. The first impression he generally conveyed was, that he had stated the case of his adversary better and more forcibly, than his opponent could state it himself. He then answered that state of facts fairly and fully, never passing by, or skipping over a bad point. When this was done, he presented his own case. There was a feeling when he argued a case, in the mind of any man who listened to him, that nothing had been passed over; yet if he could not answer the objections he argued in his own mind and himself arrived at the conclusion to which he was leading others; he had very little power of argumentation. The force of his logic was in conveying to the minds of others the same clear and thorough analysis he had in his own, and if his own mind failed to be satisfied, he had no power to satisfy any body else. His mode and force of argument was in stating how he had reasoned upon the subject and how he had come to his conclusion, rather than original reasoning to the hearer, and as the mind of listener, followed in the groove of his mind, his conclusions were adopted. He never made sophistical argument in his life, and never could make one. I think he was of less real aid in trying a thoroughly bad cause, than any man I was ever associated with. If he could not grasp the whole case and master it; he was never inclined to touch it.

From the commencement of his life to its close, I have sometimes doubted whether he ever asked anybody's advice about anything. He would listen to everybody; he would hear everybody, but he never asked for opinions. I never knew him in trying a law-suit to ask the advice of any lawyer he was associated with. As a politician and as President he arrived at all his conclusions from his own reflections, and when his opinion was once formed he never had any doubt but what it was right.

You ask me whether he changed his religious opinions towards the close of his life. I think not. As he became involved in matters of the gravest importance, full of great responsibility and great doubt, a feeling of religious reverence, and belief in God—his justice and overruling power—increased upon him. He was full of natural religion; he believed in God as much as the most approved Church member; Yet he judged of Providence by the same system of great generalization as of everything else. He had in my judgment very little faith in ceremonials and forms. Whether he went to Church once a month or once a year troubled him but very little. He failed to observe the Sabbath very scrupulously. I think he read "Petroleum V. Nasby" as much as he did the Bible. He would ridicule the Puritans, or swear in a moment of vexation; but yet his heart was full of natural and cultivated religion. He believed in the great laws of truth, the rigid discharge of duty, his accountability to God, the ultimate triumph of right, and the overthrow of wrong. If his religion were to be judged by the line and rule of Church Creeds and unexceptionable language, he would fall far short of the standard; but if by the higher rule of purity of conduct, of honesty of motive, of unyielding fidelity to the right and acknowledging God as the Supreme Ruler, then he filled all the requirements of true devotion and love of his neighbor as himself.

One great public mistake of his character as generally received and acquiesced in:—he is considered by the people of this country as a frank, guileless, unsophisticated man. There never was a greater mistake. Beneath a smooth surface of candor and an apparent declaration of all his thoughts and feelings, he exercised the most exalted tact and the wisest discrimination. He handled and moved man *remotely* as we do pieces upon a chessboard. He retained through life, all the friends he ever had, and he made the wrath of his enemies to praise him. This was not by cunning, or intrigue in the low acceptation of the term, but by far seeing, reason and discernment. He always told enough only, of his plans and purposes, to induce the belief that he had communicated all; yet he reserved enough, in fact, to have communicated nothing. He told all that was unimportant with a gushing frankness; yet no man ever kept his real purposes more closely, or penetrated the future further with his deep designs.

I wish I had time to add some things and on the whole to make this shorter and better, but I have not.

I shall try, if desirable, to give you points from time to time, but you will please remember they are confidential.

Yours Truly
Leonard Swett

From Douglas L. Wilson and Rodney O. Davis, eds., *Herndon's Informants: Letters, Interviews, and Statements about Abraham Lincoln* (University of Illinois Press, Chicago, 1998), 162–68.

Notes

For an expanded version of the notes, with longer excerpts from sources, see www.theintimateworldofabrahamlincoln.com.

INTRODUCTION

1 Kinsey, *Sexual Behavior in the Human Male*, 638.
2 Pinsker, *Lincoln's Sanctuary*, 84.

PREFACE

1 James (Jim) Kepner's writings up to 1971 are housed in the ONE, Inc., archives at the University of Southern California, and are summarized in *From the Closet of History*, privately published by Kepner in 1984.

2 The Sandburg reference to the homosexuality of Lincoln and Speed was in his 1926 edition of *The Prairie Years*; the homosexual reference to Lincoln, but not that of Speed, was removed by Sandburg from his 1954 abridged edition. Yet the abridged edition was the only one cited by Kepner—and all his copiers, thus giving themselves away.

At least one article, apparently independent of Kepner, was "Lincoln's Other Love," by Dennis Doty, *Chicago Gay Crusader*, 26 (April 1976). It is based on excerpts from the Lincoln-Speed letters in the *Collected Works of Abraham Lincoln*.

3 More specific and more useful to modern scholars than Doris Faber's book is a later compilation by Rodger Streitmatter: *Empty Without You: The Intimate Letters of Eleanor Roosevelt and Lorena Hickok*.

4 For example: "Lincoln's sexual imagination is tinged with asshole images." (p. 81) Even if a more polite "anal image" had been used, the quote would still have retained one fairly serious error, namely, the implication that *anal* was somehow Lincoln's personal emphasis. But the fact is, for reasons still not fully understood, nearly all sexual ribaldry has an anal emphasis (see Debbie Nathan and Michael Snedeker, *Satan's Silence*, x).

5 Donald, *Lincoln*, 55.
6 Sandburg, *Abraham Lincoln: The Prairie Years*, vol. 1, xii.
7 Ibid., 264.

8 Ibid., 266.

9 Kincaid, *Joshua Fry Speed: Lincoln's Most Intimate Friend*, 12–14.

CHAPTER ONE

* From 1996 to 2000, C. A. Tripp worked with Philip Nobile on the early drafting of this book, principally of this chapter, the original draft of which was written by Mr. Nobile. After disagreement on various points of interpretation, methodology, and wording, the relationship came to an end.

1 A portion of the Leech quote appears in Charles Shively, *Drum Beats*.

2 Chamberlin, *History of the One Hundred and Fiftieth Regiment*, vi–vii.

3 Ibid., 41–42.

4 Turner and Turner, *Mary Todd Lincoln*, 475.

5 From "The President's Guard," 1888 *Tribune* article by Derickson, in Burlingame, *Ida Tarbell: Notes and Letters*, 112.

6 Tarbell, *The Life of Abraham Lincoln*, vol. 2, 155.

7 Ibid., 156.

8 Whitney, *Life on the Circuit With Lincoln*, 54.

9 Noah Brooks, "Personal Recollections of Abraham Lincoln," *Harper's New Monthly Magazine*, 31 (July 1865): 222–30.

10 Lamon, *Recollections of Abraham Lincoln*, 304.

11 Fehrenbacher and Fehrenbacher, *Recollected Words of Abraham Lincoln*, 43.

12 Derickson, "The President's Guard," 112.

13 Ibid.

14 Ibid., 85.

15 Tarbell, *Life of Abraham Lincoln*, vol. 2, 156.

16 Kinsey, et al., *Sexual Behavior in the Human Male*, 638.

17 Ibid.

18 David V. Derickson to AL, Headquarters of the Provost-Marshall, Twentieth District, Meadville, Pennsylvania, June 3, 1864, Lincoln MSS, Library of Congress.

19 Sandburg, *The War Years*, vol. 4, 406.

CHAPTER TWO

1 Kunhardt, Jr., et al., *Lincoln: An Illustrated Biography*, 35.

2 Lincoln, *Collected Works of Abraham Lincoln*, vol. 4, 62.

3 Herndon and Weik, *Herndon's Life of Lincoln*, 275–76.

4 Ibid., p. 27.

5 Ibid., 29.

6 Ibid.

7 Ibid.

8 Hertz, *The Hidden Lincoln*, 353, plus Herndon notes on his interview with Mrs. Thomas Lincoln, Sept. 8, 1865, Herndon–Weik Collection, p. 6 of transcript, Library of Congress.

9 Hertz, *The Hidden Lincoln*, 350–53; with editing corrections from Herndon notes, Sept. 8, 1865, Herndon–Weik Collection, p. 6 of transcript, Library of Congress.

10 Kinsey, et al., *Sexual Behavior in the Human Male*, 457.

11 Kinsey, *Male*, 168.

12 Wilson and Davis, *Herndon's Informants*, 120. Herndon interview of David Turnham, Sept. 15, 1865. Wilson and Davis's transcription of the original reads as follows: "long tall dangling award drowl looking boy."

13 Kinsey, *Male*, 325. It was no surprise to find that the vigor of a sexual substrate that drives toward an early puberty should also carry easy and abundant sexual response, but that the pattern should last a lifetime was a great surprise.

14 Kinsey, *Male*, 187.

15 Herndon, *Life of Lincoln*, 25.

16 Sandburg, *Abraham Lincoln: The Prairie Years*, vol. 1, 43.

17 Kinsey, *Male*, 182.

18 Ibid., 303.

19 Kinsey, *Male*, 311, 507. Prepubertal masturbation does, indeed, imply the presence of a highly and easily aroused sexual substrate, but it is not just pleasure in stimulation. Such masturbatory events amount to full though "dry" orgasms.

20 Kinsey, *Male*, 309.

21 Ibid., 325.

22 Wilson and Davis, *Herndon's Informants*, 443.

23 Herndon, *Life of Lincoln*, 343.

24 The joke is mentioned in Shively, *Drum Beats*.

25 Wilson and Davis, *Herndon's Informants*, 174.

26 Hertz, *Hidden Lincoln*, 400.

27 Herndon, *Life of Lincoln*, 94. Ward Hill Lamon quote is from his biography, *Life of Abraham Lincoln*, page 478.

28 Whitney, *Life on the Circuit With Lincoln*, 66.

29 Herndon, *Life of Lincoln*, 42.

30 Wilson and Davis, *Herndon's Informants*, 442. H. E. Dummer statement to Herndon.

31 Herndon, *Life of Lincoln*, 473.

32 Fehrenbacher and Fehrenbacher, *Recollected Words*, 438.

33 Herndon, *Life of Lincoln*, 45.

34 Beveridge, *Abraham Lincoln 1809–1858*, vol. 1, 92.

35 Wilson and Davis, *Herndon's Informants*, 152.

36 Kinsey, et al., *Sexual Behavior in the Human Female*, 213n; also, Harvey R. Greenberg, H. Robert Blank, and Daniel P. Greenson. "The Jelly Baby: Conception, Immaculate and Non Immaculate," *Psychiatric Quarterly* 42 no. 1 (1968).

37 Hertz, *Hidden Lincoln*, 362. See also Shively, *Drum Beats*.

38 Ibid., 366.

39 Wilson and Davis, *Herndon's Informants*, 169.

40 Donald, *Lincoln's Herndon*, 340. See also Shively, *Drum Beats*.

41 Hertz, *Hidden Lincoln*, 243.

42 Angle, *Herndon's Life of Lincoln*, xxxiv–xxxv. See also Shively, *Drum Beats*.

42 Hertz, *Hidden Lincoln*, 19.

CHAPTER THREE

1 Herndon and Weik, *Herndon's Life of Lincoln*, 66.

2 Wilson and Davis, *Herndon's Informants*, 8–9. Mentor Graham to Herndon.

3 Lamon, *The Life of Abraham Lincoln*, 89; Mentor Graham to WHH, Wilson and Davis, *Herndon's Informants*, 9.

4 Beveridge, *Abraham Lincoln*, vol. 1, 109.

5 Duncan and Nickols, *Mentor Graham*, 125.

6 Ibid.

7 Ibid.

8 Lincoln, *Collected Works*, vol. 4, 63.

9 Wilson and Davis, *Herndon's Informants*, 17. When Herndon wrote out Greene's statement in haste, he spelled "thighs" "thigs." Like any other small error in Herndon's hasty writing, the missing "h" was easy enough to read in, but "thighs" seemed so meaningless, a question mark was placed by it and remains in the Library of Congress transcript. As shown, its meaning is entirely clear in sex research.

10 Kinsey, et al., *Sexual Behavior In the Human Male*, 69. Femoral intercourse is seldom an initial preference. Thighs hold no masculine magic on their own, as evidenced by their rare appearance in dreams or in sex fantasies. They gain their bloom of high significance only through the kinds of pleasurable conditioning Billy no doubt gained from his early experience with femoral intercourse.

11 Duncan and Nickols, *Mentor Graham*, 140.

12 Wilson and Davis, *Herndon's Informants*, 10, Mentor Graham to Herndon, May 29, 1865.

13 Beveridge, *Abraham Lincoln*, vol. 1, 133–34; Reep, *Lincoln at New Salem*, 30; Sandburg, *Abraham Lincoln: The Prairie Years*, vol. 1, 139.

14 Tarbell, *Life of Abraham Lincoln*, vol. 1, 67.

15 While "autodidact" only means self-taught, in practice it means considerably more. While an ordinary mind tends to be stopped in its tracks by a missing bit of crucial information (say, in math or logic), an autodidact can read or act quite past the missing information, assembling the whole picture later when more is known. Isaac Newton, Charles Darwin, and Albert Einstein notably had this talent, as Lincoln certainly did. It allowed him to sweep ahead in his reading and his understanding of people past all sorts of words and concepts that were neither in his experience nor in the small dictionary he sometimes used.

16 Oates, *The Man Behind the Myths*, 48.

17 Sandburg, *Abraham Lincoln: The Prairie Years*, vol. 1, 19.

18 Beveridge, *Abraham Lincoln*, vol. 1, 54.

19 Whitney, *Life on the Circuit With Lincoln*, 184.

20 Duncan and Nickols, *Mentor Graham*, 140.

21 Ibid., 144.

22 "Miss Ann Rutledge & Lincoln," W. H. Herndon, monograph. Herndon–Weik Collection, Library of Congress, p. 3 of transcript.

23 Wilson and Davis, *Herndon's Informants*, 402.

24 Duncan and Nickols, *Mentor Graham*, 261. Kunigunde Duncan's own special note.

25 Herndon and Weik, *Herndon's Life of Lincoln*, 68.

26 Wilson and Davis, *Herndon's Informants*, 9. Mentor Graham to Herndon.

27 Lincoln, *Collected Works*, vol. 4, 64. From Lincoln's short campaign autobiography written in the third person.

28 Ibid.

29 Ibid.

30 Ibid., 65.

31 Ibid.

32 Beveridge, *Abraham Lincoln*, vol. 1, 135.

33 Herndon, *Life of Lincoln*, 90.

34 Lincoln, *Collected Works*, vol. 4, 65.

35 Ibid.

36 Dr. John Allen's statement, *The Lincoln Papers*, vol. 1, 157.

37 Herndon, *Life of Lincoln*, 91.

38 Ibid., 88–89.

39 Ibid., 101.

40 Ibid., 101–2.

41 Hertz, *The Hidden Lincoln*, 122–23. Herndon to C. O. Poole, January 5, 1886.

42 Donald, *Lincoln*, 55.

43 Duncan and Nickols, *Mentor Graham*, 141.

44 That is, the Lincoln/Tripp Database, which contains the full text of many volumes on Abraham Lincoln and/or on the period. The keyboarding of every volume has been done in India, where experience has shown that the demands of precision are much better met than elsewhere, including America, China, Latin America, or the Philippines. The database is available at the Abraham Lincoln Presidential Library and Museum in Springfield, Illinois.

45 Maltby, *The Life and Public Services of Abraham Lincoln*, 27.

46 Donald, *Lincoln's Herndon*, 315.

47 Ibid., 15.

48 Abner Y. Ellis, Statement for William H. Herndon, January 23, 1866, in Wilson and Davis, *Herndon's Informants*, 171.

49 Hertz, *The Hidden Lincoln*, 247. Letter from Herndon to Weik, January 23, 1890.

50 W. H. Herndon to James H. Wilson, September 23, 1889, in *Herndon-Weik Collection*, Library of Congress.

51 Masters, *Lincoln the Man*, 145.

52 Herndon, *Life of Lincoln*, 163.

53 Neely, Jr., *The Abraham Lincoln Encyclopedia*, 248.

54 Having reached a peak of respect and popularity as the father of psychoanalysis, Freud came to lose credibility along with much of psychoanalysis itself. This is

important to Lincoln's psychology for two reasons. First, many of Freud's theories of sex in general and homosexuality in particular tend to live on in popular sexual conceptions, though they are sharply at odds with newer concepts. Second, in professional circles, too, it is necessary to "clear the decks" before introducing newer ideas that have reversed many Freudian notions.

55 Lincoln, *Collected Works*, vol. 4, 62.

56 Strozier, *Lincoln's Quest For Union*, 26. The original story of Lincoln and the wild turkeys, sans psychoanalysis, is in Lincoln, *Collected Works*, vol. 4, page 62.

57 Strozier, *Lincoln's Quest for Union*, 44.

CHAPTER FOUR

1 William H. Herndon, "Abraham Lincoln, Miss Ann Rutledge, New Salem, Pioneering & The Poem." A lecture delivered at Springfield, Illinois, November 16, 1866, p. 57. From a photostat of the original broadside of the lecture, courtesy of Dr. Thomas F. Schwartz and the Abraham Lincoln Presidential Library.

2 Paul M. Angle, "Lincoln's First Love?" Bulletin No. 9, Lincoln Centennial Association, Dec. 1, 1927, p. 5.

3 Randall, "Sifting the Ann Rutledge Evidence," in *Lincoln the President*, vol. 2, 321–342.

4 Hertz, *The Hidden Lincoln*, 310.

5 Randall, "Sifting the Ann Rutledge Evidence," 329.

6 Hertz, *The Hidden Lincoln*, 236.

7 Wilson and Davis, *Herndon's Informants*, 252.

8 Ibid., 253.

9 Ibid.

10 Beveridge, *Abraham Lincoln 1809–1858*, vol. 1, 148.

11 Randall, "Sifting the Ann Rutledge Evidence," 331.

12 Wilson and Davis, *Herndon's Informants*, 237; testimony of Mrs. William Rutledge on Rutledge family memories of correspondence between Lincoln and Ann. David Donald, *Lincoln*, 56, on the cessation of letters from McNamar to Ann.

13 The historian William E. Barton comments: "If Lincoln ever wrote to Ann while he was away [at Vandalia], the Rutledge family did not preserve his letters, and they were accustomed to save their correspondence." *The Women Lincoln Loved*, 178.

14 Randall, "Sifting the Ann Rutledge Evidence," 335.

15 Thomas, *Abraham Lincoln*, 51.

16 Wilson and Davis, *Herndon's Informants*, 108.

17 Ibid., 455.

18 Ibid., 105.

19 Ibid., 123.

20 Ibid., 518.

21 Ibid., 170.

22 Wayne C. Temple, "Lincoln and the Burners at New Salem," *Lincoln Herald*, 67 note 2 (Summer 1965).

23 Wilson and Davis, *Herndon's Informants*, 91.

24 Donald, *Lincoln*, 55.

25 Wilson, *Lincoln Before Washington*, 79. Originally published as "Abraham Lincoln, Ann Rutledge, and the Evidence of Herndon's Informants," in *Civil War History*, 36 (December 1990).

26 Wilson and Davis, *Herndon's Informants*, 525.

27 Beveridge, *Abraham Lincoln 1809–1858*, vol. 1, 39.

28 Rankin, *Personal Recollections of Abraham Lincoln*, 73.

29 Ibid., 74.

30 Shutes, *Lincoln and the Doctors*, 18.

31 Rankin, *Personal Recollections of Abraham Lincoln*, 82.

32 *Bulletin No. 12*, Lincoln Centennial Association, Sept. 1, 1928, 8.

33 Hardin Bale to William H. Herndon (in Herndon's handwriting), May 29, 1865, Herndon-Weik Collection, Library of Congress.

34 Wilson and Davis, *Herndon's Informants*, 604.

35 Donald, *Lincoln*, 55–56.

36 Lincoln, *Collected Works*, vol. 1, 118.

37 Ibid., 466. To Mary Todd Lincoln, April 16, 1849.

38 Tarbell, *Life of Abraham Lincoln*, vol. 1, 180.

39 Herndon monograph on "Miss Rutledge & Lincoln" (c. 1887) Herndon-Weik Collection, p. 9 of transcript, Library of Congress.

40 Shutes, *Lincoln's Emotional Life*, 45.

41 Wilson and Davis, *Herndon's Informants*, 73.

42 Randall, "Sifting the Ann Rutledge Evidence," 333.

43 Wilson and Davis, *Herndon's Informants*, 557. Elizabeth Abell to WHH.

44 Wilson and Davis, *Herndon's Informants*, 168. Leonard Swett to WHH.

45 Herndon, *Life of Lincoln*, 473.

46 Wilson and Davis, *Herndon's Informants*, 23.

47 Wilson and Davis, *Herndon's Informants*, 557. Elizabeth Abell to WHH.

48 Herndon, *Life of Lincoln*, 114.

49 Shutes, *Lincoln's Emotional Life*, 143. "Willie's body was disinterred from an above-ground mausoleum, in keeping with Lincoln's great discomfort at the thought of rain seeping into an underground grave of a loved one."

50 Lamon, *Life of Abraham Lincoln*, 504.

51 Stevens, *A Reporter's Lincoln*, 12.

52 Whitney, *Life on the Circuit With Lincoln*, 169.

53 Wilson and Davis, *Herndon's Informants*, 408.

54 Donald, *Lincoln's Herndon*, 231.

55 Wilson and Davis, *Herndon's Informants*, 743.

56 Herndon's Isaac Cogdal interview was dated 1865–66; thus the ambiguity as to whether four or five years had elapsed.

57 The spelling Cogdal himself used.

58 Wilson and Davis, *Herndon's Informants*, 440.

59 Randall, "Sifting the Ann Rutledge Evidence," 335.

60 Wilson, *Lincoln Before Washington*, 88.

61 Wilson, *Lincoln Before Washington*, 21–36. Originally published as "William H. Herndon and His Lincoln Informants," *Journal of the Abraham Lincoln Association* (Winter 1993), 15–34. Quote at hand: 31.

62 Angle, "Lincoln's First Love?"

63 Wilson, "Herndon's Legacy," 31.

64 John Y. Simon, "Abraham Lincoln and Ann Rutledge," *Journal of the Abraham Lincoln Association*, II (1990), 13–33.

65 Burlingame, *The Inner World of Abraham Lincoln*, xxiii. Note especially the "Court of Law" charge that critics of Randall like to cite. But Randall never used the phrase. The nearest he came was to once speak of the "law of evidence," which he specifically defined as demanding "that testimony ought to come straight. If witnesses arrange their recollections so as to make them agree, or if they seek to build them up where they admit uncertainty, the result lacks the validity of statements obtained from witnesses separately and unretouched." Randall, "Sifting," 329.

66 Donald, *Lincoln*, 58. In two of his earlier books, *Lincoln's Herndon* and *Lincoln Reconsidered*, Donald offered no accepting words, and mostly sharp derision, for both the legend and for Herndon's presentation of it. Remarkably, in his 2001 revision of *Lincoln Reconsidered* he retains unchanged his comments on Ann Rutledge, gently conceding (p. 186): "I have come to adopt a more tolerant view of the (Ann Rutledge) episode, which I have presented in my *Lincoln.*"

67 Clarence A. Tripp, Fritz A. Fluckiger, George H. Wei, "Measurement of Handwriting Variables," *Perceptual and Motor Skills, Monograph Supplement*, 5 (1957).

68 Randall, "Sifting," 334–35.

CHAPTER FIVE

1 Herndon and Weik, *Herndon's Life of Lincoln*, 120.

2 Herndon, *Life of Lincoln*, 116.

3 Lincoln, *The Collected Works of Abraham Lincoln*, vol. 1, 117.

4 Herndon, *Life of Lincoln*, 118.

5 Reep, *Lincoln at New Salem*, 83.

6 Herndon, *Life of Lincoln*, 119.

7 Quoted in Shively, *Drum Beats*.

8 Herndon, *Life of Lincoln*, 121; Hertz, *The Hidden Lincoln*, 302.

9 Herndon, *Life of Lincoln*, 120; Lamon, *The Life of Abraham Lincoln*, 174.

10 This and other Browning quotes are from Orville Browning himself, who on June 17, 1875, was interviewed by one of Lincoln's former secretaries, John Nicolay. It became one of "The Springfield Interviews" now in *An Oral History of Abraham Lincoln: John G. Nicolay's Interviews and Essays*, edited by Michael Burlingame, 4.

11 Lamon, *Life of Abraham Lincoln*, 180–81.

12 Reep, *Lincoln at New Salem*, 83.

13 Burlingame, *Inner World of Abraham Lincoln*, 138.

14 *The Basic Writings of Sigmund Freud*, originally published in German (1905).

The present English edition (Modern Library) was translated and edited by A. A. Brill. Book IV, cited here, is from "The Technique of Wit," Parts II and III in *Wit and Its Relation to the Unconscious*. Heine citation is on page 673 in all editions before 1995, and on page 641 in all subsequent editions and printings. The plates are identical for all copies; however, the pagination was changed by the present publisher's decision to delete a useful thirty-two-page introduction by A. A. Brill.

Freud's writings—*The Psychology of Wit, Psychopathology of Everyday Life*, and most of his *Interpretation of Dreams*—unlike his psychiatry, fully hold up to this day.

15 Whitney, *Life on the Circuit With Lincoln*, 174.

16 Rice, *Reminiscences of Abraham Lincoln*, 240. From Titland J. Coffey's contribution.

17 Rice, *Reminiscences of Abraham Lincoln*, 1909 ed., 240.

18 Herndon, *Life of Lincoln*, 479.

19 Hertz, *Hidden Lincoln*, 415. Anyone wishing to delve further into Herndon's rich thoughts and observations beyond their relatively narrow coverage here will find more in Emanuel Hertz's *Hidden Lincoln*, 412–16, and in Francis Carpenter, *Six Months at the White House*, 327–28. Herndon also included more in his own biography of Lincoln, 475–76, although Weik seems to have edited out much of it.

20 Herndon, *Life of Lincoln*, 475.

21 Lincoln, *Collected Works*, vol. 1, 54.

CHAPTER SIX

1 Randall, *Colonel Elmer Ellsworth*, ix.

2 Ibid., 43.

3 Ibid., 44f.

4 Ibid., 46.

5 Ibid., 47.

6 Ibid., 48.

7 Ibid., 179.

8 Ibid., 49.

9 Randall, *Lincoln's Sons*, 79.

10 In her biography of Elmer Ellsworth, Ruth Painter Randall bestows a certain dignified formality on "General John Cook" by constantly referring to him as "General." But, in fact, even the title of colonel appears to have been hardly more than honorary; in *Collected Works of Abraham Lincoln* Cook is identified before the war only as "one of Springfield's leading businessmen" (vol. 2, 292n). Considerably later (March 3, 1862) Lincoln appointed Cook as "Brigadier General of Volunteers" (vol. 5, 142).

11 Randall, *Ellsworth*, 163.

12 Ibid., 164.

13 Ibid., 167–86.

14 Ibid., 4.

15 Ibid., 6, 7.

16 Ibid., 210.

17 Ibid., 134–35.

18 Ibid., 210.

19 Whitney, *Life of Lincoln*, vol. 2, 87.

20 Randall, *Ellsworth*, 218.

21 Lincoln, *Collected Works*, vol. 4, 273.

22 Ibid., 291.

23 Ibid., 333.

24 Randall, *Ellsworth*, 258.

25 Ibid., 259.

26 Ibid., 260–61.

27 Ibid., 261f.

28 Miers, et al., *Lincoln Day by Day*, vol. III, 43.

29 Shutes, *Lincoln's Emotional Life*, 139.

30 Randall, *Ellsworth*, 271.

31 Lincoln, *Collected Works*, vol. 4, 385.

32 Randall, *Ellsworth*, 266.

33 Ibid., 252.

34 Ibid., 254.

CHAPTER SEVEN

1 Speed, *Reminiscences of Abraham Lincoln*, 1884, 22.

2 John G. Nicolay and John Hay, *Abraham Lincoln: A History* (1917), vol. 1, 194.

3 Speed, *Reminiscences of Abraham Lincoln*, 17–18; Wilson and Davis, *Herndon's Informants*, 589.

4 Baker, *Mary Todd Lincoln*, 109.

5 Quoted in Shivley, *Drum Beats*.

6 Yes, "four years," as both Speed and Lincoln himself referred to it—and as gay rights advocacy writers repeatedly remind us. Actually, Lincoln and Speed occupied the room alone for only two years. After that young Billy Herndon and Charles R. Hurst shared Speed's room, though not his bed.

7 Turner and Turner, *Mary Todd Lincoln*, 20.

8 Ibid., 27.

9 Hertz, *The Hidden Lincoln*, 374.

10 More interesting than the story itself is an important side fact. It has become something of a litmus test for a certain brand of honesty among Lincoln scholars. All agree that the story is untrue—and when pressed, all would agree that Elizabeth Edwards inserted the distortion for still unknown reasons. In 1883, Jesse Weik reinterviewed Elizabeth Edwards; she told the story exactly as she had to Herndon years before (see Weik, *The Real Lincoln*, 63). A main reason for wanting to "blame" the defaulting bridegroom story on Herndon has been to discredit his depiction of the Lincoln marriage, or of Mary Lincoln, or both—when, in fact, he was trusting the accuracy of Mary's sister. Who better?

11 Turner and Turner, *Mary Todd Lincoln*, 27.

12 Beveridge, *Abraham Lincoln 1809–1858*, vol. 1, 317.

13 The numbered Lincoln letters (all but one of Speed's letters to Lincoln are lost) are frequently cited in these pages; beyond that, they are important documents in themselves and touch on many nearby issues. Consequently, they are presented here for easy access in Appendix 2.

14 Katz, *Love Stories*, 18. See also Shivley, *Drum Beats*, 77–78.

15 Simon, *Lincoln's Preparation for Greatness*, 239.

16 Letter from James C. Conkling to Mercy Levering, January 24, 1841, cited in Sandburg and Angle, *Mary Lincoln: Wife and Widow*, 179.

17 Lincoln, *Collected Works*, vol. 1, 229.

18 Sandburg and Angle, *Mary Lincoln*, 47–48. James Conkling to Mary Levering, March 7, 1841.

19 Kincaid, *Joshua Fry Speed*, 15. See also Shivley, *Drum Beats*.

20 Beveridge, *Abraham Lincoln*, 320.

21 Lincoln, *Collected Works*, vol. 1, 265.

22 Ibid., 266.

23 Wilson and Davis, *Herndon's Informants*, 431.

24 Lincoln, *Collected Works*, vol. 1, 305.

25 Nicolay and Hay, *Abraham Lincoln*, vol. 1, 194.

26 Lincoln, *Collected Works*, sup. 1, 54n.

27 Kincaid, *Joshua Fry Speed*, 23.

28 Ibid., 24.

29 Ibid., 25–26.

30 Ibid., 26, 28.

31 Speed, *Reminiscences*, 26.

32 Ibid., 12.

CHAPTER EIGHT

1 Hertz, *The Hidden Lincoln*, 208. William H. Herndon to William O. Bartlett, October 1887. Also, Donald, *Lincoln Reconsidered*, 2002 ed., 171.

2 Donald, *Lincoln Reconsidered*, 171.

3 Wilson and Davis, *Herndon's Informants*, 444.

4 Sandburg and Angle, *Mary Lincoln*, 333. Almost identical to Wilson and Davis, *Herndon's Informants*, 477.

5 Herndon and Weik, *Herndon's Life of Lincoln*, 168; also Wilson and Davis, *Herndon's Informants*, 477.

6 Herndon, *Life of Lincoln*, 168–69.

7 Wilson and Davis, *Herndon's Informants*, 251. James H. Matheny's account to Herndon, May 3, 1866.

8 Wilson and Davis, *Herndon's Informants*, 475. Joshua F. Speed to Herndon.

9 Herndon, *Life of Lincoln*, 249.

10 Willard L. King to Ruth Painter Randall, Chicago September 21, 1953, cited in Burlingame, *Inner World of Abraham Lincoln*, 321.

11 Turner and Turner, *Mary Todd Lincoln*, 6.

12 Reminiscences of Mr. Beck, as told in Sparks, *Stories of Abraham Lincoln*, 20–21, cited by Burlingame, *Inner World of Abraham Lincoln*, 280n.

13 Wilson and Davis, *Herndon's Informants*, 617.

14 Donald, personal communication, 1995.

15 Leech, *Reveille in Washington*, 286.

16 Keckley, *Behind the Scenes*, 135–36.

17 Randall, *Mary Lincoln*, 148.

18 Baker, *Mary Todd Lincoln*, 186.

19 Stoddard, *Inside the White House*, 87–88. Historians who seek an example of Mary's selflessness often cite these pages as evidence, although White House secretary Stoddard said nothing of either the newspaper reports that did appear or her lack of visits after 1862.

20 Lincoln resisted greatly but eventually gave in when she threw one of her "hysterical fits." Herman Kreismann was waiting to see Lincoln, who explained, "Kreismann, she will not let me go until I promise her an office for one of her friends." Michael Burlingame, "Honest Abe, Dishonest Mary," 10. Hertz, *The Hidden Lincoln*, 260, 344. Henderson received the appointment but was later indicted by a federal court for using his customs post to defraud the U.S. government.

21 Keckley, *Behind the Scenes*, 151.

22 Keckley, *Behind the Scenes*, 204. For validation of the Illinois governor's yearly salary of fifteen hundred dollars, see Donald's *Lincoln's Herndon*, 192.

23 Burlingame, "Honest Abe, Dishonest Mary," 20.

24 Ibid., 19.

25 Baker, *Mary Todd Lincoln*, 187.

26 Marks and Shatz, eds., *Narrative of William Walkins Glenn*, 296, cited by Burlingame, "Honest Abe, Dishonest Mary," 19n.

27 Browning, *Diary*, March 3, 1862.

28 The quotations in this paragraph are taken from Ruth Painter Randall's *Mary Lincoln*, 264–65. For the slightly more accurate though less well-worded original, see page 362 of Benjamin Brown French, Donald B. Cople, and John J. McDonough, *Witness to the Young Republic: A Yankee's Journal; 1828–1870*. The Benjamin French solution is from Leech, *Reveille in Washington*, 295.

29 French, *Witness to the Young Republic*, 382.

30 Browning, *Diary*, vol. 1; originally censored text now restored in the computerized *Browning Diary* for March 3, (1862). See Lincoln/Tripp Database, (cited in chapter 3, n. 45), 532.

31 Burlingame, "Honest Abe, Dishonest Mary," 16.

32 Ibid., 17.

33 Ibid., 19.

34 Ibid., 20.

35 Stoddard, *Inside the White House*, 62–63.

36 Leech, *Reveille*, 286.

37 Hay, *At Lincoln's Side*, 20.

38 Burlingame, *Inner World of Abraham Lincoln*, 286.

39 This entire story is in a thirty-seven-line entry for March 3, 1862, in *The Diary of Orville Hickman Browning*, vol. 1, page 532. Note: This is not in the printed version of the diary, having been censored out at the time of printing. However, it was recently reinserted into the Browning Diary MSS, not yet in published form, but in the Lincoln/Tripp Database.

40 Keckley, *Behind the Scenes*, 129.

41 Lincoln, *Collected Works*, vol. 6, 50.

42 Burlingame, "Honest Abe, Dishonest Mary," 18.

43 John Hay diary, February. 13, 1867, Hay Papers, Hay Library, Brown University, cited in Leech, *Reveille in Washington*, 301, and in Burlingame, "Honest Abe, Dishonest Mary," 18.

44 Hay, *At Lincoln's Side*, 199.

45 Villard, *Memoirs*, vol. 1, 156–57.

46 Leech, *Reveille*, 298.

47 From Benjamin Perley Poore, *Perley's Reminiscences of Sixty Years in the National Metropolis*, vol., 143 (New York: AMS Press, 1971) 21.

48 Smith, *Sunshine and Shadow in New York*, 289.

49 Wilson and Davis, *Herndon's Informants*, 360. Herndon's interview with Mary Lincoln.

50 Baker, *Mary Todd Lincoln*, xiii.

51 The scholars who were invited to answer questions on camera included Jean H. Baker, David Herbert Donald, Doris Kearns Goodwin, David E. Long, James M. McPherson, Donald L. Miller, Mary Genevieve Murphy, Mark E. Neely, Charles B. Strozier, Linda Levitt Turner, Margaret Washington, Frank J. Williams, and Douglas L. Wilson.

52 "Conversation with Hon. O.H. Browning at Leland Hotel, Springfield, June 17, 1875." A manuscript in John Nicolay's hand, John Hay Papers, Brown University Library. Cited in Wilson, *Lincoln Before Washington*, 109n. Wilson credits Michael Burlingame for the discovery of Nicolay's interviews.

53 Badeau, *Grant In Peace*, 356–62.

54 Joseph Schafer, ed., *Intimate Letters of Carl Schurz, 1841–1869* (New York: Da Capo, 1970), 326–27. From Carl Schurz's letter to his wife, April 2, 1865, as quoted in Randall, *Mary Lincoln*, 374.

55 Turner and Turner, *Mary Todd Lincoln*, 211.

56 Lincoln, *Collected Works*, vol. 8, 384.

57 Lincoln, *Collected Works*, vol. 8, 381. Note: At source this telegram appears to be marked in error "7:45 [A.M.]" instead of 7:45 P.M., a change evidenced both in the content and in the fact that Lincoln was not likely to have sent Mary a message full of military details before she sent him her wire requesting "all the news." For further substantiation of the error in time, see David Homer Bates's *Lincoln in the Telegraph Office*, page 347, where an actual facsimile of Lincoln's handwritten despatch "to Mrs. Lincoln of 7:45 P.M., April 2, 1865," is shown.

58 Keckley, *Behind the Scenes*, 134.

59 Herndon, *Life of Lincoln*, 344; Hertz, *Hidden Lincoln*, 177. Details about Lincoln's hat and books from Hertz.

60 Weik, *The Real Lincoln*, 90–91. John T. Stuart and Judge David Davis never asked to dinner: Wilson and Davis, *Herndon's Informants*, p. 77.

61 Wilson and Davis, *Herndon's Informants*, 444–45.

62 Hertz, *Hidden Lincoln*, 375; also Wilson and Davis, *Herndon's Informants*, 444.

CHAPTER NINE

1 Wilson and Davis, *Herndon's Informants*, 108.

2 Hertz, *Hidden Lincoln*, 209.

3 Wilson and Davis, *Herndon's Informants*, 576.

4 Herndon and Weik, *Herndon's Life of Lincoln*, 356.

5 Bayne, *Tad Lincoln's Father*, 183: "Back in that day many families conducted some sort of family worship . . . but I do not remember that the Lincoln family did, although both the President and his wife were scrupulous in most of the outward observances of religion and attended church regularly." Then, on the following page: "There is a good deal on record about [Lincoln] being a man of prayer but I never heard him pray or saw him in the attitude of prayer, although I have seen him in moods when he might well have been struggling in silent prayer."

6 Letter from O. H. Browning to Isaac N. Arnold, Quincy, November 25, 1872, in Sandburg MSS, Illinois Historical Society. Cited in Donald, *David Donald's Private Collection of Lincoln Notes*, 11, 179, Lincoln/Tripp Database.

7 Keckley, *Behind the Scenes*

8 Herndon, *Life of Lincoln*, 360.

9 Guelzo, *Abraham Lincoln*, 320. From Lincoln, *Collected Works*, vol. 4, 271.

10 Stevens, *A Reporter's Lincoln*, 12.

11 Simon, *Lincoln's Preparation For Greatness*, 257. This was not the only such instance; "Lincoln consistently opposed adjourning on Christmas Day," page 275.

12 Kinsey, et al., *Sexual Behavior in the Human Male*, 309.

13 This brisk headway was particularly apparent in Lincoln's first-day "seduction" of Derickson; it appears as well in his first night with Billy Greene. In any case, Lincoln's modus operandi seems to have been based much more on a mutually arrived at backing and filling than on any kind of seduction, not only with Derickson but undoubtedly so with Henry Whitney. With the likes of Billy Greene and A. Y. Ellis, propositions (if they deserve to be called that) were apparently delivered more to Lincoln than vice versa.

14 As early as the 1850s Lincoln made suggestions to a young friend (John Langdon Kaine) on the art of delivering an oration: "Try to think [of borrowed phrases as if] they're your own words and talk them as you would talk them to me." And on the oratorical uses of literature: "It is a pleasure to be able to quote lines to fit any occasion . . . the Bible is the richest source of pertinent quotations." Fehrenbacher and Fehrenbacher, *Recollected Words of Abraham Lincoln*, 273.

15 Lincoln, *Collected Works*, vol. 5, 420.

16 Lincoln, *Collected Works*, vol. 7, 282. From a letter Lincoln wrote to Albert G. Hodges, April 4, 1864.

17 Lincoln's "Meditation on the Divine Will," September 2, 1862(?) *Collected Works*, vol. 5, 403–4. For a clearer view of this meditation, see it in Nicolay and Hay's *Abraham Lincoln*, vol. 6, 342, where it is pointed out that "[I]t was *not* written to be seen of men" but in connection with his trying to come to terms with the facts. The authors seem to think Lincoln was "trying to bring [himself] into closer communication with his Maker"—a strange interpretation. Rather, Lincoln was puzzling over the curious injustice and passivity of an onlooking Almighty, but had not yet invented the notion of the angry, retaliative God he later postulated as demanding "exact restitution" for the long past sins of slavery.

18 Lincoln, *Collected Works*, vol. 8, 356. These quoted words are from a Lincoln letter to Thurlow Weed, Mach 15, 1865.

19 Donald, *Lincoln*, 566–67.

20 This letter to Thurlow Weed is in Lincoln, *Collected Works*, vol. 8, 356, with a footnote from the editors indicating that Lincoln may also have "misread or misrecollected" Weed's note of March 4, the very day of the inaugural. Weed evidently meant his kind words for Lincoln's "reply to the Committee of Congress, informing of your re-election" (what Lincoln here speaks of as his "little notification speech"). However, Weed makes no mention of the Inaugural Address in his note. In fact, Weed's comment on "[t]he sour weather [having] spoiled the Celebration"—along with not a word of Lincoln's address—suggests that Weed missed the entire event, and thus never heard the speech. (Moreover, the celebration was far from "spoiled" by the weather. At 11:40, just as Lincoln was about to speak, "the clouds parted, and sunshine streamed [down] to fall upon the head of the newly consecrated President." Whitney, *Lincoln the President*, 304; Keckley, *Behind the Scenes*, 156.

21 Donald, *Lincoln*, 568.

CHAPTER TEN

1 Keckley, *Behind the Scenes*, 101. Worth noting, too, is an error in the literature. Albert Beveridge, in his *Abraham Lincoln*, vol. 1, 51n, cites a note from William Faux (a kind of early traveling sociologist) that in pioneer cabins, "[m]ales dress and undress before the females and nothing is thought of it." It may have seemed so to Faux, but Alfred Kinsey discovered that not even flashes of nudity occur in such lower-level situations. Rather, with their extraordinary dread of nudity lower-level individuals manage to "acquire a considerable knack of removing daytime clothing and putting on night clothing, without exposing any part of the body." Kinsey, et al., *Sexual Behavior in the Human Male*, 367.

2 As reported, for instance, in Herndon and Weik's *Herndon's Life of Lincoln*, 274–75. And by David Davis himself in Wilson and Davis, *Herndon's Informants*, page 350. For especially loud spell-outs, see Michael Burlingame's chapter "Lincoln's Anger and Cruelty" in *The Inner World of Abraham Lincoln*, 147f.

3 Arnold, *Life of Abraham Lincoln*, 416.

4 N. M. Knapp to Ozias M. Hatch, 12 May 1859, cited in Burlingame, *Inner World of Abraham Lincoln*, 8. Also cited in *David Donald's Private Lincoln Notes*, 12, Lincoln/Tripp Database.

5 Herndon and Weik, *Herndon's Life of Lincoln*, 432. Also Wilson and Davis, *Herndon's Informants*, 168. The full letter is in Appendix 3 of the present volume.

6 Lincoln's victory "had been a rankling disappointment" to Seward, Chase, Cameron, and Bates. And as Margaret Leech further noted, Secretary of the Navy Gideon Welles "was unique among the Cabinet members [in that] he did not think himself a better man than the President." Leech, *Reveille*, 40.

7 Lincoln's handling of this entire Chase and Seward conflict, which is pivotal for still other reasons yet to be examined, has been described in three biographies, each with slightly different details: (1) Nicolay and Hay, *Abraham Lincoln*, vol. 4, 253–72 (the quotations in this paragraph are from Nicolay and Hay, 268, 271); (2) Thomas, *Abraham Lincoln: A Biography*, 350–55; (3) Donald, *Lincoln*, 377–406.

8 Nicolay, *Personal Traits of Abraham Lincoln*, 242.

9 This and previous quotations in this paragraph are from Nicolay and Hay, vol. 4, 270–71.

10 The first and primary definition of "tact," as given in the *Random House Unabridged Dictionary*.

CHAPTER ELEVEN

1 Speed, *Reminiscences*, 26–28.

2 Turner and Turner, *Mary Todd Lincoln*, 296.

3 Hertz, *The Hidden Lincoln*, 384. James Gourley's statement to Herndon.

4 These events took place at the Institute for Sex Research almost exactly a year before I first met Kinsey and became part of the inner sanctum, but Beach's words and experiments were still very much the talk of the place in February 1948. The same month Kinsey wrote his comments on sexual inversion into his volume *Sexual Behavior in the Human Male*, pages 612–15, the last page of which contains Beach's seminal observation on inversion, namely "that the males who most often assume the female type of behavior are the ones who 'invariably prove to be the most vigorous copulators' when they assume the more usual masculine role in coitus." In short, inversion not only means a sex-role reversal, but when a male returns to his ordinary behavior, he is more vigorous than males without the capacity for inversion.

5 For readers interested in the technical side of these issues, two extra observations apply:

> (1) The connection between inversion and sexual intensity was established by Beach as early as his 1942 paper (see Bibliography). The nub of his finding was that *inversion rides the peaks and not the troughs of the androgen curve*. Thus, when rats or dogs are castrated, their first loss is inversion (sooner than their drop in the sex rate). Conversely, when blood levels of male hormone were

gradually restored to normal, so was the original behavior, with inversion being the last to return—thus the peaks versus troughs observation.

(2) Whether or not inversion *requires* the presence of any homosexual element has not yet been determined. My own guess is that it does not. In any case, the matter still requires careful historical checking. For instance, if a careful historical study were to turn up little if any inversion among, say, the citizens of Ancient Rome (or in other societies where overt homosexuality is both ubiquitous and subject to minimal taboos), this would suggest that the connection often found in the inversion/homosexual tie in our own society is less related to sexual orientation than to the resistance against it (its taboo status). Conversely, if inversion was found to have existed approximately as easily in Roman society as in our own, this would tend to increase the relevance of the homosexual component.

6   Most details on Churchill's early sex life would not be known had they not been researched and revealed in an English television documentary, *Secret Lives*, in the 1990s. The Somerset Maugham detail is from Ted Morgan, *Maugham: A Biography*, p. 152.

7   Much interesting and relevant material on both Roosevelt and Churchill is particularly well detailed by Joseph E. Persico, *Roosevelt's Secret War: FDR and World War II Espionage*.

8   The estimate figured and quoted by Tony Sale for the Bletchley Park Trust in the two-hour American television documentary *Nova: Decoding Nazi Secrets.*

9   Hodges, *Alan Turing: The Enigma*, 25.

10   Hodges, *Alan Turing*, 6 (You'll be a good boy, won't you?). Other quotes from ages 13 to 16, 25–33.

11   Turing often demonstrated a kind of instant insight in math. On January 19, 1943, when he visited secret facilities at Bell Laboratories in New Jersey devoted to the electronic technology of speech encipherment, engineers showed him a problem that had taken them a week to solve. Turning's quick response was that it should have given them 945 codes. When asked how he had arrived at the answer so fast, Turing simply noted that their formula boils down to 9 x 7 x 5 x 3.

12   Hodges, *Alan Turing*, 221.

13   Shades of Lincoln's experience. Throughout the Civil War he was repeatedly furious and disappointed when one general after the other, with no such advantage as Montgomery had, failed to follow up a victory by wiping out a retreating army and thus ending the war (as when Lee retreated from Gettysburg).

The "disastrous consequences all over the globe" of Montgomery's near traitorous military neglect are outlined in Hodges's biography, *Alan Turing*, page 245. Or one can hear it spelled out in greater detail in the 1999 American television documentary *Nova: Decoding Nazi Secrets.*

14   None of this material seems available in American reports. Even in Joseph Persico's *Roosevelt's Secret War: FDR and World War II Espionage* Admiral King is mentioned ten times with not a word of these facts, probably because no record of

them was found. Nor does any of this material appear in the American *Nova* documentary. For years it was sequestered in the private files of Bletchley Park, finally being released (1997–98) for use in the British documentary *Station X: The Ultra Secret*, the British version of Bletchley Park, the Enigma, Alan Turing, Churchill, and much else. It contains every detail mentioned here, even Eisenhower's diary entry and original Nazi footage of the decoration of submarine crews back at the German naval base.

15 Persico, *Roosevelt's Secret War*, 147–48.

16 Many of Turing's problems with the police extend beyond what is relevant here but were important in his life. He had been having an affair with a young man named Arnold, a friend of whose robbed Turing's house. Turing reported the theft to the police, who quickly found Turing's relationship with Arnold of greater interest than the theft. Turing, feeling no homosexual guilt, naively supplied a detailed account of what he and Arnold had done in bed. This incriminated him, and in the end he was convicted and offered a choice between imprisonment or a year-long course of treatment with female hormones to "castrate" his sexual desires. Turing chose the hormones, with the result that he grew breasts. Oddly enough, he seemed not to be greatly disturbed by this, though it reads like a nightmare to modern medical opinion. Just over a year later, however, he committed suicide by eating a cyanide-laced apple.

Some observers, noting that he did not seem particularly depressed, have questioned whether he intended to kill himself. But two factors suggest that he did. One, he had prelaced the apple with cyanide. And two, the decision could have been the result of a not unusual back-and-forth rehearsal of saving oneself versus ending it all—that is, an impulsive action far away from depression or premeditated intention. In any case, his legal troubles and his demise just shy of age forty-two add up not only to the premature loss of a great genius, but also to a major societal ingratitude.

17 A seeming exception sometimes cited is the Austrian spy Alfred Redl, who in 1912 accepted hush money from Russia, but who, in fact, instantly turned himself into a double agent, paying back his blackmailers by supplying them with a stream of wrong information during World War I. For more on this and the whole psychology surrounding would-be sexual blackmail, see Tripp, *The Homosexual Matrix*, Chapter 10, "The Politics of Homosexuality."

18 Lt. Col. Wayne Sharks, spokesman for the Language Institute, explained that it was U.S. policy to discharge anyone who was either found or known to be homosexual. As he put it, "We just enforce that policy." Sounds very much like what the British police said when they arrested Alan Turing for his homosexual admission with no other complaint against him—a flagrant contradiction of common sense or, indeed, to any sense. But it is morality on the march.

AFTERWORD I

1 Simon, "Abraham Lincoln and Ann Rutledge," 33.

2 Wilson, *Lincoln Before Washington: New Perspectives on the Illinois Years*, 100.

3 Donald, *Lincoln Reconsidered: Essays on the Civil War Era; Lincoln; "We Are Lincoln Men": Abraham Lincoln and His Friends; Lincoln at Home: Two Glimpses of Abraham Lincoln's Domestic Life.*

4 Herndon to Jesse W. Weik, Springfield, 8, 15, 16 January 1886, Herndon-Weik Collection, Library of Congress; Herndon to C. O. Poole, Springfield, 5 January 1886, in Hertz, ed., *The Hidden Lincoln: From the Letters and Papers of William H. Herndon*, 122; Herndon to Truman Bartlett, Springfield, 22 September 1887, Bartlett Scrapbooks, Massachusetts Historical Society; Herndon, "Analysis of the Character of Abraham Lincoln," 1865 lecture, *Abraham Lincoln Quarterly* 1 (1941): 419n.

5 Carl Schurz, interview with Ida M. Tarbell, 6 November 1897, Ida M. Tarbell Papers, Allegheny College.

6 John G. Nicolay to John Hay, Washington, 29 January 1864, in Burlingame, ed., *With Lincoln in the White House: Letters, Memoranda, and Other Writings of John G. Nicolay, 1860–1865*, 125.

7 John Hay to John G. Nicolay, Washington, 5 April 1862, in Burlingame, ed., *At Lincoln's Side: John Hay's Civil War Correspondence and Selected Writings*, 19.

8 Dr. Stone paraphrased in the manuscript diary of John Meredith Read, Jr., U.S. minister to Greece, quoted in Old Hickory Book Shop (New York) catalog, n.d., clipping, Lincoln files, "Wife" folder, Lincoln Museum, Lincoln Memorial University, Harrogate, Tennessee.

9 B. B. French to his son Frank, Washington, 9 July 1865, French Family Papers, Library of Congress.

10 Dr. Tripp frequently cites my pamphlet "Honest Abe, Dishonest Mary." A revised and expanded version of that paper, "Mary Todd Lincoln's Unethical Conduct as First Lady," can be found in Burlingame, ed., *At Lincoln's Side*, 185–203.

11 Rice, ed., *Reminiscences of Abraham Lincoln by Distinguished Men of His Time*, 241.

12 Donald, *"We Are Lincoln Men,"* 38–39.

13 Washington correspondence, 8 April 1863, San Francisco *Daily Evening Bulletin*, 15 May 1863, in Burlingame, ed., *Lincoln Observed: Civil War Dispatches of Noah Brooks*, 253n4.

14 Statement Speed made "some years" before his death in 1882, quoted in a Washington letter, n.d., to the Louisville *Courier-Journal*, copied in the Bloomington, Illinois, *Pantagraph*, 17 January 1884.

15 "Lincoln, Speed, Hurst & I slept in the same room for a year or so." Herndon to John E. Remsburg, Springfield, 10 September 1887, copy, privately printed by H. E. Barker of Springfield, 1917. See also Herndon to Ward Hill Lamon, Springfield, 25 February 1870, Lamon Papers, Huntington Library, San Marino, California, and Angle, ed., *Herndon's Life of Lincoln: The History and Personal Recollections of Abraham Lincoln as Originally Written by William H. Herndon and Jesse W. Weik*, 150. Born in Philadelphia, Hurst (1811–81) settled in Springfield in 1834. After working for Speed a few years he bought the store in 1841 and held it until 1877.

16 Herndon interviewed in the Cincinnati *Commercial*, 25 July 1867.

17 Donald, *"We Are Lincoln Men,"* 145, 146.

18 Pinsker, *Lincoln's Sanctuary: Abraham Lincoln and the Soldiers' Home,* 57, 98.

19 Strozier, *Lincoln's Quest for Union: A Psychological Portrait,* 2nd ed., rev., 58–59.

20 David Davis, interview with Herndon, 20 September 1866, Wilson and Davis, eds., *Herndon's Informants: Letters, Interviews, and Statements about Abraham Lincoln,* 50.

21 Lincoln told this to James A. Briggs, a Cleveland attorney and businessman who served as the Ohio state agent in New York and was a Republican party leader and orator. Cincinnati *Commercial,* n.d., copied in the Belleville, Illinois, *Advocate,* 8 June 1866, copied in the card catalogue of Lincolniana, microform division, Illinois State Historical Library, Springfield. It was reprinted with the wrong date (8 *July* 1866, a day on which the weekly paper was not published) in *The Journal of the Illinois State Historical Society* 32 (1939): 399. Lincoln commended Briggs to the attention William Henry Seward, saying "I know James A. Briggs, and believe him to be an excellent man." Lincoln to Seward, Washington, 11 August 1862, *The Collected Works of Abraham Lincoln,* ed. Basler et al., 5:367.

22 Herndon to Jesse W. Weik, Springfield, 23 January 1890 and January 1891, and Herndon to James H. Wilson, n.p., 23 September 1889, all in the Herndon-Weik Collection, Library of Congress.

23 Herndon to Jesse W. Weik, Springfield, 5 January 1889, Herndon-Weik Collection, Library of Congress. Douglas L. Wilson sensibly observed that these "stories of overnight encounters on the road with young women" were "probably based on real incidents," though they "may have been colored by the familiar genre of stories about 'the farmer's daughter.'" Douglas L. Wilson, "Keeping Lincoln's Secrets," *The Atlantic Monthly,* May 2000, 81.

24 N. W. Branson to Herndon, Petersburg, Illinois, 3 August 1865, Wilson and Davis, eds., *Herndon's Informants,* 90.

25 John Todd Stuart, interview with Herndon, [1865–66], Wilson and Davis, eds., *Herndon's Informants,* 481.

26 Herndon's account in Caroline Dall, "Journal of a tour through Illinois, Wisconsin and Ohio, Oct. & Nov. 1866," entry for 29 October 1866, Dall Papers, Bryn Mawr College.

27 Herndon to Jesse W. Weik, Springfield, 10 December 1885, Herndon-Weik Collection, Library of Congress.

28 Speed, interview with Herndon, 5 January 1889, Wilson and Davis, eds., *Herndon's Informants,* 719; Herndon to Jesse W. Weik, Springfield, 5 January 1889, Herndon-Weik Collection, Library of Congress. Herndon added, "Lincoln went out of the house, bidding the girl good evening and went to the store of Speed, saying nothing. Speed asked no questions and so the matter rested a day or so. Speed had occasion to go and see the girl in a few days, and she told him just what was said and done between herself & Lincoln; and Speed told me the story and I have no doubt of its truthfulness."

29 On Speed's romantic propensities, see Joshua Speed to Mary L. Speed, Springfield, 31 October 1841, Speed Family Papers, Filson Club, Louisville, Kentucky.

30 Joshua Speed to Eliza Speed, Springfield, 12 March 1841, Speed Papers, Illinois State Historical Library, Springfield.

31 The best accounts of the relationship between Matilda Edwards and Lincoln are Wilson, *Honor's Voice: The Transformation of Abraham Lincoln*, 219–42 and Wilson, "Abraham Lincoln and 'That Fatal First of January,'" in Wilson, *Lincoln Before Washington: New Perspectives on the Illinois Years*, 99–132. See also J. Bennett Nolan, "Of a Tomb in the Reading Cemetery and the Long Shadow of Abraham Lincoln," *Pennsylvania History* 19 (July 1952): 262–306; Orville H. Browning, interview with John G Nicolay, Springfield, 17 June 1875, in Burlingame, ed., *An Oral History of Abraham Lincoln: John G. Nicolay's Interviews and Essays*, 1–2; Harry O. Knerr, two essays, both entitled "Abraham Lincoln and Matilda Edwards," enclosed in Knerr to Ida M. Tarbell, Allentown, 26 October 1936, Ida M. Tarbell Papers, Allegheny College; Allentown (Pennsylvania) *Morning Call*, 9 February 1936; Herndon to Ward Hill Lamon, Springfield, 25 February 1870, Lamon Papers, Huntington Library, San Marino, California; Jane D. Bell to Anne Bell, Springfield, 27 January 1841, copy, Lincoln files, "Wife" folder, Lincoln Memorial University, Harrogate, Tennessee; Albert S. Edwards in Stevens, *A Reporter's Lincoln*, ed. Burlingame, 113; Octavia Roberts, "'We All Knew Abr'ham,'" *Abraham Lincoln Quarterly* 4 (1946): 27; Stoddard, *Abraham Lincoln: The True Story of a Great Life*, 122.

32 Caroline Owsley Brown, "Springfield Society before the Civil War," [Edwards Brown, Jr.], *Rewarding Years Recalled* (privately published, 1973), 33–34.

33 Alice Edwards Quigley, niece of Matilda Edwards, to "Dear Sir," Alton, Illinois, 22 March 1935, Allentown, Pennsylvania, *Morning Call*, 9 February 1936; Virginia Quigley to [Octavia Roberts] Corneau, Alton, Illinois, 13 July [1939?], F. Lauriston Bullard Papers, Boston University; Orville H. Browning, interview with John G. Nicolay, Springfield, 17 June 1875, Nicolay, *Oral History of Lincoln*, ed. Burlingame, 1; Albert S. Edwards, in Stevens, *A Reporter's Lincoln*, ed. Burlingame, 113.

34 *Berks and Schuylkill Journal*, 8 February 1851, quoted in Nolan, "Of a Tomb in the Reading Cemetery," 292.

35 James C. Conkling to Mercy Levering, Springfield, 7 March 1841, Sandburg and Angle, *Mary Lincoln: Wife and Widow*, 180.

36 Jennie Edwards Nisbet to William E. Barton, La Jolla, California, 8 January 1927, Barton Papers, University of Chicago. Matilda Edwards's niece told Octavia Roberts Corneau: "Never did any one have so many offers of marriage as Mathilda did" during that winter. Roberts, "My Townsman—Abraham Lincoln," typescript of a talk given to the Lincoln Group of Boston, 18 November 1939, 12, Abraham Lincoln Association Reference Files, "Reminiscences," folder 5. Cf. Virginia Quigley to [Octavia Roberts] Corneau, Alton, 13 July [1939?], F. Lauriston Bullard Papers, Boston University.

37 Jane Hamilton Daviess Bell to Anne Bell, Springfield, 27 January 1841, copy, Lincoln files, "Wife" folder, Lincoln Memorial University, Harrogate, Tennessee. Jane Bell, wife of Joseph Montgomery Bell, was a half-sister of Mary Montgomery

Helm, who wed Joshua Bell, after whom Bell County, Kentucky, was named. Anne Bell, recipient of this letter, was Joshua Bell's sister; she married Ormond Beatty, who became president of Centre College in Kentucky. Mary M. B. E. Jackson (Mrs. Henry Jackson) to John B. Clark, Danville, Kentucky, 25 August 1948, copy, ibid. Jane Bell probably got her information from Speed. Wilson, *Honor's Voice*, 237.

38 Octavia Roberts Corneau, "My Townsman—Abraham Lincoln," typescript of a talk given to the Lincoln Group of Boston, 18 November 1939, Abraham Lincoln Association Reference Files, "Reminiscences" folder 5, p. 11; Octavia Roberts Corneau, "The Road of Remembrance," unpublished manuscript, 119, Corneau Papers, Illinois State Historical Library, Springfield.

39 Virginia Quigley to [Octavia Roberts] Corneau, Alton, Illinois, 13 July [1939?], F. Lauriston Bullard Papers, Boston University.

40 Orville H. Browning, interview with John G. Nicolay, Springfield, 17 June 1875, in Nicolay, *Oral History of Lincoln*, ed. Burlingame, 1.

41 Mrs. Benjamin S. Edwards to Ida M. Tarbell, Springfield, 8 October 1895, copy, Ida M. Tarbell Papers, Allegheny College.

42 James H. Matheny, interview with Herndon, 3 May 1866, Wilson and Davis, eds., *Herndon's Informants*, 251.

43 Joshua F. Speed, interview with Herndon, [1865–66], Wilson and Davis, eds., *Herndon's Informants*, 475.

44 Herndon to Ward Hill Lamon, Springfield, Illinois, 25 February 1870, Lamon Papers, Huntington Library, San Marino, California.

45 Ninian W. Edwards, interview with Herndon, 22 September 1865, Wilson and Davis, eds., *Herndon's Informants*, 133.

46 Elizabeth Todd Edwards, interview with Herndon, [1865–66], Wilson and Davis, eds., *Herndon's Informants*, 444.

47 Green, "New Cases of Women's Influence over Lincoln," *New York Times*, 11 February 1923, sec. 8, p. 1.

48 Interview with Hardin's sister, Mrs. Alexander R. McKee (née Martinette Hardin), "A Romance of Lincoln," clipping marked "Indianapolis, January 1896," Lincoln Museum, Fort Wayne, Indiana.

49 Unidentified newspaper article by Frank G. Carpenter, [1891], Lincoln Museum, Fort Wayne, Indiana. Carpenter's source was Judge Daniel H. Solomon of Iowa, whose wife (née Elizabeth Hardin at Jacksonville in 1839) was the daughter of John J. Hardin's sister, Lucy Jane.

50 Donald, *Lincoln*, 612n.

51 Wilson, *Honor's Voice*, 355.

52 Donald, *Lincoln*, 612n.

53 Donald, *"We Are Lincoln Men,"* 101–39.

54 Strozier, *Lincoln's Quest for Union*, 2nd ed., 49–50.

55 Orville H. Browning, interview with John G. Nicolay, Springfield, 17 June 1875, in Burlingame, ed., *Oral History of Lincoln*, 1–2; Browning to Isaac N. Arnold, Quincy, Illinois, 25 November 1872, Arnold Papers, Chicago Historical Society.

56 John M. Lockwood to Jesse W. Weik, Mount Vernon, Indiana, 4 January 1896, and two letters to Mr. J. A. Stuart of Indianapolis, dated Princeton, Indiana, 25 and 26 January 1909, one from an unknown correspondent and the other from "Hastings," in Jesse W. Weik, *The Real Lincoln: A Portrait*, ed. Burlingame (1922; Lincoln: University of Nebraska Press, 2002), 365–67.

57 Sandburg and Angle, *Mary Lincoln*, 54–55, 344–50, and Gary Lee Williams, "James and Joshua Speed" (Ph.D. dissertation, Duke University, 1971), 19–25.

58 Sarah A. Rickard Basset to Herndon, Connors, Kansas, 3, 12 August 1888, Wilson and Davis, eds., *Herndon's Informants*, 663–64, 665; Anna Miles Herndon, interview with William Herndon, [13 September 1887], *ibid.*, 640; Herndon to Jesse W. Weik, Springfield, 8 August 1888, Herndon-Weik Collection, Library of Congress; interview with Sarah Rickard Barrett by Nellie Crandall Sanford, Kansas City *Star*, 10 February 1907. Jesse W. Weik interviewed Sarah Rickard about the courtship and was told that her elder sister had opposed the match because of the girl's youth. Weik, *Real Lincoln*, ed. Burlingame, 66–68. After the spring of 1841, when Speed returned to Kentucky, Lincoln roomed as well as boarded with the Butlers. William J. Butler, grandson of William Butler, in the *Illinois State Journal* (Springfield), 28 February 1937. See also John G. Nicolay's interview with William Butler, Springfield, June 1875, Burlingame, ed., *Oral History of Lincoln*, 22–24.

59 William E. Barton, memorandum of a conversation in Springfield with Mrs. Charles Ridgely, [1921], Barton Papers, University of Chicago. Mrs. Ridgely said that Sarah Rickard, her sister-in-law, "told me Lincoln proposed to her. But she did not take it very seriously. . . . [W]hen he came to be famous she spoke jokingly of it without regret. Held him in high honor but no real affection, and she was very young."

60 William G. Greene quoted in George A. Pierce, "Lincoln's Love," dispatch dated "on the cars," 16 April, Chicago *Inter-Ocean*, 23 April 1881.

61 Herndon's essay, "Lincoln's Courtship with Miss Owens," excerpted in R. Gerald McMurtry, appendix in Olive Carruthers, *Lincoln's Other Mary* (Chicago: Ziff-Davis, 1946), 209.

62 Lincoln to Mary Owens, Vandalia, 13 December 1836, Basler, ed., *Collected Works of Lincoln*, ed. Basler, 1:54–55.

63 Parthena Hill, interview with Walter B. Stevens, 1886, in Stevens, *A Reporter's Lincoln*, ed. Burlingame, 10.

64 Wilson, *Lincoln Before Washington*, 81–82.

65 Interview with Nancy Rutledge Prewitt, conducted by Margaret Flindt, Fairfield, Iowa, correspondence, 10 February, Chicago *Inter-Ocean*, 12 February 1899; interview with Nancy Rutledge Prewitt, conducted by E. E. Sparks, *Los Angeles Times*, 14 February 1897; Sarah Rutledge Saunders, interview with William E. Barton, Lompoc, California, correspondence, 14 January, *Illinois State Journal* (Springfield), 15 January 1922; Sarah Rutledge Saunders, interview with Katherine Wheeler, *Chicago Tribune* magazine, 22 February 1922; Mrs. Samuel Hill, in Laura Isabelle Osborne Nance, *A Piece of Time (In Lincoln Country)*, ed. Georgia Good-

win Creager (n.d. [ca. 1967]), 26; reminiscences of E. J. Rutledge, Ottumwa, Iowa, *Courier*, n.d., typed copy, clipping collection, Lincoln Museum, Fort Wayne, Indiana.

66 "Sifting the Ann Rutledge Evidence," in Randall, *Lincoln the President: Springfield to Gettysburg* (2 vols.; New York: Dodd, Mead, 1945), 2:342.

67 Ruth Painter Randall, *I, Ruth: Autobiography of a Marriage* (Boston: Little, Brown, 1968), 165; James G. Randall to Francis S. Ronalds, n.p., 3 February 1945, copy, Randall Papers, Library of Congress.

68 Simon, "Abraham Lincoln and Ann Rutledge," *Journal of the Abraham Lincoln Association* 11 (1990): 13–33; Wilson, "Abraham Lincoln, Ann Rutledge, and the Evidence of Herndon's Informants," *Civil War History* 36 (1990): 301–23. Wilson's piece also appears in his collection of essays, *Lincoln Before Washington*, 74–98.

69 Urbana: University of Illinois Press, 1993.

70 Burlingame, "The Authorship of the Bixby Letter," in Hay, *At Lincoln's Siide*, ed. Burlingame, 169–84.

71 Fehrenbacher, *Lincoln in Text and Context: Collected Essays*, 278. See also D. E. Fehrenbacher and V. Fehrenbacher, eds., *Recollected Words of Abraham Lincoln*, liii.

72 Wilson, *Lincoln Before Washington*, 86–88.

AFTERWORD II

1 Gay used as a noun dates from the 1950s, but its use as an adjective goes back to the 1930s for men, and by the early 1800s for women prostitutes. J. E. Lighter, ed., *Random House Historical Dictionary of American Slang* (New York: Random House, 1994), 1:871.

2 Donald, *"We Are Lincoln Men,"* 35. I was a graduate student of Donald's at Johns Hopkins and Harvard, where I completed my doctoral dissertation under his direction in 1978.

3 Ibid.

4 Herndon and Weik, *Herndon's Life of Lincoln*, 471–75.

5 For the ongoing debate see Jean H. Baker, "The Lincoln Marriage: Beyond the Battle of Quotations," Thirty-eighth Annual Robert Fortenbaugh Memorial Lecture, Gettysburg College, 1999; recycled as "Mary and Abraham: A Marriage," in Boritt, ed., *The Lincoln Enigma*, 36–55. See also Burlingame, *The Inner World of Abraham Lincoln*, and Wilson, *Honor's Voice*. Since the distinguished LaWanda Cox, author or coauthor with her husband, John H. Cox, of many works on Lincoln's political leadership and the issues of slavery, race, and Reconstruction, there may not be a prominent published woman scholar who has focused primarily on any aspect of Lincoln's life or career.

6 *Herndon's Life of Lincoln*, 117–29.

7 Masters, *Lincoln the Man* (London: Cassell and Co., 1931), 51–62.

8 Philip S. Klein, *President James Buchanan* (University Park, Pa.: Pennsylvania State University Press, 1962), 28–34, 111; Warren Johansson and William A. Percy, *Outing: Shattering the Conspiracy of Silence* (New York: Haworth Press, 1994), 233–34; Carl Sferrazza Anthony, "Was James 'Aunt Fancy' Buchanan Our

Gay President?" *The Advocate* 571 (Feb. 26, 1991): 50–53. Noted Southern historian J. Mills Thornton III writes, "King formed a close and affectionate relationship with James Buchanan. . . . The two lifelong bachelors shared the same views on most public questions and in private life held each other in the highest regard. It is not clear whether the friendship had a sexual component, although contemporaries sometimes implied that it did. The relationship was never overtly a political issue." *American National Biography* (New York: Oxford University Press, 1999) 12:720–21.

9 Douglas L. Wilson, "Abraham Lincoln, Ann Rutledge, and the Evidence of Herndon's Informants," *Civil War History* 36 (Dec. 1990): 301–24; *Honor's Voice*, 114–26; and Walsh, *The Shadows Rise*. For a critical view of the Rutledge revivalists, see Lewis Gannett, "'Overwhelming Evidence' of a Lincoln–Ann Rutledge Romance?: Reexamining Rutledge Family Reminiscences," forthcoming in the *Journal of the Abraham Lincoln Association*.

10 Baker, "Mary and Abraham," 39–40.

11 One could start with Baker's *Mary Todd Lincoln*; and J. G. Turner and L. L. Turner, eds., *Mary Todd Lincoln: Her Life and Letters*.

12 Donald, *Lincoln*, 335; Baker, *Mary Todd Lincoln*, 195–96; "Mary and Abraham," 49–50.

13 Donald, *Lincoln*, 324–25, on Wikoff; no mention of Wood; on Mary's dislike of Seward, 427; Baker, *Mary Todd Lincoln*, on Wikoff, 218, 231–32; on Wood, 184–85, 187–89, 191, 205, 301. See also Sandburg and Paul M. Angle, *Mary Lincoln*, 113, 205–06; Sandburg, *Abraham Lincoln: The War Years*, 1:35 ; and Winkler, *The Women in Lincoln's Life*, 157, 160. It is hard to find information on Wood, a crony of Seward, whom Mary Lincoln disliked. Why, then, did the Lincolns appoint him to manage the president-elect's railroad entourage on its way east from Springfield in 1861? A check of Glyndon G. Van Deusen's *William Henry Seward* (New York: Oxford University Press, 1967) ; John M. Taylor, *William H. Seward* (New York: HarperCollins, 1991); earlier biographies by Frederic Bancroft, and Thornton Kirkland Lothrop, *American National Biography*, and several other biographical references found nothing on Mr. Wood. The three mentions of Wood in *The Collected Works of Abraham Lincoln* 4:326, 528; 5:71, n., are tantalizing in their details, as are those in the Turners' *Life and Letters*, 83, 100–04, 110.

14 Deborah Hayden, *Pox: Genius, Madness, and the Mysteries of Syphilis* (New York: Basic Books, 2003), 120–32; Wilson, *Honor's Voice*, 126–29, 182–85, 348n.36.

15 Browne, *The Every-Day Life of Abraham Lincoln*, 151–53; Donald, *Lincoln*, 66.

16 See Donald's detailed treatment of Speed and Lincoln, "He Disclosed His Whole Heart To Me," chapter 2 in *"We Are Lincoln Men,"* 29–64.

17 Ibid., 51–64.

18 Along with Herndon, biographies that have considerable detail about Speed and Lincoln's sleeping arrangement, and their friendship, beyond a mere mention, include those by Sandburg, Oates, Strozier, Donald, and Wilson.

19 Baker, "Mary and Abraham," 45.

20 "Most men were eager—and sometimes desperate—to get married. Typically, young men responded to letters from their beloveds much more quickly than the young women responded in turn, and also wrote longer love letters than they received . . . marriage was a mark of full manhood, and manhood was a status to which males urgently aspired. Especially for young men whose careers were starting to take shape, wedded life completed the social identity of a male adult." E. Anthony Rotundo, *American Manhood: Transformations in Masculinity from the Revolution to the Modern Era* (New York: Basic Books, 1993), 114—16. In 1890 the median age for men was 26.1 years. United States Bureau of the Census, *The Statistical History of the United States From Colonial Times to the Present* (New York: Basic Books, 1976), Series A, 158–159, "Median Age at First Marriage, by Sex: 1890 to 1970," 19.

21 J. G. Holland, Francis Fisher Browne, James G. Randall, Benjamin P. Thomas, and Richard N. Current have only passing mention of Ellsworth; Herndon, and especially Carl Sandburg and Stephen B. Oates, go into considerable detail, Donald somewhat less so, and not at all in *"We Are Lincoln Men."* Two psychobiographies, George B. Forgie's *Patricide in the House Divided* (New York: W. W. Norton, 1979), and Strozier's *Lincoln's Quest for Union* fail to mention Ellsworth.

22 See http://www.pa-roots.com/~pacw/150thcok.html for the roster of the 150th Pennsylvania. Derickson appears as captain, Co. K, under Brig. Gen. J. H. Martindale, District of Washington, 31 March 1863, and was honorably discharged 10 Nov. 1865. *Official Records*, I:25, pt. II, 183; III:5, 899. Service confirmed in Janet B. Hewett, ed., *The Roster of Union Soldiers, 1861–1865: Pennsylvania*, vol. 1 (Wilmington, N. C.: Broadfoot's Bookmark, 1998), 385.

23 I checked biographies by Holland (1866), Browne (1886), Herndon (1889), Charnwood (1916), Sandburg (1926–39), Randall (1945–55; fourth and final volume completed by Richard N. Current), Thomas (1952), Current's essays, *The Lincoln Nobody Knows* (New York: Hill & Wang, 1958), Oates (1970), Forgie (1979), Strozier (1982), and Donald (1995).

24 Tarbell, *The Life of Abraham Lincoln*, 3:153–57; Leech, *Reveille in Washington, 1860–1865*, 303; Sandburg, *Abraham Lincoln: The War Years*, 2:211, 4:306.

Bibliography

Note: Items followed by an asterisk are included
in the Lincoln/Tripp Database.

Angle, Paul M., ed. *The Lincoln Reader.* New Brunswick, N. J.: Rutgers University Press, 1947.

Angle, Paul M. "Lincoln's First Love?" Bulletin No. 9, Lincoln Centennial Association, Dec. 1, 1927.*

Angle, Paul M., and Earl Schenck Miers, eds. *The Living Lincoln: The Man, His Mind, His Times, and the War He Fought, Reconstructed From His Own Writings.* New Brunswick, N. J.: Rutgers University Press, 1955.

Angle, Paul M., Benjamin P. Thomas, and Harry E. Pratt. *Bulletins of the Abraham Lincoln Association, 1923–1937, Numbers 1 to 50.* Springfield, Ill.: The Abraham Lincoln Association, 1938.

Arnold, Isaac N. *The Life of Abraham Lincoln.* Lincoln, Neb.: University of Nebraska Press, 1994. Reprint of the original edition from A. C. McClurg & Company, Chicago, 1884.

Badeau, Adam. *Grant In Peace: From Appomattox to Mount McGregor, a Personal Memoir.* Hartford, Conn.: S. S. Scranton, 1887.

Baker, Jean H. *Mary Todd Lincoln: A Biography.* New York: W. W. Norton, 1987.

Barton, William E. *Abraham Lincoln and Walt Whitman.* Indianapolis: Bobbs-Merrill, 1928.

Barton, William E. *President Lincoln.* 2 vols. Indianapolis: Bobbs-Merrill, 1933.

Barton, William E. *The Women Lincoln Loved.* Indianapolis: Bobbs-Merrill, 1927.

Bates, David Homer. *Lincoln in the Telegraph Office: Recollections of the United States Military Telegraph Corps during the Civil War.* Lincoln, Neb.: University of Nebraska Press, 1995.

Bates, Edward. *The Diary of Edward Bates 1859–1866.* Volume IV of the Annual Report of the American Historical Association for the Year 1930, edited by Howard K. Beale, Washington: U. S. Government Printing Office, 1933.*

Bayne, Julia Taft. *Tad Lincoln's Father.* Boston: Little, Brown, 1931.

Beach, Frank A. "Analysis of Factors Involved in the Arousal, Maintenance and Manifestation of Sexual Excitement in Male Animals." *Psychosomatic Medicine*, Vol. 4, No. 2, April 1942.

Beach, Frank A. "Bisexual Mating Behavior in the Male Rat: Effects of Castration and Hormone Administration." *Physiological Zoology* 18, 1945.

Beach, Frank A. "Execution of the Complete Masculine Copulatory Pattern by Sexually Receptive Female Rats." *Journal of Genetic Psychology*, 60, 1942.

Beach, Frank A. "A Review of Physiological and Psychological Studies of Sexual Behavior in Mammals." *Physiological Reviews*, Vol. 27, No. 2, April 1947.

Beach, Frank A. "Sexual Behavior in Animals and Man." Harvey Lecture, May 20, 1948.

Beach, Frank A., and A. Marie Holz-Tucker. "Effects of Different Concentrations of Androgen Upon Sexual Behavior in Castrated Male Rats." *Journal of Comparative and Physiological Psychology*, Vol. 42, 1948.

Beach, Frank A. and Julian Jaynes. "Effects of Early Experience Upon the Behavior of Animals." *Psychological Bulletin*, Vol. 51, No. 3, May 1954.

Beveridge, Albert J. *Abraham Lincoln 1809–1858.* 2 vols. Boston: Houghton Mifflin, 1928.*

Booker, Richard. *Abraham Lincoln in Periodical Literature 1860–1940.* Chicago: Fawley-Brost, 1941.

Boritt, Gabor, ed. *The Lincoln Enigma: The Changing Faces of an American Icon.* New York: Oxford University Press, 2001.

Brooks, Noah. *Lincoln Observed: Civil War Dispatches of Noah Brooks,* edited by Michael Burlingame. Baltimore: Johns Hopkins University Press, 1998.

Browne, Francis Fisher. *The Every-Day Life of Abraham Lincoln.* Lincoln, Neb.: University of Nebraska Press, 1995. Reprinted from the 1887 edition published by Northwestern Publishing, Minneapolis, based on the original edition published by N. D. Thompson Publishing, New York, 1886.

Browne, Robert H. *Abraham Lincoln and the Men of His Times.* 2 vols. Cincinnati: Jennings and Pye, 1901.

Browning, Orville Hickman. *The Diary Of Orville Hickman Browning, Volume I, 1850–1864,* edited by Theodore Calvin Pease and James G. Randall. Springfield: Illinois State Historical Society, 1925.*

Burlingame, Michael. "Honest Abe, Dishonest Mary." Historical Bulletin Number 50. Racine: Lincoln Fellowship of Wisconsin, 1994.*

Burlingame, Michael. *The Inner World of Abraham Lincoln.* Chicago: University of Illinois Press, 1994.*

Carman, Harry J., and Reinhard H. Luthin. *Lincoln and the Patronage.* New York: Columbia University Press, 1901.*

Carpenter, Francis B. *Six Months at the White House with Abraham Lincoln.* New York: Hurd and Houghton, 1867.*

Chamberlin, Thomas. *History of the One Hundred and Fiftieth Regiment Pennsylvania Volunteers, Second Regiment, Bucktail Brigade.* Philadelphia: F. McManus, Jr., 1905. Reprinted by Butternut and Blue, Baltimore, 1986.*

Current, Richard N. *The Lincoln Nobody Knows*. New York: McGraw-Hill, 1958.

Donald, David Herbert. *Charles Sumner*. New York: Da Capo Press, 1996.

Donald, David Herbert. *David Donald's Private Collection of Lincoln Notes*. Nyack, New York: Lincoln/Tripp Database, 2001.*

Donald, David Herbert, ed. *Inside Lincoln's Cabinet: The Civil War Diaries of Salmon P. Chase*. New York: Longmans, Green & Co., 1954.*

Donald, David Herbert. *Lincoln*. New York: Simon & Schuster, 1995.*

Donald, David Herbert. *Lincoln*. London: Jonathan Cape, 1995.

Donald, David Herbert. *Lincoln at Home: Two Glimpses of Abraham Lincoln's Family Life*. New York: Simon & Schuster, 2000.

Donald, David Herbert. *Lincoln Reconsidered: Essays on the Civil War Era*. New York: Vintage, 2001.*

Donald, David Herbert. *Lincoln's Herndon*. New York: Alfred A. Knopf, 1948.*

Donald, David Herbert. *"We Are Lincoln Men": Abraham Lincoln and His Friends*. New York: Simon & Schuster, 2003.

Duncan, Kunigunde, and D. F. Nickols. *Mentor Graham: The Man Who Taught Lincoln*. Chicago: University of Chicago Press, 1944.

Fehrenbacher, Don E., ed. *Lincoln: Selected Speeches and Writings*. New York: Vintage Books, 1992.

Fehrenbacher, Don E. *Lincoln in Text and Context: Collected Essays*. Stanford, Calif.: Stanford University Press, 1988.*

Fehrenbacher, Don E. *Prelude to Greatness: Lincoln in the 1850's*. Stanford, Calif.: Stanford University Press, 1962.

Fehrenbacher, Don E., and Virginia Fehrenbacher, eds. *Recollected Words of Abraham Lincoln*. Stanford, Calif.: Stanford University Press, 1996.

French, Benjamin Brown. *Witness to the Young Republic*. Donald B. Cole and John J. McDonough, eds. Hanover, N. H.: University Press of New England, 1989.

Freud, Sigmund. *The Basic Writings of Sigmund Freud*, edited by A. A. Brill. New York, Modern Library, 1995.

Freud, Sigmund. *The Standard Edition of the Complete Psychological Works of Sigmund Freud*. 24 vols. London: The Hogarth Press and the Institute of Psycho-Analysis, 1966.

Gannett, Lewis A. "Scandal Brewing in Lincoln Country." *The Gay & Lesbian Review*, Vol. 11, No. 2, March–April 2004.

Green, Horace. "New Cases of Women's Influence over Lincoln." *New York Times*, 11 February 1923.

Guelzo, Allen C. *Abraham Lincoln: Redeemer President*. Grand Rapids, Mich.: Eerdmans Publishing, 1999.*

Guelzo, Allen C. *Edwards on the Will: A Century of American Theological Debate*. Middletown, Conn.: Wesleyan University Press, 1989.

Hay, John. *At Lincoln's Side: John Hay's Civil War Correspondence and Selected Writings*, edited by Michael Burlingame. Carbondale, Ill.: Southern Illinois University Press, 2000.

Hay, John. *Inside the White House: The Complete Civil War Diary of John Hay*, edited by Michael Burlingame and John R. Turner Ettlinger. Carbondale, Ill.: Southern Illinois University Press, 1997.

Helm, Katherine. *The True Story of Mary, Wife of Lincoln.* New York: Harper & Brothers, 1928.

Herndon, William H. "Abraham Lincoln, Miss Ann Rutledge, New Salem, Pioneering and *The Poem.*" Broadsheet of a lecture privately printed by Herndon. Photostat of the broadsheet courtesy of Dr. Thomas F. Schwartz and the Illinois State Historical Library. Reprinted by H. E. Barker, Springfield, Illinois, 1910.*

Herndon, William H., and Jesse W. Weik. *Herndon's Life of Lincoln: The History and Personal Recollections of Abraham Lincoln as Originally Written by William H. Herndon and Jesse W. Weik*, edited by Paul M. Angle. New York: A. & C. Boni, 1930.

Herndon, William H., and Jesse W. Weik. *Herndon's Life of Lincoln.* Greenwich, Conn.: Fawcett, 1961.

Herndon, William H., and Jesse W. Weik. *Herndon's Life of Lincoln.* New York: Da Capo Press, 1983.*

Hertz, Emanuel, ed. *The Hidden Lincoln: from the Letters and Papers of William H. Herndon.* New York: Viking, 1938.*

Hertz, Emanuel, ed. *Lincoln Talks: A Biography In Anecdote.* New York: Viking Press, 1939.

Hickey, James T. *The Collected Writings of James T. Hickey from Publications of the Illinois State Historical Society, 1953–1984.* Springfield, Ill.: Illinois State Historical Society, 1990.

Hodges, Andrew. *Alan Turing: The Enigma.* New York: Simon & Schuster, 1983.

Holzer, Harold, ed. *Dear Mr. Lincoln: Letters to the President.* New York: Addison-Wesley, 1993.

Holzer, Harold, ed. *The Lincoln-Douglas Debates.* New York: HarperCollins, 1993.

Hurt, James. *Writing Illinois: The Prairie, Lincoln, and Chicago.* Chicago: University of Illinois Press, 1992.

Jaffa, Harry V. *Crisis of the House Divided: An Interpretation of the Issues in the Lincoln-Douglas Debates.* Chicago: University of Chicago Press, 1973.

Jennison, Keith W. *The Humorous Mr. Lincoln.* New York: Thomas Y. Crowell, 1965.

Katz, Jonathan Ned. *The Invention of Heterosexuality.* New York: Dutton, 1995.

Katz, Jonathan Ned. *Love Stories: Sex Between Men Before Homosexuality.* Chicago: University of Chicago Press, 2001.

Keckley, Elizabeth. *Behind the Scenes: Thirty Years a Slave, and Four Years in the White House.* Salem, N. H.: Ayer, 1985. Reprint of the original edition from the New York Printing Company, New York, 1868.*

Kincaid, Robert L. *Joshua Fry Speed: Lincoln's Most Intimate Friend.* Harrogate, Tenn.: Department of Lincolniana, Lincoln Memorial University, 1943.*

Kinsey, Alfred C., Wardell B. Pomeroy, and Clyde E. Martin. *Sexual Behavior in the Human Male.* Philadelphia: W. B. Saunders, 1948.*

Kinsey, Alfred C., Wardell B. Pomeroy, Clyde E. Martin, and Paul H. Gebhard. *Sexual Behavior in the Human Female.* Philadelphia: W. B. Saunders, 1953.*

Kunhardt, Philip B., Jr., Philip B. Kunhardt III, and Peter W. Kunhardt. *Lincoln: An Illustrated Biography*. New York: Alfred A. Knopf, 1992.

Lamon, Ward Hill. *The Life of Abraham Lincoln: From His Birth to His Inauguration as President*. Lincoln: University of Nebraska Press, 1999. Reprint of the original edition from James R. Osgood, Boston, 1872.*

Lamon, Ward Hill. *Recollections of Abraham Lincoln*, edited by Dorothy Lamon Teillard. Lincoln: University of Nebraska Press, 1994. Reprint of the expanded Second Edition, 1911.*

Lee, Elizabeth Blair. *Wartime Washington: The Civil War Letters of Elizabeth Blair Lee*, edited by Virginia Jeans Laas. Chicago: University of Chicago Press, 1991.

Leech, Margaret. *Reveille in Washington 1860–1865*. New York: Harper & Brothers, 1941.*

Lewis, Lloyd. *Myths After Lincoln*. New York: Press of the Readers Club, 1941.

Lincoln, Abraham. *The Collected Works of Abraham Lincoln*, edited by Roy P. Basler. 8 vols. plus index. New Brunswick, N. J.: Rutgers University Press, 1953–55.*

Lowry, Thomas P. *Don't Shoot That Boy! Abraham Lincoln and Military Justice*. Mason City, Iowa: Savas, 1999.

Lowry, Thomas P. *The Story the Soldiers Wouldn't Tell: Sex in the Civil War*. Mechanicsburg, Penn.: Stackpole Books, 1994.

Maltby, Charles. *The Life and Public Services of Abraham Lincoln*. Stockton, Calif.: Daily Independent Steam Power Print, 1884.*

Masters, Edgar Lee. *Lincoln, the Man*. New York: Dodd, Mead, 1931.

Masters, Edgar Lee. *Spoon River Anthology*. New York: The Macmillan, 1964.

Matthews, Elizabeth W. *Lincoln as a Lawyer: An Annotated Bibliography*. Carbondale, Ill.: Southern Illinois University Press, 1991.

Mearns, David C. *The Lincoln Papers*. 2 vols. Garden City: Doubleday, 1948.*

Miers, Earl Schenck, William E. Baringer, and C. Percy Powell, eds. *Lincoln Day by Day: A Chronology 1809–1865*. Dayton, Ohio: Morningside, 1991.*

Mitgang, Herbert, ed. *Abraham Lincoln: A Press Portrait*. Chicago: Quadrangle, 1971.

Monaghan, Jay., ed. *Lincoln Bibliography 1839–1939*. 2 vols. Springfield: Illinois State Historical Library, 1943–1945.

Morgan, Ted. *Maugham: A Biography*. New York: Simon & Schuster, 1980.

Neely, Mark E. *The Abraham Lincoln Encyclopedia*. New York: Da Capo Press, 1982.*

Newton, Joseph Fort. *Lincoln and Herndon*. Cedar Rapids, Iowa: Torch Press, 1910.*

Nicolay, Helen. *Personal Traits of Abraham Lincoln*. New York: Century, 1912.

Nicolay, John G., *An Oral History of Abraham Lincoln: John G. Nicolay's Interviews and Essays*, edited by Michael Burlingame. Carbondale: Southern Illinois University Press, 1996.

Nicolay, John G. *With Lincoln in the White House: Letters, Memorabilia, and Other Writings of John G. Nicolay, 1860–1865*, edited by Michael Burlingame. Carbondale: Southern Illinois University Press, 2000.

Nicolay, John G., and John Hay. *Abraham Lincoln: A History*. 10 vols. New York: Century, 1917 (reprint of the 1886 edition).

Niven, John. *The Salmon P. Chase Papers, Volume 1: Journals, 1829–1872*. Kent, Ohio: Kent Sate University Press, 1993.*

Oates, Stephen B. *Abraham Lincoln: The Man Behind The Myths*. New York: Harper & Row, 1984.

Oates, Stephen B. *With Malice Toward None: A Life of Abraham Lincoln*. New York: HarperPerennial, 1994. Originally published by Harper & Row, 1977.

Onstot, T. G. *Lincoln and Salem: Pioneers of Menard and Mason Counties*. Forest City, Ill.: Self-published by Onstot, 1902.*

Persico, Joseph E. *Roosevelt's Secret War: FDR and World War II Espionage*. New York: Random House, 2001.

Pinsker, Matthew. *Lincoln's Sanctuary: Abraham Lincoln and the Soldiers' Home*. New York: Oxford University Press, 2003.

Randall, J. G. *Lincoln the President*. 4 vols. New York: Dodd, Mead & Company, 1944–1955.

Randall, J. G. "Sifting the Ann Rutledge Evidence," Appendix to *Lincoln the President: Springfield to Gettysburg*. New York: Dodd, Mead, 1945.*

Randall, Ruth Painter. *Colonel Elmer Ellsworth*. Boston: Little, Brown, 1960.*

Randall, Ruth Painter. *The Courtship of Mr. Lincoln*. Boston: Little, Brown, 1957

Randall, Ruth Painter. *Lincoln's Sons*. Boston: Little, Brown, 1955.

Randall, Ruth Painter. *Mary Lincoln: Biography of a Marriage*. Boston: Little, Brown, 1953.*

Rankin, Henry B. *Intimate Character Sketches of Abraham Lincoln*. Philadelphia: J. B. Lippincott, 1924.

Rankin, Henry B. *Personal Recollections of Abraham Lincoln*. New York: G. P. Putnam's Sons, 1916.*

Reep, Thomas P. *Lincoln at New Salem*. Petersburg, Ill.: The Old Salem Lincoln League, 1927.*

Rice, Allen Thorndike, ed. *Reminiscences of Abraham Lincoln by Distinguished Men of His Time*. New York: North American Review, 1888.*

Sachs, Benjamin D., Richard J. Valcourt, and Henry C. Flagg. "Copulatory Behavior and Sexual Reflexes of Male Rats Treated with Naloxone." *Pharmacology, Biochemistry & Behavior*, Vol. 14, pp. 251–53.

Sandburg, Carl. *Abraham Lincoln: The Prairie Years*. 2 vols. New York: Charles Scribner's Sons, 1940.*

Sandburg, Carl. *Abraham Lincoln: The War Years*. 4 vols. New York: Charles Scribner's Sons, 1940.

Sandburg, Carl. *Mary Lincoln, Wife and Widow*. Bedford, Mass.: Applewood Books, n.d. Originally published by Harcourt, Brace, New York, 1932.

Sandburg, Carl, and Paul M. Angle. *Mary Lincoln: Wife and Widow*. New York: Harcourt, Brace, 1932.

Shively, Charley. *Drum Beats: Walt Whitman's Civil War Boy Lovers*. San Francisco: Gay Sunshine Press, 1989.

Shutes, Milton H. *Lincoln and the Doctors.* New York: Pioneer Press, 1933.*

Shutes, Milton H. *Lincoln's Emotional Life: A Medical Narrative of the Life of Abraham Lincoln.* Philadelphia: Dorrance, 1957.*

Simon, John Y. "Abraham Lincoln and Ann Rutledge." *Journal of the Abraham Lincoln Association,* 11, 1990.*

Simon, Paul. *Lincoln's Preparation for Greatness: The Illinois Legislative Years.* Chicago: University of Illinois Press, 1971.

Smith, Jean Edward. *Grant.* New York: Simon & Schuster, 2002.

Smith, Matthew Hale. *Sunshine and Shadow in New York.* Hartford: J. B. Burr, 1868.

Speed, Joshua F. *Reminiscences of Abraham Lincoln and Notes of a Visit to California.* Louisville: John P. Morton, 1884.*

Steers, Edward, Jr. *Blood on the Moon: The Assassination of Abraham Lincoln.* Lexington: University Press of Kentucky, 2001.

Stephenson, Nathaniel Wright. *An Autobiography of Abraham Lincoln.* Indianapolis: Bobbs-Merrill, 1926.

Stephenson, Nathaniel Wright. *Lincoln: An Account of His Personal Life, Especially of Its Springs of Action as Revealed and Deepened by the Ordeal of War.* Grosset & Dunlap, 1934.

Stevens, Walter B. *A Reporter's Lincoln,* edited by Michael Burlingame. Lincoln: University of Nebraska Press, 1998. Originally printed in 1916.*

Stoddard, William O. *Abraham Lincoln: The True Story of a Great Life.* New York: Ford, Howard, & Hulbert, 1884.

Stoddard, William O. *Dispatches from Lincoln's White House: The Anonymous Civil War Journalism of Presidential Secretary William O. Stoddard,* edited by Michael Burlingame. Lincoln: University of Nebraska Press, 2002.

Stoddard, William O. *Inside the White House in War Times.* New York: Charles L. Webster, 1890.

Strong, George Templeton. *The Diary of George Templeton Strong,* edited by Allan Nevins and Milton Halsey Thomas, abridged by Thomas J. Pressly. Seattle: University of Washington Press, 1988.

Strozier, Charles B. *Lincoln's Quest for Union: Public and Private Meanings.* New York: Basic Books, 1982.*

Tarbell, Ida M. *Abraham Lincoln & His Ancestors.* Lincoln: University of Nebraska Press, 1997 . Originally published as *In the Footsteps of the Lincolns,* Harper & Brothers, 1924.

Tarbell, Ida M. *Ida Tarbell: Notes and Letters.* An Unpublished Collection from Michael Burlingame. Nyack, N.Y. Lincoln/Tripp Database, 2001.*

Tarbell, Ida M. *The Life of Abraham Lincoln.* 2 vols. New York: Lincoln Memorial Association, 1900.

Temple, Wayne C. *Abraham Lincoln: From Skeptic to Prophet.* Mahomet, Ill.: Mayhaven Publishing, 1995.

Temple, Wayne C. "Lincoln and the Burners at New Salem." *Lincoln University Herald,* 67:2, Summer 1965.

Thomas, Benjamin P. *Abraham Lincoln.* New York: Alfred A. Knopf, 1952.*

Thomas, Benjamin P. *"Lincoln's Humor" and Other Essays,* edited by Michael Burlingame. Chicago: University of Illinois Press, 2002.

Thomas, Benjamin P. *Lincoln's New Salem.* New York: Alfred A. Knopf, 1954.*

Thomas, Benjamin P. *Portrait for Posterity.* New Brunswick, N.J.: Rutgers University Press, 1947.

Thomas, Benjamin P., and Harold M. Hyman. *Stanton: The Life and Times of Lincoln's Secretary of War.* New York: Alfred A. Knopf, 1962.

Thomas, John L., ed. *Abraham Lincoln and the American Political Tradition.* Amherst: University of Massachusetts Press, 1986.

Tripp, C. A. *The Homosexual Matrix.* New York: McGraw-Hill, 1975.

Tripp, C. A. "The Strange Case of Isaac Cogdal." *Journal of the Abraham Lincoln Association,* Vol. 23, No. 1, Winter 2002.

Tripp, C. A., Fritz A. Fluckiger, and George H. Wei. "Measurement of Handwriting Variables," *Perceptual and Motor Skills,* Monograph Supplement 5, 1957.

Turner, Justin G., and Linda Levitt Turner, eds. *Mary Todd Lincoln: Her Life and Letters.* New York: Alfred A. Knopf, 1972.*

Villard, Henry. *Memoirs of Henry Villard, Journalist and Financier.* 2 vols. Boston: Houghton Mifflin & Co., 1904.*

Walsh, John Evangelist. *The Shadows Rise: Abraham Lincoln and the Ann Rutledge Legend.* Chicago: University of Illinois Press, 1993.*

Warren, Louis A. "The Ann Rutledge Myth." *The Lincoln Kinsman,* 35, May 1941.

Warren, Louis Austin. *Lincoln's Parentage & Childhood.* New York: Century, 1926.

Waugh, John C. *Reelecting Lincoln: The Battle for the 1864 Presidency.* New York: Crown Publishers, 1997.

Weik, Jesse W. *The Real Lincoln: A Portrait.* Boston: Houghton Mifflin, 1922. Rev. ed. edited by Michael Burlingame. Lincoln: University of Nebraska Press, 2002.

Whitney, Henry C. *Life of Lincoln.* New York: Baker & Taylor, 1908.*

Williams, Frank J. *Judging Lincoln.* Carbondale: Southern Illinois University Press, 2002.

Williams, Gary Lee. *James and Joshua Speed: Lincoln's Kentucky Friends.* Doctoral Dissertation, Duke University, 1971, Facsimile from UMI Dissertation Services, 1996.

Wilson, Douglas L. "Abraham Lincoln, Ann Rutledge, and the Evidence of Herndon's Informants." *Civil War History* 36, 1990.

Wilson, Douglas L. *Honor's Voice: The Transformation of Abraham Lincoln.* New York: Knopf, 1998.*

Wilson, Douglas L. "Keeping Lincoln's Secrets." *Atlantic Monthly,* May 2000.

Wilson, Douglas L. *Lincoln Before Washington: New Perspectives on the Illinois Years.* Chicago: University of Illinois Press, 1997.*

Wilson, Douglas L., and Rodney O. Davis, eds. *Herndon's Informants: Letters, Interviews, and Statements about Abraham Lincoln.* Chicago: University of Illinois Press, 1998.*

Wilson, Rufus Rockwell, ed. *Intimate Memories of Lincoln*. Elmira, N.Y.: Primavera Press, 1945.

Wilson, Rufus Rockwell, ed. *Lincoln Among His Friends*. Caldwell, Idaho: Caxton Printers, 1942.

Winkle, Kenneth J. *The Young Eagle: The Rise of Abraham Lincoln*. Dallas: Taylor Trade Publishing, 2001.

Winkler, Donald H. *The Women in Lincoln's Life*. Nashville, Tenn.: Rutledge Hill Press, 2001.

WPA. *Annals of Sangamon County, 1831–1860*. Springfield: Federal Works Agency, Works Projects Administration of Illinois. Nyack, N.Y.: Lincoln/Tripp Database, 2001.*

Zall, P. M., ed. *Abe Lincoln Laughing: Humorous Anecdotes from Original Sources By and About Abraham Lincoln*. Berkeley: University of California Press, 1982.

Acknowledgments

The Estate of C. A. Tripp wishes to thank the following individuals for their assistance:

Lewis Gannett
Christopher Mee
Celia Tripp Reid
Richard Milner
Daniel Gwin
Herb Atkin
Barbara Wersbra
Alice Fennessey
Patrick J. Finnegan

George Weinberg
Julia Heiman
Tom Schwartz
Donald Farber
Roz Lichter
Don Slawsky
Jonathan Ned Katz
Peter Havel

Index

About the Author

C. A. TRIPP passed away in May 2003, just two weeks after completing the manuscript of *The Intimate World of Abraham Lincoln*. A psychologist, therapist, and sex researcher, he worked with Alfred Kinsey in the late 1940s and 1950s before obtaining a Ph.D. in clinical psychology from New York University. He maintained a private practice of psychology for years, and taught at the State University of New York, Downstate Medical Center, from 1955 to 1964. The author also organized the Charles Darwin database now in use by Darwin scholars and at the core of the research effort of the Charles Darwin Correspondence Project at the Cambridge University Library.